Praise for *The Solace of Fierce Landscapes*

"Lane, a Presbyterian minister teaching theology at a Catholic University, makes some of the rich tradition of the Christian people available to us in a uniquely powerful way because he has allowed it to live in his own life and has an artist's ability to make that experience present to us. This is theology at its most fruitful best and an exquisitely beautiful read."—The late M. Basil Pennington, O.C.S.O., St. Joseph's Abbey, Spencer, Massachusetts

"This is a beautifully written book in which the author describes and unfolds the mutually illuminating interaction in himself between his profound sensitivity to place, especially the hard places of this earth, and his experience of one of the hardest of life's losses. Lane uses his wide and deep knowledge of the mystical tradition to interpret this experience in such a way that the reader is enlightened and encouraged. Reading this book is an experience of the human engagement with the Mystery of God as lived by the author."—Sandra M. Schneiders, Professor of New Testament and Christian Spirituality, The Jesuit School of Theology at Berkeley

"Belden Lane is a storyteller. Here he tells the story of the relationships between inner and outer wilderness. The landscape is an integrant of selfhood. To be 'in the desert' is to want something—water, promise of exodus. But there is no replenishment of these desires. The imagination and the 'self' are transfigured—given illumination—when the desert has its way. In the emptiness, the Voice says, 'stay with me; talk with me, not about me or you. This is my body, along with the echoes from yonder mountain.' This is what Belden Lane teaches us."—Richard E. Wentz, Professor of Religious Studies, Arizona State University, author of *John Williamson Nevin, American Theologian*

"Pushed by God, deserts, and death to the limits of human life, the spiritual seeker is relieved of worry over her own anxious ego—'the things that ignore us save us'—and the reader, in turn, comes away soothed by a fine illustration of the intimate connection there can be between abstract ideas and the daunting realities of life. In the vast desert of pop spirituality, Lane's book is an oasis."—*Kirkus Reviews*

THE SOLACE OF FIERCE LANDSCAPES

· **Exploring Desert and Mountain Spirituality** ·

BELDEN C. LANE

OXFORD

UNIVERSITY PRESS

OXFORD
UNIVERSITY PRESS

Oxford University Press, Inc., publishes works that further
Oxford University's objective of excellence
in research, scholarship, and education.

Oxford New York
Auckland Cape Town Dar es Salaam Hong Kong Karachi
Kuala Lumpur Madrid Melbourne Mexico City Nairobi
New Delhi Shanghai Taipei Toronto

With offices in
Argentina Austria Brazil Chile Czech Republic France Greece
Guatemala Hungary Italy Japan Poland Portugal Singapore
South Korea Switzerland Thailand Turkey Ukraine Vietnam

Copyright © 1998 by Beldon C. Lane

First published by Oxford University Press, Inc., 1998
198 Madison Avenue, New York, NY 10016
www.oup.com

First issued as an Oxford University Press paperback, 2007
ISBN 978-0-19-531585-1

Oxford is a registered trademark of Oxford University Press

The Library of Congress has cataloged the hardcover edition as follows:
Lane, Belden C., 1943–
The solace of fierce landscapes:
exploring desert and mountain
spirituality / Belden C. Lane
p. cm. Includes bibliographical references and index.
ISBN 0-19-511682-8
1. Spiritual life—Christianity.
2. Wilderness (Theology).
3. Deserts—Religious aspects—Christianity.
4. Mountains—Religious aspects—Christianity.
5. Lane, Belden C., 1943–
I. Title.
BV4501.2.L31834 1998 248.4—dc21
98—10842

Pages xi-xii constitute an extension of the copyright page.

1 3 5 7 9 8 6 4 2
Printed in the United States of America
on acid-free paper

Contents

Acknowledgments

I have to acknowledge, before anything else, my debt to the landscape itself—to those empty places surrounding Mount Sinai, Ghost Ranch, and Christ in the Desert Abbey that have been life-giving for me in the process of this work. These are places increasingly at risk, threatened by the expansion of developers, tourists, even occasional retreatants like myself. The ecological concern of this book is not often emphasized in what follows, but one could argue that the apophatic tradition has (and must) support the preservation of fierce landscapes in the process of extolling the solace they provide. These are places most important for what *isn't* there. "To those devoid of imagination," wrote Aldo Leopold in his *Sand County Almanac*, "a blank place on the map is a useless waste; to others, the most valuable part."

Books are written out of a long loneliness, sustained and encouraged at times by communities of hope. The groups of support to which this book is indebted, through various stages of its growth, include the third-floor residents of the Colonial Health Care Center in Saint Louis, Missouri, the Dominican community of the École Biblique in Jerusalem, the Benedictine community of Christ in the Desert Monastery near Abiquiu, New Mexico, the Presbyterian community of Ghost Ranch down the Chama River Valley from the Benedictines at Christ in the Desert, and the Jesuit community of Saint Louis University.

Scholars who have offered criticism and encouragement along the way include Bernard McGinn of the University of Chicago, Philip Sheldrake of the Cambridge Theological Federation, Regina Siegfried, A.S.C. of the Aquinas Institute, and most particularly my friend Douglas Burton-Christie of Loyola-Marymount University. While their insights have helped immeasurably in writing and revising the book, I alone am responsible for its faults. Bob Raines of Kirkridge, Steven Berry of the First Congregational Church of Los Angeles, and David Douglas of Santa Fe have also helped through their invitations to participate in seminars and workshops on desert and mountain spirituality.

Friends, students, and graduate assistants who have offered insight and assistance along the way are too many to number. I am grateful to Saint Louis University and the chairperson of the Department of Theological Studies, Bill

Shea, for support in allowing time for writing, and to Gin O'Meara, R.C.S.J. and Joan Chamberlain, trusted guides through the deep canyons of the soul. Cynthia Read at Oxford University Press, along with Jeannette Batz and Ann Weems, offered invaluable editorial assistance.

Finally, to my children, Kate and John, and most especially my wife, Patricia, I give thanks for their loving me most when I least knew how to love in return. In the apophatic tradition, the one about whom the least is said is always most important. Such is the case with this woman who's shared my life these last thirty years. The book belongs at last to my mother and father, Jane E. Lane and Edward H. Lane, who through their dying offered me most of what they had to teach about living.

Illustrations

1 · Saint Catherine's Monastery at the foot of Mount Sinai, author's photograph, appearing in the text on p. 60.

2 · *Moses Leading the Children of Israel Through the Wilderness,* engraving by Hans von Windsheim?, 1481/82. Used by permission of the Staatliche Graphische Sammlung, Munich, appearing in the text on p. 97.

3 · The employment of inverse perspective and the curvature of mountains in an icon of the Holy Trinity, Novgorod school, late fifteenth century. Used by permission of the Temple Gallery, London, appearing in the text on p. 127.

4 · *The Meeting Between St. Anthony and St. Paul,* a fresco by Pinturicchio (Bernardino de Betto), ca. 1493, Appartamenti Borgia. Used by permission of the Monumental Musei e Gallerie Pontificie, Vatican, appearing in the text on p. 198.

5 · The chapel at Christ in the Desert Abbey, Abiquiu, New Mexico, author's photograph, appearing in the text on p. 226.

Permissions

"Stalking the Snow Leopard: A Reflection on Work," January 4–11, 1983.

"Desert Terror and the Playfulness of God," September 30, 1987 and October 14, 1987.

"Fierce Back-Country and the Indifference of God," October 11, 1989.

"Grace and the Grotesque," November 14, 1990.

"Dragons of the Ordinary: The Discomfort of Common Grace," August 21–28, 1991.

"Transformation at Upper Moss Creek," September 8–15, 1993.

"Imaginary Mountains, Invisible Landscapes," January 18, 1995.

THE SOLACE OF FIERCE LANDSCAPES

Introduction

I write these words at dusk far up the Chama River Canyon, surrounded by red sandstone cliffs in a landscape that bleeds. The Spanish named the mountains nearby the Sangre de Christo range, and on evenings when a wine-dark sun shines through dust-laden sky, the blood of Christ seems smeared over every rock. From the Mexican Penitentes to Georgia O'Keeffe, people have recognized this beautiful, haunting land as a place of death that is able also to heal. Like the red rocks of Sedona, Arizona or Ayers Rock in central Australia, the lifeblood of mother earth seems to have risen to the surface here.

I sit in the courtyard of the small guest house at Christ in the Desert Monastery, a Benedictine abbey some twenty-five miles north of Abiquiu in the high desert country of northern New Mexico. It's a remote place, located at the end of Forest Service Road #151, a deeply rutted path sometimes inaccessible, even with four-wheel-drive vehicles. The emptiness here is vast, the silence at first disconcerting, though it sinks its way slowly into the soul as one submits to the monastic pattern of chanted psalms, work, and prayer.

This is a place where desert and mountain meet, a terrain not unfrequented in the history of Christian spirituality. Indeed, in the Coptic language, the single word *toou* is used to refer to mountain and desert alike, suggesting that for early Egyptian monasticism all terrain beyond the safety of the Nile was regarded as equally hazardous, a place of brokenness where divine mercy must suffice.[1] I've come to such a place to finish this book, asking how my own experience of desert and mountain emptiness can be understood over against a tradition stretching back through John of the Cross and Meister Eckhart to Evagrius and the Cappadocian fathers. If in certain respects this is a fool's errand, it's one anchored in deep longing for the truth that the desert teaches.

The project began several years ago, out of the effort to comprehend the meaning of my mother's prolonged death by cancer, an experience that sent both of us on a journey into fierce and unfamiliar desert country. A crisis like this offers an opportunity for rethinking all of the dyings in one's life. My father's catastrophic death when I was hardly more than a child, the recent death (also by cancer) of a graduate student I'd known well, the frequent loss of new friends at the nursing home where my mother lived—all these became part of the desert-mountain experience to which I was ineluctably drawn.

Over the last half-decade I've found myself physically and symbolically attracted to fierce landscapes in a way I haven't entirely understood. I've been driven to the desert mountains of New Mexico on many occasions, as well as to Mount Sinai in Egypt and dry stretches of the Negev in Israel. Such places symbolize much of the pain, and also the healing, made possible by wilderness. Thoreau was right: "We need the tonic of wildness."[2]

This love of unsafe terrain has led me also to the study of desert and mountain imagery in the history of the Christian apophatic tradition. The apophatic way, familiarly known as the *via negativa,* is a tradition in spirituality that rejects all analogies of God as ultimately inadequate.[3] God is greater than any language we might ever use to speak of God. Ironically, however, in the history of this tradition a few lean and spare landscape images have frequently been employed to challenge the very use of images themselves. These include the desert, the mountain, and the cloud—porous, "aniconic images" used, on the one hand, to question the overconfidence in words that sometimes characterizes the theological enterprise, and, on the other hand, to suggest metaphorically the deepest, virtually indescribable, human experiences of pain and joy.[4] These landscape images derive their energy from the archetypal experience of Moses in the desert at Sinai. They recur repeatedly in mystical writers of the apophatic tradition, from Gregory of Nyssa to Thomas Merton.

This book makes no claim to be a thoroughgoing historical-critical study of the apophatic tradition. Nor does it offer an ethnographic analysis of specific cultural understandings of desert and mountain environments. What it attempts, instead, is something of a performance (rather than a mere description) of apophatic spirituality, inviting the reader's entry into those rare events of "apophatic fusion" that sometimes occur in human life—when we're driven like Moses to wonderment, beyond the distinctions we ordinarily make between subject and object, ourselves as knowers and that which we seek most passionately to know.[5] Mystics have continually resisted defining their subject of discourse, insisting that God is ever beyond language, even beyond their "experience" of God. "Rather than pointing to an object, apophatic language attempts to evoke in the reader an event that is—in its movement beyond structures of self and other, subject and object—structurally analogous to the event of mystical union."[6]

The book, therefore, invites the reader into several of the pivotal texts (and contexts) out of which such events of vulnerability and union have repeatedly been generated in the history of the tradition. Its purpose is to allow these texts (and this terrain) to engage the reader at a deep level of personal risk, through the intimate involvement of the interpreter's own voice in the process of saying and unsaying what is otherwise wholly unavailable to discourse. Only at the periphery of our lives, where we and our understanding of God alike are undone, can we understand bewilderment as occasioning another way of knowing.

Mine is a highly textured, multidimensional reading of the apophatic tradition. Its narrative structure draws heavily, with a naked honesty at times, from my own experience. I simply don't know any other way of doing it. Yet this unusually personal involvement of the author in his research raises important hermeneutical questions.[7]

The self-implicating character of research in religious-history–writing is increasingly a subject of current debate.[8] Reluctantly or not, the academy continues to probe the permeable boundaries between critical scholarship and lived experience. Walter Brueggemann distinguishes between the "scribes" who stringently maintain the integrity of a text, permitting it to linger in the ongoing life of a tradition, and the "agents of the imagination" who periodically allow the text to explode into new meaning, recovering its ability to startle in a way that necessarily moves beyond critical insight.[9] Brueggemann himself embodies both tasks in his own work as a scholar. I, too, am interested in the scribal labor of attending to texts and the settings in which they are read, but in this particular study I function more as an *agent provocateur,* daring to let the text "explode" in my own hands in the process of offering it to the reader.

I write as a self-identified Christian, though one burned out (like a lot of people) on shallow religion. I've found more life, risk, and daring in the church's ancient traditions of prayer than in what's available in most contemporary spiritualities. Introduced several years ago as a Presbyterian minister teaching at a Roman Catholic University who had come to tell Jewish stories at the Vedanta Society, I've come to value many of the great, if forgotten, traditions of prayer. While the person of Christ remains pivotal to my own faith commitment, apophatic spirituality occasions a wide arena for dialogue among world religions, and I welcome that.[10] In this book I write not only for people in the academy, but for pastors and laypeople hungry for something of substance on the subject of spirituality, for desert-lovers who can't figure out why they're so drawn to wild and empty terrain, for those left numb by the sustained weariness of death experienced at close hand.

This book aims at resolute honesty to the inconsolable human experience of death, grief, and recovery. Its theological reflection on the apophatic tradition is filtered through a single pilgrim's experience of loss and his effort to pray, often in the absence of viable images of God. It is selective, deeply personal, and provisional, as all theology must be. It draws on the teaching authority of those on the margins—persons who are dying, residents of nursing homes, the poor, people who trace the edges of sanity and despair. These are the ones whose experience of limit, desperation, and persistent hope authenticates as genuine their bold reading and living of the truth.[11]

The book asks how the experience of place affects (and is affected by) the images of God found in the history of Christian spirituality. It examines, with the eye of a naturalist, the geographical and psychological matrix out of which desert and mountain spiritualities emerge. What is the impact on the spiritual imagination of a barren and threatening environment—a land studded with rocky crags, arroyos that fill with the rush of sudden rains, creosote bush, mountain lions? Desert and mountain places are often associated with the "limit-experiences" of people on the edge, people who have run out of language in speaking of God, people whose recourse to fierce landscapes has fed some deep need within them for the abandonment of control and the acceptance of God's love in absolute, unmitigated grace.

The reader is drawn up the slopes of Mount Sinai above Saint Catherine's monastery, into the lonely cells of desert fathers and mothers in ancient Egypt, up remote canyons in the high desert country of New Mexico, into a small and solitary room in Jerusalem, along corridors in a Saint Louis nursing home where my best teachers have been "desert Christians" who perceive abandonment not only as loss, but also as grace.

The book is organized after a classic pattern in the history of Christian spirituality, the three stages of the spiritual life generally described as purgation, illumination, and union. These are symbolized, respectively, in the experience of the desert, the mountain, and the cloud. One initially enters the desert to be stripped of self, purged by its relentless deprivation of everything once considered important.

The first part of the book invites the reader into the deep sense of relinquishment the desert demands. It examines the psychological and spiritual impact of wild terrain on the human spirit, as well as the recurrence of desert imagery in the apophatic tradition.

In the next stage of spiritual growth, one ascends the mountain, seeking illumination from the greater perspective its height affords. The knowledge of God increases as one waits like Moses on the barren mountain slope. The second part of the book reflects on this dominance of the Sinai image within the apophatic tradition. It explores the longing that Moses experienced, and Gregory of Nyssa after him, for an ever-expanding apprehension of the vision of God, a gradual movement "from glory to glory."

At the height of spiritual encounter, people have also spoken of being lost in a dark cloud on the mountain's slope, losing their separate identity within it, being enveloped by a love defying explanation. In that moment, in what mystics describe as a "brilliant darkness," God alone shines in the soul. The third part of the book examines the character of this love as it takes shape in a desert-mountain landscape of abandonment. It focuses on the experience of the early desert fathers and mothers, asking how their discipline of *apatheia* (or indifference) gives birth to *agape* (or love).

Each of the three parts of the book begins with a description of experience, tracing the steps of my mother's movement toward apophasis and death. They advance from her first entry into the desert of surgery and radiation oncology, to the long process of waiting by the third-floor window of her room in a nursing home, to her final release in a dying that seemed an unflinching surrender to love.

Interspersed among the substantive chapters about the apophatic tradition in the history of spirituality are shorter pieces I call "mythic landscapes." These are more personal efforts to comprehend the nature of each successive movement by reference to my own experiences in desert and mountain terrain. I separate them in order to distinguish (to some extent, at least) the scribal work of text analysis from the more imaginative work of text appropriation. Bringing the two together enhances the "intertextuality" of the whole.[12] Underlying the entire work is a conviction that the physical experience of desert-mountain territory and the personal experience of "spiritual dryness" are mutually illuminative horizons of meaning. Each interprets the other.

The first chapter addresses important questions about how one "reads" a rugged landscape, how it has to speak with its own integrity even as one inevitably subjects it to cultural and religious meanings. This chapter discloses my own bias as an author, raising central issues about the nature of environmental interpretation. Readers with little patience for methodological concerns may feel free to dance their way through it lightly. Others will find its prominent themes of participation and risk to be woven throughout the rest of the book.

· 1 ·

Connecting Spirituality and
the Environment

Geography is simply a visible form of theology. —Jon Levenson[1]

We live in the description of a place and not in the place itself. —Wallace
Stevens

Talk about God cannot easily be separated from discussions of place.
A desert-mountain environment (or any landscape, for that matter) plays a central role in constructing human subjectivity, including the way one envisions the holy. The place where we live tells us who we are—how we relate to other people, to the larger world around us, even to God. Meaningful participation in any environment requires our learning certain "gestures of approach" or disciplines of interpretation that make entry possible. All these are matters essential to the analysis of any spirituality.

In the aboriginal lands west of Alice Springs in the desert of central Australia, one easily recognizes a connection between geography and the spiritual life. Aboriginal peoples traverse the sacred landscape by following invisible songlines, singing—as they walk—the songs first sung by their ancestors in an ancient dreamtime beyond memory. They name (and "re-create") every characteristic of their hard and thirsty land—rocks, caves, desert brush, and waterholes—through the *habitus,* or ritualized way of perceiving reality, they bring to it.[2] They know that to "dwell" in a place creatively over an extended period of time is to conduct oneself according to a custom or habit that draws meaning from the particularities of the environment.

Bruce Chatwin, a British travel writer fascinated with Australia, tells of giving a ride in his Land Cruiser to an aboriginal friend on a dusty road in the outback. The aboriginal man was on pilgrimage, engaged in a dream trek aimed at restoring meaning to his own life as well as to the landscape. Driving at twenty-five miles an hour, Chatwin noticed the man frantically jumping back and forth from one window to the other, chanting the place-names of his songline as quickly as possible. Suddenly he realized his mistake as a driver, and slowed the car down to the four-mile-an-hour pace of a walker so that the man's song could be sung at a proper and comfortable rate. Only in this way could the land be adequately honored and their entry into it together made spiritually possible.[3]

This intimate connection between spirit and place is hard to grasp for those of us living in a post-Enlightenment technological society. Landscape and spirituality are not, for us, inevitably interwoven. We experience no inescapable linkage between our "place" and our way of conceiving the holy, between habitat and *habitus,* where one lives and how one practices a habit of being.[4] Our concern is simply to move as quickly (and freely) as possible from one place to another. We are bereft of rituals of entry that allow us to participate fully in the places we inhabit.

We have lost the ability even to heed the natural environment, much less perceive it through the lens of a particular tradition. Modern Western culture is largely shorn of attentiveness to both habitat and *habitus.*[5] Where we live—to what we are rooted—no longer defines who we are. We have learned to distrust all disciplines of formative spiritual traditions, with their communal ways of perceiving the world. We have realized, in the end, the "free individual" at the expense of a network of interrelated meanings.

Without a *habitus*—particularly one that is drawn, at least in part, from the rhythm of the land around us—our habitat ceases to be a living partner in the pursuit of a common wholeness. We become alienated from an environment that seems indifferent, even hostile. Habitat turns into scenery, inconsequential background. *Habitus* is reduced to a nonsacramental, individualistic quest for transcendent experience. We lose any sense of being formed in community, participating in a tradition that allows us to act unconsciously, with ease and delight, out of a deep sense of what is natural to us and to our milieu.[6] We are, in short, a people without "habit," with no common custom, place, or dress to lend us shared meaning.

Aboriginal people know that land is necessarily approached by a vision appropriate to it. They understand their habitat only by reference to its *habitus,* the way one rightly behaves with respect to it. But to appreciate this, one probably has to move at a four-mile-an-hour pace, intimately attending to the landscape and the habitude it fosters. The intention of this book is to explore a particular habitat that has exercised extraordinary influence in the history of Christian spirituality: the lean and austere terrain of the desert mountain.

Why has such a landscape so often gripped the Christian imagination? What *habitus* gives it meaning? The apophatic tradition's spare way of thinking draws energy from the imaginal poverty of a dry and barren land. The *via negativa* finds symbolically written across a frugal desert topography all of the emptiness necessary for beginning a life of prayer. As Michael Ondaatje puts it in his novel *The English Patient,* "A man in a desert can hold absence in his cupped hands knowing it is something that feeds him more than water."[7] This book does not argue that apophatic thinking is inevitably linked to a desert or mountain setting. Ideas are never rigidly rooted in geography. Yet the symbolic terrain preferred by teachers of the apophatic way is inevitably a land that is stingy, uncluttered, and empty.

Given my own particular attraction to desert terrain, I have to ask myself four questions in beginning this work: What sort of spiritual experience (what *habitus* or pattern of prayer) do I bring to the desert as a way of interpreting it? Do I fool myself in thinking the desert is able automatically to grant me spiritual insight? How do I participate in the construction of the desert as a work of the human imagination? Finally, what personal risk is required in exploring this nexus where desert geography and spiritual growth converge?

The Desert Habitus of Contemplative Prayer

My own approach to desert experience is formed, in large part, by a fledgling practice of contemplative prayer, rooted in early desert writers such as Evagrius and John Cassian. These desert Christians practiced a particular *habitus,* a way of ordering one's life around silence which was shaped by the desert-mountain terrain in which they lived. Calling themselves to a poverty of language and self, as well as goods, they plowed ground for the later growth of the apophatic tradition.

Denys Turner summarizes the historical development of that later tradition as an interplay between metaphors of ascent and inwardness, mountain and desert realities, the story of Moses meeting God on Sinai and Plato's allegory of the cave, intersecting biblical and Neoplatonic themes.[8] But the desert experience of silence was the soil out of which everything else eventually grew. The *habitus* of the early desert Christians allowed them to read from the landscape itself a particular vision of God, a conception of the human self, and a discipline necessary for the joining of the two. Through subsequent development in the tradition, it came to be articulated as follows:

1. God is a desert whose fullness of glory is hidden from human sight, known only in an unknowing and risking of love.

2. The self is a desert that must be stripped and made empty before God can be found at its center.

3. The realization of God's love at the heart of one's being is inseparably related to ascetical and liturgical performances (which are themselves suggested by desert experience).[9]

This "habit of being" outlines a model for growth in the spiritual life drawn from the desert itself, suggesting a pattern of behavior passed on in the community's history through its teachings on contemplative prayer.

My own efforts at appropriating this *habitus* over the last several years have involved a regular nightly practice of "desert prayer," routine participation in the liturgical life of a faith community, periodic backpacking trips alone into the wilderness, consistent work with an insightful spiritual director, and a disciplined pattern of reading in the classics of the tradition. This may sound like a labor-intensive method for realizing certain paradigmatic desert experiences in my own practice. One might imagine that in pretending to be a desert monk in the city my goal is to achieve particular states of desert consciousness. But the long-standing insistence of the tradition is that there is no "experience," no achievement of "consciousness" to be sought in any of this. The desert practice of contemplative prayer abandons, on principle, all experiences of God or the self. It simply insists that being present before God, in a silence beyond words, is an end in itself.

God cannot be *had,* the desert tradition affirms, if this means laying hold of God by way of concept, language, or experience. God is a desert, ultimately beyond human comprehension. John Cassian defined contemplative prayer as an imperfect yet "astonished gaze at God's ungraspable nature, something hidden" finally from human sight.[10] Evagrius advised his students that "when you are praying, do not shape within yourself any image of the Deity."[11] He knew that the God revealed in Jesus Christ is known ultimately only along the dry desert path of faith.

While this actual metaphor of "God as desert" may not appear before the sixth century (in Pseudo-Dionysius), it stands in concert with earlier teachings of Gregory of Nyssa and is developed later in John Scotus Eriugena, Thomas Gallus, and Meister Eckhart.[12] They unhesitatingly describe God as a desert mountain, high above all understanding.[13]

Still other teachers in the contemplative tradition echo the author of *The Cloud of Unknowing* in emphasizing the need to love God "with a naked intent," completely apart from any of God's attributes or benefits. God is a desert to be entered and loved, never an object to be grasped or understood.[14] In the end, we are no more able to "possess" God than we are able to possess ourselves. It is only as we abandon every effort to control God by experiencing God, relinquishing even the grasping self (always anxious to add the Deity to its store of personal acquisitions), that the mystery of meeting God beyond experience ever becomes possible.

Hence, a second dimension of this desert *habitus* is its conception of the human self as an inner desert of its own, stripped of worldly care, delighting in silence. Eucherius of Lyon was one of the earliest in the Latin West to emphasize this theme.[15] To become an inner desert is to abandon the rampant race of thoughts, feelings, and worries that continually distract the soul from attentiveness to God. Evagrius himself had understood the "putting away of such thoughts" as the essence of prayer.[16]

In the practice of contemplation, one comes eventually to embrace an apophatic anthropology, letting go of everything one might have imagined as constituting the self—one's thoughts, one's desires, all one's compulsive needs. Joined in the silence of prayer to a God beyond knowing, I no longer have to scramble to sustain a fragile ego, but discern instead the source and ground of my being in the fierce landscape of God alone. One's self is ever a tenuous thing, discovered only in relinquishment.[17] I recognize it finally as a vast, empty expanse opening out onto the incomparable desert of God.[18]

Given this emphasis, the modern reader searching for new techniques of spiritual "self-discovery" will largely be disappointed in the desert tradition of the apophatic way. Classical writers in this *habitus* could not be more indifferent to the modern search for "experiences of the sacred" that enhance self-realization. They would never, in the private, psychologizing way so familiar to contemporary spirituality, be anxious to add an encounter-with-God-through-contemplative-prayer to their collection of previous meditative accomplishments. As if one could then say, "Been there, done that!" to yet another personal success achieved through Zen attentiveness, transcendental meditation, or even centering prayer. The self is not "realized" in contemplative prayer; it is a desert one learns to ignore.

Having said this, however, it is important to note that the desert tradition never seeks the destruction of the self. Indeed, in early monastic terms, trying to live without a self is a temptation of its own, making the love of others impossible.[19] In the life of prayer, I am invited to realize my identity as "a unique self-determination of the image of God," able to love others only because of being loved myself. The goal of the spiritual life, therefore, is "a kenosis [an emptying] of the ego that opens one to being more fully possessed by a God whom one has never lacked," but who is known far more intimately in the joining through prayer of God and the self.[20]

Finally, the ordinary means by which these two deserts (of God and the self) are joined is a discipline shaped by the community's ascetic and liturgical life, anchored in the imitation of Christ. While teachers in the tradition insist that contemplation (and union with God) is a gift having nothing to do with human accomplishment, they also stress that attentiveness to the Word in *lectio divina,* the Liturgy of the Hours, the celebration of the Eucharist, and even the discipline of the body are intimately a part of the purgative and illuminative process by which one moves toward oneness with God. Sometimes spiritual methods are reduced to the very simplest performances, as in the silent repetition of a single word for dispelling thoughts and entering into stillness.[21] Yet the exercise of the discipline necessarily remains centered in the broader liturgical life of the faith community.

Devotional exercises thus have value in the practice of contemplative prayer. They frame it within a larger context of word and sacrament. But they certainly are not aimed at achieving what one may think of as devotional experiences of inner personal awareness. Even the most deeply moving thoughts and feelings about God can get in the way of meeting God most intimately in shared silence. Union with God is an apophatic event beyond experience and proof, beyond every individualistic, privatized way of knowing.[22]

This explains the antidevotional tendency of so many figures in the history of the apophatic tradition. The fourteenth-century author of *The Cloud of Unknowing* wanted nothing to do with the prolonged "sweet feelings and weepings" so characteristic of his contemporary Richard Rolle. John of the Cross remained resolutely critical of all extraordinary visions and raptures, even when proclaimed by his esteemed colleague Teresa of Avila. Denys Turner points to an astringently negative anti-mysticism (in Eckhart and others), aimed at "deconstructing what they think of as a baroque, over-florid, technology of spiritual experientialism."[23]

A religion of *pure experience* is typically a modern phenomenon, which often entails searching for religious encounters separate from any particular faith commitment.[24] The contemporary seeker, for example, might even suspect that a book like this—with its emphasis on the symbolic significance of desert-mountain terrain—could suggest ways of extracting desired psychological states from the natural environment itself.[25] Yet the *habitus* by which I approach this landscape has to insist that there *is* no free-floating desert-mountain "consciousness," certainly not apart from those communal traditions able to give it meaning.

For that matter, much of the experience I try to share in this book is, at its deepest level, inaccessible. I am not able to distill from either my mother's encounter with death or my own exposure to desert-mountain terrain any universal insights about the wonder-evoking power of fierce landscapes. I am left, ultimately, at an end of language, having nothing more than my own emptiness to report, though gradually coming to recognize emptiness itself as a profound and wonderful gift.

This is a book that attends at last to what Sherlock Holmes once described as the problem of the dog barking in the night, referring—of course—to the curious matter of the dog's not barking in the night. Sometimes the absence of sound and meaning, where normally most expected, may be itself full of significance.[26]

Desert Habitat and Environmental Determinism

People like myself may have a tendency to view a desert landscape as inherently suggesting the spiritual value of emptiness. Is it true, as some have argued, that the desert *qua* desert is inevitably a breeding ground for spirituality? Does it necessarily raise questions of God in a way that other landscapes do not? Or do I fool myself in imagining some automatic connection between geography and moral insight?[27]

In the history of environmental determinism, some writers have argued that prolonged desert experience irrevocably inclines the soul to questions of faith. Geographer Ellen Churchill Semple boldly proclaimed in 1911 that human beings are inescapably "a product of the earth's surface."[28] She urged in particular that along "waterless tracts of the desert," where the watching of grazing herd gives . . . leisure for contemplation, and the wide-ranging life a big horizon, . . . ideas take on a certain gigantic simplicity; religion becomes monotheism, God becomes one, unrivalled like the sand of the desert and the grass of the steppe, stretching on and on without break or change.[29]

"Le dèsert est monothéiste," Ernest Renan had declared in the late nineteenth century.[30] In arid landscapes of the Middle East—a land of few interruptions, where a wide, incendiary sky reaches out to a distant, unified horizon—he saw a stark simplicity to rule, thoughts turning inexorably to the mystery of One.[31]

So the argument has gone. Yahweh (and Allah) emerged as a function of desert reflection. A vast uncluttered landscape operated on the human mind to give rise to a singularity of vision. In actuality, however, desert life—absorbed constantly with questions of survival—has ever required attention to a multitude of details, never focused on simply one.

To survive at all, the desert dweller—Tuareg or Aborginal—must . . . forever be naming, sifting, comparing a thousand different "signs"—the tracks of a dung beetle or the ripple of a dune—to tell him where he is; where the others are; where rain has fallen; where the next meal is coming from. . . .[32]

Life in the desert is never simple. More than one conclusion can be drawn from it. As Bruce Chatwin observes, "desert people themselves show an indifference towards the Almighty that is decidedly cavalier." They are not particularly awestruck at the immense majesty of the divine. "We will go up to God and salute him," said a bedouin to an anthropologist in the nineteenth century, "and if he proves hospitable, we will stay with him: if otherwise, we will mount our horses and ride off."[33]

It is impossible, therefore, to attribute any facile geographical necessity to certain religious ideas or preferences in spirituality. The old adage that "basalt is conducive to piety" simply does not hold.[34] Monotheism is not inevitably a desert belief. Neither are saints an automatic product of desiccated land. Ed Abbey would have scoffed at the very idea. The desert, as he saw it, was as likely to produce outlaws as it was contemplatives—a distinction, by the way, that Thomas Merton would happily have found unnecessary. Holiness has never been a predetermined result of topography. Nor, for that matter, has orneriness.

The danger of a simplistic geographical determinism in the spiritual life is that it makes everything too easy. I do not have to assume the discipline or embrace the *habitus* if merely "going" to high desert country irresistably draws me to an uncomplicated wholeness. I can imagine that finding the right desert monastery, making the best mountain retreat, will occasion in itself involuntary holiness. But the desert, the mountain, offer no such guarantee. Physically being there is never enough. Growth in the spiritual life requires adopting a conscious "habit of being." Far too easily do we embrace the illusion that changing places is the simplest way of changing ourselves.

On the other hand, this does not mean that the landscape fails to exert an important, sometimes commanding influence upon us. "The spirit of place," D. H. Lawrence insisted, has an undeniable effect upon all of the ideas, as well as art and literature of a people.[35] Desert and mountain terrain may not carry a preordained necessity, but its power of suggestion is great. Antoine de Saint-Exupéry would have been an altogether different author had he worked as a train engineer in rainy Scotland. Georgia O'Keeffe would not have been the artist she became had she never gone to New Mexico. One cannot imagine Tony Hillerman writing detective stories from the ambience of a New England village. High desert country may not dictate ways of thinking, but it indelibly influences everything it touches.

In his stories, Hillerman places his protagonists, Navajo Tribal Police detectives Joe Leaphorn and Jim Chee, within a compellingly beautiful landscape of dread. Unsolved murders unfold within a fierce terrain of tall mesas and lifeless volcanic rubble—*malpais*, or "bad country," as the Spanish described it.[36] The land looms powerfully in the background, as do the arcane rituals of Navajo witchcraft. Yet Leaphorn and Chee, as good detectives, are reluctant to attribute foul play to Navajo "skinwalkers" drawing power from the earth. Keen judges of human nature, they know that crime can always be more readily ascribed to human turpitude. They realize that the land carries no irresistible or fatalistic influence of its own.[37] The landscape gives life, but it does not compel.

Participating in the Interpretation of Landscape

How do I participate in the construction of landscape as a work of the human imagination? Desert or mountain terrain is never simply "there." I manufacture it in the process of reading cultural meanings back onto the natural world.[38] I give it shape, even as it exerts its own influence on the imagining process I bring to it.

This tendency to read wilderness landscapes out of the collective memory of a people is seen in the way artists through the centuries have depicted desert background in portraits of Saint Anthony of Egypt. They delineate a stylized terrain that changes according to varied cultural conceptions of nature. Pinturicchio and Francesco Traini picture the saint against a wild, rocky terrain where desert foxes prey on unsuspecting birds. Pisanello places a thick woods in the background; Hubert and Jan van Eyck paint dark bushes, their leaves illuminated by a holy light. Albrecht Dürer puts the desert father in civilized Bavaria, with the castle of Nuremburg in the distance.[39] Landscape interpretations continually change, in art and spirituality alike, as the ongoing work of imagining the environment continues.

Given the fact that there are no "primordial places" intuitively perceived apart from the cultural construction of reality, this poses sharply the question of hermeneutics, the very nature of landscape interpretation.[40] How does one participate intimately in a given landscape—listening to it, being joined to its movements, letting it sink deeply into the pattern of one's being—without also distorting it, reading one's own subjective meanings back into its mystery?[41]

Deborah Tall is sensitive to this tension in her captivating interpretation of the Finger Lakes region of western New York. Her book, *From Where We Stand: Recovering a Sense of Place,* analyzes the landscape between Syracuse and Rochester as a paleographer might examine an ancient palimpsest, peeling away the successive messages of writers who through the years have inscribed new texts on the half-erased pages of old ones.

She reads the land through the eyes of the Iroquois, the raiding army of General Sullivan after the Revolutionary War, the long succession of farmers and merchants that followed. Yet she interprets all this from a very personal horizon of meaning, concerned to grasp the significance of her own dwelling in that place. Consequently, there is a constant danger of reducing the actual landscape to a metaphor of the identity she seeks: "I go out with the lamp of myself shining brightly, illuminating a clearing, but I remain, implacably, its center. My fear is that I violate topography as I describe it, that I inject my own dream into what is, simply, there."[42]

I too am aware of the danger of reading desert and mountain landscapes allegorically, seeing them through the particular lens of my own mother's slow dying. The geography described in this book is a single individual's rendering of a particular terrain, skewed by hopes and fears. The eye tries to be honest, but sees with its own idiosyncrasy.

The challenge is to honor the thing itself, as well as the thing as metaphor. When Emerson declared in 1836 that "every natural fact is a symbol of some spiritual fact," he sent people racing to the woods, anticipating the voice of God in the call of every thrush.[43] But too often they paid scant attention to the songbird in their anxiousness to hear some transcendent message. They returned home full of nothing but themselves, their pockets stuffed with metaphors. As the imagination reaches relentlessly for a timeless, interior soulscape, it is easy to sail over the specificity of particular landscapes.[44] The tendency to "reach through" every concrete detail of the environment—looking for God under every bush and twig, "injecting one's dream into what is, simply there"—is to fall into Ruskin's pathetic fallacy, betraying the "true appearance of things" under "the influence of emotion."[45]

This book of necessity walks a thin line between distance and participation.[46] Trying to balance critical analysis with the intimate experience of place, it merges three horizons of meaning, each hopefully serving as check on the other.[47] The first horizon is an acute, personal longing for fierce terrain. I come with a sufficient sense of loss to make a landscape of abandonment particularly compelling. A craving for wilderness, a love of backpacking alone in high desert country, has accompanied a need in recent years for letting go of many things in my life.

Having begun at that point, two other horizons of meaning are important in judging my experience of arid land, lest I simply read into it what I am already expecting to find. One is the meticulous attentiveness the naturalist gives to the self-evident "thereness" of desert-mountain terrain. I have to take seriously the landscape on its own terms—its geological and topographical details, its flora and fauna, its climate and precipitation. I must let the land speak in all its bewildering otherness. If home, as Joseph Wood Krutch once said, is "the place where one opens one's eyes without surprise," then the naturalist can never properly be at home, must be continually astonished and challenged.[48]

If the eye of the naturalist provides one important corrective, another comes from those who have adopted a particular way of living in desert and mountain places over a long period of time. Certain monastic communities in the history of Christian spirituality have developed rules for the ordering of life "on the edge," physically removed from the influence of a dominant culture. They have gathered through the years a corporate wisdom, drawn from the community's history and the landscape alike, which allows them to question the authenticity (or aberrance) of any given individual's practice of the desert way. This, too, serves as a check on the conclusions I draw about a spirituality rooted in wild terrain. I have had to write this book with field guides to desert ecology piled on one side of the desk and copies of Evagrius, Basil the Great, and Gregory of Nyssa on the other. Both are necessary if I am to be kept honest.

The study of spiritual traditions vis-à-vis their particular geographies is a fairly recent phenomenon. Philip Sheldrake urges research in this direction in *Spirituality and History* and goes on to exemplify it in his subsequent study of Celtic spirituality and place.[49] Keith Basso's analysis of landscape and the construction of identity among the Western Apache in Arizona offers an excellent example of ethnographic inquiry into the spiritual meanings of place.[50] Earlier accounts of desert spirituality, seen in the work of Derwas Chitty, Alan Jones, and Henri Nouwen, have been (respectively) historical, psychological, and pastoral in character, not attending necessarily to questions of geography or place.[51] Douglas Burton-Christie explores the connection between spirituality and landscape among contemporary nature writers, an interest growing out of his earlier analysis of desert monasticism.[52] Finally, authors such as Terry Tempest Williams and Kathleen Norris probe, in a finely crafted way, the healing character of fierce terrain in its relationship to experiences of personal loss.[53]

This book is an effort to wed these various approaches in a joining of scholarly research with engaged personal reflection. Sandra Schneiders affirms spirituality as an academic discipline, saying that research in this field is "self-implicating, often at a very deep level."[54] How one accomplishes this task without sacrificing the canons of scholarship is not yet entirely clear.

Beginning at the Desert's Edge

A bedouin story from the Sinai peninsula underscores the idea that what one brings to the desert—one's personal way of seeing it, even of walking through it—is crucial to the way one understands it. A Westerner entering the desert beyond Nuweiba once asked an English-speaking bedouin how far it was to the nearest oasis. The man did not respond. "How far is it to Ein El Furtaga?" the traveler asked more loudly, distinctly mouthing the words. But the bedouin still said nothing. Shouting his question a third time into the man's face, and receiving only silence yet again, the traveler finally shook his head and started walking away. "About four hours!" the bedouin then called out, in answer to his question. "Why didn't you tell me that the first time?" the Westerner asked. "I couldn't say," the man responded, "until I knew how fast you were accustomed to walking."[55] Answers to desert questions often depend upon what one brings in coming, how one may be accustomed to moving through anything.

The beginning place for my own work on desert-mountain spirituality has to be a point of profound vulnerability. Risk is the way I have become "accustomed to walking" in recent years. This is the only answer I have for the last question posed by the book, the question about personal risk and one's starting point in research. The terrain itself demands such a response. Embracing desert and mountain spirituality requires assuming the hazards of a rugged land, remaining open to the threat it poses. There may be no substitute for the instructive power of place. The only other heuristic aid of penetrating importance might be the simultaneous experience of loss in one's personal life. Certain truths can be learned, it seems, only as one is sufficiently emptied, frightened, or confused.

Accompanying my mother through cancer surgery, the prolonged experience of a nursing home, and the onslaught of Alzheimer's disease presented exactly such an opportunity, if not one of my own choosing, for examining death (and life) at very close range. During my mother's slow journey into emptiness, I found myself increasingly drawn to the threat and allure of wilderness. I read everything available on desert terrain, making more and more frequent trips into the wilds, hungry for the solace of empty spaces. An inexplicable correspondence emerged between the nursing home's freakish embrace of unconventionality and the desert's vacant sense of abandonment. Each place carried its own harsh honesty, its uncomfortable silences and grotesque extremes of behavior. Each helped in understanding the other.

Perhaps one flees to landscapes of abandonment in times of loss, like a person half conscious of his sickness drawn unexplainably to homeopathic cures. In the practice of homeopathy, a physician prescribes minuscule doses of an improbable medicine in order to produce symptoms closely resembling those of the disease being treated.[56] If one applies the same mysterious logic to landscape, then sheer cliffs and alkali flats may keenly suggest themselves to those for whom deprivation or loss have become harsh realities. Emptiness offers answers of its own. Deep speaks to deep.

Extremity is the necessary, even normative starting point for understanding what William James described as the strenuous character of the spiritual life. Yet most popular literature on desert spirituality speaks very little of risk and rarely attends to desert topography. All things harsh and threatening are missing. There are no vultures on the wing, no relentless sun, no smell of death in the air. In accounts of the desert experience of God,

> The term *desert* is often used metaphorically and psychologically, not geographically or ecologically. The so-called desert is any place of solitude, simplicity, and emptiness—a barren wasteland, figuratively—to which one withdraws for undistracted communication with God. One closes one's eyes and blocks out the other senses in order to experience the Spirit with utmost clarity. The process is seemingly transcendental rather than sacramental.[57]

Spiritual insights of the desert Christians (from Anthony of Egypt to Charles de Foucauld) are lifted out of the earthy, boulder-strewn world in which they were formed, becoming otherworldly and abstract, separated from the senses. We lose the sacramental affront of the place itself, its sense of danger, its powerful critique of language, its irrepressible challenge to human frailty.

My fear is that much of what we call "spirituality" today is overly sanitized and sterile, far removed from the anguish of pain, the anchoredness of place. Without the tough-minded discipline of desert-mountain experience, spirituality loses its bite, its capacity to speak prophetically to its culture, its demand for justice. Avoiding pain and confrontation, it makes no demands, assumes no risks. It betrays Saint Jerome's critique of the soft life and is horrified at Ed Abbey's Monkey Wrench Gang, sabotaging the "developers" of wilderness. It resists every form of desert perversity, dissolving at last into a spirituality that protects its readers from the vulnerability it was meant to provoke. The desert, in the end, will have none of it.

In his *Seven Pillars of Wisdom,* British adventurer T. E. Lawrence ("Lawrence of Arabia") wrote of his years in the Hejaz along the Red Sea. In the naked desert's night, he said, "we were stained by dew, and shamed into pettiness by the innumerable silences of stars." He found in the desert something that cut to the bone, reducing his soul to a thinness he would spend the rest of his life trying to recover. Despite a Eurocentric romanticism he never overcame, his description of desert life suggests the leanness sought by early desert Christians. "The desert Arab found no joy like the joy of voluntarily holding back. He found luxury in abnegation, renunciation, self restraint. He made nakedness of the mind as sensuous as nakedness of the body."[58] The mystery celebrated by the apophatic tradition is precisely this sensuous "nakedness of the mind" before God. It is where I have to begin this book.

Awad Afifi the Tunisian was a nineteenth-century dervish teacher who drew his wisdom from the wide expanse of desert North Africa. He once shared with his pupils a story that began with a gentle rain falling on a high mountain in a distant land. The rain was at first hushed and quiet, trickling down granite slopes. Gradually it increased in strength, as rivulets of water rolled over the rocks and down the gnarled, twisted trees that grew there. The rain fell, as water must, without calculation. The Sufi master understood that water never has time to practice falling.

Soon it was pouring, as swift currents of dark water flowed together into the beginnings of a stream. The brook made its way down the mountainside, through small stands of cypress trees and fields of lavender-tipped purslane, down cascading falls. It moved without effort, splashing over stones—learning that the stream interrupted by rocks is the one that sings most nobly. Finally, having left its heights in the distant mountain, the stream made its way to the edge of a great desert. Sand and rock stretched beyond seeing.

Having crossed every other barrier in its way, the stream fully expected to cross this as well. But as fast as its waves splashed into the desert, that fast did they disappear into the sand. Before long, the stream heard a voice whispering, as if coming from the desert itself, saying, "The wind crosses the desert, so can the stream." "Yes, but the wind can fly!" cried out the stream, still dashing itself into the desert sand.

"You'll never get across that way," the desert whispered. "You have to let the wind carry you." "But how?" shouted the stream. "You have to let the wind absorb you." The stream could not accept this, however, not wanting to lose its identity or abandon its own individuality. After all, if it gave itself to the winds, could it ever be sure of becoming a stream again?

The desert replied that the stream could continue its flowing, perhaps one day even producing a swamp there at the desert's edge. But it would never cross the desert so long as it remained a stream. "Why can't I remain the same stream that I am?" the water cried. And the desert answered, ever so wisely, "You never can remain what you are. Either you become a swamp or you give yourself to the winds."

The stream was silent for a long time, listening to distant echoes of memory, knowing parts of itself having been held before in the arms of the wind. From that long-forgotten place, it gradually recalled how water conquers only by yielding, by flowing around obstacles, by turning to steam when threatened by fire. From the depths of that silence, slowly the stream raised its vapors to the welcoming arms of the wind and was borne upward, carried easily on great white clouds over the wide desert waste.

Approaching distant mountains on the desert's far side, the stream then began once again to fall as a light rain. At first it was hushed and quiet, trickling down granite slopes. Gradually it increased in strength, as rivulets rolled over the rocks and down the gnarled, twisted trees that grew there. The rain fell, as water must, without calculation. And soon it was pouring, as swift currents of dark water flowed together—yet again—into the headwaters of a new stream.[59]

Awad Afifi refused to say what the story "meant," how it should be interpreted. He simply pointed his students to the desert nearby and urged them to find out for themselves.

Part I

PURGATION

Emptiness in a Geography of Abandonment

Nudos amat eremos [The desert loves to strip bare.] —Saint Jerome, letter to Heliodorus

The emptiness of the desert makes it possible to learn the almost impossible: the joyful acceptance of our uselessness. —Ivan Illich, Foreword to Carlo Carretto's *Letters from the Desert*

The desert says nothing. Completely passive, acted upon but never acting, the desert lies there like the bare skeleton of Being, spare, sparse, austere, utterly worthless, inviting not love but contemplation. —Edward Abbey, *Desert Solitaire*

I have it in me so much nearer home / to scare myself with my own desert places. —Robert Frost, "Desert Places"

The *vast* and the dreadful have a great affinity to one another . . . a wild solitude where we are afraid of being alone. . . . Savage lands that are uncultivated, landscapes ruined by the desolation of war, lands forsaken and abandoned—all partake of the quality of *vastness* which gives rise to a sense of secret horror within us. . . . —Seigneur de Saint-Evremond, *Dissertation sur le Mot de Vaste*

Coyote is always out there, and he is always hungry. —Tony Hillerman, *Coyote Waits*

The desert of the divine nature [is] an inexpressible height removed from all things. It is "deserted" by every creature, because it surpasses all intellect, although it does not "desert" any intellect. . . . It is in the very desert of divine height that the Word, through whom "all things were made," cries out. —John Scotus Eriugena, *Commentary on the Gospel of John*

[In the desert] ... the world is flat, empty, nearly abstract and in its flatness, you are a challenging upright thing as sudden as an exclamation point, as enigmatic as a question mark. —Wallace Stegner, *Wolf Willow*

The significance of desert and mountain is not who resides here, but what we ourselves have left behind in coming. —David Douglas, *Wilderness Sojourn: Notes in the Desert Silence*

In the beginning you weep. The starting point for many things is grief, at the place where endings seem so absolute. One would think it should be otherwise, but the pain of closing is antecedent to every new opening in our lives.

When my mother was diagnosed with bone cancer, she was given six months to live. It seemed such a sudden and abrupt ending, so inarguable. But she was eighty years old and signs of Alzheimer's disease had begun already to appear. The doctor's words were given with what he meant to be a comforting assuredness, and I wanted to receive them as such. There was comfort in thinking limits were being assigned to her pain, as well as to my grief. I'd feared for some time that her body might go on for years longer than her mind could last.

In the coming weeks I would travel with her through surgery, radiation treatments, the painful experience of being uprooted from her house and placed in a nursing home. Roles were reversed, as I (an only child, the last of my family) became mother to my mother, wondering at midlife who would be left to mother me. It was an experience of discovering an unlikely grace in a grotesque landscape of feeding tubes and bed restraints, wheelchairs and diapers, nausea and incontinence.

During those first few months I watched my mother work as hard at dying as I'd ever seen her work at anything in her life. I sat beside her bed, wondering at this middle passage through which she journeyed, looking for hints from the other side, listening for the wisdom she was weaving from the gathered threads of a long and troubled life. I was studying an athlete in training, a desert monk wholly absorbed in *ascesis,* the intimate exercise of holy living (and holy dying).

It was not easy for either of us. She longed to have the work done, seeking release from the burden of death. I, too, wished to put it behind me, hating the pitch of uncertainty at which my life was now lived. But I also valued our times together in silence. The opportunity for prolonged grief was somehow good, inviting me to the letting go of other things in my life. A keen sense of immediacy, a vulnerability that sharpened life's intensity, a capacity to discern what was and wasn't important, all these were occasioned by the proximity of death. I wondered at times if I could begin living always as if someone dear to me were dying.

In the beginning you weep. This is what the teachers of the spiritual life insist. In the first canto of Dante's *Inferno,* the pilgrim is lost in a *gran diserto.* It's the same desert through which the children of Israel passed on their way from Egypt to the Promised Land. It's a place of brokenness, a desert through which we've all passed (or will pass) in our journey from bondage toward hope. There Dante meets Virgil, the one who'll guide him through the corridors of hell and up the slopes of Mount Purgatory, where he'll meet yet another guide—the sweet Beatrice—who carries him on to Paradise. The road to Paradise always begins with tears.

This threefold pattern of the spiritual life, from mourning to insight to glory, came to be described early in the church's history, following the apostle Paul's distinctions of spiritual childhood, adolescence, and maturity.[1] Gregory of Nyssa characterized growth in faith as entry into a moonlit desert night, then movement to a fog-covered mountain and, finally, into the impenetrable darkness of a thick cloud. The more darkness faith could embrace, he thought, the greater light it gave.

Bernard of Clairvaux preferred the imagery of three kisses given to one's beloved. The penitent's kiss on the feet is followed by the seeker's kiss on the hand and subsequently the lover's kiss on the mouth.[2] This movement from one stage (or one kiss) to the next— from desert to mountain to cloud—was never seen as fixed, nor even guaranteed. Elements of each stage might be present along the way. Threat and promise could recur at every level. It was understood that we grow, to our chagrin, by fits and starts throughout our lives.

Increasingly, my own experience was one of being called to this erratic kind of growth, stumbling slowly with a dying parent along the desert's purgative way. After the immediate threat of death had lessened and it became apparent that my mother and I were in for a longer haul than first expected, a sabbatical semester made it possible for me to satisfy my increasing need for wilderness, for a sprawling geography of emptiness. I made a month-long trip to Israel and Egypt, going for the first time in my life to the Holy Land. It was a pilgrimage that echoed my mother's own long journey into relinquishment and loss. The desert of the Sinai is a perfect place for confronting deep fears and feelings of abandonment. Loneliness there is a constant companion, one who insists on being honored if not also loved.

My time was divided between research in the library of the École Biblique in Jerusalem and various excursions into the Judean desert and beyond. The most important of these was an eight-day hiking trip into the Sinai wilderness. In that austere landscape, I realized more than ever before the healing capacity of fierce terrain. The desert did for me what the nursing home had begun to do for my mother at home. It invited me out of myself, out of my fears and need for control, out of a self-absorption wary of opening itself to intimacy.

The way of purgation involves an entry into what is unnerving, even grotesque in our lives, into what quickly reveals our limits. It seems at first, like most beginnings in the spiritual life, a mistake, a false start, an imperfection in God's planning, a regression in our own growth. Only through hindsight do we recognize it for the unexpected gift that it is.

Grace and the Grotesque

Reflections on a Spirituality

of Brokenness

The grotesque is a game with the absurd, in a sense that the grotesque artist
plays, half laughingly, half horrified, with the deep absurdities of existence.
—Philip Thomson[1]

I sat in a chair next to my mother's bed in the nursing home to
which she'd been brought from the hospital early that morning. The
doctors didn't expect her to live long. I'd been assured that this
starkly simple white room would be only temporary. Meanwhile, a
nurse stabbed at my mother's arm with a needle, searching for a vein
that long ago had collapsed. I thumbed nervously through a large-
print edition of the *Living Bible* on the stand beside her bed, pretending not to notice. It held two unanswered letters and an old
Mother's Day card. Other than this and a familiar pair of false teeth
in a plastic container nearby, there was nothing in the room that
made it my mother's. I felt the prolonged and insistent probing of
the needle as if it were my own arm, indeed, my own soul.

This was the beginning of an end that would take much longer
than I expected. I had no way of knowing that morning how many
months, even years, it would finally be. Flannery O'Connor once
remarked that "sickness is more instructive than a long trip to Europe." She spoke out of her own prolonged and agonizing experience with lupus, the disease from which she died at age thirty-nine.
Having learned so much from her "grand tour" of the continent of
pain, she confessed that "sickness before death is a very appropriate
thing and I think those who don't have it miss one of God's mer-
cies."[2]

It would take me a long time to grasp the meaning of this strange
truth. But gradually I came to find a peculiar, unanticipated comfort
in the grotesque world of O'Connor's fiction, mirroring as it did the
baroque character of my mother's illness. In O'Conner's stories one
finds lonely, twisted people running from their brokenness, denying
their sinfulness, terrified of death and change. They learn that God's

grace seldom comes in a form they might welcome; it demands the abandonment of every security to which they've clung. Only in accepting the vulnerability that grace demands do they find themselves invited back to wholeness.

Such was the hazardous desert terrain into which I was led by this unintelligible thing the doctors referred to as metastatic breast cancer. My mother and I had no way of understanding it. We feared the loss of memory, the intense pain that is a part of proliferating bone cancer, the long hours spent in the waiting room of radiation oncology, the dread (and longing) for the morphine shunt that mercifully but terrifyingly dulls the mind, the wish simply to know when to expect the end. Not that I was ready, in any way, to deal with my mother's dying. It reminded me too much of my father's death, and even my own. I wasn't ready for any of this, least of all for the truth that grace would be found, not apart from but wholly within the experience. The grotesque mask of death forced me toward a new honesty—about God, myself, all the fears and denials to which I'd clung. It offered a grace I would much rather not have received at the time.

The Art of the Grotesque

The art of the grotesque, in literature and in life, can suggest, for those who embrace it, a healing spirituality of brokenness. Its unexpected combinations of revulsion and amusement, disgust and delight, open up disconcerting but highly imaginative possibilities. My teachers in those early months were the people I met in hospital cancer wards and nursing homes. These seasoned travelers in grief became a source of improbable grace, like the bizarre characters of O'Connor's short stories, the sideshow freaks and dwarfs photographed with compassion by Diane Arbus, the people with mental and physical disabilities of whom Jean Vanier writes so poignantly. When life confronts us with our limits, those who have lived with limits all their lives instruct us most profoundly.

Christianity has long been fascinated with the grotesque in art and literature. The accounts of Jesus' suffering and death, followed so closely by the ludicrous joy of Easter, occasioned a vivid coincidence of opposites in the early Christian imagination. This emerged as a pattern in Christian spirituality, flouting with levity the terrors of death.[3] It recurred in the medieval practice of dressing the skeletons of saints in bright clothing, in the *danse macabre* and *flagelantes* of Baroque Spanish devotion.

As early as the second century it could be seen in Polycarp of Smyrna's almost comic martyrdom. Threatening him with lions, unsuccessfully burning him at the stake, finally stabbing him with a dagger, the Romans found him practically impossible to kill. His story was retold with zest and grisly detail by persecuted Christians everywhere. They knew that horror is accompanied by laughter in a resurrection faith. This is a truth later echoed in Francis of Assisi's kiss of the leper on the road to Perugia, in the comic and monstrous figures of Renaissance painter Hieronymus Bosch, in variations on the theme of

Beauty and the Beast from Andrew Lang to the *Elephant Man* and *Phantom of the Opera.*

Yet any theoretical discovery of grace in the grotesque could be dangerous if divorced from the palpable experience of pain, the mundane smell of urine and despair. A saccharine, easy grace is no grace at all. I sat beside my mother's bed on that first day in the nursing home, seeing her as grotesque, almost unrecognizable. There was nothing romantic about her suffering. Black spots and purple splotches covered her hands and feet where needles had searched for shriveled veins. A feeding tube hung from her nose. Her lips were dry and peeling, her breath foul. She'd been tied to the bed because she didn't know where she was and repeatedly tried to get up to leave. Yet there in the twisted shape of my mother's body I stumbled upon an unguessed wholeness.

It was Wednesday of Holy Week, her first day in the nursing home. She was in tears, working at dying, yet unable even to wipe her nose because of the feeding tube. She tried unconsciously to pull it out, but I stopped her, calling for help. When the nurse came, she explained that my mother would need the "mittens," and proceeded to tie large gauze boxing gloves on her hands, preventing her from touching anything. What had I done? I asked myself. There she lay—miserable, stripped of dignity, incapable of helping herself in the least way—and now betrayed by a son whose best intentions had only made things worse. I left the room, choking on my own helplessness.

But the unexpected occurred that afternoon when I returned to the nursing home. My mother was resting quietly by then, the gloves removed. She looked up and said to me gently, in an unusual moment of lucidity, "Don't cry, Belden. It's natural to have to do this. It's all a part of dying." With those words a window suddenly opened. By an unanticipated grace, I found healing through the one I'd meant to comfort.

Through that Holy Week I was shown pierced hands and feet as I'd never seen them before. I was brought face to face with my own death. Guilt and hurt were mixed with love, a crazy humor pervading it all. My mother's hallucinations were sometimes hilarious; we often knew laughter through tears. Embarrassment brought a fool's comedy of its own. I would brush her false teeth or change a bed pan as quickly as possible, hoping no one would walk by the room and think me daft or some sort of pervert. Sickness before death is filled with ambivalences, a crazy-quilt of all we'd known in life.

Why are we drawn to the grotesque, to those freakish ambiguities that set our lives on edge? German critic Wolfgang Kayser suggests a definition of the grotesque style as exemplified in the art of Bruegel and Goya, the fiction of Kafka and Edgar Allen Poe. The grotesque is born, he says, out of the dislocation that people feel in an estranged world. In periods of personal or cultural crisis, human beings experience a loss of control in a universe that's no longer reliable. The grotesque mirrors their fear of the incomprehensible; it recalls to mind an ominousness they cannot name.[4]

But the grotesque is also a daring exercise in summoning the absurd, making fun of what is feared. Its goal is to defeat, at least in the space of a brief moment's laughter, the powers of darkness. It's "an attempt to invoke and subdue the demonic aspects of the world," says Kayser. Theologically, this is the heart of Paul's argument for folly in his first letter to the Corinthians, culminating in the absurd, apocalyptic declaration that "death is swallowed up in victory" (I Cor. 15:54). Thomas Mann wasn't far wrong when he said that the grotesque is "the only guise in which the sublime may appear." He knew the heart's deepest longing for a bloodied, ragged truth that comes staggering from behind to startle and win. No other truth is worthy of the risks that life demands.

Grace as a Harsh and Dreadful Thing

The grotesque reminds us of the *via negativa,* the discovery of God's presence in brokenness, weakness, renunciation, and despair. It exposes our compulsive fears of being vulnerable in a society that values only competence. Our temptation is always to flee the monstrous terror of our own deformity, but by confronting it we discover a spirituality that exults in woundedness. This poses a radical challenge to our culture, however, and necessitates a rethinking of our twisted images of God, grace, and human nature. A spirituality of brokenness shows us how to live in the face of death and all the other threats of the grotesque. Yet it requires of us three acts of extraordinary difficulty in our society.

First, it forces us to admit that grace rarely comes as a gentle invitation to change. More often than not it appears in the form of an assault, something we first are tempted to flee. Such was the prophetic experience of Jonah and Jeremiah. For them, receiving God's grace was more like being hit on the head with a book and called a warthog from hell, Ruby Turpin's disconcerting experience in Flannery O'Connor's story "Revelation." God's grace comes sometimes like a kick in the teeth, leaving us broken, wholly unable any longer to deny our need.

The grotesque form is powerfully able to communicate this difficult truth, forcing on us the inescapability of our sin. It serves, therefore, a prophetic function, disturbing us into accepting our condition. It can't be "nice." Only in harshness can it heal. Flannery O'Connor tried to explain this to those readers (including her own mother) who thought she ought to write pleasant things that people would like. She despaired of the idea, however, that good "Christian" stories should offer instant uplift, happy endings and easy transitions that leave the reader undisturbed and feeling good.

The irony of the gospel is that it becomes truly "good news" only for those immersed in the bad news of their normal experience. It has to come as shocking surprise, something so irregular that it may at first seem repulsive. O'Connor observed, "Our age not only does not have a very sharp eye for the almost imperceptible intrusions of grace, it no longer has much feeling for the nature of the violences which precede and follow them."[5] Meeting God's grace can be like seeing an unloved son in a threatening murderer (as in "A Good Man is Hard to Find") or like hearing the affirming words "God made me thisaway" randomly spoken in a lewd show at a carnival (as in "A Temple of the Holy Ghost").[6] Grace bursts forth from absurd sources.

A Redefinition of Humanity

A spirituality of brokenness demands, secondly, a rethinking of what it means to be human. The grotesque forces us, as we gawk at what is abnormal, to clarify what constitutes the essence of personhood. "To be able to recognize a freak, you have to have some conception of the whole man," said O'Connor.[7]

Photographer Diane Arbus offers a deeply compelling artistic reflection on the nature of our humanity. What is shared in common, she asks, by a Jewish giant at home with his parents in the Bronx, a Mexican dwarf in his hotel room on 42d Street, and a tattooed man at a carnival in Maryland? Why are we so irresistably drawn to the weird and bizarre?

"There's a quality of legend about freaks," she suggests, "like a person in a fairy tale who stops you and demands that you answer a riddle."[8] We look at ourselves through a distorted mirror in a circus fun house and grasp for a truth that lies hidden in the glass. We study a photograph of a retarded girl from New Jersey in an oversized dress, holding a hat on her head and looking curiously toward the camera. What do we see reflected in her face if not our own vulnerability and our own wholeness as well? The very image of God, disguised perhaps by nervous laughter, stares back at us in silence. We're known, stripped of all masks, reduced to an identity no longer subject to harm. This is the creaturehood for which we've been brought into being.

But it remains distorted by "the sumptuous arrogance of a world in which death has no place."[9] Our culture substitutes the glamorous for the grotesque, denying this awkward vision of the *imago Dei*. Our definitions of the human rule out bizarre and broken forms. People dying of cancer possess none of the power or beauty that we assume to be the principal marks of human worth. If we define the person exclusively in terms of rational ability and productivity, someone with Down's syndrome will inevitably appear less than whole. The eccentric, the ugly, the abnormal lie beyond the measure of our societal norms. We're left with a stylized and truncated humanity, dangerously imagining itself complete.

Jean Vanier, the French-Canadian founder of the l'Arche communities around the world, argues for a radically different conception of humanity. He finds that people who are most severely disabled, both physically and mentally, provide a truer measure of humanity than any image held by our dominant culture. Not only do the handicapped teach those who help and support them in the l'Arche communities, but the most severely handicapped teach those who are less impaired. The inordinantly marginal and despised possess an undiminished capacity for touching others.[10]

Michael Downey speaks of this in his book *A Blessed Weakness: The Spirit of Jean Vanier and l'Arche*.[11] Downey lived for several months in the l'Arche community of Trosly-Breuil in France. Finding it difficult to adjust to a new language and culture, he was invited one night to read the French Bible at Evening Prayer. He was very self-conscious, "fumbling on every line, stuttering and massacring that beautiful language of the angels." But he noticed that Alain, the most severely impaired person in the house (one who usually responded to very little), began to follow his haltering effort with the greatest attention. Alain recognized something of his own deep and lifelong struggle in this "unimpaired" man's painful effort to read, and he gave in return a respect and encouragement drawn from the deep wells of his own attentiveness. Downey's vulnerability, his weakness, is what occasioned the human contact. Allegedly "disabled" people would teach us that we most encounter wholeness when "we recognize our poverty and not our capacity."

Consequently, we need to measure ourselves by something other than performance, despite what our culture has taught us. "The handicapped, the elderly, the marginalized, and the weak have little sense of competition," writes Downey. "These people call the healthy and the robust to a life of sharing, where individuals are valued for themselves in their uniqueness. There is, we learn from them, no need to conform—we are already one in our fragility and in our being toward death."[12] They invite us, at last, to accept ourselves and each other, to be no more (nor less) than what we were created to be.

Rediscovering a Broken God

The third and last requirement of a spirituality of brokenness is its call to reconsider the ways we've learned to picture God. In a world of elaborate computer images, it's immensely difficult to grasp the subtle simplicity that characterizes God in biblical faith. This is the "scandal" of the gospel that Paul describes in I Corinthians. God is not what we expect. We may be ready like Peter on the mount of transfiguration to concede God's presence in stupefying splendor, perhaps even to publicize and market it to our own advantage (Matt. 17:1–8). But we flee with terror when following God leads to the smell of prison and the anger of authorities armed with steel (Luke 22:54–60). Our image of God doesn't prepare us for a truth realized in brokenness. We need to be shaken out of our expectations. "To the hard of hearing you shout, and for the almost-blind you draw large and startling figures," O'Connor wrote.[13]

The grotesque reminds us who we are, but even more it discloses the mystery of God's presence. Repeatedly in biblical faith we discover a broken and despised people calling upon a God made accessible in pathos and tears. God is never what Pharoah, Ahab, and Herod expect. There's a shocking, almost comic quality about the annunciations one finds in scripture. Angels announce to shepherds standing in a field of sheep dung the birth of a king clothed in rags. A figure clad in white announces to John of the Apocalypse the majestic Lion of the Tribe of Judah, but when he turns to look there's only a slain and bloody lamb (Rev. 5:5–6). In biblical experience, what you see isn't necessarily what you get. This is the mystery of God as *Deus absconditus*.

The God of scripture is equally revealed in vulnerability and in triumph. This is because both actions are rooted in love. God wills us to be broken for the sake of a strength to make whole. Divine love is incessantly restless until it turns all woundedness into health, all deformity into beauty, all embarrassment into laughter. In biblical faith, brokenness is never celebrated as an end in itself. God's brokenness is but an expression of a love on its way to completion. Hence we never can accept, much less romanticize, the plight of a people rejected by the world as aberrant and unfit. They invite us to share in the "groaning of all creation" for a redemption yet to be revealed (Rom. 8:19–21). The paradox of the grotesque is that it summons those who are whole to be broken and longs for those who are broken to be made whole.

This paradox forces me back to the nursing home where my mother waited through that first season of Lent several years ago. All theologizing, if worth its salt, must submit to the test of hospital gowns, droning television sets, and food spilled in the clumsy effort to eat. What can be said of God that may be spoken without shame in the presence of those who are dying? At the time, that was my one test of theological method. I met a woman by the elevator each day whose mouth was always open wide, as if uttering a silent scream. In a bed down the hall lay a scarcely recognizable body, twisted by crippling arthritis—a man or woman I'd never met. Another woman cried out every few moments, desperately calling for help in an "emergency" that never ebbed. Who *were* these people?

They represented the God from whom I repeatedly flee. Hidden in the grave-clothes of death, this God remains unavailable to me in my anxious denial of aging and pain. He is good news only to those who are broken. But to them he's the Lion of the Tribe of Judah, lurking in the shadows beyond the nurses' desk, promising life in the presence of death. This is the last place I might have sought him. I found myself wanting often to run from that gaping mouth, the twisted body, the cries that echoed through the halls. I resisted going to the nursing home. Yet at the same time, I was drawn there.

I know why Francis of Assisi had to kiss the leper, why Mother Teresa reached out to those dying on the streets of Calcutta, why Jean Vanier gives himself without restraint to the handicapped. It has nothing to do with charity. It's a concern to touch—and to be touched by—the hidden Christ, the one found nowhere else so clearly. It's a longing to reach out to the grotesque, stroking the bloodied head of a slain lamb as its image gradually changes into the fierce and kindly face of a Lion whose name is love.

On that first day in the nursing home, as my mother lay dying, we waited together, as if something or someone were coming for both of us. I adjusted uneasily to my vulnerability, learning what it meant to be grotesque, slowly abandoning all my theoretical questions of God and grace and human pain. Reading Laura Gilpin's poem "The Two-Headed Calf" would later bring an unusual sense of recognition. In my deepening understanding of my mother's situation, she and I had begun changing places. The differences between deformity and wholeness had begun to fade. I'd almost grasped (or was it *remembered?*) what it meant for myself to be born into brokenness.

> Tomorrow when the farm boys find this
> freak of nature, they will wrap his body
> in newspaper and carry him to the museum.
>
> But tonight he is alive and in the north
> field with his mother. It is a perfect
> summer evening: the moon rising over
> the orchard, the wind in the grass. And
> as he stares into the sky, there are
> twice as many stars as usual.[14]

Perhaps we all live in such a short span of time, knowing ourselves broken, yet content for now to be alive, mothered by something we cannot fully name, looking out in silence at the stars.

Apophatic spirituality has to start at the point where every other possibility ends. Whether we arrive there by means of a moment of stark extremity in our lives, or (metaphorically) by way of entry into a high desert landscape, the sense of naked inadequacy remains the same. Prayer without words can only begin where loss is reckoned as total.

· 2 ·

Places on the Edge

Wild Terrain and the
Spiritual Life

A person is forced inward by the spareness of what is outward and visible in all this land and sky. The beauty of the Plains is like that of an icon.... what seems stern and almost empty is merely open, a door into some simple and holy state. —Kathleen Norris[1]

Wild places have always tantalized the human imagination, captivating even as they unnerve. Vast and indifferent landscapes, from the Sinai Peninsula in a bitter February to the rugged coast of Iona in rainy August, have a way of disarming one by with their austere beauty. In the eyes of poet and mystic, they become bearers of a forgotten yet insistent truth. Lawrence Kushner argues that:

> The memories of a place become a part of it. Places and things never forget what they have been witnesses to and vehicles of and entrances for. What has happened there happened nowhere else. Like ghosts who can neither forget what they have seen nor leave the place where they saw it, such are the memories tied to places of ascent.[2]

Mountain and desert territory connects people symbolically, if not literally, to places of ascent (or places of threatening expanse). They remind them of things they would rather forget, taking them to edges from which the human psyche normally recoils. Such places have nothing to do with comfort. Martin Marty speaks of a "wintery spirituality," with its shrill cry of absence, frost, and death, contrasting this to a "summery spirituality" of artificial warmth, easy exuberance, and a glib certainty of the divine presence.[3] Mountain and desert experience is a "wintery" phenomenon, more kenotic than pleromic, more given to being emptied than to being filled. It is harsh, lean in imagery, beggarly in its gifts of love. Yet, as Hosea and Jeremiah knew well, no love is deeper nor more honest than desert love.[4] Fierce landscapes remind us that what we long for and what we fear most are both already within us.

Another way of saying this is that desert and mountain terrain provokes the identification and reordering of boundaries. It confronts people with their edges.[5] In wild places, terror and growth-toward-wholeness walk hand in hand.

"We need to witness our own limits transgressed," wrote Henry David Thoreau.[6] Deserts, accordingly, confront us with a vast horizontal edge, a horizon of emptiness into which we find ourselves absorbed and lost. The desert is intrinsically hostile to the ego, threatening to swallow it up in its endless expanse of nothingness. Mountains, by contrast, provide—both physically and metaphorically—a decisively *vertical* edge. Standing at the top of a great cliff, plunging a thousand feet into the chasm below, one knows the unholy dread felt by creatures without wings. The abyss threatens to consume everything.

In desert and mountain wilderness, people discover liminal places suggesting thresholds between where they have been and where they are going.[7] Whether they experience these places as dream symbols or rites of passage, whether they physically travel through wild, disorienting terrain or enter it metaphorically through an experience of profound crisis, such sites mark important points of transition in their lives. Out on the edge—in the desert waste or suspended between earth and sky—they transgress the limits of culture, language, all the personal boundaries by which their lives are framed. In whatever form one may find it, "the desert loves to strip bare," as Saint Jerome insisted.[8] The desert reduces one to a rawboned simplicity. Life out there is lawless. The structured patterns of civilization do not extend that far. Law and order break down. You quickly come to the end of what you have depended upon to give continuity and meaning to your life.

These are potentially dangerous landscapes, beyond the boundaries of a safe, inhabitable world. By definition, a desert is an arid region where annual rainfall remains less than ten inches. Some deserts average only half an inch a year, with parts of the Sahara not receiving a drop of rain for more than twenty years.[9] There are places where only "ghost rain" falls, evaporating before it reaches the ground, where temperatures of rocks at ground level can approach two hundred degrees Fahrenheit, where wind and dust storms cause the human body to lose as much as a quart of moisture an hour.

Mountains, by definition, are rugged land forms that offer a minimal local relief (an immediate rise above the surrounding terrain) of between three hundred and nine hundred meters. Their slope angles fall between ten and 30 degrees, with successive levels of elevation providing significantly different climates and ecological environments. Some mountains even produce their own weather systems.[10] One geographer suggests, however, that a mountain is defined as much by the stories told about it—the way it enters into the imagination of the people living in its shadow—as by its shape or size.[11] Tales of lost climbers, storms and avalanches, unusual light effects, spirit beings dwelling at its peak—all of these add to the aura of mountain angst and mountain glory.[12]

They form a forbidding, even belligerent province, these worlds of desert and mountain ascendency. Few people, if any, live far up in the hills or deep in the wilds. And the ones who do tend to be caricatured as renegades and fools, crazy people not accustomed to polite society. They do not fit in easily. They can even be terrifying and menacing, as in James Dickey's novel *Deliverance,* awakening within us impulses we are reluctant to face.[13]

In wilderness extremity, people find themselves running out of language, driven to silence. Ordinary speech seems inappropriate. Mountain and desert people do not talk much. Their words are measured by the leanness of the land. In short, the liminality of desert and mountain terrain redefines every boundary giving shape to one's life.[14]

The Psychology of Extreme Landscapes

These varied effects upon people of exposure to unusual and threatening land-scapes is a concern of researchers in the relatively recent fields of environmental psychology and psychogeography.[15] They ask why some of us tend to be drawn to such places and what physical or psychological effects they have upon us.

In his study of the 1963 American Mount Everest expedition, for example, James Lester analyzed the personality type of those attracted to the most demanding levels of mountain climbing. He found a self-confident and assertive individuality to be the most prevalent characteristic of the group. These were no-nonsense people of action. Yet he was amazed at the mystical, self-transcending experiences reported at high altitudes by those not normally inclined toward transcendent experience at all. Bivouacked at night on a snow-covered ledge at twenty-eight thousand feet, some of them sustained out-of-body experiences and a sense of oneness with everything in the universe. They exulted in their personal limits' being overrun. His conclusion was that the appeal of mountain experience to climbers is rooted not only in its challenge to self-assertiveness but also in its possibilities for occasioning self-forgetfulness. "The devotee of climbing seems . . . to exemplify often the most exquisitely balanced struggle between 'proving' self and 'losing' self, with every action serving both ends."[16]

This explains much of the appeal of desert and mountain topography in the history of spirituality, from Egyptian hermits in the fourth century to contemporary pilgrimages up Croagh Patrick in Ireland today.[17] In stretching the self to its edges, the geography helps in forcing a breakthrough to something beyond all previously conceived limits of being.[18]

Psychologists observe that challenging terrain evokes a high commitment of personal energy because of the uncertainty it poses. Human motivation thrives on uncertainty. If a desert trek or mountaineering expedition seems guaranteed of success (or guaranteed of failure), motivation will never be as high as when there is genuine doubt of the outcome. As a result, group conversation on a mountaineering expedition will tend to maintain or maximize uncertainty as a way of sustaining motivation. The pleasure obtained from climbing a mountain "is not in reaching the summit but in carrying on the task in the face of doubt as to whether the summit will be reached or will prove unattainable."[19] The human spirit delights in the exercise of uncertainty.

Yet another researcher attributes the seductive attraction of wild landscapes to the sense of "flow" sometimes experienced by rock climbers or desert trekkers as they methodically and painstakingly work their way across the terrain.[20] "Flow" is a term coined by University of Chicago social psychologist M. Csikszentmihalyi in describing the holistic sensation we experience whenever we act with total involvement. It can happen in an athletic event, an artistic performance, or a religious ritual. In an experience of flow, one action follows another without need for conscious intervention. There is a loss of ego, a diminished sense of control. Little distinction is made between the self and the environment, as everything moves together in unforced harmony. "While an actor [or climber] may be aware of what he is doing, he cannot be aware that he is aware, or the flow will be interrupted."[21] This loss of self-consciousness, experienced by intimate involvement with a demanding landscape, is not unlike the classic virtue of *apatheia* taught by desert monks.

Interaction between the human psyche and a harsh geography is invariably reciprocal. On the one hand, environmental conditions associated with the extremities of the land impact human consciousness by means of excessive temperatures, physical exhaustion, isolation, stress, or a lack of variation in physical and social stimuli.[22] The severity of desert and mountain travel has a significant effect on the way people perceive what they experience there.[23] Yet on the other hand, as psychogeographers remind us, the external landscape is also a projected map of internal states of consciousness. "We project psychic contents outward onto the social and physical world and act as though what is projected is in fact an attribute of the other or outer."[24] We imagine the desert, for example, to be possessed of the inherent hostility and malevolence many tend to associate with it, when of course the desert itself remains wholly disinterested, neither hateful nor loving. We simply respond to a projection of our own fearfulness.

The interaction of these two realities—the physical stress posed by a rugged environment and the interior interpretative process of the psyche—can result in a wide range of psychological and spiritual experience. Charles Lindbergh, flying alone over mountains of cloud at ten thousand feet on his transatlantic flight, spoke of spirit beings or "ghostly presences" that came to his aid in the process of his journey.[25] Such experiences of a "sensed presence" in unusual environments, from Moses on Mount Sinai to solitary sailors circumnavigating the globe, do not have to be interpreted as psychiatric aberrations.[26] They exemplify the highly imaginative convergence of threatening terrain and the rich vulnerability of the human spirit in the face of the unknown.

Peaks and Vales on the Metaphorical Map of the Psyche

Desert and mountain landscapes, as read by the human mind, are always symbolic as well as geodetic, suggesting unexplored interior regions of the subconsious. Fierce landscapes serve as metaphorical maps of the life of the spirit. De-

serts and mountains of the psyche can be traced throughout the history of mythology, the writings of the mystics, and the work of psychologists exploring
landscape symbols in folklore and dreams. Apophatic spirituality frequently
employs the imagery of empty and dangerous terrain, though it never presumes
that physical entry to such places is the only way of learning their truth. Saint
John of the Cross knew and wrote about desert-mountain experience better
than most people in the history of spirituality, yet he spent little, if any, time in
starkly arid or elevated country.[27] The mountains and deserts that move us most
are those of the spirit.

Archetypal psychologist James Hillman has characterized the exploratory
edges of human consciousness as a tension between peaks and vales, between
the heights of the spirit and the depths of soul.[28] Metaphorically speaking, the
human psyche repeatedly finds itself ascending the mountain of ecstasy or ven-
turing into the desolate vale of tears. The mountain is where one seeks to tran-
scend ordinary human experience; the desert is where one enters it most deeply.

I am uncomfortable with trying to distinguish too neatly between desert and
mountain experiences as identifiably separate "psychological states." Largely in
this book, desert and mountain spirituality refers simply to a common experience of "wilderness," not to distinct motifs one might try to differentiate in the
spiritual life.[29] Yet the recurrence of these archetypal images in Western myth is
a compelling phenomenon worth considering here, at least briefly.

Abraham Maslow developed the image of "peak experience" to describe
those rare, exciting moments that offer an enhanced perception of reality. They
are powerfully self-validating, yielding a sense of wonder, awe, and reverence,
suggesting the exaltation of ascension.[30] This was the experience of the eighth-
century Japanese poet who found himself at a loss for words in the presence of
the sacred mountain. "It baffles the tongue, it cannot be named, it is a god mysterious."[31]

To begin the path up the mountain, says Hillman, is to embrace the impulse
of the *puer aeternus,* the childlike wonder that draws us ever upward to glory,
like Icarus with his wings, Phaethon driving the chariot of the sun, Bellerophon
ascending on his winged horse. The way of the mountain is the way of ecstasy,
prophetic insight, the white-hot coals of inspiration, the long-distance vision
that the towering peak affords. Here the spirit is given flight. It longs to soar,
viewing everything from aloft, placing all of life's details within universal patterns of clarity. This is one way of going to the edge, surpassing the ordinary by
ascending the mountain.

By contrast, the way of the soul is the descent into the vale, the desert, the
cave, the labyrinth. The vale draws us into the depths of the earthy and ordinary,
into the dark night, into the desolation that is dreadful but also anchors us in
the place where we are given new life. Thomas Moore speaks of the soul's preference for "details and particulars, intimacy and involvement, attachment and
rootedness. . . . To the soul, the ordinary is sacred and the everyday is the pri-

mary source of religion."[32] The desert is the path taken by this life-embedded soul, the *anima,* into the long, hollow depression of the commonplace, mundane, and vernacular. This is Theseus entering the labyrinth, Orpheus descending to underworld, Osiris encountering death in the sands of Egypt. It poses a very different edge to which the psyche is also drawn.

Hillman and his student Moore caution against separating the flight of the spirit from the descent of the soul. The spiritual life involves more than soaring to the heights, like Peter Pan, the eternal boy, without the constraints and commitment of family to tie him down. Spirituality is not the sublime transcendence of everything trivial and matter-of-fact. In the Western spiritual tradition, the journey of the soul into the vale of ordinariness is an equally good, if not surer, route to holiness.[33] This is the way of being wounded, of being committed to the concrete, of being bound to the familiar.

The two, of course, ultimately feed each other. The spirit longs to carry the soul beyond the prosaic, to the highest reaches of the sublime. The soul forces the spirit back into the valley of pain and experience, teaching it to connect, to be involved, to be grounded. Both journeys are necessary. In the language of landscape symbolism, the mountain cannot be ascended without going also through the desert. Moses scales the heights of Sinai only after tasting the bitter waters of Marah, experiencing hunger in the wilderness of Sin, angrily striking the rock in Horeb.[34] John of the Cross knows that the ecstasy of Mount Carmel is reached only by way of the *nada,* the nothing of the immense, unbounded desert.[35] In the Muslim Sufi tradition, Mount Qaf surrenders its wisdom only to those who pass through the seven valleys of the barren waste which precede it.[36] The epiphany on the mountain's height is inseparable from struggle and temptation on the desert floor.

In each of these movements—through the desert and up the mountain path—there is an unavoidable encounter with the savage, fierce, and merciless. Entering the valley of the shadow of death or spending the night on Bald Mountain with its witches' sabbath are equally terrifying experiences.

Throughout much of the history of Western culture, mountains have been viewed as physically threatening, aesthetically distasteful, even morally reprehensible. They were guardians of the gates of Dante's hell. Mount Pilatus in the Swiss Alps was a place of dread, where the body of Pontius Pilate had allegedly been cast in punishment for the crucifixion of Christ. The modern Romantic fascination with mountain terrain is a relatively recent development in Western thought.[37] Mountains were largely avoided, not climbed, until the fifteenth century. They were frequently maligned as ugly protuberances or unsightly blemishes on the earth's beauty. Augustine suggested that mountains were not a part of the original creation but resulted only after the Fall. Accordingly, they were scorned as proud, insolent, sky-threatening, and aloof. Seventeenth-century travellers felt only terror in crossing the Alps, closing their eyes when possible as they traversed the high passes.[38]

In a similar way, deserts have been viewed with fear and contempt as the snare of the devil, the abode of dragons, or the lair of the lawless.[39] As wilderness, *wüste,* waste, the desert becomes the haunt of demons—at best a "negative landscape" or "realm of abstraction," located outside of the ordinary sphere of existence, susceptible only to things transcendent.[40] In early Christian tradition, the desert was perceived ambiguously, usually as an unfriendly, intimidating domain; but for those able to endure its purifying adversity, an image also of paradise.[41] If desert terrors can be sustained as the self is laid bare under its harsh scrutiny, dry land becomes an avenue of hope.

The dainty and delicate will not thrive well in desert-mountain terrain. A life that is too comfortable or too safe will avoid such landscapes at all cost. Wild places are uncompanionable to the qualmish, to those compulsively anxious to please. They disclaim the false niceties of home, the small lies and pretences by which an entire life can sometimes be shaped. In fierce landscapes one knows that "being good, being sweet, being nice will not cause life to sing."[42] There the fragile ego loses its props and supporting lines. Its incessant need for validation is ignored. Count on it, says Gary Snyder, "Great insights have come to some people only after they reached the point where they had nothing left."[43]

Biblical Perspectives on Desert-Mountain Experience

Biblical religion, from ancient Israel to the early church, takes shape in a geographical context dominated by desert-mountain topography. Yahweh is a God who repeatedly leads the children of Israel into the desert, toward the mountain. Of the recurring traditions that undergo transformation in Israel's life, the wilderness motif is one of the most significant. At every subsequent period of testing—from Assyrian threat to Babylonian invasion and beyond—the Jews interpret the loss and possibilities of the present in light of their collective memory of the wilderness experience.[44] Having once been taken to the edge, they view all succeeding passages into the wilds of unpredictability in light of that metaphorical paradigm.

The God of Sinai is one who thrives on fierce landscapes, seemingly forcing God's people into wild and wretched climes where trust must be absolute.[45] In the Talmudic tradition of the rabbis, this geographical preference on God's part came to be discussed in connection with a difficult text in Exodus 13:17. The text affirms, in its most usual English translation, that when Pharoah let the people of Israel go, Yahweh did not lead them by way of the land of the Philistines, although that would have been closer; they were not taken along the Mediterranean coast and into Palestine by the easier, more direct route to the north. Instead, they were pointed toward a longer route, further south, more deeply into the desert, toward Mount Sinai.

The argument of the rabbis hinged on how the Hebrew word *ki* should be understood in this passage. Usually the term is taken to mean that God chose not to lead the Israelites by the northern route "although" (*kî*) it was the shorter, less-troublesome way. Yet *kî* can also be translated "because," suggesting something far more provocative in the context of the passage. If this is the meaning, then God decided against the shorter route *because* (or for the very reason that) it was easier and less-demanding.[46] God intentionally opted for the more difficult landscape, as if this were habitually the divine preference.

God's people are deliberately forced into the desert—taking the harder, more onerous and hazardous route—as an exacting exercise in radical faith.[47] They are shoved down the difficult path so there will be no thought of ever turning back. They cover grueling miles of terrain so tortuous they will never be tempted to recross it in quest of the leeks and onions they remembered in Egypt. Perhaps others can go around the desert on the simpler route toward home, but the way of God's people is always through it.[48]

The gospel of Mark draws on this same tradition when it speaks of Jesus himself being "driven" into the desert. The Greek word *ekballó* in Mark 1:12 is a harsh word, having a sense of being roughly thrown or violently propelled.[49] Jesus, like all of Israel before him, is forced to take the hard way, going directly from his baptism into the wilderness of temptation. Being thrust into the desert and its promise of death, he sounds in advance the keynote of his whole mission.[50] The Son of God, still wet from the waters of the Jordan, impelled now into the wilds, is going to his death, headed already toward the cross.

Mark is preeminently a desert gospel. All the images of deserted wilderness (*erēmos*) in the first half of its narrative prepare the reader for the suffering that moves to fulfillment in its second half. The desert in Mark is a place of death. It foreshadows the cross. Yet ironically, Jesus also finds solace and comfort there, going often to places on the edge, retreating to the *erēmos topos*, the site of abandonment. Indeed, in the topographical schema of Mark's gospel, the customary pattern of chaos and order (deserted waste versus habitable terrain) comes to be reversed. The place of death in the desert becomes the place of miraculous nourishment and hope, while the order and social stability of Jerusalem leads only to the chaos of the cross.[51] Places in the second gospel are given provocative new meaning in light of Jesus and his mission.

Repeatedly he invites his listeners into the disturbing (and liberating) reality of his message through an unanticipated experience of place. As often as he retreats to the desert, seeking respite from the crowds, people follow him—curious, captivated, drawn to the edge.[52] In the bright light of day, with plenty of company, the wilderness is an adventure, a place for seeking out this strange healer who seems so at home on the boundaries. But with the coming of evening, they find themselves out in the desert waste without resources, far from town. Uneasiness grows. The desert begins to reveal itself for what it is, a place without kindness. The spirit of carnival turns to discomfort, then anxiousness. People confront limits they were reluctant to face.

Yet it is here—in the desert, of all places—that people are fed, five thousand of them at a time. Here a new community takes shape, a community formed in brokenness, constituted on the edge. It is a community defined by the exigencies of the place. In the presence of Jesus, the desert evokes a sharing and openness that, back home, would be repudiated by every social and economic distinction.[53] The place of scarcity, even death, is revealed by Jesus as a place of hope and new life.

If Mark is the desert gospel, Matthew is more fascinated with mountains. For Matthew, the mountain is invariably a place of expectation, a hazardous and remote locale where an eschatological community is gathered around Jesus as Messiah. Only there can people recognize the intriguing figure from Galilee, the one so comfortable with boundaries, as the central focus of Israel's messianic hope.

Terence Donaldson's study of mountain topography in the first gospel argues that the six mountain stories of Matthew provide a literary schema giving order to the entire gospel.[54] The drama builds from the mount of temptation in chapter 4, where Jesus refuses the messianic power prematurely offered him by the tempter, to the mount of commissioning at the gospel's end, where he declares to his disciples that all power in heaven and earth has now been given to him. In between are four other mountain narratives in which Jesus teaches the ethic of the coming kingdom (in the sermon on the mount), prefigures its messianic banquet (on the mount of feeding), anticipates its eschatological glory (on the mount of transfiguration), and describes the time of its coming (in the Mount of Olives discourse).

In each case, the recipients of hope are drawn geographically to the edge. An eschatological community takes shape on the boundaries, at the liminal place on the mountain's slope. The established order breaks down, a company of the future is formed, new rules are adopted. Jesus repeatedly leads people into hostile landscapes, away from society and its conventions, to invite them into something altogether new.

Matthew incorporates a much older mountain motif traceable through the whole of Israel's history.[55] The most common word for mountain (*hār*) appears no less than 520 times in the Hebrew scriptures.[56] The religion of Yahweh takes form in a Palestinian topography distinguished by two ridges of mountains, extending down either side of the Jordan River. These mountains offer refuge and security for a people threatened by their enemies. Indeed, the Israelites become so identified with mountain ascendancy that advisors to the Syrian King warn him: "Their gods are gods of the hills, and so they were stronger than we; but let us fight against them in the plain, and surely we shall be stronger than they" (I Kings 20:23). In the rugged mountains of Judea, God's power is recurrently exercised on behalf of displaced peoples.

There on the mountain, one meets the God of the unexpected. Yet Israel always held back from attributing a sense of automatic sacrality to mountain terrain. If a mountain was sacred, it was not because of its impressive height or any noumenal quality inherent in the place itself, but because Yahweh consented to be met there. The sacredness of Mount Sinai or Mount Zion is not rooted in a cosmic mountain theology, but in the freedom and power of the divine choice.[57] God chooses to be revealed there, beyond the range of Canaanite and Syrian sovereignty, at the place where a broken company is made into a community of promise.

Desert and mountain places, located on the margins of society, are locations of choice in luring God's people to a deeper understanding of who they are. Yahweh frequently moves to the boundary in order to restore the center, calling a broken people back to justice and compassion. When Ahab brings the worship of Baal into the court of Israel, God sends fire on the mountain to refocus the direction of Israel's praise (I Kings 18).[58] At the peripheral place, unsettling and "eccentric" as it may be, the core of a people's identity is reconceived.

Scholars sensitive to the function of place in biblical narrative observe that Jesus, in a similar way, frequently presses the people closest to him into places they find threatening.[59] Jesus is always redefining the nature of "center." He moves regularly beyond the safety and exclusiveness of the Jewish homeland in Galilee to include Gentiles in outlying regions where his disciples are reluctant to go. He functions repeatedly as a boundary crosser, pushing his disciples to edges they find exceedingly uncomfortable. In Mark 6:45 he uses the harsh language of a sailor in forcing them to cross the Sea of Galilee, raising sail for Gentile Bethsaida.[60] "Just shut up and get in the boat," he seems to be saying. They don't want to go, but Jesus insists.

He knows that places on the edge, those considered God-forsaken by many, are where his identity as Messiah has to be revealed. Out in the wilds anything can happen. He pushes to the east coast of the Sea of Galilee, to the swine-herding country of the Gerasenes to heal the demoniac (Luke 8:26–39). He goes north over the border into Tyre and Sidon to affirm the faith of the Syrophoenician woman and cure her daughter (Matt. 15:21–28). He heals in Decapolis, on the far side of the Jordan. He feeds a multitude on the eastern or foreign side of the lake, even as he had done on the western or Jewish side (Mark 8:1–10). Ever dragging his disciples away from the familiarity of home, he declares present the power of the kingdom in the alien landscapes of another land.[61]

Images of Wilderness in the History of Spirituality

In turning, at last, to mountain and desert imagery in the history of Christian spirituality, we discover a continuation of this biblical preoccupation with places on the edge. Saint John of the Cross made it plain, in discussing the role of place in the spiritual life, that fierce landscapes are always preferred in achieving that "spiritual nakedness" which communion with God requires.

In his *Ascent of Mount Carmel*, John speaks of "three different kinds of places by which God usually moves the will."[62] The first is typically a beautiful site, characterized by a variegated landscape with trees. It easily awakens the senses. But its danger is that it distracts by its charms; it discourages self-forgetfulness. Far better, he says, is the second kind of place, a solitary and austere topography, such as desert terrain or a barren mountain. Here in the wilderness one is stripped of all distractions. Like Abba Simon, the desert father in his narrow cell, one is virtually "tied with a cord so as not to use up more space or go farther than the cord allowed."

Yet a third category of places described in John's typology refers to those chosen by God for a particular revelation of the divine presence. These too, he observes, are most often mountain and desert locales, including those at Sinai, Horeb, or Mount Garganus in the legend of Saint Michael. Once again, the divine preference for self-disclosure in space is declared to be an austere, deserted, feral terrain.

This is especially apparent in the history and geography of Christian monastic movements. People seeking new vitality in the spiritual life continually retreat to wild and undeveloped landscapes, seeking new meaning along the outer margins of familiarity. There, in places of abandonment—the desert, the highlands—they establish a community rooted in the spirit of wilderness saints before them. But after having made this new land habitable, beginning to look upon it with a pastoral eye, they sense the danger of losing the sharp edge and hardiness the original landscape had suggested.

Subsequent movements of reform, therefore, set off in search of still other wild and remote regions to begin anew. Or they preserve within the present terrain an archetypal or metaphorical landscape symbolizing the wilderness enclave the community still aspires to become.[63] Repeatedly, therefore, the "desert ideal" of fourth-century monasticism in Egypt, Syria, and the Wilderness of Judea served to inspire successive movements of spiritual renewal.[64]

Basil of Caesarea visited Syria and Egypt in the year 357 to observe the characteristic marks of fourth-century desert monasticism. He returned to his familiar but haunting rockscape of Cappadocia to establish a small monastery of his own in the Pontine Hills along the River Iris. Cappadocia eventually became known for its unique rock churches and monasteries, literally carved out of the fortlike crags that mark its landscape.[65] In this "naked and mournful" land, Basil duplicated the desert pattern, developing a monastic rule that encouraged liturgical prayer, manual labor, and care for the poor—all within a community of strict obedience.[66]

When John Cassian made a similar trip to the desert monks at Scete in Egypt in the late fourth century, he too was taken by the undomesticated, even monstrous landscape in which they lived. Abba Paphnutius, the one they nicknamed Bubalis or the Wild Roamer, impressed him because of his love of the desert's inaccessible regions, where risk of snakebite and death were high.[67] John had been warned about the lethal poison of the basilisk and other desert snakes.[68] When he later founded a monastery in Marseilles in southern France, he extolled the desert ideal, seeking the solitude he had remembered from Egypt on the lonely Iles de Lerins nearby. He wrote books on Egyptian monasticism that became standard reading for centuries in the West, exerting enormous influence on the Benedictine tradition.[69]

The desert ideal reemerged with renewed vitality in the West in the eleventh-century renaissance, with the rise of Camaldolese, Carthusian, and Cistercian forms of monastic life.[70] Saint Romuald began reading the lives of the desert hermits as a young man and proceeded by 1023 to found the monastery of Camaldoli in the thickly forested and snow-covered Tuscan mountains of northern Italy near Arezzo. It brought together two different styles of ascetic life, the eremetic (or solitary) and the cenobitic (or communal), with hermits trained in the larger community living higher up on rocky crags.

In a similar way later in the century, Saint Bruno—influenced by his reading in the sources of Egyptian monasticism—led a handful of French monks to the "mountain desert of the Chartreuse" in the Alps north of Grenoble.[71] There, between enormous slabs of rock and frequent avalanches, they began the first community of the Carthusian order. Thomas Gray, a later visitor, would speak of the "magnificent rudeness" of the path to the isolated monastery, "on one side the rock hanging over you, & on the other a monstrous precipice." This seventeenth-century English poet complained that the place "carries the permission mountains have of being frightful rather too far."[72]

William of Saint-Thierry, writing to his sister community at Mont Dieu, later spoke of the Carthusians as those by whom "the light of the East and ancient fervor of Egypt was introduced to our Western darkness and cold of France."[73] The earliest sites chosen for these new monasteries were selected because of their difficulty of access. Indeed, the infamous Mount Inaccessible, first climbed in the fifteenth century, stood only a few miles away. Barbarous landscape can serve many purposes in the monastic life, from modeling an earlier desert ideal to escaping the influence of undesired ecclesiastical authority.[74]

When Saint Bernard, in the year 1115, led twelve of his brother monks out of Citeaux to establish a new monastery for the Cistercian community, they traveled north, beyond the source of the Seine, through "thick umbrageous forests," into a dark terrain marked by "gloom and wildness." At first they called it "the valley of Wormwood," this abode along the upper reaches of the Aube River. Only later was it named Clairvaux, as they planted the surrounding mountain slopes with grapevines and corn, managing the water supply and creating in Benedictine fashion a cultivated landscape from the brutish wilderness. Bernard spoke of the place as eminently able to "soothe weary minds, to relieve anxieties and cares."[75] Wilderness remained in the background as a reminder of danger and risk, but the foreground disclosed a pastoral landscape more like the garden of paradise.

The desert tradition further expressed itself with the founding of the Carmelites in the twelfth century. Gathered around Saint Berthold on Mount Carmel in Palestine in 1155, these hermits claimed as their heritage a succession of monks going back to the prophet Elijah, the "founder" of desert monasticism. Much later, in the wake of sixteenth-century reforms initiated by Teresa of Avila and John of the Cross, Carmelite "deserts" began to reappear. These were small communities of hermits living in remote, wild areas in order to preserve the original desert way. The first Carmelite desert of Bolarque was established in a rocky Castilian valley in the summer of 1592.[76]

Yet another expression of preference for untamed landscape (at least metaphorically) can be found in the Beguine spirituality of Germany and the Low Countries in the thirteenth century. Hadewijch of Brabant spoke of finding God's love in the "deepest abyss," "in the deepest and most dangerous waters, on the highest peaks."[77] God is a mystery personified as Love, found only on the outer edges of human experience.

> For I can know her only as she is in herself,
> Whether she commands in storm or in stillness.
> This is a marvel beyond my understanding,
> Which fills my whole heart
> And makes me stray in a wild desert.[78]

The wild desert was, for her, a place of love and delight, burgeoning with life.

John Ruusbroec, another Dutch mystic, felt the same way about rough mountainous terrain. Looking toward the foothills of the Ardennes from his window in the church of Saint Gudula in Brussels, he proclaimed:

> In mountainous country, in the central part of the earth, the sun shines upon the mountains and brings about an early summer, with much good fruit, strong wine, and a land full of joy. . . . A person who wishes to experience the radiance of the eternal sun, which is Christ himself, must have the power of sight and must make his abode in mountainous country by gathering together all his powers.[79]

Tracing the spiritual appeal of wilderness into the twentieth century focuses on the work and influence of people such as Charles de Foucauld, Carlo Carretto, and Thomas Merton. Former aristocrat and officer of the French Foreign Legion, Charles de Foucauld went as a priest to the Algerian desert in 1901. There he established a remote hermitage at Tamanrasset, almost a mile high in the rugged Hoggar mountains of the central Sahara. Working with the poor of the Tuareg, he sought "a hidden life among the least of his brothers," like earlier desert Christians before him.[80] The Congregation of the Little Brothers of Jesus resulted from his labors.

Another Frenchman, Carlo Carretto, would join this community in 1954, popularizing the desert experience in his writings for a whole generation of lay readers. "If you cannot go into the desert," he said, "you must nonetheless 'make some desert' in your life."[81] In the Sahara he would find his own purgatory and dark night, his own place for learning to simplify and deintellectualize his faith, for discovering love and embracing the poverty of others. As he explained, the desert "is immeasurable and contains every other gift within itself."[82]

Perhaps no one has done more to renew the wells of monasticism in the twentieth century than Thomas Merton, the Trappist monk living in the woods of central Kentucky who wrote continually of deserts and mountains. Echoing the double image of wilderness that recurs throughout the monastic tradition, he argued that "[t]he *Erēmos*, the desert wilderness 'where evil and curse prevail,' where nothing grows, where the very existence of man is constantly threatened, is also the place specially chosen by God to manifest Himself in His 'mighty acts' of mercy and salvation."[83] What appealed to him most, given the pressures of a twentieth-century commodity culture, was the desert's capacity to "reject completely the false, formal self, fabricated under social compulsion in the world."[84] The desert father, he argued, living in a trackless wilderness, "had to be a man mature in faith, humble and detached from himself to a degree that is altogether terrible." He was forced by the terror of the landscape to abandon altogether the ego, "like bones whitening in the sand," in order to be clothed anew in "the hidden reality of a self that was transcendent, mysterious, half-known, and lost in Christ."[85] With Merton, the process of interiorizing desert experience, described by George Williams as a dominant trend in the Western spiritual tradition, would find its most recent and imaginative expression.[86]

In all these ways—from the psychological appeal of hazardous landscapes to the mythology of peak-and-vale experience in Western symbolic life, from the use of wilderness motifs in the Bible to desert and mountain imagery in the history of spirituality, a craving for the wild splendor of God recurs repeatedly in the recesses of the human soul. When people are drawn geographically to the remote edges of our world, they are carried metaphorically to the edges of themselves as persons, invited to an emptiness as exhilarating as it is frightening. Encountering overwhelming fierceness at the end of all possibilities, they know themselves to be loved in wild and unanticipated grace.

This was the experience of Anthony in the dry desert of Egypt, of Basil in the rockscape of Cappadocia, of Francis of Assisi amid the jagged cliffs atop Mount La Verna in the Apennines.[87] Mechthild of Magdeburg declared love to be the last of the twelve lessons taught her by wilderness.[88] To find oneself expended—lost at the end of the trail, without hope of return—and to be met there unexpectedly by grace is the soul's deepest longing. As David Douglas suggests, "the crops of wilderness have always been its spiritual values—silence and solitude, a sense of awe and gratitude—able to be harvested by any traveler who visits."[89]

Fierce Back-Country and the Indifference of God

The Bible abounds in references to the desert and the wilderness. Encounters with God, both directly and through prophetic voices, took place in scenes of desolation. God spoke on an empty stage, knowing how easily the sound of rivers diverted human attention. —Yi-Fu Tuan[1]

I awoke before dawn in freezing cold. The camels near the tent were asleep, covered with blankets. Yet even by starlight one could recognize the nearby pinnacle of rock, known on the Israeli maps we carried as Jebel Aum Dachnah. We'd camped for the night at a small oasis near a bedouin cemetery, some eight miles north of Saint Catherine's monastery beneath Mount Sinai.

Climbing alone in the darkness that morning, I moved more quickly with the break of day, trying to keep warm. On the high plain of the Upper Sinai Massif, Aum Dachnah rose some six hundred meters above the center of a huge cirque of rugged mountains. Surrounded by empty wadis, almost entirely devoid of vegetation, this was a raw moonscape, relentless and indifferent. A lone hawk flew across the eastern sky in advance of the rising sun. Rocks passed through slowly changing shades of mauve and salmon. My breathing became heavier the higher I climbed.

On reaching the top, the blood pounding in my ears, I thought again of why I'd come to the Sinai. In search of an ancient silence and the fierce love of God, I'd traveled three days with a group of Austrian climbers heading toward Jebel Mussa, the Mountain of God. Feeling lonely, cut off by language from everyone around me, I'd needed to be completely alone that morning, moving as close as possible to the edge of that wild and desolate landscape.

From the high cliff in the sunlight of dawn I took stock of my surroundings. Three hundred and sixty degrees of nothing. A huge circle of weathered rock, two miles in diameter. One hawk. A tiny cluster of tents far below, hardly noticeable beside a handful of palm trees. Otherwise . . . nothing.

Gradually, the distant sound of movement drifted up from the camp below—people rising, a fire being started. These remote human noises were the only sounds to break the immense silence of that morning. They seemed but a tiny presence encroaching upon some huge and unmanageable absence. Walking twenty feet to the other side of a large boulder on the crest of the ridge, I lost even those faint noises in the depths of a soundlessness I'd never heard or even imagined. The shape of the surrounding terrain formed an acoustical vacuum, absorbing all sound in a silence both grand and disturbing.

Was this, I wondered, what Elijah had experienced, not far from this place, many centuries before, in the wake of a passing earthquake, wind, and fire (I Kings 19:12)? Was this anything like the compelling absence, the *kōl demamah dakah* or "sound of sheer silence" that had cut through Elijah like a knife, penetrating and close, bringing with it a terror laced with love? Whatever it was, this silence (and this place) has been one to which I've returned again and again in the dark, lonely nights of the imagination. The Sinai wilderness has become a haunting metaphor of the loss of language and personal abandonment to which, for the last several years, my whole life has been drawn.

I still don't entirely understand my irresistable attraction to this wild and unwelcome land. Travel agents, especially those arranging religious tours, rarely book passage to the kinds of places I've most needed to go. Their itineraries don't generally include roaming the sparse desert of Sinai, trekking the mountain passes on the road from Lhasa, or walking the Scottish Highlands on a wintery day as cold wind sweeps down from the Hebrides. Yet these are places where human beings have frequently encountered a God of seemingly fierce indifference, a God that seized their imagination as none other.

This is the God of Abraham's children, Tibetan devotees of the Dalai Lama, and even Scots Presbyterians who made their way to New England in the seventeenth century. In each case, their God was no less foreboding and captivating than the landscape through which they moved. Their haunting vision of the holy, growing out of such austere spaces, reminds one of the inevitable correlation that exists between a person's spirituality and his sense of place. "Tell me the landscape in which you live," wrote Ortega y Gasset, "and I will tell you who you are." There is a special intrigue in the images of God that come out of harsh and rugged landscapes, those that remain so utterly indifferent to pressing human concerns. People are sometimes pulled, both spiritually and geographically, to that which most ignores them.

I often tell my students that if I weren't a Christian raised in the Reformed tradition, I'd probably be a Jew, and if I weren't a Jew, I'd be a Buddhist. These three traditions engage me by the power of their stories, the seriousness with which they address the meaning of suffering, and their strange, even vehement, attitude toward God. The people of these faiths, formed by mountains, desert, and rough terrain, celebrate, oddly enough, a sense of God's indifference to all the assorted, hand-wringing anxieties of human life. In their grand notions of divine sovereignty and the embrace of the void (with its prerequisite emptying of the self), they undercut altogether the incessant self-absorption that preoccupies the American mind. They discover in the vast resources of divine disinterest a freedom and a joy that is missing in much of contemporary pop theology.

I'm increasingly uncomfortable with current images of God found in books and workshops that mix popular psychology with a theology wholly devoted to self-realization. They seem to reverse the first question of the catechism I studied as a child, declaring that "the chief end of God is to glorify men and women, and to enjoy them forever." I really don't want a God who is solicitous of my every need, fawning for my attention, eager for nothing in the world so much as the fulfillment of my self-potential. One of the scourges of our age is that all our deities are house-broken and eminently companionable. Far from demanding anything, they ask only how they can more meaningfully enhance the lives of those they serve.

John Updike has carried on a running argument with this prevalent theologizing. In *A Month of Sundays*, the Rev. Thomas Marshfield, a lapsed vicar who longs for transcendence, attacks the marshmallowy immanence of his younger assistant, Ned Bork. He speaks of "his limp-wristed theology, a perfectly custardly confection of Jungian-Reichian soma-mysticism swimming in a soupy caramel of Tillichic, Jasperian, Bultmannish blather, all served up in a dime-store dish of his gutless generation's give-away *Gemütlichkeit*." Marshfield wants nothing of religion made amenable to human demands. "Let us have it in its original stony jars or not at all!" he insists.[2] Why does such a harsh and unmeasured Connecticut-Calvinist outburst strike within us a deep prophetic chord? In a society that emphasizes the limitless possibilities of the individual self, it comes as a strange freshness to be confronted by an unfathomable God, indifferent to the petty, self-conscious needs that consume us.

The three landscapes and three traditions mentioned earlier call people back to the *mysterium tremendum* evoked by Yahweh, Kali, the Great Mother, and Calvin's God of sovereign majesty. They suggest much about the renewed importance of an apophatic spirituality with its recovery of the *via negativa*, its attention to renunciation, its emphasis on the importance of being drawn beyond oneself into the incomprehensible greatness of God. "The world is charged with the grandeur of God," declared Gerard Manley Hopkins. "It will flame out, like shining from shook foil." But people in a postmodern world haveforgotten. The austere, unaccommodating landscapes of desert, mountain, andheath recall once again the smallness of self and the majesty of Being. Such places bring to mind what theologians once described as the aseity of God, a divine indifference having as its goal the ultimate attraction of that which it initially repels.

The Fierce Bodhisattvas of Tibetan Buddhism

Occasioning this whole line of thought for me is a phrase that has rumbled for several years in and out of my consciousness like a nagging koan. "We are saved in the end by the things that ignore us." I found it in a book by Andrew Harvey, an Englishman from Oxford writing about Buddhist meditation, the landscape of northern India along the borders of Tibet, and his own pilgrimage in search of a self he meant to lose.[3] Near the Land of Snows, at the roof of the world, he traveled with eager anticipation from one monastery to another, passing rows of large stone stupas erected along the high passes, spinning the copper cylinders or "prayer wheels" that symbolically intone the ancient mantra *om mani padme hum.*

Moved by the magnificence of mountain landscape and the esoteric mystery of the lamas, he found himself searching for a Great Experience, wanting to be transformed by what he saw, desiring as a tourist some deep, spiritual memento of his trip. Yet this self-obsessed "wanting" was precisely what kept him from obtaining enlightenment.

Only as the vast grandeur of the land drew him beyond himself did he begin to discover what he sought. Walking one day toward a remote monastery at Rde-Zong, he was distracted from his self-conscious quest for spiritual attainment by the play of the sun on stones along the path. "I have no choice," he protested, "but to be alive to this landscape and this light." Because of his delay, he never arrived at the monastery. The beauty of the rocks in the afternoon sun, the weathered apricot trees, the stream along which he walked, all refused to let him go. He concluded that "to walk by a stream, watching the pebbles darken in the running water, is enough; to sit under the apricots is enough; to sit in a circle of great red rocks, watching them slowly begin to throb and dance as the silence of my mind deepens, is enough."

Most compelling to his imagination was the fact that the awesome beauty of this fierce land was in no way conditioned by his own frail presence. It was not there for *him.* The stream would continue to lunge over the rocks on its way to the valleys below long after he'd gone. The apricot trees would scrape out a spare existence and eventually die entirely apart from any consideration of his having passed that way. Only in that moment of afternoon sunlight in Ladakh, as he abandoned any thought of hurrying on to the monastery, did he receive back something he'd already unconsciously offered. Hence he declared, "The things that ignore us save us in the end. Their presence awakens silence in us; they refresh our courage with the purity of their detachment." Becoming present to a reality entirely separate from his own world of turmoil strangely set him free. By its very act of ignoring him, the landscape invited him out of his frantic quest for self-fulfillment.

There's something clean and spare about this invitation to relinquish self and desire. But for people like myself, so anxious to experience and possess everything, it's also fraught with terror. This is why, in the spirituality of Tibetan Buddhism, there are so many fierce Bodhisattvas, saintlike figures who harshly treat the ego with indifference. In their earthly lives the Bodhisattvas had extinguished the candle of desire, but instead of relishing *nirvana* they returned to help others along the same path.

These peaceful representations of fulfillment in the spiritual life sometimes also manifested themselves as Terrifying Ones. The unsettling consternation they evoked was but another form of compassion—warding off evil, establishing justice in the world, giving courage to the fearful. Yamantaka, for example, the most powerful of the "eight dreadful deities" in tantric lore, was pictured with flailing arms in an aura of red flames and smoke. He could evoke a sense of menacing terror in those clinging to their own ego, but his purpose was to "rouse the deluded spirit to inward contemplation and reversal, to purification and, after the conquest of fear, a safe passage through terror."[4]

In the frightening experience of having our fragile egos ignored, we're thrust beyond fear to a grace unexpected. Such, at least, was the experience of Andrew Harvey in the mountain-enclosed desert of rock that is Ladakh. Called away from the self-dramatizing intensities by which he had lived, he was stunned by the quiet joy of self-forgetfulness.

From Job to Calvin: God's Harshness as Grace

Judaism and Christianity both view the divine *apatheia* as a richer and subtler way of teasing us out of ourselves and into relationship with God. The book of Job poignantly addresses the nagging question of God's apparent indifference. Why does God seem to ignore Job altogether? I asked that question often in the initial stages of my mother's illness. The answer given toward the end of Job's book, weak as it may at first appear, is directly connected with the fierceness of landscape.

When God finally speaks out of the whirlwind, it is to conduct a tour of the harsh Palestinian countryside. God points to the wine-dark sea, the towering clouds over a desolate land, the storehouses of snow and hail in the distant mountains. God asks Job what all this has to do with him. Does the wild ox pay him any attention? Does the calving of a mountain goat on a rocky slope depend in any way on his frail knowledge? Does the eagle mount up at his command to make its nest in the tall cedars? Does Leviathan speak to him a single word?

The answer, in every case, is that the rich mystery of life continues, stubbornly separate from all of Job's anxious longings. His anxieties are absorbed into a dread landscape that goes on perfectly well without him, even though it surely seemed in the bleak corridors of his own imagination that *nothing* could have continued beyond the enormity of his suffering.

This ultimately, of course, isn't an answer. But somehow, for Job, it's enough. It drives him outside of himself and his need for vindication and fulfillment. In the silence that's left when the whirlwind subsides, Job finds what he'd most sought all along. "I had heard of thee by the hearing of the ear," he cries, "but now my eye sees thee." Job is given no answer, but in being drawn out of himself he's met by God.

This is a strange dimension in Jewish spirituality. It's the experience of Moses at Sinai, of Elijah in the cave on Mount Horeb, of Second Isaiah as he offers Israel the "comfort" of a God entirely removed from the vanity of human fretfulness (Isa. 40). This God "sits above the circle of the earth, with all of its inhabitants like grasshoppers." One might easily lose the subtlety of this religious conviction by dismissing it as a scaremongering patriarchal primitivism. But there's more to it than that. What ancient Israel found in its context of untamed landscapes was a Fierce Mother as well as Gentle Father, who woos her children to a relationship of deeper maturity. Standing nakedly before the divine resplendence, they discover the indifference of God to be yet another form of God's insistent love.

Within Christianity this theme of divine majesty is celebrated characteristically in the Reformed tradition. From Calvin to Barth there echoes a thundering fugue of recurring counterpoints on the glory of God. Calvin found in Job and Isaiah some of the finest examples of God's praise being echoed in the turbulence of sea and sky.[5] He knew the God of wilderness to be one who "comes with might," "who has measured the waters in the hollow of his hand and marked off the heavens with a span" (Isa. 40:12).

On the wide heaths of Scotland and the rocky shorelines of New England, a baroque grandiosity became the hallmark of Reformed spirituality. In its excesses it led to those exulting in their willingness to be damned for the glory of God. But its finest exemplars, such as Jonathan Edwards, never viewed the divine indifference as an end in itself. Walking over his father's farm in the western Massachusetts woods, he found grace rather than fear in the unleashed grandeur of sudden thunderstorms.[6]

There is more than a worn-out devotion to a stern God of patriarchal splendour in the idea of divine sovereignty found at the heart of Reformed spirituality. Ernst Troeltsch argued that such a theology is rich in implications for the understanding of the self. A focus on the divine majesty brings with it a corresponding tendency to de-emphasize the ego and its inordinant concern for self-aggrandizement. In Calvinist spirituality "a constant preoccupation with personal moods and feelings is entirely unnecessary."[7] For Calvin, the chief concern wasn't with a self-centered personal salvation but with the glory of God.

This offers an important corrective to many of the simplistic self-help theologies in religious circles today. To be engrossed in the self is, paradoxically, to lose it altogether, as Jesus suggested (Mark 8:35). Reformed theology insists that the liberation of the true self in Christ comes only by ignoring the false self, overshadowed and driven to utter silence by a God "in light inaccessible, hid from our eyes." When the self (curved-in-on-itself) has been wholly abandoned, only then is there the possibility of seeing it restored in Christ. What had been lost irretrievably then comes rushing back as divine gift.

Jesuit Anthony de Mello describes the paradox of the frangible self in this way. "Before I was twenty," he says, "I never worried about what other people thought of me. But after I was twenty I worried endlessly—about all the impressions I made and how people were evaluating me. Only sometime after turning fifty, did I realize that they hardly ever thought about me at all."[8] So often people presume themselves to be at the center of everyone else's attention, performing for an audience that isn't there. Their chief loss, in the process, is missing the gift of blessed indifference that was being offered to them all along. "We are saved in the end by the things that ignore us."

The Gift of Nothingness in a Desert Landscape

Nowhere is this truth more readily apparent than in a lean desert topography. The Sinai wilderness, as well as the high desert country of the Four Corners region in the American southwest, has taught me as much about self-forgetfulness as I've ever learned from Meister Eckhart or *The Cloud of Unknowing*. The huge kivas of the lost Anasazi at Chaco Canyon, the dwelling place of the Kachina spirits in the San Francisco Peaks, the healing properties of El Santuario de Chimayo north of Santa Fe—these are holy sites that rekindle life by their proximity to death. But as impressive as they may be, the plain, unadorned desert itself is always sufficient for unraveling and redefining one's life. Its inattentiveness to human anxiety provides an inexplicable healing.

Meinrad Craighead found this in her experience among the sandstone flats and underground kivas of the Pueblo Indians. "When I came to New Mexico in 1960," she writes, "I found the land which matched my interior landscape. The door separating inside and outside opened. What my eyes saw meshed with images I carried inside my body. Pictures painted on the walls of my womb began to emerge."[9] She discovered the Great Mother in the awesome beauty of the desert, brooding over a world still in the process of being born. She found hope where others might have experienced only despair. In being ignored, she was unexpectedly given back her truest self.

I know this experience of being strangely welcomed by seemingly unreceptive terrain. But, like many other people, I'm not able to travel very frequently to the land that curiously feeds me. I lack regular access to the desert. I can't readily absorb the power of precariousness from nearby mountains. Living in urban Saint Louis, I seldom get to the rugged terrain that lures me most. But I seek its equivalent every night in the dark sky of my own backyard.

For several years I've made a practice of climbing into an old sleeping bag behind my house between nine and ten o'clock or so each evening. There's little to distract me there. Nothing takes note of me in the dark. I'm ignored by the overhanging trees, the passing clouds illuminated by city lights, the stars shining for anyone who might be watching (never lit for me in particular). It's an ideal place for the letting go of thoughts, for the exercise of contemplative prayer.

I've learned to love the night, to delight, like John of the Cross, in its desert-like quality of indifference. None of the solicitudes of the day seem nearly as significant in the backyard under the stars at night. There I can yield more readily to the same will of God to which the night also abandons itself. A deep desire surfaces there, to be present to the night and to the God who hides, like the Song of Song's elusive lover, within it.

God's indifference to all the cares brought with me from the day's events—an indifference mediated through the dark, slim images of night—makes possible a lighter touch on everything I'd considered important. It draws me out of myself into an indifference of my own, an ability to remain neutral and unruffled before all the various obsessions of the day. This is the abandon of which Jean-Pierre de Cassaude wrote so compellingly in his *Abandonment to Divine Providence*. It's the "holy indifference" that Francis de Sales extolled in his *Treatise on the Love of God*. "The indifferent heart," Francis affirmed, "is a ball of wax in the hands of its God . . . ; it is a heart without choice, equally disposed for everything, having no other object of its will than the will of its God. . . ."[10]

In the ersatz desert that I enter each night behind my house, this truth makes sense in a way that I never grasp so easily elsewhere. The night gives it persuasiveness. I find in that desert an immense empty space opening out onto something unnameable, eliciting a desert within me as well. The paths of these remote, converging deserts wind through long, rust-red canyons, passing huge boulders, up narrow draws ever leading into nothingness. I don't know why I find such joy (even unabashed desire) in this time spent each evening at being ignored, at doing absolutely nothing. But I do.

There's comfort in the fact that Ed Abbey had just as much difficulty accounting for his own improbable love of desert terrain. He thought people must be half crazy to think of going into the desert, given all the dangers and discomforts of the place. He wondered why he even bothered writing about it. Yet something irrational and unexplained required it of him.

Visiting the remote gorge of Nasja Creek in Arizona one summer, Abbey walked along its amber stream, canyon walls towering hundreds of feet above on either side. He made his way through the afternoon shadows in a slow ascent up a narrow trail on the east wall toward the distant sun. No human being had been that way for years, he thought, maybe never. But as he reached the canyon rim, breaking into the bright light of the vast desert floor, he saw the remains of an arrow design laid in broken stone near the edge. It pointed off to the north, toward more of the same purple vistas and twisted canyons that he'd seen for the past week or more.

He searched in that direction for some irregular line on the distant horizon, an old ruin or sacred site to which the ancient arrow might have pointed. Yet there was nothing. Nothing but the desert . . . and its blessed indifference. Nothing but a desolate silence that filled the earth with its emptiness. Nothing. With a savage and unaccountable joy, he descended the gorge once again, knowing why it was that he had to walk and write about deserts. The sheer nothingness of it refused to let him go.[11]

The power of Abbey's encounter, and others like it, is found in the fact that what is met can't be named. It perhaps can be painted, as Georgia O'Keeffe learned, giving a spare beauty to the dry bones of the New Mexican desert she'd come to love. But it can't be named. In the end, I suspect, that's what pulls me irresistably to God, finding myself speechless before a mystery I'm able to love though never fully comprehend.

Stretched out over the edge of a deep precipice, one hand clutching the branch of a blue juniper tree growing from the rock, I peer down as far as I dare. My eyes catch the motionless soaring of red-tailed hawks in the canyon far below. Sensing an invitation to emptiness, I'm drawn there by an indifference whose other name is love. It begins to grow within me, like a vast, insistent silence. There's fear, knowing that in hanging there I'll eventually be destroyed. The roots of the juniper begin already to loosen from their crevice in the rock.

Yet a senseless joy bids me stay. And when I fall, it's in a long, slow descent, feathers being unfamiliar to me. I wing my way across the borders of an unaccustomed consciousness, adjusting uneasily to warm-air currents drifting upward. The circling hawks I'd studied from above have drawn me by their indifference far more than I'd imagined. With them, I become part of a great remembered wholeness that's strangely akin to love. The sky opens out into a thin, orange line over the dark horizon and I head with the others toward home. "We are saved in the end by the things that ignore us."

I learned this truth more engagingly in the Sinai desert than anywhere else I've been. I'll never forget the tiny trail camp of Sheikh Awade, bitterly cold on the February night we stumbled into it, having worked our way up and down high ridges all day. We'd traveled many miles beyond the rocky pinnacle of Jebel Aum Dachnah with its awesome silence, camping once again beside a bedouin cemetery. This time a low stone enclosure, used for keeping sheep, helped to shield us from an icy wind sweeping over the plains.

Our trip was nearing its end. The next day we would make the final ascent of Mount Sinai, walking in the steps of Moses to the Mountain of God. For nearly a week we'd eaten only flat bread and cheese, cucumbers and tea, traveling light as pilgrims must. Wanting to celebrate our long trek that night, our Jebeliya guides had bartered for a lamb with local bedouins. Huddled over a small fire around a pot of lamb stew, we passed a bottle of Tia Maria, singing songs in half a dozen languages.

But the cold was insistent, sending everyone to bed early, though with little sleep. Bitter wind dislodged nightmares clinging to the stones of the nearby cemetery. The desert was restless. I dreamt of death, recalling images of my

Saint Catherine's Monastery at the foot of Mount Sinai.
(Photograph by author)

father's sudden, unexplained dying when I was young, of my mother's slower death by cancer continuing at that very moment. I dreamed of someone like myself being stalked in the night on those high desert plains.

A mountain lion's assault on its prey can be a fearful thing to watch, I'm told. Having tracked a nervous mule deer along a canyon creek for several hundred yards, the cat suddenly springs in a swift and uninterrupted motion. Its huge front paws sink their hooked nails into the deer's back, while the jaws anchor themselves in the nape of its neck. The large incisors pick up the gap between vertebrae as the teeth slide in. The lion swings its jaws fiercely from side to side, the neck snaps, the kill is complete.[12] I could feel the entire pattern unfold from where I lay in the cold half-sleep of the desert night, almost sensing the lion's warm breath on my neck.

The next morning at dawn, I walked outside the enclosure, thankful for the arrival of day and passing of the night. On the ground beyond the wall, I noticed the entrails and blood of the slaughtered lamb from the night before, bright red in the morning sun. It reminded me of my dream. I thought of myself tracked as prey over the desolate waste through which we'd come, hunted by the Lion of the Tribe of Judah. That Hound of Heaven had been sharp on my heels in the night just past, its "strong Feet following . . . with unhurrying chase and unperturbed pace."[13]

But I couldn't imagine then, like John of the Apocalypse, that in turning to face the fierce countenance of that pursuing Lion, I'd be shown instead a lamb slain, a lamb of unfathomable love, worthy to receive blessing, honor, glory, and power. In many ways, death would have been far easier to accept than love. It always is. Ever distrustful of grace, I assent more readily to being destroyed than to being loved. It's too much to presume that I might be the object of God's deepest longing, profoundly loved by that which frightens me most.

Why am I drawn to desert and mountain fierceness? What impels me to its unmitigated honesty, its dreadful capacity to strip bare, its long, compelling silence? It's the frail hope that in finding myself brought to the edge—to the macabre, stone-silent edge of death itself—I may hear a word whispered in its loneliness. The word is "love," spoken pointedly and undeniably to me. It may have been uttered many times in the past, but I'm fully able to hear it only in that silence.

How, then, is desert terror dissolved into desert love? At what point does the mountain's immovable indifference make possible the deepest caring? In what way do wry, disturbing images of fierce landscapes—carrying us beyond language, into the unintelligible mystery of God—occasion for us an intimacy we might never have dreamed? These are the questions to which this book struggles to be faithful. They're the most important questions of my life.

· 3 ·

Prayer Without Language in the Mystical Tradition *Knowing God as "Inaccessible Mountain"—"Marvelous Desert"*

> When we give a thing a name we imagine we have got hold of it. We imagine that we have got hold of being. Perhaps we should do better not to flatter ourselves too soon that we can name God. —Gregory of Nyssa[1]

> God, who has no name—who is beyond names—is inexpressible. —Meister Eckhart[2]

Karl Barth once remarked that doing theology is like trying to paint a bird in flight.[3] It is always a hazardous task, one that never improves on the original. Perhaps the first danger of the theologian is being able to write without astonishment. "Wonder" is the only adequate category by which theologians properly begin and end their work.

It was for this reason that the apophatic tradition arose early in the history of Christian thought.[4] Emphasizing the importance of reaching "beyond" (*apo*) every "image" (*phasis*) one might use to speak of God, the movement emerged as a prophetic critique of theological presumption.[5] It insisted that any similarity one might find between the Creator and some aspect of creation could not be expressed without acknowledging a still greater dissimilarity.[6] God may be like a rock in the way Yahweh stands firm for Israel, but there are far more ways in which God is not like a rock. Modesty of expression, therefore, must be the hallmark of theological language.

This continuing exercise in theological deconstruction, known also as the way of negation or via *negativa*, never became a clearly defined movement or "school" in its own right, either in theology or in spirituality. But its influence remained enormous in both areas. Its bold proclamation that "less is more" came to be applied not only to the wordiness of theologians, but also to the complexity of one's life. It played a double role of nurturing humility in the academy and encouraging an emptiness of self in Christian living.

As a mode of speaking about God, the apophatic tradition guarded the boundaries of the theological enterprise, emphasizing the ineffable and incomprehensible character of the divine. As a mode of contemplative ascent to God, it taught spiritual poverty and the imitation of Christ's self-emptying love.[7] Always its goal was the wonder and simplicity of "less," both in the exercise of language and the relinquishment of self. The purpose of this chapter is to introduce the essential themes of the tradition, as it has been taught and lived by those who practice it as a life of prayer.

The apophatic tradition has roots in the biblical theology of both Old and New Testaments. The experience of Moses on Mount Sinai became a definitive event in developing the negative way. There on the desert peak, Moses learned that God dwells in "thick darkness" (Exod. 20:21), hidden behind an impenetrable cloud (Exod. 24:15). In disclosing the divine glory, God also necessarily hides its fullness from human view. No one can see God and live. At best Moses only glimpsed a passing shadow of God's grandeur from his hiding place in the cleft of the rock (Exod. 33:21–23). Whoever tries to comprehend the majesty of the divine ends up confessing with Job, "I have uttered what I did not understand, things too wonderful for me, which I did not know (Job 42:3)."

In the New Testament Paul underscores the transcendent glory of God, the one who "dwells in unapproachable light, whom no one has ever seen or can see" (I Tim. 6:16). God's unsearchable judgments and inscrutable ways are beyond all human comprehension (Rom. 11:33). Even when the divine glory is revealed in full splendor—on the mount of transfiguration—the disciples are left speechless, instructed in being still about what they do not understand (Matt. 17:1–9). Jesus is the only clear image of God offered in the gospels, yet even he remains hidden, emptied of his glory (Phil. 2:5–11). Moreover, his continued presence in the world after his death and resurrection is by way of a Spirit who is both unseen and unknown (John 14:17). In such a way, believers are continually pointed beyond all images and concepts to a glorified Christ. God ultimately remains "more" than anything our language (or hearts) can bear.

Because of the deliberate hiddenness of God's grandeur, biblical religion demands the repudiation of idols, of every word and likeness that might presume to guarantee the glory of divine presence. God can only be met in emptiness, by those who come in love, abandoning all effort to control, every need to astound. The presence of God may, as often as not, be perceived as an absence.[8] God is revealed in what others may blithely disregard as a barren nothingness. Such was the mystery disclosed to Moses in the specifications for the Ark of the Covenant.

> The Mercy Seat in the Temple at Jerusalem was a vacant space, between the cherubim in the Holy of Holies. This "great speaking absence between the images" signified both Israel's repudiation of earthly representations of the deity and the imageless space into which they sought to come by prayer and devotion. In the New Testament, the empty tomb is similarly eloquent in its absence of presence.[9]

The God of the Bible is ever an elusive one. The only guarantee of divine availability is God's own promise to be present to those who empty themselves in perfect trust.

The Emergence of a Tradition

In the history of Christianity the origins of the apophatic tradition can be traced back to the fourth century. It emerged as an argument in theological debate, not only in response to the Neoplatonism of Plotinus and Porphyry,[10] but also in Gregory of Nyssa's reaction to the heresy of Eunomius, a fourth-century Arian theologian who audaciously claimed the divine nature to be entirely knowable by the human mind.[11]

Gregory pointed to Moses' profound experience of unknowing (*agnōsia*) on Mount Sinai as a way of emphasizing the inability of the intellect to comprehend the mystery of God.[12] He and his brother Basil the Great, also from the scorched and rocky landscape of Cappadocia, stressed God's inexhaustible nature, something never fathomed by human understanding. Reticence, they insisted, always befits the theologian.

As an approach in spirituality, the apophatic tradition can be traced to yet another source in the fourth century. The monastic experience of early desert dwellers like Evagrius of Pontus gave rise to a discipline of prayer which paralleled the negative way. Living at Nitria in the wilderness west of the Nile, desert silence and simplicity taught him the relinquishment of self that accompanies the renunciation of language. "Strive to render your mind deaf and dumb at the time of prayer," he wrote, "and then you will be able to pray."[13] Only as one abandons mental images in the practice of still prayer can the self be sufficiently emptied to be filled with God.

The desert fathers and mothers were among those most insistent on the limits of language in attempting to speak of divine things. Abba Pambo remained mute when a celebrated prelate came to him for a lesson in holiness, saying later that if His Eminence were not edified by his silence, he certainly would not be instructed by his words. Abba Agathon kept a pebble in his mouth for three years, learning restraint in speech as a route to growth in the spiritual life.[14] Reaching beyond language, beyond the capacity of the mind to entertain the divine mystery, became the chief impulse of the apophatic tradition, both in theological method and in the practice of a life of prayer.

If the apophatic tradition was born in the fourth century, it apparently had no name until the early sixth century. At that time, a Syrian monk calling himself Dionysius the Areopagite first made the distinction between apophatic and kataphatic approaches in a theology of prayer. Pseudo-Dionysius, as he is commonly known, defined kataphatic or affirmative theology as that which makes generous use of metaphor and analogy in describing the mystery of God. It is concrete and incarnational, speaking of the divine by way of vivid imagery and storytelling. It operates "according to" (*kata*) the "image" (*phasis*), emphasizing the metaphorical character of all thought. God is father and lover, judge and friend, raging fire and still small voice—all of these, and yet none of them. Franciscan and Ignatian spiritualities, with their love of nature and imaginative use of the five senses, are good examples of this approach as expressed in the kataphatic tradition.

By contrast, Pseudo-Dionysius defined apophatic or negative theology as that which recognizes the utter poverty of all language about God. When we encounter the matchless glory of the divine, we "find ourselves not simply running short of words but actually speechless and unknowing."[15] Being stripped of images, therefore—standing naked before God without the protective interference of language—is as important to the practice of contemplative prayer as the use of images may be in reaching that point where silence begins. Metaphorical images can bring us to God, but once we stand face to face with God's imageless glory, we realize the impoverishment of all imagination. Carmelite spirituality, seen in Teresa of Avila and John of the Cross, as well as the mysticism of *The Cloud of Unknowing* express this concern in the history of the apophatic tradition.

Like Gregory of Nyssa before him, Dionysius pointed to the pivotal experience of Moses on Mount Sinai as a way of describing what can and cannot be said about the mystery of God's being. There on the mountain, "beyond the summit of every holy ascent," Moses was plunged into a "truly mysterious darkness." He could not gaze upon the splendor of God's invisible majesty, but was able only "to contemplate the place where God dwells."[16] This distinction between God's essence and God's "place," the one wholly unknowable and the other more accessible to human sensitivity, is based on the biblical text in Exodus 33:21 and recurs often in the tradition.[17]

It is impossible for human intelligence to comprehend God, yet certain places may allow people to experience the necessary risk that opens them, body and soul, to what their minds cannot entertain. God's places, in scripture and in the history of spirituality, are frequently fierce landscape settings like the storm-beaten slopes of Mount Sinai. God is "an inaccessible and pathless mountain," as Philo described the peak Moses ascended in fear and trembling.[18] Such liminal places are able, symbolically if not physically, to put people on edge, driving them beyond all efforts to control reality (and even God) by means of the intellect.

A central argument of this book is that the apophatic tradition, despite its distrust of all images about God, makes an exception in using the imagery of threatening places as a way of challenging the ego and leaving one at a loss for words. If we cannot know God's essence, we can stand in God's place—on the high mountain, in the lonely desert, at the point where terror gives way to wonder. Only there do we enter the abandonment, the *agnōsia*, that is finally necessary for meeting God.

The apophatic tradition will argue that language simply is not enough. God is "unknowable and inaccessible to all and altogether beyond understanding," argued Maximus the Confessor, a seventh-century theologian whose stand for the words of the orthodox creed had led to the loss of his right hand and tongue.[19] Even this man, who knew to the extent of martyrdom the importance of language, was aware also of its limits.

A Recovery of the Apophatic Way

A number of factors have contributed to a renewed interest in this ancient tradition in the twentieth century. Much of Western culture, in philosophy and the arts, has been preoccupied with the inability of language to do all that we once expected it to do. From abstract expressionism in art to the theater of the absurd, the tendency of our culture has been toward a minimalism of image, a post-Enlightenment stripping away of fixed, rational structures by which meaning can be measured. We no longer trust the word absolutely, but recognize its hollowness—from popular media images to political discourse.

In the logical positivism of A. J. Ayers, the language analysis of Martin Heidegger, and the more recent hermeneutics of postmodernist deconstruction, philosophers in this century have argued over what is and is not sayable in theological utterance.[20] Theologians such as Karl Rahner and writers in spirituality such as Thomas Merton have done much to foster the apophatic critique of language, even as historians such as Vladimir Lossky and Bernard McGinn have given new attention to classical figures within the tradition.[21]

Furthermore, the increased interest in spirituality on the part of lay Christians in the late twentieth century has brought about a revival of the discipline of apophatic prayer. The popularity of Eastern spiritualities, especially Zen Buddhism with its emphasis upon wordlessness, has pointed Western Christians back to traditions in their own past that develop the idea of *kenosis* or self-emptying.[22] This interest ranges from the popularity of the simple Jesus Prayer, as taught in *The Way of a Pilgrim* (a nineteenth-century Russian classic), to workshops on centering prayer offered by contemporary Cistercians such as Thomas Keating and Basil Pennington.[23] People worn out by cheap language have found themselves drawn to contemplation, moving beyond an excess of words to an emptiness where God is met in silence. For many reasons, therefore, the ancient appeal of apophaticism has been given new life.

Christian prayer has traditionally involved a four-step pattern, moving back and forth from a dependence upon language to an abandonment of words altogether. Prayer begins with *lectio,* the practice of spiritual reading in the scriptures and classic Christian texts. From there one turns to *meditatio* (the ruminative reflection on what has been read) and *oratio* (an expression of praise and intercession growing from that reflection). These, in turn, lead to a fourth form of prayer, *contemplatio,* in which one passes beyond all the words and images of the earlier stages to embrace a deep silence in the presence of God.[24] This is where apophatic prayer begins, but not where it ends. Never becoming a goal in itself, apophatic prayer serves ultimately to recycle the process, moving back through the earlier stages in a dynamic rediscovery of the word.

We can summarize the principle themes of the apophatic tradition by tracing them as movements within the life of contemplative prayer. They begin with an embrace of silence—relinquishing language, along with its powers of naming, entitling, and possessing. This leads, in turn, to the letting go of one's thoughts, the emptying of the self, the act of loving in silent contemplation what cannot be rationally understood, even a new freedom with respect to others and one's life in the world.

The rest of this chapter will explore these particular movements in the exercise of apophatic prayer, using representative figures from the tradition to exemplify how the truth is conveyed. Teaching silence and the surrender of language seems an impossible task, yet these teachers do so by the thinnest of images, many of them drawn, curiously enough, from desert and mountain sources.

They make use of word-knots that jumble the sounds and meanings of terms, poetry and paradoxical speech, images that readily empty themselves into something else. They play with simple metaphors like a juggling magician, inviting their readers to watch something that seems to disappear before their eyes. Continually referring to the paradigm of Moses ascending the mountain, like their predecessors Gregory and Dionysius, they carry their listeners into a mind-boggling desert and mountain landscape, suggesting loss of control, loss of words, loss of self.

This is T. S. Eliot's "wasteland," where language breaks down and relationships shatter—a desert so utterly threatening, and yet familiar, to modern consciousness. It is a bitter end, but it offers a new beginning. We cannot imagine letting go of the mastery of reality that our words once occasioned for us; and yet we know our words to be hollow. We long for silence, realizing that our only way out of the desert is to go deeper into it, beyond the breakdown of language to the "still point" where God meets us in emptiness.

The recovery of the apophatic tradition at the end of the twentieth century is part of a much larger distrust of words in our culture. It is an effort to quell the verbiage that limits genuine discussion of what is most important. For theology it demands a return to fundamental discourse. "The accent on the apophatic," says Jaroslav Pelikan, has throughout Christian history "functioned as a check, and one that was often necessary, on the pretensions of theologians."[25]

In spirituality it is also a summons to the simplicity of life that flows from the relinquishment of language. It is a longing to see ourselves and our world transformed—to find speech renewed, relationships restored, a new vision of God made possible through the recognition of our limits. This is the thirst that prompts the current popularity of contemplative prayer, whether sought in Eastern mysticism or the Christian apophatic tradition.

Julian of Norwich: The Abandonment of Control

A first characteristic of the apophatic way, and the starting point of contemplative prayer, is the recognition that language is inescapably an agent of control. In revealing the mystery of God, words also inevitably limit. God overflows every analogical notion we might use to describe God. The mind is always lured forward, toward that which cannot (as yet, or perhaps ever) be seized. Augustine argued, "If you have understood, then this is not God. If you were able to understand, then you understood something else instead of God. If you were able to understand even partially, then you have deceived yourself with your own thoughts."[26] The hazards of language must be acknowledged by all those who are tempted to speak where they had best keep silent.

Julian, the fourteenth-century English anchoress who lived in a cell attached to the parish church of Norwich in the East Midlands, began her *Revelations of Divine Love* with an account of her own most vivid experience of apophatic prayer. Over a three-day period when she was thirty years old, she appeared to have been struck with a sudden illness in which she could not speak. She struggled to focus her attention on a crucifix as her sight failed and the room grew dark around her. She was given up for dead and received the last rites of the church. Yet during this time of utter silence and complete loss of control, she experienced something she would spend the rest of her life trying to describe.

It was an experience of knowing herself as "nothing," being wholly stripped of language and identity. Yet this experience-that-was-not-an-experience joined her more closely to Christ than anything she had ever known. It was the deepest participation in his suffering on the cross. In the playfulness of language that came to characterize her subsequent work, she made use of punning word-knots to describe this knowing, noughting, nothing, no thing, this coming to naught in which she found her greatest joy.[27] She understood it as a sharing in the emptiness (the nawtedness) of Jesus. "Thus was our lord Iesus nawted for us, and we stond al in this manner nowtid with hym."[28]

The only way she knew how to convey what she had experienced was to offer tiny images that reduced language to a bare minimum. To enter into the mystery of prayer, she said, is to recognize oneself as "something small, no bigger than a hazelnut." Such a little thing "could have fallen into nothing because of its littleness," yet only because of being loved by God does it exist.[29] To pray without language is like meeting God in nothing but a "point," in the smallest interval possible where God holds together all that is.[30] To share in apophatic prayer is to enter a "barren and waste desert, alone in the wilderness," where the Lord is found waiting for his wounded servant with loving regard.[31]

Julian recognized that prayer is always a summons to silence and impotence, to the awareness of one's utter poverty in speech. As she put it in her play with words, our "menie meanes" are too mean to grasp the meaning of what he meant.[32] To submit to silence in prayer is to admit that we stand naked before God, without even words to cover ourselves. Words are the fig leaves we continually grasp in the effort to clothe our nakedness. Sam Keen has argued:

> A psychoanalysis of chatter would suggest that our over-verbalization is an effort to avoid something which is fearful—silence. But why should silence be threatening? Because words are a way of structuring, manipulating, and controlling; thus,

when they are absent the specter of loss of control arises. If we cannot name it, we cannot control it. Naming gives us power. Hence, silence is impotence, the surrender of control. Control is power, and power is safety.[33]

Apophatic prayer invites us to a vulnerability—to a radical interruption of speech—that is highly disconcerting.[34]

Yet it does more than observe the brokenness and inadequacy of human language. Lao-tzu had done as much centuries ago in the Chinese tradition of the *Tao Te Ching*. Apophatic prayer insists that language must also be redeemed. If it is true that words, because of their limits, can rarely convey the depth of experience, it is also true that speech is unavoidably necessary—because God has spoken first, disclosing himself as "the Word made flesh."[35] We *must* speak yet we *cannot* speak . . . without stammering. This is the bold insistence of the apophatic way. It stalks the borderland of the limits of language, using speech to confound speech, speaking in riddles, calling us to humble silence in the presence of majesty. This is what Julian does with such playfulness and grace.

God, in short, refuses to be "tamed" by any human tongue. Yet God, in God's deep compassion, enters like a grieving mother into loving conversation with those who know themselves as wounded and dumb. The route to knowing and speaking of God is invariably the way of abandonment, the way of the cross.

Meister Eckhart: Letting Go of Thoughts

If apophatic prayer begins with the embrace of silence, its second movement involves a letting go of the restless activity of the mind, putting less stock in the concepts by which we label everything we know. At the beginning levels of a life of prayer, thoughtful images are useful, even necessary, ways of referring to a reality beyond ourselves, but we come to depend on them too much to frame (and limit) our understanding of God. The *via negativa,* therefore, rejects every mental image taken from the natural world that might be used to speak of divine things, even while it insists—on account of the incarnation—that every aspect of the created world be taken seriously. All of our thoughts about God, being limited, are subject to negation. Yet given the need in this life to speak in shadows and figures, total negation is impossible.

How far, then, does one go in abandoning distinctions and concepts, images and analogies which—by their fragmentary character—veil as much as they reveal the divine glory? Two answers to this question are found in the history of the apophatic tradition.

Psuedo-Dionysius, Meister Eckhart, and, to some extent, the author of *The Cloud of Unknowing* are much more radical in their abandonment of images. They speak of approaching a naked God, stripped of all distinctions, leaving behind "everything perceived and understood."[36] They describe the highest level of prayer as a process of "denudation," of radical poverty, letting go of every concept of God. One is invited to forget everything—one's sins, one's self, all that one supposedly knows to be objectively true. "I pray God that he may quit me of God," said Eckhart.[37] Who wants an abstraction, he asks, when the living reality is present?

This German mystic and Dominican preacher of the early fourteenth century sought more than anything else to realize the unmediated union that exists between God and the human soul. Eckhart wanted nothing to do with God as a concept, a mental category that could be entertained or rejected at will. Yahweh is not a subdivision within a class, something to be labeled alongside other examples within a larger category of "gods." The "Abyss," the "Source," the "Silent Desert" that is God is never discovered in pursuing "thoughts about God," but in recognizing the intimate unity already present between God and all created beings.[38]

Human existence began in the divine "womb" prior to its actual creation, said Eckhart. The original "me" was an idea in God before it was anything else; it was not separate from God. No one thought of "God" and the "self" as distinct categories. The creature could not even be conceived of apart from its existence in the divine. This sounds like the Johannine mysticism one finds in passages such as John 17:22–23 or Paul's language of union in Galatians 2:19–20. Yet in his enthusiasm, Eckhart was prone at times to erase all distinctions between God and the soul. Because of this, some of his ideas were condemned as heretical after his death in 1329.[39]

However one judges the adequacy of Meister Eckhart's mystical language, the effort to realize the unity of God and the soul is the purpose of apophatic prayer. To pray silently and without the objectification of thought is to leave ourselves defenseless against a God who longs to make us one with Godself. In the mystical intensity of such prayer, Eckhart spoke with poetic ecstasy: "The eye with which I see God is the same eye with which God sees me; my eye and God's eye are only one eye and one seeing and one knowing and one love."[40]

His German sermons are full of striking images and teasing paradoxes, used to invite his listeners into the emptiness of apophatic knowing.[41] He refers to the joining of God and the human soul, for example, as a movement into a desert. God's innermost being is discovered by us as a "solitary wilderness," a "vast wasteland."[42] The desert into which Yahweh invites Israel in Hosea 2:14 is the hidden mystery of God's most intimate self.

Using landscape imagery like others in the tradition, Eckhart speaks of God as a mountain to be ascended without activity, a "marvelous desert" into which the human soul must venture.[43] Only as I have "desertified" myself, as it were—making myself a desert, stripped of everything but the spark of the soul within—am I fit to meet that Desert which is God. With word play and poetry, Eckhart dissolves these images into nothingness as he models the radical relinquishment of thought necessary if one is to be joined to God.

This is a severely rigorous rejection of mental images, much akin to that of

Pseudo-Dionysius. It moves even "beyond the sacraments, beyond Christ in his humanity, beyond God himself conceived as person, to enter the abyss of God-head."[44] If lifted out of its original context in the liturgy of the monastic life, it could lend itself to an esoteric speculativeness, especially since its understanding of God and the soul owes as much to Neoplatonic mysticism as it does to the Bible.[45]

By contrast, others in the apophatic tradition—Maximus the Confessor, John of the Cross, and Thomas Merton—are less concerned to rid the mind of every possible image in approaching God.[46] They retain a deeply Christological focus to their apophaticism, emphasizing the self-corrective role necessarily played by the image of Jesus in any negative theology. The quest for a more immediate access to God than that offered by Christ and the cross must be judged hazardous and presumptive. The God who is met in the darkness of unknowing is none other than the One already revealed in Jesus at Gethsemane.

In popular spirituality today, there is an increased fascination with imageless meditation, both Eastern and Western.[47] The temptation is for people to seek an instant encounter with unmediated power and wonder, grasping a "naked God" apart from the spiritual disciplines necessary for such an encounter. In response to this quest, the apophatic tradition cautions that a commitment to prayer has to be rooted, not in intellectual curiosity, but in a deep longing for God alone, as found in the cross. There is no cheap and easy access to divine majesty.[48]

In the exercise of contemplative prayer, one comes to abandon thoughts, even "good thoughts" about the passion of Christ and the graciousness of God. Yet in this abandonment "a little word" continues to be used in focusing one's attention on the darkness of the divine being. The name of Jesus is repeated over and over again as a way of stilling the mind, bringing it to a stop in the presence of mystery.[49] The emptying to which Christians are called is always one patterned after the quintessential emptying, the *kenosis*, of Jesus Christ as Lord (Phil. 2:5–11).

Author of *The Cloud of Unknowing:* Emptying of the Self

In the practice of apophatic prayer, one first learns silence in the outward sense, through the cessation of speech, and then silence in the inward sense, through the relinquishment of thoughts. The monotonous repetition of a single word or phrase often helps drive away intruding thoughts as it moves one toward a deep sense of self-forgetfulness. At this point, getting oneself out of the way becomes the central concern of contemplative prayer.[50] The author of *The Cloud of Unknowing* insists that true contemplation is never manipulated. There is nothing one can do to "achieve" the experience, to force it to happen. All one can do is try not to interfere should it arise in the exercise of silent prayer. "Simply try to be the wood," he urges, "and let it be the carpenter."[51]

This anonymous author of *The Cloud of Unknowing* may have been a fourteenth-century English Carthusian living in the Fens district of the East Mid-lands.[52] His work was written for a younger monk, offering instruction in the exercise of apophatic prayer. The Fens was a marshy region, stretching from Lincolnshire to Norfolk, its land later drained and reclaimed for farming in the seventeenth century. In the fourteenth century, it was a terrain given to thick fog and dark clouds sweeping in from the North Sea. The author was naturally drawn by his environment, therefore, to Moses' entry into the cloud on Mount Sinai as a metaphor of our reaching out in prayer to a God we cannot see.[53]

A dark cloud always separates the believer from her deepest desire, a God beyond the reach of human reason. It is a frustrating darkness through which the mind cannot see, yet it serves to intensify longing for that which is loved. The only way the thick cloud can be pierced is by "a sharp dart of longing love," by utterly forgetting oneself in the quest for what is loved above everything else.[54] In order to focus on this dark cloud behind which God hides for the sake of love, one must cultivate yet another cloud of forgetfulness to be placed between oneself and the world of distractions. Everything must be forgotten in the process of yearning for God.[55]

Yet the self is the hardest thing to forget. The *Cloud* author knows the human ego to be ravenously hungry for experience, always grasping "like a greedy greyhound" for something to claim as its own.[56] Entering into a cloud of forgetfulness begins to still this frantic restlessness. The dog is given something to do—reciting a little word, concentrating on the name of God. The repetition of the name functions as a piece of meat thrown to the dog, keeping it busy while the heart is free to seek its love.

Ego dormio, sed cor meum vigilat, Saint Bonaventure declared in his *Journey of the Soul to God.* As the ego sleeps, the heart remains vigilant. Indeed, the more self-outpouring we are, abandoning the ego and all its frenzied needs, the more truly we become ourselves, taken to the heart of our deepest being in God.[57]

Something inexplicable happens in this self-forgetfulness of prayer. Absorbed in the repetition of the single word, releasing every thought as it comes, one may suddenly discover that significant periods of time have elapsed without any conscious awareness—as if one had gone somewhere, lost in a presence-almost-experienced-as-absence. There is no memory of an "experience" as such, no encounter to describe; only a simple restfulness richer than sleep, a sense of having been held in the arms of something wonderfully unknown.[58]

Thomas Merton made use of the distinction between true and false selves as a way of explaining the forgetfulness sought in this exercise. Contemplative prayer, he argued, ignores the external, false self which draws its life from artificial distractions, in order to concentrate on a deeper, truer self constituted by God at the center of one's being. God "begins to live in me," Merton explains, "not only as my creator, but as my other and true self." This true self remains ultimately as hidden and unknown as God; it too can be known only apophatically, in darkness and in trust.[59]

This hiddenness of the self in the apophatic tradition is also nurtured by its impulse to anonymous authorship. The incognito of the spiritual teacher is viewed as an appropriate dimension of the nature of the truth that he communicates. The sixth-century monk who speaks of himself pseudonymously as Dionysius the Areopagite points his reader beyond himself to the Athenian worshipper of an unknown God (Acts 17:16–34), while at the same time exemplifying the apophatic experience through his own ambiguous identity.[60] The author of *The Cloud of Unknowing* enters so fully into the process of self-forgetting that his name no longer matters. Maximus the Confessor detracted from his own scholarly renown by attributing his finest insights to an anonymous and "blessed old man."[61] In each instance, the teacher of emptiness teaches best by the negation of his own self-consciousness.

John of the Cross: Loving What Cannot Be Understood

The ego is relinquished, along with its constant flow of chatter and illusion of control, so that love may happen. Love, after all, is the only way God can be known. In the stillness of prayer, the heart and the will can accomplish what human reason never could attain. While God cannot be thought, God can be loved, the *Cloud* author declared.[62] This capacity of love to grasp what the mind cannot is emphasized repeatedly in the tradition. "Love," says Merton, "enters the darkness and lays hands upon what is its own! Love astounds the intellect with vivid reports of a transcendent Actuality which minds can only know, on earth, by a confession of ignorance. And so, when the mind admits that God is too great for our knowledge, love replies: `I know Him.'"[63]

It is a deep mystery that love is born in the mind's (and body's) experience of emptiness and loss. The longing of the soul, made sharper by the painful absence of that which it loves—by its inability to close on what it desires—reaches in darkness for a beloved who comes unannounced and without guarantee. God reaches through the dark night of the senses, as John of the Cross would express it, to offer freely in love what no human effort could buy.

If God is to be loved as God loves, it will happen only in the dark corridors of emptiness. Only in devastating loss—beyond all security of language and identity, in despairing ever of obtaining the glory first sought—only then does a truth too wondrous to be grasped come rushing back out of the void. Love takes wing where calculation ends.

The sixteenth-century Spanish Carmelite reformer John of the Cross came to understand this truth during nine months of solitary confinement in a dark Toledo prison cell. We find ourselves truly free and capable of loving God, he argued, only as we experience the deprivation of all other things we may have depended upon for comfort, security, and self-esteem.[64] What happens when one is suddenly stripped of everything that lends meaning to life—reputation, the worth of one's work, father, mother, the familiarity of home? In John's case, the pain and self-doubt of deprivation were made worse by the fact that his own confreres had imprisoned him in violent reaction to his reforming zeal. What is left to one's life, he asks, when everything external is taken away?

For John of the Cross, growth in the life of apophatic prayer is aided by experiences of loss. Indeed, tragedy in one's personal life can be trusted as a gift of God's unfailing presence far more than trances, raptures, or visions received in so-called mystical experiences. He points to the desert imagery of scripture in his insistence that a loving knowledge of God is not found in "spiritual delights and gratifications," but in "the sensory aridities and detachments referred to by the dry and desert land." God leads us into "a land without a way."[65] This only is the path to love, being "led into a remarkably deep and vast wilderness . . . , an immense, unbounded desert, the more delightful, savorous, and loving, the deeper, vaster, and more solitary it is."[66]

It is only in the wasteland of the dark night, in the letting go of everything, that love—like a night-blooming cereus in a tropical garden—is able to blossom. John expresses it in exquisite poetry, reflecting the Song of Songs:

> There in the lucky dark,
> stealing in secrecy, by none espied;
> nothing for eyes to mark,
> no other light, no guide
> but in my heart: that fire would not subside.
>
> That led me on—that dazzle truer than high noon is true
> to where there waited one
> I knew—how well I knew!—
> in a place where no one was in view.[67]

God hides from us in an act of loving play, wooing us to the very abandonment that makes love possible. Love cannot exist so long as it remains an object to be possessed. It is born only in the letting go of all grasping and being grasped. The way up the mountain of God's love, as John describes in *The Ascent of Mount Carmel,* is the way of "*nada, nada, nada.*"[68]

John Ruusbroec had spoken of God being revealed in "darkness, bareness, and nothingness," the believer feeling completely lost in the very moment of being found. "In the nothingness all his activity fails him, for he is overcome by the activity of God's fathomless love. . . ."[69]

Thomas Merton similarly recognized the insoluble connection between love and brokenness. In one of his "Night Letters," written to the nurse with whom he had fallen in love in the summer of 1966, he said:

> Love is not itself
> Until it knows it is frail
> And can go wrong
> It does not run

> Like a well-oiled machine . . .
> Love runs best
> when it seems to break down . . .[70]

Intimacy in all human relationships—especially with God—can occur only as vulnerability and inadequacy are owned. "To be reduced to nothingness in Love," wrote Hadewijch, "is the most desirable thing I know."[71]

John of the Cross would go on to describe carefully the stages by which one moved from this initial night of the senses to a subsequent night of the spirit in which love became more fully realized. Both stages involved an active participation of the believer in the self-discipline of prayer, as well as a passive night in which God brings—by external circumstances or interior sterility—the anguished sense of absence necessary for the deepest experience of love. This, finally, is where everything ends for the "doctor of nothingness." "At the end of the day," he proclaimed, when all the school books are closed, "the subject of examination will be love."[72]

Thomas Merton: The Power of Acting while Expecting Nothing

One who has learned to distrust language and self in the discipline of apophatic prayer, having experienced love in the midst of emptiness, is not able to remain "alone with the Alone," Thomas Merton contended. True contemplation can never fulfill itself in "the false sweetness of a narcissistic seclusion."[73] It has to re-enter the world of others with its newly won freedom. In Christian mysticism, apophatic experience is never completed until it returns to kataphatic awareness and the exercise of a compassion whose shape is justice. Meister Eckhart insisted that "if a person were in a rapture as great as St. Paul once experienced and learned that his neighbor were in need of a cup of soup, it would be best to withdraw from the rapture and give the person the soup he needs."[74]

The contemplative returns to the ordinary, not in spite of her detachment from it, but *because* of that detachment. No longer driven by fear of rejection and loss, she is able now to love others without anxiously needing anything in return. She looks disinterestedly at who needs to be loved and asks the most important question of compassion: How is justice distributed? The author of *The Cloud of Unknowing* argued that the person steeped in apophatic prayer is able to love everyone, without "special regard for any individual, whether he is kinsman or stranger, friend or foe."[75] Where one is free from the need to impress the one or to fear the other, all can be loved.

Eckhart said that people who, through prayer, have become dead to all things and in touch with nothingness, become powerfully and perhaps even dangerously free. They are able to "aim at nothing in their works, to intend nothing in their minds, seeking neither reward nor blessedness."[76] They move through the world with a compassionate indifference to all its threats and promises.

As a Trappist monk writing his autobiography, *The Seven Storey Mountain*, from a Kentucky monastery in 1947, Merton came to describe the monk as a true prophet in American society, the only one who is free to do nothing without feeling guilty about it. There is a certain nonacquiescence, a noncooperativeness that is the common outgrowth of a life of contemplative prayer. Its grounding in silence and nothingness makes it far less susceptible to the ego-driven restlessness of contemporary culture.

The truest impulse toward work for social justice, therefore, grows not out of an anxious sense of pity for others or a grandly noble desire to serve, but out of the abandonment of the self in God. A love that works for justice is wholly uncalculating and indifferent, able to accomplish much because it seeks nothing for itself. Eckhart, in one of his sermons on justice and poverty, said it well:

> If you want to live and want your works to live, you must be dead to all things and have become nothing. It is a characteristic of creatures that they make something out of something, while it is a characteristic of God that he makes something out of nothing. Therefore, if God is to make anything in you or with you, you must first have become nothing.[77]

Becoming "nothing" before others is the natural concomitant of having been met by God in emptiness. One's way of responding to everyone else is radically changed.

In the apophatic way, love is not directed toward an attractive, lovable object. Indeed, it is drawn to that which appears as nothing, to that which is least in this world, as Julian (and Thérèse of Lisieux) insisted.[78] A love such as this, Father Zossima argued in *The Brothers Karamazov*, is "a harsh and dreadful thing." It flourishes in receiving no response, expecting nothing in return. Merton described this almost Buddhist approach of "action as nonaction" in a letter he wrote to a young activist engaged in work for peace:

> When you are doing the sort of work you have taken on, essentially an apostolic work, you may have to face the fact that your work will be apparently worthless and even achieve no result at all, if not perhaps results opposite to what you expect. As you get used to this idea, you start more and more to concentrate not on the results but on the value, the truth of the work itself.[79]

Merton's call for social justice in the 1960s was no faddish participation in the restive activism of the decade, but a natural consequence of his commitment to contemplation. He knew, for example, that disciplined and creative nonviolent action is only possible for those who have begun a journey into emptiness.

The freedom to act while expecting nothing in return is only gained in the wilderness of apophatic prayer. "The ordinary way to contemplation lies through a desert without trees and without beauty," Merton claimed.[80] The desert, with its scarce and brackish water—smelling "poisonous as tar"—becomes not only a place of self-deprivation, but also "a base for observation of a corrupt society."[81] Its parched dryness offers the perspective of distance, both internally and externally. There the Christian contemplative is called "to penetrate the wordless darkness and apophatic light of an experience beyond concepts."[82]

When he returns from that vacant place to the world of others, he is equipped to enter their darkness and pain as well. This participation in each other's experience of desert ultimately becomes its own reward. Whether one "succeeds" or "fails" in the work of justice makes no difference. The end is a sharing of emptiness. For this reason, apophaticism may have richer resources for nurturing justice than one often finds in the kataphatic way. One's work for social change, when rooted in such a truth, becomes altogether free—released from all the illusions and expectations we usually bring to our service of others.

Conclusion

The apophatic tradition is one that serves, intellectually, as a theological corrective, summoning theologians to a posture of humility. It reminds us that theology must ever be an extension of the life of prayer. We speak always, and with profound trepidation, of that which is beyond all knowing. Be careful how you theologize, Evagrius warned. "Never define the divine." Definitions are only appropriate to created beings. No one names God but God.[83] The apophatic way begins in the absence of language, with what seems to be the obscurity and unresponsiveness of God. It reaches, gropingly and at great risk, for a truth gathered from the night, clearer than words, sharper than sight. "It is when from the uttermost depths of our being we need a sound which does mean something—when we cry out for an answer and it is not granted—it is then that we touch the silence of God."[84]

God's silence, as Simone Weil knew, is a function of our broken capacity to hear, joined with the awesome mystery of the divine. At that point in human experience where language ends, we find ourselves at the foot of an inaccessible mountain, at the edge of a marvelous desert. We enter with Moses into a dark cloud of unknowing. Yet the abandonment experienced in these threatening places may prove more fruitful than we ever expected. We may find ourselves, in fact, proclaiming with poet May Sarton, "I am lavish with riches made from loss."

This is the paradox of the negative way: it always points back to affirmation. "No Christian mysticism is totally apophatic," as William Johnston suggests.[85] Apophatic and kataphatic ways continually critique and revitalize each other. Thomas Merton argued:

> We must affirm and deny at the same time. One cannot go without the other. If we go on affirming, without denying, we end up by affirming that we have delimited the Being of God in our concepts. If we go on denying without affirming, we end up by denying that our concepts can tell the truth about Him in any sense whatever.[86]

This is the dilemma of theology and prayer alike—always wanting to speak, but lacking any adequate words.

Yet the experience itself is a sharing in the very emptiness of God, in that embrace of vulnerability and need that God as Holy Trinity has made the heart of God's own being. "'God is most God on the cross and most Man in the resurrection,' wrote Karl Barth. It is in the cry of dereliction that God is most deeply revealed, for dereliction is God's experience of God. Even God has to let go God's ultimate idea of God in the divine *kenosis*."[87]

Here the apophatic tradition leads us into the astounding mystery that God's very nature is disclosed in spirit-crushing poverty, among those experiencing deepest loss, at the point where life and sanity are most threatened. There, in a silence shorn of all meaning, God's heart remains stubbornly and painfully open to love. God's whispered speech, in the giving (and breaking) of God's son, emerges from that still point.

Art Spiegelman, contemporary cartoonist and son of a Holocaust survivor, admits that nothing can be said to explain the horrors of history, including events like those of Nazi Europe. Some silences seem endless. "Every word is like an unnecessary stain on silence and nothingness," Samuel Beckett once insisted. But after pondering Beckett's truth for a long time, Spiegelman adds, with a spark of humor if not hope, "On the other hand, he SAID it."[88] To speak, even in brokenness, is a deep, inexorable need of the human heart, and the final goal of the apophatic way. To make response—reaching by fragile faith through the dark cloud of unknowing—is the most profound impulse of our humanity.

There are no guarantees; yet in that nothingness one may discover, like Dionysius the Areopagite, the "dazzling obscurity of the secret silence outshining all brilliance with the intensity of its darkness."[89] This is a language of mystics, perhaps too playful in its paradoxes. It can be spoken too glibly by those who have not experienced pain, but it points, at last, beyond the outer edges of the theologian's quest to the place where all efforts to know are absorbed in a love surpassing all knowing.

Stalking the Snow Leopard

A Reflection on Work

The secret of life is to have a task, something you devote your entire life to, something you bring everything to, every minute of the day for your whole life. And the most important thing is—it must be something you cannot possibly do! —Sculptor Henry Moore[1]

Halfway through the school year—the bone weariness of work robbing the world of mystery—I find myself reaching for metaphor, stalking an image that might give life. My desk is piled with papers to grade, rank and tenure files to review, scattered notes for miscellaneous research projects. Every year at this time the work expands as the space in my office simultaneously shrinks, becoming oppressive, confining. I push aside notes for tomorrow's classes, uncovering a photograph of the southern slope of Machapuchare in the Annapurna Range. It lies in sunlit splendor under the glass on the top of my desk. At this time of the semester I find it easy to fantasize about untaken trips to the Himalayas.

My eyes wander among the travel books on a shelf across the room, noticing the story of another man's work, a half-metaphysical reflection on vocation sliding under the surface of an adventure tale. Several years ago Peter Matthiessen set out on a trek some 250 miles across the Himalayas with biologist George Schaller. Ostensibly they went to study the migratory and mating patterns of the Himalayan blue sheep, a scientific investigation of reputable merit. But there was also the elusive possibility along the way of seeing the rarest and most beautiful of the great cats, the snow leopard. On that possibility hinged the author's deepest intrigue as well as his book's eventual title.[2]

The snow leopard is a symbol of ultimate reality, that fleeting beauty we see only in occasional snatches. Hiding behind gnarled trees and granite cliffs at four thousand meters, it may never truly be seen by any of us. As Schaller says, "Maybe it's better if there are some things that we don't see." Yet it's the seldom-seen snow leopard that forms the nub of Matthiessen's search. The demographic study of Himalayan blue sheep is simply a cover, an excuse—something that lets him look legitimate in the eyes of society while he searches on his own for what matters most.

The metaphor is rich in nuance for a consumer society where one's job becomes the primary measure of one's worth. As writer-interviewer Studs Terkel observed, work for Americans is frequently a mechanism for transcendence, a means of quantifying self-esteem. To consider one's labor as penultimate—as a mere cover, an acceptable facade—seems almost blasphemy. Yet I feel that blasphemous need, like "a pagan suckled on a creed outworn." William Wordsworth was right; in getting and spending we do lay waste our powers. In our jobs we look for an ultimacy they can never provide. The holy is seldom captured in the places where we seek it most. While we're preoccupied with Himalayan blue sheep, it slips onto the periphery of our vision in the furtive silhouette of a great cat.

One's Job as Cover for One's Work

I'm intrigued by this often paradoxical relationship of labor and mystery. William Least Heat Moon explored the connection between the two on his own journey into out-of-the-way parts of America. From Columbia, Missouri, where his teaching contract had been left unrenewed, he set out on the back roads of the national consciousness—the ones marked in blue by Rand McNally, the ones spurned so adamantly by the devotees of interstate arteries. Near Hat Creek, California, he met an old man traveling with a dog and a German woman, having left his job behind as well. Waiting for the dog to wet, the old man said reflectively,

> A man's never out of work if he's worth a damn. It's just sometimes he doesn't get paid. I've gone unpaid my share and I've pulled my share of pay. But that's got nothing to do with working. A man's work is doing what he's supposed to do, and that's why he needs a catastrophe now and again to show him a bad turn isn't the end, because a bad stroke never stops a good man's work.[3]

There's an important distinction implied here between one's work and a job. The two words ought not to be used interchangeably. Another of Moon's characters says, "A job's what you force yourself to pay attention to for money. With work, you don't have to force yourself." Work is paying attention to what matters most. A job can only be tangential to that. But it takes the perspective of mountains, if not a catastrophe, to realize that truth.

We all need to experience the desacralization of our jobs from time to time, being reminded of the mystery they cannot entirely embrace. Yet it's never enough simply to complain of the workplace, then hit the open road where magic abounds. William Least Heat Moon found himself ultimately drawn back to the Native American wisdom that all things of substance are done in a circle. Having traveled the full rim of the national geography, he returned to where he began—back to Columbia, back to the job, back to the self he'd been and still was. He knew there is always a dialectical tension between the dull ordinariness of one's job and the vivid encounters sought in one's work. The trick is finding the hinge on which the paradox swings.

Again Matthiessen may point the way in his metaphor of the mountain cat. He observes that only a handful of people have ever seen a snow leopard in its natural habitat. It hides so well one might be staring at it only yards away and not see it. Curiously, most Westerners who have seen the beast have done so by accident, inadvertently—in the process of observing the bharal, or blue sheep. Since the leopard principally feeds on these animals, it can best be seen by those who give up looking for it and devote their attention to the sheep instead. The gift of mystery often comes indirectly, as a function of plodding, inglorious labor. The vision is distinct from the job; it happens of its own accord. But it comes in the very process of attending to the job, with all its aching drudgery.

Cotton Mather, good Calvinist that he was, put it this way: every Christian has two callings, one general and the other personal. The first is that primary task of seeking Christ in all his glory; the second is one's particular employment, the peculiar lot in which he finds himself. "A Christian at his *Two Callings,* is a man in a Boat, Rowing for Heaven. . . . If he mind but one of his *Callings,* be it which he will, he pulls the *Oar,* but on *one side* of the boat, and will make but a poor dispatch to the Shoar of Eternal Blessedness."[4] In other words, the work and the job are inseparable, two oars to be pulled in concert.

My own particular cover is that of a university professor. It's a way of looking responsible while attending to much more important things. I appear to be respectably observing blue sheep—gainfully employed, engaged in reputable endeavors, locked into acceptable categories. I manage to satisfy my employer, meet society's expectations, sign paychecks, keep house. But it's all more or less a mask for the basic task of stalking the snow leopard, something more often seen in *not* being seen.

This is a crucial insight for those who've been taught to expect transcendent meaning in their jobs. Surprisingly, it sometimes happens. A class will click, a story connect. But there's more absurdity than glory in the idea that I convey Truth three times a week in every class as students sit in rapt wonder. Most of my best teaching happens inadvertently, before class begins or after it ends. As Kierkegaard knew, truth comes indirectly—sneaking in endwise, engaging us often where we least expect it.

This is important to remember, especially for those whose jobs take them close to the environs of the holy. The jobs of people in ministry suggest their being "in control" of sacred things. Yet the monk, the priest, the teacher never do more than skirt the truth. They mask as much as they reveal. For them, the need to distinguish their jobs from their work is absolutely necessary; otherwise they run the risk of idolatry. I love my job, but I do it well only so long as it remains secondary to something else.

Describing that something else, that holy work to which I'm called first, is always elusive. It's much easier to define the parameters of my job than to speak precisely and unmetaphorically about my work. The job comes with its own set of stock expectations. One knows not only what a professor does, but even how he or she ought to look.

Max Weber taught us about the sense of "worldly asceticism" that has marked Protestant views of vocation since the sixteenth century. We've performed our jobs in the world with the same spiritual fervor once thought possible only for those in the cloister. From seventeenth-century Puritanism to the present, we've celebrated the active virtues, insisting that our jobs be characterized by a deliberate and holy relevance. In such a climate, even the most mundane tasks become devotional.

Celebrating Irrelevance

Against this backdrop of sacralizing one's job, it sounds more than vaguely heretical to speak of it as simply preparatory to one's work. There's a disreputable, subversive quality to this quest for the snow leopard. Responsible people don't escape to the mountains in search of unlikely splendor. One's true work seems to lack accountability; it has no quantifiable purpose, serves no apparent end. Thomas Merton spoke of a "deliberate irrelevance" lying at the heart of the monk's vocation. Mountain spirituality witnesses to that which seems irresponsible to people on the plains.

Great is the need in my own uncontemplative life for spheres of deliberate irrelevance. So much of my existence is motivated by the pragmatic, calculative values of the job. Even when I set aside time to be "wasted," I try to waste it in the most profitable way. In years past, I'd walk my children to the neighborhood playground, wanting to take out appropriate time for "fathering," but I'd also carry a book under one arm, just in case they began playing with others and I found myself with nothing to do. Even in deciding to go to a movie with my wife (for the sheer deliberate irrelevance of it), I unconsciously ask myself which film might offer insights useful in teaching or writing. Quintessential American that I am, I do everything for the worth that's in it, relating it to my job and the meaning I hope to derive from it.

I'm stricken with terror when I realize how little I know about the truly irrelevant work of watching for snow leopards. I keep returning to the basic Zen (and Christian) truth that it takes phenomenal skill to do *nothing* well. In his *Autobiography*, G. K. Chesterton shuddered at seeing people throw away their hard-won holidays by doing something, filling in the time with something relevant. "For my own part," he said, "I never can get enough Nothing to do."

The art of living well is to accomplish one's job without diminishing the priority of one's work. Yet the temptation for me (and others) is always to confuse the cover with the ultimate concern, as if higher education or a church vocation were alone able to fulfill my deepest needs or those of my students. There's a danger for all of us in looking for more meaning in our jobs than they can provide. One is never fulfilled by one's job, only by one's work.

Yet there's a necessary and startling connection between the two. The very work that by its nature is so intangible and ethereal is indirectly but repeatedly encountered though the job—with all its dull, mundane, and painfully routine details. I discover the holy not *sub specie aeternitas* (by assaulting heaven in all its glory), but peering under the edges of the ordinary. Stalking the snow leopard is not so much an exercise in grasping the numinous as in paying attention to the prosaic. Full awareness of the unnoteworthy immediate moment is the grandest and hardest of all spiritual exercises.

Simone Weil recognized this in her essay "Reflection on the Right Use of School Studies with a View to the Love of God."[5] There she said that prayer consists simply in giving to God all the careful attention of which the soul is capable. The purpose of school exercises or of one's job ought to be an increase in the power of attention that will be available at the time of prayer.[6] Learning to focus one's attention in any single sphere (no matter how mundane or commonplace) is a training in the attention needed for more important encounters.

Martin Buber tells of the Hasidic rabbi once approached by a pious soul complaining of certain Jews who were staying up all night playing cards. His response was, "That's good. They're learning great concentration and becoming skilled at remaining awake for long hours. When they finally turn to God, see what excellent servants they'll make for him." In the mountains of Nepal, Peter Matthiessen learned that "the purpose of meditation practice is not enlightenment; it is to pay attention even at unextraordinary times, to be of the present, nothing-but-in-the-present, to bear this mindfulness of *now* into each event of ordinary life."[7]

Hiddenness and Sign

Yet discovering this mindfulness through the workaday routine of the job isn't easy. It's only as one turns to solitude that the truth becomes apparent. That's why I took two days recently to concentrate on my work at the nearby village of Elsah, Illinois, overlooking the Mississippi near its union with the Illinois River. Amidst nineteenth-century Victorian houses, shaded by tall bluffs and sycamores, I sought again to reach under the surface of things—genuinely to pay attention to all that was there. Time away like this is a chance to realize that everything is a mask of something else. There's a great sacramental mystery to the world. Beauty and wonder are conveyed through it in such a way that new value is given to the mask itself. That's how the Eucharist grants new holiness to ordinary bread and wine, or the hidden presence of the snow leopard gives new importance to blue sheep. That's how the job can occasion my best work.

In the woods that afternoon, taking a path up along the bluffs overlooking the river, I took time to notice things—the dusty moss on a dry stream bed, a spider eating a huge beetle caught in its web; a vine girdling a tree and then finding itself snapped by the tree's persistent growth; a doe and two fawns crossing a remote road. In each there was *res* and *signum*—an object of significance hidden under a translucent cover whose frayed edges could be peeled up to reveal the wonder beneath. Maybe it's precisely along these edges that one almost glimpses the great cat. In deciding on paths to take, I kept looking for ravelings, points from which fore and back sides of the reality could both be seen.

I wasn't able to maintain this sensitivity for long. It was hot; flies, mosquitoes, and persistent spider webs kept me plunging through the woods in quest of a way back to the cabin. I should have stopped and calmly paid attention to where I was. But the woods gradually became more threatening. Wild berry bushes grew thickly along the stream beds I tried to follow. Before long I was seeing nothing, rushing recklessly over territory I didn't know. Mud, thorns, the twisting course of rock-filled creeks—all seemed to laugh at my hurried fear. Keep the sun on the right, I said to myself. The next hollow must lead back to the river. Finally the sound of a car to the left revealed that I'd been zigzagging parallel to a country road traveling ever so gently in precisely the wrong direction. I never would have gotten home that way.

Again the *signum* and *res*. This is a mask of what I've done so often in my life; suspecting I'm on the wrong path, I go faster in hopes of proving it to be right after all. Never stopping to pay attention, I race from one experience to the next. Only in Elsah, thirty miles from home, do I again see clearly.

Having returned from the woods, the difficult task is to plod along on the right path here at home, in front of the computer, at the desk where I work each day. Can I learn alertness in this place, finding here the edges rolled up on reality? I met Peter Matthiessen in Saint Louis some time ago. For a moment I wished I had walked in his wind-beaten skin or run through half the worlds he's seen. For a moment I despised the limits of my own job, my own experience. But I know it's not in Nepal, nor in far Tortuga, nor even at play in the fields of the Lord where I find the cat that I seek. It's here, at *this* desk, with *these* people, in the drudging necessity of *this* sometimes-dull present. The mystery comes as a by-product of my attention to all of this.

Peter Matthiessen himself never saw the snow leopard—at least, he hasn't yet. Ironically, it was George Schaller, the one *not* looking for the great cat, who saw it, two weeks after Matthiessen had left the high country. The one making all those meticulous observations of blue sheep was the one who finally saw the snow leopard. Perhaps Abraham Maslow was right; those most likely to have what he called "peak experiences" are the ones most able to engage themselves in ordinary things without being bored.

At the climax of his pilgrimage in search of the snow leopard, Matthiessen met the lama of Shey Gompa, a monastery on the slopes of the Crystal Mountain, high on the Tibetan plateau. He asked the lama if he was happy there, where he'd lived for years in seclusion. Now old and crippled, he would never again be able to cross the high passes to the outside world. With arms flung to the sky the lama answered, "Of course I'm happy here! It's wonderful! *Especially* when I have no choice!" There's the hinge of the paradox. Can I learn to say the same, here in the caughtness of where I am? Seeing *this* job as able to occasion the holy? Wishing for nothing else. "Especially when I have no choice!"

There's a rare snow leopard at the Saint Louis Zoo, a trapped lion of the tribe of Judah. I seldom stop to look at the cage; it seems too painful an intrusion. I sometimes wonder at what price rare animals should be preserved from extinction. It's enough for me that a few of these great beasts still stalk the high country of the Himalayas, like ancient griffins and dragons roaming free and seldom being seen. The memory, the story is mystery enough.

The wizard Sparrowhawk, in Ursula LeGuin's *The Farthest Shore,* expressed it well: "Though I came to forget or regret all I have ever done, yet would I remember that once I saw the dragons aloft on the wind at sunset above the western isles; and I would be content."[8] Tell the story, then, but don't cage the dragon and charge admission. Wendell Berry wrote his poem "To the Unseeable Animal" in response to his young daughter's concern for the privacy and respect that properly belong to hidden mysteries. "I hope there's an animal somewhere that nobody has ever seen," she said. "And I hope nobody ever sees it."[9]

Let me observe, even domesticate, Himalayan blue sheep. But not the snow leopard. Let him be seen only along the edges of reality, where a cultivated attention awaits his passing. He can't be neatly contained, the truth kept under glass, behind wire. In stalking the snow leopard, I'm made aware, even as I search, of being stalked myself—"down the nights and down the days . . . down the labyrinthine ways of my own mind." It's the ancient paradox of being found rather than finding. Unable to trace the fearful symmetry of that great beast, I'm driven to a fear mixed with joy.

He is the Tiger, Tiger, burning bright; Aslan's flashing eyes and flowing mane; a Christ fierce with love. Let me then insist on the priority of that which can't be seen on demand, the power of that feline mystery which bends my world to itself, an odd mystery which crouches in ordinariness. Through all the tedium and anxious compulsions of the workplace, let him reign—wild and awesome—at the center of my fevered imagination.

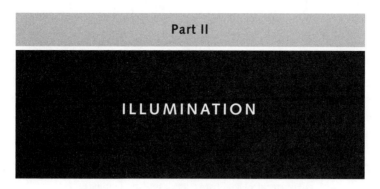

Part II

ILLUMINATION

Waiting in a Silence Beyond Language

Kilimanjaro is a snow-covered mountain 19,710 feet high, and is said to be the highest mountain in Africa. Its western summit is called by the Masai "Ngàje Ngài," the House of God. Close to the western summit there is the dried and frozen carcass of a leopard. No one has explained what the leopard was seeking at that altitude. —Ernest Hemingway, "The Snows of Kilimanjaro"

It was cold. Space, the air we breathed, the yellow rocks were deadly cold. There was something ultimate, passionless, and eternal in this cold. It came to us as a single constant note from the depths of space; we stood on the very boundary of life and death. —Frank Smythe, *Camp Six: An Account of the 1933 Mount Everest Expedition*

The mountain stands for the goal of the pilgrimage and ascent, hence it often has the psychological meaning of the self. —Carl G. Jung, "The Phenomonology of the Spirit in Fairy Tales"

In several traditions, the Cosmos is shaped like a mountain whose peak touches heaven: above, where the heavens and the earth are reunited, is the Center of the World. This cosmic mountain may be identified with a real mountain, or it can be mythic, but it is always placed at the center of the world. —Mircea Eliade, *Patterns in Comparative Religion*

Plants and animals change as one goes up the mountain, and so apparently, do people. —Diana Kappel-Smith, *Desert Time: A Journey Through the American Southwest*

Don't point at the mountain! It's rude! —an Athapaskan mother to her young daughter

There is another side of Kanchenjunga and of every mountain—the side that has never been turned into postcards. That is the only side worth seeing. —Thomas Merton, "Asian Notes"

There may be more to learn by climbing the same mountain a hundred times than by climbing a hundred different mountains. —Richard Nelson, *The Island Within*

The most spiritual people on this planet live in the highest places. —The Fourteenth Dalai Lama, letter to Peter Goullart

Considering the rugged form of Monte Verna in northern Italy and marvelling at the exceeding great clefts and caverns in its mighty rocks, St. Francis of Assisi betook himself to prayer and it was revealed to him that those clefts had been miraculouly made at the hour of the Passion of Christ when, according to the gospel, the rocks were rent asunder. —*The Little Flowers of St. Francis*

To the one who knows nothing, mountains are mountains, waters are waters, and trees are trees. But when he has studied and knows a little, mountains are no longer mountains, water is no longer water, and trees are no longer trees. But when he has thoroughly understood, mountains are once again mountains, waters are waters, and trees are trees. —Zen Buddhist saying

My mother did not die within the six months the doctors had predicted. Life often refuses to be cheated of its final energies. Having in the first few months struggled her way over the lip of a ragged outcropping of rock, she found herself on a wide plateau where she remained for another three years. The place was desolate and gaunt, but offered a long view and adequate time for reflection. In retrospect, they may have been some of the gentlest and most healing years of her life. She was able to let go of a need for control that had kept her so often from joy. I watched her slowly release her grip on anger, then fear, even her need to earn love. Most important for me, for the first time in her life she ceased expecting anything of her son. This gave me a freedom (and love) that I'd never known from her before. While we never finally crossed that chasm separating parent and child, we spent countless hours together in a silence that had a way of mending us both.

If in the beginning you weep, then subsequently you learn to wait. This is true in the spiritual life as well as the shared experience of cancer. It seemed to last forever, this time spent with my mother in the succeeding months of confusion, deciding whether she should work at dying or consent to continue still to live. Her adjustment to the nursing home went very slowly, as if exploring the physics of a whole new universe. In her world of terrifying forgottenness, she never had a place of her own, she was ever being introduced yet again to her roommate, bills were always waiting to be paid. Day after day, I would calm her fears, reminding her that "This is your bed. This is where you'll sleep tonight. That's where Millie will sleep in the bed next to you. It's all paid for; you don't have to worry about a thing."

As time wore on, my mother's condition somewhat improved. She no longer vacillated on the brink of death. What had at first seemed to us so bizarre gradually became ordinary. Physically at least, it looked as though she might even rally. But instead of happiness or relief, I felt confusion—almost disappointment, to be honest. Why was I so ambivalent about the possibility of her "getting well?"

I suppose I'd concluded, along with the rest of my culture, that the only life capable of meaning is a life open to the fullness of mental and physical health. I viewed any marginal physical improvement as merely temporary, a cruel joke at best. However long the quantity of her life might be extended, I presumed its quality had slipped beyond the point of redemption. I couldn't imagine that my mother's humanity remained intact, wholly apart from her ability to get her mind and body to do what she wanted. This deeper knowledge about the core of what it means to be human would come only through long waiting in a silence beyond language.

I also realized that by this time my mother's dying had ceased to be "exciting." The initial intensity of the threat of death had given way to the dull ordinariness of a long and exhausting wait. I no longer teetered on the threshold between life and death, caught up in a tragic immediacy that gave meaning and pathos to life. I was no longer the bearer of profundity, a person made powerful by my proximity to pain. Instead, I felt only the anguish, weariness, and anger that often accompany protracted illness.

Anger was stirred by the fact that while my mother tried so hard to die, to release her hold on life, other people around me were doing it with extraordinary ease and unwillingness. A graduate student about whom I'd cared deeply was suddenly diagnosed with cancer of the throat. She would die within the year, leaving a husband and a three-year old son whom she feared would grow up never remembering his mother. She wrote poetry in those last few months as a way of leaving him something of herself. Some of these poems reflected on conversations she'd had with him about her cancer. He called it her "hamster." "Does your hamster hurt you today, Mom?" And she would say yes, for she was always honest with him.[1] I couldn't understand why my friend had to die so young, having begged to be able to live—while my mother still lived, having begged to be able to die.

Nor would I understand, during this same period, why the baby of our next door neighbors (and dear friends) would also die under tragic circumstances. For nine months they had joyfully awaited the coming of this unexpected child, appearing late in their marriage. The pregnancy had been flawless, but the day before the baby was to have been delivered, she suddenly died. The umbilical cord had wrapped itself twice around her neck and she had choked to death in her mother's womb. Why, I asked, was the baby taken and my mother spared? The only answer was silence.

The confusion, weariness, and anger of these drawn-out months were all absorbed into that prolonged silence. I learned that if any wisdom were to be found, it would take its own good time in being revealed. I was slowly climbing an immense mountain, waiting there for an illumination that might or might not ever come—and if it did, probably not in any recognizable way.

Of the three stages of growth in the spiritual life, the second stage of illumination is the one most akin to the experience of the season of Ordinary Time in the Christian calendar. It requires the long and agonizing patience of waiting. After the desert of purgation, the ascent of the mountain symbolizes for the illuminative way the acquisition of a deeper knowledge of God's mysteries. It seldom comes with the certainty of immediate insight. Moses had to wait forty days on Mount Sinai in the process of receiving all God had to teach him. In the Japanese tradition of Zen, a classic haiku speaks of the snail as it "slowly, O so slowly, climbs Mount Fuji." Illumination can't be rushed. Neither can death. Each of them keeps its own timetable.

During this middle period of my mother's long and wearisome task of dying, I became fascinated by some of her "dry runs" at death, her dress rehearsals for what would be the final performance of her life. It was as if she were in training, exercising unfamiliar skills at letting go that she'd seldom put to use earlier in her life. I was watching a butterfly methodically working at releasing itself from its cocoon.

Still at other times it seemed as if some operation of "cosmic play" were at work. Little things would happen, allowing us to laugh at what previously had appeared unqualifiedly dreadful. In Hindu spirituality, the divine *lila* (the "playfulness" of God) can involve death making light of itself, God's telling us in absurd and comic ways not to take death nearly so seriously.[2]

Late one afternoon, for example, we received a surreal phone call from the nurses' desk on my mother's floor. A voice explained that she had just died and that we should come to see her, if we wanted to, before the car from the funeral home arrived to claim her body. I rushed to the nursing home. But on arriving there, I found her—to my amazement and laughter—sitting up in her wheelchair as usual, looking curiously at me and my surprise, completely unaware of her reputed demise. The message was a mistake; death had made its call for someone else that day. In freakish, strangely hilarious ways like this we learned something of the prolonged agony (and even playfulness) that waiting on the mountain of illumination often entails.

Dragons of the Ordinary

The Discomfort of
Common Grace

> We were talking of DRAGONS, Tolkien and I
> In a Berkshire bar. The big workman
> Who had sat silent and sucked his pipe
> All the evening, from his empty mug
> With gleaming eye glanced towards us:
> "I seen 'em myself!" he said fiercely.
>
> C. S. Lewis[1]

Sitting in my mother's room at the nursing home, as months dragged into years, I sometimes read to her. Usually the Bible, but also other stories—as if we'd changed places and I'd become the parent reading bedside tales to a child.

One day I'd brought along a children's book, telling a story of dragons from the ancient Chinese city of Wu in the mountains of northern China. When wild horsemen from the north once threatened the city, the local mandarin sought deliverance, praying for help to the Great Cloud Dragon. Having never actually seen a dragon before, he didn't know what form it might take in coming. But when a little man—short, fat, and bald—knocked on the city gates, announcing that he'd arrived in response to the mandarin's request, the ruler of the city was very sure that this couldn't be a dragon. Dragons were proud lords of the sky, coming with power and might. This little man of inconsequence was nothing of the sort.

But when dark riders descended upon the city of Wu and everything seemed lost, the little fat man who called himself a dragon puffed out his cheeks and blew a long, sustained breath. He sprang into the air as his form suddenly changed. His coat turned to the color of sunset shining through soft rain. Scales formed on his huge body, and his eyes shone like those of a proud horse. The mandarin had never seen anything more beautiful or more frightening in all his life. The city was promptly saved, and in the process the mandarin learned at last what a dragon looks like—nothing less than a small, fat, bald old man.[2]

My mother and I read stories of dragons like this one, engaged as we were in our own search for deliverance from wild horsemen from the north. We, too, hoped for miraculous rescue from proud lords of the sky. What we discovered was something far more ordinary.

This tension between the dramatic and the commonplace is one familiar to biblical theology and human experience alike. It appears in the alternate poles of prophecy and wisdom literature, resurrection and incarnation, the excitement of the Exodus and the boring years of wilderness wandering. One pole celebrates life at the center of action and change; the other speaks of the monotony of day-to-day affairs. We continually find ourselves torn between the two. David excelled as killer of giants, caught up in the high drama of battle with the Philistines. But he failed utterly in the day-to-day demands of fathering and building relationships. Peter was ecstatic about seeing Jesus transfigured on the mount. But he found it impossible to accept the quiet inevitability of Jesus' suffering and death. Like many of us, including the mandarin in the Chinese tale, he balked at ordinariness.

This truth impressed me as I continued to participate in my mother's painfully slow process of dying. Having survived the initial shock of her battle with cancer, I learned quickly that life (and death) goes on. We adjust to traumatic experiences more readily than we might expect. Crisis brings its own rush of energy. Remembering that first long, slow ascent of the roller coaster ride, we know we can get through anything so long as we hold on tight and it doesn't last long. There's a strange comfort about the extraordinary, even the extraordinarily *bad*. We're convinced that it simply cannot last.

But sometimes it does. There are times when life fails to deliver that long-awaited, glorious moment of conclusion and release. Sometimes the height of drama drags into tedious repetition. Such was the case with my mother's illness. Leaving her half alive, the cancer seemed to have gone into temporary remission. She exchanged the imminent threat of death by cancer for the slow dying of the mind by Alzheimer's disease. Having prepared myself for a dramatic deathbed scene, I instead had to watch my mother slowly adjust to a life that refused to end. Yet through it all I experienced an inexplicable gentleness as well as the undeniable discomfort of unexceptional grace.

Difficult as it was, at first, to discern grace in the grotesque, it became even more difficult to discover grace in the prolonged redundancy of ordinariness. How could I adjust to life's untheatrical regularity when I'd been prepared for grand opera and dark tragedy? I could handle bad news. I'd worked at it all of my life. Crisis is the only invariable constant for people schooled in codependency. But how would I deal with the uneventful and commonplace? It was the disconsolation of the ordinary that I found most difficult to accept. I needed a book about When Ordinary Things Happen to Average People. I needed a spirituality of the uneventful, of the low places in one's life that are neither deep nor exhilaratingly high.

Death Has Worn Two Faces

The first death I faced was my father's, which came with sudden, frightening violence when I was thirteen years old. At that time the dread beast, its wings flapping and breath foul as hell, took by two shots in the chest the one I'd loved and feared most in all the world. This death had been the monster of chaos, intruding into life in a dramatic way. It left me locked in combat, teaching me to expect tragedy, prepare against sudden loss, and endure pain by making myself numb.

In the gradual dying of my mother, however, death was very different. It came slowly as a teacher and distant friend, offering passage through the wide, gray terrain of the mundane. It didn't threaten so much as it tired.

I've seen these two deaths in a series of lithographs that German artist Käthe Kollwitz made between the wars. One drawing represents death as a terrifying, skeletal figure, snatching a young child from its mother's clutching arms. In another drawing, titled *Death Recognized as a Friend,* an old woman reaches out with joy and release to grasp a dark figure.[3] I noticed that expression at times in my mother's eyes. It spoke of a quiet acceptance I couldn't understand. Some graces spill out drop by drop, as though through an intravenous tube on slow delivery.

Looking into the tired and ancient eyes of the dragon, I began to discern a wisdom I'd never known before. It grew slowly, feeding on ordinariness. The dragon has long served as a metaphor of death in Western mythology. We fear the dragon like nothing else, seeking its defeat at every turn. "I never yet met anyone who really believed in a pterodactyl," writes Kenneth Grahame. "But everyone believes in dragons in the back-kitchen of his consciousness."[4]

Dragons are the unacknowledged shadow against which we all do battle. But only in the years of my mother's dying did I discover the important differences between Western and Eastern dragons. While the former terrifies with its melodramatic fury, the other teaches with its prosaic commonness. I suspect these are two sides of a single truth. Yet Western thought, with its pervasive denial of death, is in deep need of the corrective that Eastern dragons provide.

Western dragons are ugly and vicious. Dwelling in dark caves and flying only at night, they breathe fire on terrified villagers. Never sleeping, they guard their unused treasure with bloodshot eyes. Occasionally they escape to swallow a live elephant or feed on the unsuspecting daughter of a king. This is the unspoken terror at the end of every Western nightmare. It strikes unexpectedly, like Freddy Krueger, Hannibal Lecter, or the dark beings in a Stephen King thriller. We feed on their horror—dramatizing the confrontation with darkness, fantasizing our own heroism or helplessness, projecting outside of ourselves all that is evil. In biblical mythology, this dragon is Leviathan, "the coiled one," described in

Isaiah 27:1 as the twisting serpent of chaos, ultimately destroyed by Yahweh.[5]

By contrast, Eastern dragons—as portrayed in China, Japan, and Indonesia—are beautiful, gentle, and friendly. They may bring change and even death, but they do so as promise instead of threat. They symbolize an ancient wisdom, the quiet rhythms of nature as opposed to the savagery of disorder. Appearing in the convoluted shapes of clouds, they breathe a drizzling mist that waters the earth and brings forth life. Eastern dragons feed on tender bamboo shoots and milk. Living between sky and sea, they thrive on water and offer gifts to those lucky enough to meet them. The "night-shining pearl" is the finest of the dragon's gifts. It symbolizes fecundity and the mystery of rebirth. Curiously enough, this benevolent aspect of the Eastern dragon is also pictured in the Christian scriptures. In Psalm 104:26, the very same Leviathan (elsewhere seen as a threat) is presented as a grand beast, giving God pleasure, sporting in the open sea.

What is this mystery of the dragon as a metaphor of death, simultaneously evoking images of the dramatic and the ordinary, the fearsome and the good? The dragon threatens our existence; wholly unpredictable, attacking without warning, it lurks in the shadows of our deepest fear. Yet at the same time it promises life, offers the pearl of great price which is the gradual unfolding of new possibilities in the failure of the old. This is the grand paradox of death itself, as Martin Luther well knew. He spoke of death as the final enemy to be defeated by the power of the cross. Yet in his Genesis commentary, written near the end of his life, he called death God's plaything. He understood God to have been "sporting" with Abraham in the painful journey toward Mount Moriah.[6] Death is a terrible thing, and yet it also is an ordinary dimension of our passage through life.

In a Wilderness of Ostriches and Dragons

I was reluctant at first to acknowledge the dragons of the ordinary in my mother's gradual death. I was more used to battling the frightening beast of my imagination, stealing myself against the terrors of death, feeling fully alive only in defying its power. To think of befriending the dragon was almost more fearful than imagining combat with it. Of the two dragon stories that stand out in the history of Christian myth, I'd always been prone to identify with Saint George, the knight who slew an ominous dragon with a single blow. It often seems easier to kill dragons than to deal with one's fear of them. Yet the story of Saint Martha and the dragon spoke much more directly to my need at the time of my mother's dying. Martha's winsome way of subduing the frightening dragon that threatened her village was to sprinkle its tail with holy water, then lead it peacefully out of town, using a silken cord as leash. She knew intuitively that dragons love water, that they can be handled better with gentleness than with force. Her singular triumph was in facing her own fear, even before thinking of approaching the beast.

Moses Leading the Children of Israel Through the Wilderness, engraving by
Hans von Windsheim?, 1481/82. *(Used by permission of the Staatliche
Graphische Sammlung, Munich)*

The temptation to dramatize death—to imagine ourselves defeating its claim
in the triumph of violence—is rife in our culture. Never content with ordinariness, unable to address our fears, we pump up the volume on every dramatic
(and violent) possibility. We live from one moment of fear-stifling exhilaration
to the next. Only in this way do we feel engaged with life. In our best-selling
novels, current films, and the tensions of urban life and foreign policy, the
dragons of awfulness lurk in every corner, reminding us that if we've survived
the terrors of death, we *must* be alive. *Supervivo, ergo sum.*

But when the drama fails, when we grow weary of the intense pressure of life
on the edge, we're forced to reconsider the myths by which we live. War is not
the principle metaphor of human existence. Death is not always an enemy. Life
is more than a matter of breathless contention, triumphing over obstacles, denying the monsters of our own feelings. The dragons of the ordinary invite us back
to simplicity and a quiet acceptance of life's rhythms.

The deepest joys are not so much spectacular as commonplace. "Do not forget," wrote Teilhard de Chardin, "that the value and interest of life is not so
much to do conspicuous things . . . as to do ordinary things with the perception
of their enormous value."[7] Jesus said as much in telling his disciples not to be

anxious but to consider the quiet simplicity of wildflowers blooming and dying in a field.

Such were the lessons I began to learn in my frequent visits to the nursing home. When my mother's condition leveled out and even improved in certain ways, I had to rethink the meaning I'd sought from her death. Her own acceptance of death's delay made me reconsider my restless impatience. No longer could I picture myself in tragic terms, defiantly confronting death, eager to get it over with as soon as possible. Instead, a more insistent question began to emerge. How would I cope with the uneventful, living from day to day in the absence of spectacular drama? Finding myself on the slow path to Canaan, I moved through a weary landscape strewn with ostriches and dragons (Lam. 4:3).

Only in time spent pushing a wheel chair, changing diapers, sitting through long periods of silence, and waiting for nothing can one learn the truths of ordinariness. Life is not a matter of running away from fears, denying the monstrous feelings that lie within us. Life cannot be "fixed," at least not in the compulsive and controlling way I'd often attempted. There was no cure for my mother or myself, I learned. Healing maybe, but no cure. We both were terminal cases. I even learned that I didn't need her constant approval, although I'd always sought it. My mother's approval didn't come much anymore, and maybe our relationship was cleaner and more honest as a result. All these truths offered by the dragons of the ordinary are as simple as those Robert Fulghum learned in kindergarten. They speak of slow and courageous acts of letting go.

There are graces, we all come to realize, that we'd rather not receive. Theologians used to distinguish between special grace and common grace, but we've never much valued the latter. Special grace is extraordinary; it comes with drama and flair. We are rescued, singled out in a momentous act of boldness. But common grace falls upon the just and unjust alike. It strikes us as simply too . . . ordinary.

Waiting for Epiphany

I continued to study my mother as the days went on, looking for hints of transcendence in the ordinary. I watched her at times, in her great silence. She seemed to be working on a grand solution of some sort, a way of comprehending the last great mystery—joining earth and heaven, conscious and unconscious, known and unknown. Every now and then she seemed to gain some sense of how it all tied together. A sudden wave of recognition passed over her face and then faded. The closer she got to grasping the shape of this Great Whole, the less ability she apparently had to convey its meaning, to reveal its pattern. I was left only with subtle nuances, tracking life's meaning along the slow and beaten path toward death.

One morning I told her I had a last request—that she wait for me to be there when she died, if she were able to do so. Her eyes started to tear and I said I realize we have no control over such things. But she answered quickly, "You might be surprised. It could be soon! In fact, even *now* would be a good time!" she added, speaking with an unnerving certainty that made me wish I hadn't raised the subject.

She looked me straight in the eye for a long moment and then, glancing toward the window, asked intently, "Can you hear it? The truck is here." I heard nothing, only the hum of sounds usual to the nursing home's third floor, north wing. She sat listening, and then announced assuredly, "The King is here," speaking with a confidence that made me yearn to hear as well. "The King says it's time to go," she declared. "He says it's *this* way."

I didn't know whether to laugh or to cry. My mother was going through a full-scale dress rehearsal for death, willing it with all the strength she could muster. The King had come to pick her up in his truck. Its motor was running outside. She had only to say goodbye. She told me, at last, that she would go and that I must stay for now, and come later. Then, after a prolonged silence, she rested her chin on her chest, waiting to die as she dreamed of a long ride with the King. I suspect she sat with her elbow out the truck's window, letting the wind catch her hair as flowers bloomed in the passing fields. For the rest of that morning, she went riding with the King.

I fully expected her to die that day. But she didn't. Yet she saw a clear promise of that which was to come. Such a wonderful image of death, to be fetched by the King in his pickup truck. There is drama and ordinariness in that image. Both dragons.

In C. S. Lewis's tale, *The Lion, the Witch and the Wardrobe,* the little girl Lucy is frightened by the dragonlike terrors of the White Witch. But when she hears Mr. and Mrs. Beaver speaking of the lion Aslan, a fierce king who'll come to put things to right, she's not entirely sure the unknown danger will be any better than the known. Of this Aslan, the wild and promised King, she asks with trepidation, "Is he safe?" And Mr. Beaver, as honest as he is wise, responds, "Who said anything about safe? 'Course, he isn't safe! But he's *good!* He's the King, I tell you."[8]

The goodness of this King may be slow in coming. But it's sure. Some graces appear very unexceptional at first. Yet the route to all grand things passes by way of the commonplace. My mother knew this. She waited for the sound of the truck and the voice of the King to come again, for the last drama to which her life would finally lead. Until that time, when the lights would go down and the curtains rise at last, she sat at stageside, accompanied in her silence by grand and beautiful dragons. The dragons of the ordinary.

· 4 ·

The Sinai Image in the History
of Western Monotheism

Whatever the experience of the people Israel on Mount Sinai was, it was so overwhelming that the texts about it seem to be groping for an adequate metaphor through which to convey the awesomeness of the event. . . . Fear pervades the spectacle, a fear that infects nature as much as humanity. —Jon Levenson[1]

Whereof one cannot speak, thereof one must be silent. —Ludwig Wittgenstein[2]

The austere slopes of Jebel Mussa in the desert of the Upper Sinai Massif have through the centuries exercised the apophatic imagination as much as any other place in the history of Christianity.[3] Jews and Muslims, as well as Christians, have been drawn, metaphorically if not physically, to the mountain where Moses entered into the cloud of darkness to meet a God of incomprehensible light. Whether this particular peak was the actual site of Mount Sinai is incidental to the study at hand. A case can be made for five or six different locations of the mountain that Moses ascended.[4] Of interest here is Sinai as a mountain of the imagination, an evocative image of great power that recurs repeatedly in the Christian apophatic tradition as well as in the folklore of the Abrahamic traditions generally.

Sinai—the desert and the mountain—is a symbol of fierce majesty, a landscape of terror and theophany, where Yahweh is met in the darkness of unknowing. It demonstrates the enormous energy that landscape metaphors exert on the human imagination. The long, silent contemplation of a vast, indifferent terrain has been shown, throughout human experience, to be a powerful force in subverting self-consciousness, pushing the outer edges of language, evoking the deepest desire of the human heart for untamed mystery and beauty.

Barry Lopez found this in the haunting desertlike landscapes of the arctic, even as John Van Dyke had done in the wild terrain of the American southwest.[5] Thoreau recognized, from his own forays into the dark woods of Maine, that inexplicable wilderness carried him beyond himself, beyond all illusion of mastery, into an emptiness that left him stunned, vulnerable, and open to the unexpected. "We need the tonic of wildness. . . . At the same time that we are earnest to explore and learn all things, we require that all things be mysterious and un-explorable, that land and sea be infinitely wild, unsurveyed, and unfathomed by us because unfathomable."[6]

The experience of threatening wilderness invites us to the unexplored land-scapes of an inner geography where that which is most deeply "us" is joined to what we experience as radically Other. In hostile landscapes of desert, moun-tain, and thundering clouds we are brought forcibly to the boundaries of what our minds and bodies are able to sustain. Hence Gregory of Nyssa saw the soul to be guided to the world of the invisible, "the secret chamber of divine knowl-edge," by way of the sense phenomena of desert, mountain, and cloud.[7]

Tribal peoples have known this intuitively for millennia, sensitive as they are to the healing properties of fierce landscapes—those that teach us our limits. In the Beautyway ceremony, performed by traditional singers of the Dineh, or Na-vajo people, the spiritual order and balance of the exterior landscape (with all its vast emptiness) is invoked as a way of healing the broken, interior landscape of the individual who comes in need of wholeness. Contemplating the sacred bal-ance (*hozro*) of wild desert terrain and tall mesas is recognized as purgative and therapeutic, restoring the inner geography of the soul.[8]

In a similar way, the Nepali shaman makes use of a "healing geography" in the symbolic travels he undertakes to restore wholeness to one who is ill. The shaman's spirit visits the "inner mountain snowfields" of Tibet, high cliffs in the Himalayas, or dangerous jungle terrain, which he subsequently describes and interprets to the patient as a way of cleansing and restoring health.[9] Being in-vited to the contemplation of a landscape so wild it threatens one's very being is an ancient form of therapy that doubles as worship. "Beauty," said the poet Rainer Marie Rilke, "is only the first touch of terror we can still bear and it awes us so much because it so cooly disdains to destroy us."[10]

This chapter asks how a wild landscape image such as Mount Sinai functions in radical monotheism as a way of knowing and talking about a God of utter transcendence. It considers first the enduring power of the cloud-covered mountain as an image in the history of religions. Then it traces the use of Mount Sinai as a dominant (if also reluctant) metaphor within the Christian apophatic tradition. Finally, it suggests similarities and differences in the im-agery of Sinai as found in Jewish and Muslim thought.

The Cloud-Covered Mountain as Apophatic Metaphor

The image of the cloud-covered mountain, glimpsed on the desert horizon, half-hidden from human view, is an intriguing one in the history of religions. What is *not* seen can often be more compelling to the imagination than what is seen. The metaphor of the partially disclosed mountain, alluring in its mystery and inaccessibility, has gripped the human imagination—from Plato's dream of the lost island-mountain of Atlantis to fifteenth-century descriptions of the rocky coast of Lyonesse, vanishing in the mist beyond Land's End in Cornwall.[11]

Mount Meru has functioned as cosmic center for Hindu believers, while the mysteries of Mount Kaf have been celebrated in Sufi mysticism. Far up the Yangtze River in Western China stands O-mei Shan, the highest of the four Buddhist mountains. Rising over three thousand meters on the eastern rim of the Tibetan plateau, it seems to disappear in changing clouds. Atmospheric conditions on the peak sometimes create a corona of rainbow colors known as "Buddha's Glory."[12] The semireal, semimythic mountain recurs in stories everywhere. Examples in the history of Christian spirituality can be found in Gregory and his brother Basil, in Cosmas Indicopleustes and Hildegard of Bingen, in John of the Cross, Thomas Merton, and others.

The seductive, ambivalent landscape of the half-seen mountain—able to be read but *not* read, provoking as much confusion as it does insight—is a metaphor of the effort to speak of God. In the Western monotheistic tradition, cloud-covered Sinai is where all graven images—all attempts to contain God's mystery (either in stone or in speech)—are ultimately declared inadequate. The mountain becomes a sign of contradiction, proclaiming all similes to be false. God is "like" nothing else. No single image can encompass the divine glory.

Yet, at the same time, Sinai stands as a mountain of great mythic energy, stirring the imagination, giving birth to a magnificent folklore. It discloses God's awesome character and power in revelations given to Moses and subsequently to Elijah, Catherine of Alexandria, even Muhammad.

In the twist of imagination that metaphor occasions, the mountain speaks of two things at once: its own fierce, demanding presence as a physical form, and the notion of God's incomprehensible greatness. The mind struggles, uncomfortably and simultaneously, with these two juxtaposed images. God is the *rock* of our salvation, the psalmist insists (Ps. 18:31; 78:35). Yet God obviously is not a rock, precisely speaking. The metaphor succeeds in conveying its truth only to the extent that it is recognized as literally false. It "is" yet it "isn't." The mountain discloses the divine mystery in the very process of hiding it.[13]

This is the power of metaphor as a language event.[14] Half of the content (and most of the energy) of a metaphor is found in what it does *not* say. It undermines speech in the very act of speaking. It functions in both apophatic and kataphatic ways. What the metaphor of Sinai expresses kataphatically is lean, starkly simple, barely suggestive—a landscape of nothingness. Much more important, and indeed, what is emphasized by the thin suggestiveness of the sensory landscape, is what is *not* seen. Here one discovers the metaphor's apophatic power.

Pilgrims to Mount Kailas in the Himalayas, and to other sacred peaks often shrouded in mist, speak of the mountain's powerful presence even when (or especially when) completely hidden by clouds. Young men of the Oglala Sioux, seeking a vision quest on the upper slopes of Bear Butte in South Dakota, await the darkness of night or the passing of huge thunder clouds for a message that may come for their people. In the exercise of myth, the mountain is more captivating in its darkness, in remaining hidden.[15]

Basho, the Zen poet, once described in a telling haiku his own most meaningful ascent of Japan's holiest mountain: "Delightful, in a way, / to miss seeing Mount Fuji / In the misty rain."[16] Not seeing the mountain, being frustrated in one's quest, can be far more riveting to the imagination than succeeding in beholding what one sought. This was Peter Matthiessen's experience in his search for the snow leopard along the high passes of the Himalayas. In Ku Hsi's classical pattern of Chinese landscape art, the subtle appeal of mountains is rooted in the artist's skillful craft of omission; the peaks are half-dissolved in clouds. This is why the metaphor of the cloud-covered mountain serves so well in speaking of a divine mystery beyond human comprehension.

The half-disclosed mountain is a metaphor evoking high mystery. I'll never forget an experience of my own one summer on Mount Whitney in the Sierra Nevadas of California. A friend and I were climbing the peak, finding more snow and ice above twelve thousand feet than we'd expected. The day of our final ascent to the top, from a base camp at Mirror Lake, I learned for the first time what mountain terror entails.

Clouds had been gathering all day as we worked our way up snowfields, trying to discern the switchbacks on the trail. We scrambled up ice-covered rocks I couldn't imagine coming back down again. Fear began moving like a warm cloud across my mind. I wanted only to flee, but before long we found ourselves closed in by a huge bank of ash-gray clouds towering around us. They swept in slowly at first, in beautiful wreaths flowing over the higher ridges. It was a beauty even terror could recognize. But within minutes they swept tightly around us, their thick, wet silence suffocating in its ubiquity. We couldn't see anything. We didn't dare move, for fear of stepping off the mountain.

Within ten minutes the cloud passed on, though others came swiftly behind it. We could see enough to make our descent back down the mountain, but I never made it to the top of Mount Whitney, having come so close. This splendid "failure" to succeed is a mystery that's worked its way deeply into my imagination ever since.

The cloud-covered mountain is a symbol of exquisite terror, a disorienting place intimating abandonment and delusion. This is how people have described the other-worldly haze surrounding Wu-t'ai Shan, the hauntingly beautiful peak sacred to Buddhists in northern China. It is like the Magic Mountain of Thomas Mann, full of unexpected dread. Whoever endures the horror of whiteout, the total incapacity experienced in a mountain snowstorm, or the frightening stillness of heavy fog, emerges with altogether new powers of being.[17]

There are many stories of the spiritual hero who disappears on the cloud-covered peak—passing, in the process, into a higher form of consciousness. Jesus is transfigured in the thick cloud on Mount Tabor (Mt. 17:1–9) and ascends into heaven from the cloud-covered slopes of Mount Olivet (Acts 1:9–12). King

Kay Khusraw, an Iranian hero and spiritual teacher in the Muslim tradition, is said to have disappeared in the swirling mists of Mount Kaf. The *Mahabharata,* India's epic narrative, ends with King Yudhistira's ascent into heaven from the clouds surrounding Mount Meru.

Why do these tales so readily transfix the analogical imagination? What passage from a state of "knowing" to a deeper way of "*un*knowing" is symbolized for us in the experience of being enclosed by mountain clouds?

For the first seventeen centuries of the Christian era, mountains were viewed in highly negative terms—as blisters, tumors, or warts on the face of the earth. They were objects of revulsion and fear, characterized by a dangerous and surly ambition.[18] This enduring negative connotation of the mountain in the history of myth has been highly provocative in the Western apophatic imagination. The mountain looms over the tininess of every human endeavor. Standing above all that is readily known, beyond comprehension, it threatens and deconstructs. It fosters a self-forgetfulness in the absoluteness of its indifference to human life. "One must learn to look away from oneself," said Nietzsche's Zarathustra in speaking of the skills necessary for mountain survival. "Every climber needs this hardness."[19]

The mountain terrifies, bringing the mind to a stop in the presence of great mystery. Al-Ghazzali, the eleventh-century Persian poet and Muslim theologian, described the mountain as a "great and illimitable" symbol, yet one from which "streams of knowledge pour into the mind like water into a valley."[20]

Landscape Imagery in Early Christian Apophaticism

But what of the particular irony found in the use of mountain imagery in the Christian apophatic tradition? While criticizing every image one might use to describe the unsayable mystery of God, apophatic writers have resorted again and again to the fierce metaphor of Sinai as a way of questioning and deconstructing all other images. How has the cloud-covered mountain of Moses and Elijah served to symbolize the exhaustion of language to which Christian prayer is ultimately prone?

The *via negativa,* emerging in early Christianity, was fully aware that one cannot speak of God yet must speak. There's an opaqueness and impenetrability about the divine being that resists every effort to grasp its mystery. God is inaccessible to all forms of human control, beyond every linguistic sign and image one might use as referent.[21] Language about God is as impossible as it is necessary.

Deeply sensitive to this tension, early apophatic writers adopted a twisted language of paradox and negation, using language against language. They employed lean, porous images, able to point to a mystery beyond themselves while at the same time warning of the danger of idolatry present in every image. The fathers of the Eastern church utilized fierce landscape metaphors, rooted in their own physical experience of "limit," to provoke the emptiness and poverty-of-imagination out of which God-talk is properly begun. The stark metaphor of Sinai had a way of limiting the imagination, emptying the mind of preconceived notions and stripping the self to enable one to encounter a God beyond all one might anticipate.

The context for this emerging development of the apophatic tradition takes us back to fourth-century Asia Minor, during the years following the Council of Nicea in 325.[22] In the last decades of that century, a radical Arian movement known as Anomoeanism was revived under the leadership of Eunomius, bishop of Cyzicus in Cappodocia.[23] Arguing against what he saw to be the mystifying Orthodox doctrine of the Trinity, he insisted on the perfect simplicity of the divine being, saying that God's nature can be readily defined and that God has no more knowledge of God's own substance than we do.[24] He seemed to imply that God's innermost being was perfectly accessible to human intelligence.

Orthodox theologians in Cappadocia such as Basil the Great and his brother, Gregory of Nyssa, along with John Chrysostom in nearby Antioch, reacted to this bald theological presumption as they saw it. They insisted on the incomprehensibility of God to the human mind and the necessary limits of theological discourse. In 381 Gregory followed his brother's response to the controversy with a major treatise *Against Eunomius* and John Chrysostom fired his own cannons five years later in a series of twelve homilies, *On the Incomprehensible Nature of God.*[25]

Chrysostom excoriated those "curious busybodies" who fix their eyes on the ineffable glory of God, claiming readily to understand the divine being.[26] How can anyone understand the mystery of God, he asked, when we cannot even grasp the inexplicability of nature? He pointed to certain fierce landscape images as a poignant way of silencing his antagonists.

> We wonder at the open sea and its limitless depth; but we wonder fearfully when we stoop down and see how deep it [actually] is. It was in this way that the [psalmist] stooped down and looked at the limitless and yawning sea of God's wisdom. And he was struck with shuddering.[27]

The God of the psalmist is one who "looks upon the earth and makes it tremble," who "touches the mountains and they smoke."[28] The golden-tongued Chrysostom used these threatening images of untamed nature to evoke the "limitless," "yawning," and "shuddering" character of God's numinous mystery. One's experience of wild, menacing terrain, he suggested, provides the best analogy for contemplating the otherness of God.

It is not accidental, by the way, that Rudolf Otto, in his classic study of mystical experience, drew examples from John Chrysostom and Gregory of Nyssa to describe how one's idea of the Holy involves both a sense of *mysterium tremendum* and *fascinans,* that which causes one to shudder and that which stirs delight. He says of Chrysostom, "Blank amazement is to him at the same time enraptured adoration; speechlessness in the presence of the inapprehensible passes over . . . into a humble gratitude that it is so, that it is 'fearfully wonderful.'"[29] What desert-mountain landscapes provide for these two writers is an imagery rich enough to suggest the numinous terror as well as the "exceeding greatness" of the God they sought to uphold.

Gregory of Nyssa developed the same line of argument in his *Life of Moses,* composed several years later but still reflecting this background of controversy with Eunomius.[30] Here Gregory adopted the grand metaphor of Moses entering the cloud of darkness on Sinai as a primary vehicle for expressing the idea of God's incomprehensibility and grandeur. The mountain experience of Moses had been used earlier as an apophatic metaphor by Philo, Clement of Alexandria, and Origen as they described the ineffable darkness of God's being.[31] But with Gregory of Nyssa it became an archetypal image echoed in the apophatic tradition down through the centuries.

"The knowledge of God," Gregory argued, "is a mountain steep indeed and difficult to climb."[32] "The one who is going to associate intimately with God must go beyond all that is visible and (lifting up his own mind, as to a mountaintop, to the invisible and incomprehensible) believe that the divine is *there* where the understanding does not reach."[33]

Both Gregory and his brother Basil had a deep fascination for desert-mountain terrain.[34] They loved it in the very process of being awed and terrified by it. In his *Commentary on Ecclesiastes,* Gregory pointed to the wild mountainous places of his own familiar Cappadocia to reiterate his favorite theme of God's incomprehensible greatness. Imagine, he said, a steep rocky crag of red sandstone, out in the wild, desert expanse. You stand at the top of this high ridge on the edge of a cliff, looking down into what seems a bottomless chasm below. You feel a sense of vertigo. You reach for something to hold onto, but nothing is there. Your foot begins to slip on the rock beneath you and you find yourself overwhelmed by a sense of dread. This, he insists, is what it is like to know the incomprehensible mystery of God.[35]

There is terror, he knows, in such an experience. The slipping of the foot on the edge of the cliff is an entry into darkness and fear. But the place of fearfulness—the place of risk—is also, paradoxically, the place of being known and loved. As Gregory observed in his reflections on the Song of Songs, the bride is most joyfully met by the bridegroom in the darkest part of the night—at that very point of uncanny, shuddering feeling, when she does not know who or what is there, when she expects terror but suddenly breaks into the joy of recognition and love.[36]

Gregory knew this, both in his mystical experience of God and in his practical experience of desert landscape. The towering cliff in the desert waste, forbidding as it was, had often occasioned for him a divine encounter of apprehension and joy alike. He became one of the first Christian theologians to develop a thoroughgoing theology of darkness, emphasizing that one is continually lured by God, through increasing levels of obscurity and vulnerability, to a deeper knowledge and love.[37] His concept of *epiktasis* claimed the goal of human life, in this world and in the next, to be the endless pursuit of God's inexhaustible mystery.[38] There would always be mountains of God's splendor to be climbed.

The experience of Moses on the desert mountain became, for Gregory, paradigmatic of three stages of growth in the spiritual life. God's revelation came first to Moses in the conspicuousness of light (the glory indirectly seen from the cleft of the rock), then subsequently in the richer obscurity of the cloud in which God descends, and finally in the sublime contemplation of utter darkness.[39] This is a very different pattern, of course, from the light-centered consciousness most characteristic of the kataphatic tradition in Eastern and Western Christianity.

The beginning of any true knowledge of God, Gregory knew, is found at the cliff overhanging the great abyss. This stark, troubling image assaults the proud imagination of any who might presume to lay hold of the divine being through their use of language and reason.

The Image of Sinai in the Medieval Apophatic Tradition

In the succeeding history of Christian spirituality, the image of Sinai, after the pattern of Gregory of Nyssa, continued to persist as a reminder of God's incomprehensibility to the human mind. The cloud-covered mountain became a symbol of what the heart longs for most, as well as what the mind is least able to comprehend. Pseudo-Dionysius (c. 500) would speak of the blessed Moses who "left behind every divine light, every voice, every word from heaven, to plunge into the darkness where the One dwells who is beyond all things."[40] The mountain symbolized for him the glory of God reflected in each created being, as well as the necessity of negating everything that is not God in one's ascent to the divine mystery.[41] Later in twelfth-century France, Abbot Suger would trace this same pattern of heirarchical ascent in his exposition of the new Gothic style at the Church of Saint Denis.

Maximus the Confessor (c. 580–662), one of the earliest interpreters of Dionysius to the West, stressed that one is never capable of making God's nature a subject of human thought. Returning to the metaphor of Sinai, he observed in Exodus 33:7–23 that Moses pitched "the tent of thought" *outside* the camp and only then conversed with God on the mountain. "It is precarious to attempt to speak the ineffable in verbal discourse," he warned.[42] In the mountain's thin air, one's thoughts and words—like one's breath—must be carefully measured.

Richard of Saint Victor (d. 1173) was similarly fascinated with Moses' entry into the cloud on the mountain at Sinai. In that "cloud of unknowing," Moses experienced "a dense veil of forgetting," his mind falling asleep in a supreme self-forgetfulness.[43] In Richard's thinking, this is characteristically the analogical meaning of mountains. Rams leap for joy on the mountain (as in Ps. 114:4), representing the contemplatives who leave thought and self behind in meeting God face to face. By contrast, the younger lambs remain in speculative thought on the hills, still seeing through a glass darkly.[44] How does one encounter God on Sinai? Only by entry into the cloud, says Richard, leaving one's words and concepts behind, ascending to the high place of the heart.

For Meister Eckhart, this involved meeting—like Moses—the One who is without name, who is a denial of all names.[45] While this may sound like a repudiation of any speech whatever about God, in none of these writers does the task of negation dissolve into a simplistic anti-intellectualism. Reason is essential to the work of affirming and negating all that is and is not God, but the vehicle within us by which we finally meet God is the human will, our naked intent. Thought may help us locate the mountain, but faith is what finally makes the ascent.

The *Cloud* author in fourteenth-century England, for example, spoke of ascending the cloud-wreathed mountain as a matter of learning how to know God without adjectives. Don't think anything about *what* God is, he declared, only *that* God is. Don't try to reach into God's inner mystery by subtle reasoning. Similarly, he added, don't think about what *you* are, whether focusing on your competence or incompetence, your weakness or strength. Only be content *that* you are. When you put those two things side by side—the naked fact that "God is" and that "you are"—letting the two exist together in quiet contemplation, you have entered the deepest, simplest mystery of prayer. "Take the good, gracious God, just as he is, without qualification, and bind him, as you would a poultice, to your sick self, just as you are."[46]

This is what all of the apophatic writers want to accomplish in their varying ways of employing the imagery of Sinai. They point the climber to a peak that demands abandoning all the intellectual baggage possible. The mountain's ascent requires the letting go of every pride of mastery, every naive confidence in what might once have been known. It is finally not stamina or expertise that drives the pilgrim up the mountain, but a profound, inexpressible desire for that which cannot be named.

What isn't seen directly on the mountain's peak but glimpsed only "from the back" through gathering clouds, creates an incredible longing for a deeper, more privileged knowing that is always the goal of apophatic awareness. In the ways of love, the secrecy of playful hiding is ever the servant of intimacy. Gregory of Nyssa himself could speak of the "partial seeing" of God by Moses on Sinai as, indeed, an invitation to the most intimate of relationships. He asked how Moses could have been so close to God without actually glimpsing God's face (being able only to see his back), and concluded that God must have been holding Moses on his shoulders like an infant carried piggy-back, God's right hand occasionally reaching over to touch and support the child at his back.[47] This is what draws the pilgrim to the dark crest of Sinai, a response of the will to the promise of incalculable love.

William of Saint-Thierry (c. 1085–1148) similarly understood the narrative of Moses on the mountain as occasioning unutterable love within a context of dread. Only when the human will is reduced to a naked longing, like Moses gazing from his cleft in the rock, says William, can "I see the 'back' of him who sees me; I see your Son Christ 'passing by' in the abasement of his incarnation."[48] The connection of Jesus with the mountain of Moses and Elijah occurred very early in the Christian tradition, the New Testament writers themselves interpreting the experience of Sinai in terms of the encounter at Tabor. The two mountains eventually became overlapping images in the apophatic tradition.

Jan Ruysbroec (1293–1381), writing in the Low Countries in the fourteenth century, used the metaphor of "following Christ up the mountain of our *bare mind* to a barren, secret place."[49] There on the mountain one is "free of images," gazing with "blissful yearning" for what remains unseen. Given the tradition, one might think he was speaking of Sinai, but he referred here to Tabor, viewing the one mountain through the Christological lens of the other.

While Maximus the Confessor honored Moses as one who "entered the darkness, the formless and immaterial place of knowledge," he, too, insisted that one move beyond the Moses of Sinai to the Jesus of Tabor.[50] John Climacus, abbot of Saint Catherine's monastery in the seventh century, compared the penitence of Moses' mountain with the joy of Jesus' mountain near Nazareth, providing his monks with a "ladder of divine ascent" to help in climbing both mountains of the spiritual life.[51]

All these writers claimed to have found in Christ the splendid darkness in which Moses had been met by God. In ascending the mountain, they discovered a God who "makes darkness his covering around him, his canopy thick clouds dark with water (Ps. 18:12)." But in abandoning every effort to grasp this God through thoughtful reflection, they found themselves surprised by an intimacy they never would have guessed.

Comparing Jewish and Muslim Images of Sinai

An apophatic image such as Mount Sinai brings the mind to a halt, serving ultimately to redirect and reanimate the energies of the kataphatic imagination. These two dimensions of religious insight necessarily exist in dialectical tension. An aniconic image such as Sinai has a double role of systematically discounting all images and subsequently restoring their kataphatic energy. As a metaphor, it launches a thousand ships of the imagination. Its spare, deconstructed ambiguity provokes, curiously, a language of bold exaggeration.

"How does one write about nothing?" asks Maggie Ross, speaking of the perennial dilemma of apophatic theology. "As extravagantly as possible," she answers.[52] The great mystics, from Rumi to Julian of Norwich and Isaac Luria, knew there was no language for what they wanted most to say. So they began leanly, suggesting very little, hinting—it seemed—at nothing. Yet eventually they broke into a language of allure, scattering images written as bait, attracting others to the exuberantly speechless mystery that was theirs.

Apophatic theology, holding its breath in silence for as long as it can, sometimes bursts at last into a kataphatic excess of language. It becomes, as Denys Turner argues, "a kind of verbal riot, an anarchy of discourse in which anything goes."[53] This is what happens with the image of Mount Sinai in the Western apophatic imagination. In the Jewish, Muslim, and Christian mythologies of Sinai, an incorrigible extravagance tumbles forth from this meager, stinted image.

Israel's primal, definitive experience at Sinai, for example, was typically one of terror. The people described themselves there as trembling in the presence of thunder, lightning, and thick clouds (Exod. 19:16). Touching the mountain, even looking at it, could mean their death (Exod. 19:12, 21). Jon Levenson mentions "a mysterious extraterrestrial quality to the mountain," symbolizing "the uncontrollable and unpredictable quality of God's choice of place." Yet it fascinated even as it frightened. The experience for Israel was one of "charm and threat."[54] As much as they were terrified by it, they couldn't help but be drawn into its mystery, multiplying metaphors hand over fist in the effort to comprehend a reality deeper than language could bear.

In the Midrash, for example, the whole Sinai region became, if anything, even more hostile and threatening—a surreal landscape, hideous in its details. The rabbis described it as "horrible and dreadful wilderness, full of snakes, lizards, and scorpions, extending over hundreds of miles. So deadly is the nature of the snakes that dwell in this desert, that if one of them merely glides over the shadow of a flying bird, the bird falls to pieces." This horrifying landscape served as a fitting theatrical backdrop for the even greater grace of Yahweh, seen in God's protection of the people from every harm. The rabbis remarked offhandedly that "as soon as the snakes saw the Israelites, they meekly lay down upon the sand."[55]

In the Jewish tradition one discovers an ambivalence about this Sinai image, seen in the contrast between its presentation in the *Zohar* and in the *Midrash*. In the mystical text of the *Zohar,* very little is said of Moses' profound experience inside the cloud on the mountain's top. We are told that as he ascended the peak the rainbow took off her garments and gave them to him to wear, but apart from this, we learn only that "he saw what he saw."[56]

By contrast, the *Midrash* describes in grandiose detail his entry through the cloud into paradise, where he observed a continuous stream of fire flowing from under the Throne of Glory. This awesome stream was fed by the perspiration of the holy *Hayyot,* magnificent angels who perspire fire out of their fear of God. There Moses found Yahweh occupied with the work of ornamenting the letters from which the Torah would be written. God carved little crown-like decorations for each letter as Moses looked on without saying a word.[57]

In these two very different ways, the image of Mount Sinai circumscribes as well as it sets free the powers of the religious imagination. What happened on the mountain remains wholly beyond human comprehension. One only can speak of it, therefore, by way of minimalist austerity or playful extravagance. Either one will do, but normal language will not suffice.

The Jewish tradition's use of roguish extravagance becomes especially apparent in the Midrashic tales concerning Moses' reception of the law on Sinai. We read, for example, that the mountains of Israel had fought among themselves over which should be chosen to receive the tablets of the law and the presence of God's *shekinah*. Some mountains argued for their own selection because they were taller or more beautiful, and others because they had played a more prominent role in Israel's history, but Sinai was finally adopted because it was ugly and insignificant.[58] Its barren inconsequence qualified it most readily as a place of divine revelation.

We learn further of the particular terror felt by the earth at the time of the theophany on the mountain. Fearing the end of time had come, the earth listened in breathless silence to the echoless voice of Yahweh, speaking to all the souls who had ever been (or ever would be) born.[59] The rabbis even spoke of God's lifting the mountain up off the desert floor, holding it over the heads of the people, waving it in the air to threaten them if they failed to keep the law.[60]

These tales all display an inordinate language of excess, meant intentionally, it would seem, to explode in the listeners' hearing.[61] Far from being taken literally, they are outlandish narratives aimed at astounding rather than instructing. They function as a self-subverting utterance, staggering the mind with an cacophony of contradictory sound-images, forcing both speaker and listener once again to a confused silence before the ineffable. This is the nature of theological discourse in its continual dialectic of apophatic and kataphatic motifs. As Denys Turner suggests:

> We could say that the predicament for theology is rather like that of the verbose teacher, who in shame at having talked too much in class, lapses into an embarrassed silence. . . .
>
> But that embarrassment has to be procured, and to reach that point—this is the essence of the cataphatic—it is necessary for theology to talk too much.[62]

The goal of kataphatic verbosity is ultimately to run itself out, collapsing into nervous silence in the presence of mystery.

Comparable ways of dealing with the imagery of Sinai are found in Islam. There, for example, the mountain of Moses is the one by which Muhammad swore in declaring the truth he spoke.[63] Sinai is the mountain where Allah revealed himself to Moses as Lord of the Worlds (sura 28:29–30). When Moses asked to see God face to face, Allah answered that he could witness the divine presence only indirectly as it was disclosed to the mountain. When this actually happened, however, the mountain suddenly dissolved into dust before his eyes (sura 7:139–40).

In the tales of *The Prophets of al-Kisa'i*, an Arabic text from the twelfth century, Moses and his people were allowed to see angels on the mountain, arrayed in all their finery and awesome spiritual forms.[64] We are even told of Moses' being taken on Gabriel's pearl-and-coral-studded wing to the place where Allah was preparing the law. "There Moses heard the rush of the pen across the tablet and the emerald slates. God said to the pen, 'Write!'" declaring that no human image could ever be associated with the Holy One.[65] No metaphor could ever embrace the majesty of Allah.

Rumi, the great mystical poet from Persia, spoke boldly of seeing, along with Moses, the full light of the divine epiphany on Sinai. He described the mountain as intoxicated and lit with brilliance, watching it turn into rubies and blood, becoming a perfect Sufi, beginning even to dance. The whole mountain broke into three pieces as the light of God surged upon it. The rock melted like ice beneath the feet of Moses.[66]

As a metaphor describing the unparalleled majesty of Allah, this image of Mount Sinai begins in stark simplicity but gives way at last to a language of pandemonium and excess. Jewish and Muslim writers are fiercely driven to a multiplication of metaphors—a fecundity of the imagination—in their effort to speak the unsayable. While the image of Sinai reminds them that no single metaphor is ever able to contain the divine being, they conclude that there is safety in numbers. God must be recognized in the brilliance of light and in thick darkness, in the sound of thunder and perfect silence, in images of presence and absence alike. Only a multitude of metaphors can safely embrace the greatness that is God's.

The Christian effort to comprehend the mystery of Sinai assumes a different form from that found in Jewish and Muslim sources. More than either of the other Abrahamic traditions, Christianity has long been fascinated with Mount Sinai as a site of pilgrimage, a place that sacramentally conveys the grandeur of God's majesty.

Beginning as early as the fourth century, Christians were eager to plot an intricate landscape of holy places for pilgrims to visit within the vicinity of Sinai and its monastery.[67] The site of the burning bush, the place where Moses hid in the cleft of the rock, the cave where Elijah heard the sound of Yahweh's "utter silence," the 3,700 chiseled steps leading up to the mountain's peak, the nearby slopes of Jebel Katerina to which the body of Saint Catherine of Alexandria had been miraculously conveyed—all these places (and more) would be catalogued and explained in detail to visiting pilgrims.[68]

This impulse to geographic specificity stands in stark contrast to Judaism's remarkable indifference to the location of the original revelation to Moses on Mount Sinai.[69] Jews have never been concerned with pinpointing the place. Shrines commemorating Moses and the sites of his encounters with God were never established by ancient Israel. The Torah instructed them to ignore even the place of his burial (Deut. 34:6).

Islam would demonstrate a somewhat greater interest in the location of the holy mountain. Stories are told, for instance, of the prophet Muhammad having passed through that region as a young boy. A mosque has existed on the site of Saint Catherine's Monastery since the eleventh century. In fact, to this day the monks of the monastery point to a "letter of protection" said to have been sent by the hand of the prophet himself.[70]

But Christianity's attention to geographical detail in the iconography of Mount Sinai is unique. This may be due, in part, to the Christian emphasis upon the incarnation—its sacramental, materialistic fascination with icon and place. It may also reflect the need of post-Constantinian Christianity to establish an imperial religion celebrated at sacred sites after the pattern of Hellenistic culture.[71]

Whatever the reasons, Christianity's apophatic fascination with Sinai came to be given explicit kataphatic expression in two different ways: in the multitude of biblically marked places set apart for pilgrimage, and in the remarkable icons gathered in Saint Catherine's Monastery at the mountain's foot. There, in a stunning mosaic in the apse of the monastery church, a symbolic interconnection was drawn between Sinai and Tabor, the mountain of Moses' apophatic experience and the mountain of Jesus' transfiguration in kataphatic glory.

At Sinai God would be glimpsed only in darkness—from the back side—but at Tabor, God could be seen in all the splendor of light. In this way Christianity sought to interrelate the double motion of apophatic obscurity and kataphatic clarity, the emptiness of the one preparing for the plenitude of the other. This symbolic apposition of the two mountains will be the focus of the next chapter.

Mount Sinai has never ceased through the centuries to haunt the Christian imagination. Procopius, a sixth-century Christian pilgrim, was unnerved by his visit to the awesome mountain above Saint Catherine's Monastery. He wrote, "It is impossible for a man to pass the night on the summit, since constant crashes of thunder and other terrifying manifestations of divine power are heard at night, striking terror into man's body and soul."[72]

I remember one evening standing beside the small stone chapel on the top of Jebel Mussa, looking west into the darkness where the sun had just set behind Jebel Katerina. I could appreciate the qualms of Procopius. Even in the absence of storm and thunder, the silence gathers there in a beauty that rides on fear.

If one *were* to survive the night on Sinai—and in this day of vastly increased pilgrimage, it happens all the time—the rising sun would reveal a landscape not unlike that seen along the edges of the Sea of Tranquillity on the surface of the moon. There is almost no vegetation in this geomorphological district of the southern Sinai peninsula—only Nubian sandstone and stark, red and black granite, metamorphic rock that through the ages has endured the transformation of intense heat and pressure. Looking north into the Valley of er-Raja, where the children of Israel waited while Moses ascended the peak, one senses the awe they must have felt in such a forbidding landscape.

The spiritual function of fierce terrain in the apophatic tradition is to bring us to the end of ourselves, to the abandonment of language and the relinquishment of ego. A vast expanse of jagged stone, desert sand, and towering thunderheads has a way of challenging all the mental constructs in which we are tempted to take comfort and pride, thinking we have captured the divine. "The things that ignore us save us in the end." Such is the truth of every apophatic image. Sinai, as desert and mountain, stands as a "great and terrible wilderness"—an unmistakable reminder of our grand inconsequence and the limits of all theological discourse.

Encounter at Ghost Ranch

The bones seem to cut sharply to the center of something that is keenly alive on the desert, even tho' it is vast and empty and untouchable—and knows no kindness with all its beauty. —Georgia O'Keeffe, on the dried bones in her Ghost Ranch landscapes[1]

A red hill doesn't touch everyone's heart as it touches mine and I suppose there is no reason why it should."[2] —Georgia O'Keeffe

Riding the bus north from Santa Fe along highway 84, the fierce land beyond the window threatened to burst the glass through which I looked. The brilliant red hills and black mesas, the mountain silhouette of Pedernal, the twisted trunks of old piñon trees above the Chama River—all were there just as I remembered them from the paintings of Georgia O'Keeffe. I'd come to Ghost Ranch, New Mexico, for a seminar on mountain and desert spirituality.[3] It was my first trip there, and I arrived with a bag full of mountain slides, notes on the desert fathers, and a longing for landscape. Most of all I'd come for healing, seeking respite from a mother dying of cancer, needing to let the poetry of William Butler Yeats and Robert Bly work its way into changes begun in my life. I came to the desert to find peace, to seek a safe place, to read deep consolation off steep canyon walls.

That was what I came for, but that wasn't what the desert had to teach me. One seldom learns what he thinks he most needs to be taught. I began on the first day of the seminar talking about "spirituality," a word that frankly makes a lot of people apprehensive. Too often it brings to mind a *contemptus mundi* tradition, smelling of snake-oil remedies, overly preoccupied with escape, speaking of the next world in its persistent flight from this one. Many of us at Ghost Ranch that week were looking for just such an escape, half-broken people coming to the desert to be put back together again. But as the Rev. Tom Marshfield learned in John Updike's novel, *A Month of Sundays,* the desert rarely functions as a resort.

Spirituality and the desert are alike in that regard. They share a common ambiguity, a certain difficulty of access. Their "meanings" can't be summarized in neat Cartesian categories. Their answers are painful. Barry Lopez points to the opaque way in which the desert refuses to open itself to glib analysis. "You can't get at it this way," he urges. "You must come with no intentions of discovery. You must overhear things, as though you'd come into a small and desolate town and paused by an open window."[4] As the early desert fathers and mothers knew, the wilderness possesses a stubborn indifference to one's fervid quest for solace. One's entry into the desert is marked invariably by confusion and loss. Something will always seem amiss.

I sensed that keenly during my first few days at Ghost Ranch. The group was going well. The food was good. The place was beginning to grow on us all with a deep mystery. But something still was missing. We'd not yet encountered the desert's wildness. It posed no danger to us. The structures of our world had not yet been threatened.

The Importance of Desert Irreverence

I kept thinking of three wild people who, had they been there, would have perceived the same landscape so differently from the rest of us. We were in need of a John Muir, that crazy fool who would tie himself to the top of a Douglas fir tree, riding out a fierce storm in the High Sierras as the tree whipped back and forth some thirty degrees in the wind. We needed Georgia O'Keeffe, that wonderfully irreverent saint who would have thrown up at the idea of some sappy teacher talking about the desert in a limp-wristed church camp where people were afraid of firsthand experience. And I knew what Ed Abbey would have thought of the whole thing. That wild and irascible writer of the American southwest would have growled that the desert is "nothing but a goddamned place to die"—a place where all your easy answers fall to pieces, where you yourself may end up as nothing more than buzzard meat.

These were the people we needed there in the desert, these wild, almost blasphemous people, whose fierce honesty makes them the finest teachers of all. It strikes me as odd that sometimes the most "irreverent" people are the ones most in touch with the holy. These are the wild men and women of whom Robert Bly and Clarissa Pinkola Estés speak.[5] They're a desert product, nurtured by a desolate and God-forsaken terrain. In keeping with the meaning of the Hebrew word for wilderness, *midbār*, they are "the cut-off ones," those "driven out" from society's mainstream. Like Elijah and John the Baptist, they thrive on the edges of culture, threatening its structures, speaking the language of fiery serpents and Lilith, the night hag (Deut. 8:15; Isa. 34:14). They know inherently that "it is in wildness that justice comes to live" (Isa. 32:16).

Edward Abbey came up in a conversation at lunch on Wednesday of that week. I was eating with John Fife, a Presbyterian minister from Tucson, Arizona who has been an important figure in the sanctuary movement over the last decade or more, seeking justice for Central American refugees. He's a gentle man, but more honest than some people can take. I asked if he'd ever met Abbey. He smiled widely and spoke of a letter he'd gotten some years before (at the time of his trial), one that wasn't signed and that read something like this:

> I'm just a cowpoke who's read a little about what you've been doing. I don't especially agree with you. [Abbey favored closing the U.S.-Mexican border to immigration.] But I had my bedroll out on the desert the other night, looking out at the stars. And it struck me that there's probably room enough here for anybody who wants to come. So if those government bastards come for you someday, knocking on the front door; and you can get out the back door before they kick your ass, I'd be glad to offer you a place to stay.

There was only a telephone number at the bottom of the page. No name.

Out of curiosity, John Fife called the number and learned it was Abbey. They became friends. A couple of years later, Fife invited him on a float trip down the Green River in Utah through Desolation Canyon. John told him that he would come with what he was as a theologian and Abbey could come with all his sharp edges and they'd argue their way back and forth down the river. Abbey liked the idea and they planned to go, but death intervened. Edward Abbey died on March 14, 1989.[6]

John Fife went to see him in the hospital before his death. Abbey asked him, "What the hell are you doing here? You didn't come to preach to me, did you?" "No," John answered, "I've got too much respect for you to do that. I just wanted to see you." There was something about Ed Abbey's crotchetiness and fierce indifference to unimportant things that inevitably drew people to him.

That story haunted me as I went hiking alone in the desert that afternoon. Thinking of Abbey, I determined to meet the landscape on its own terms, without expectations, submitting at last to its sublime disregard for all my petty concerns. Abandonment, after all, is what the desert teaches best. As Abbey would say, the central spiritual lesson to remember about the desert is that "it doesn't give a shit." Its capacity to ignore is immense. Yet in that very indifference, one discovers an enormous freedom.

Gary Snyder says "the wilderness can be a ferocious teacher, rapidly stripping down the inexperienced or the careless. It is easy to make the mistakes that will bring one to an extremity."[7] Being brought to the end of oneself is the terrifying (and enthralling) possibility that the desert enjoins. Here it is that we enter an interior wilderness more fearful and promising than anything charted on terrestrial maps. The wildest, most dangerous trails are always the ones within.

Desert Thunderstorm

With the sun still shining, I took the path into a box canyon several miles behind Ghost Ranch. Thunderstorms had been coming up every afternoon and people were reluctant to venture far. Yet I desperately needed the time alone, getting away far enough to approach the border of that interior landscape I'd neglected so long. It was a beautiful afternoon. A slight breeze rustled leaves on the cottonwood trees. The smell of sage was sharpened by recent rains. I followed a small creek into the canyon, noticing deer tracks along its bank. Later in the week, tracks of a mountain lion were seen along that same trail. It was a fine place for a lion to trap deer, up a narrow canyon with no escape.

By the time I'd followed the creek to the canyon's end, the cliffs had risen to a hundred feet on either side. The rock had chipped away from the edge at the top, leaving an overhang all the way around. There was no way out. Tripping over talus fragments fallen from above, I heard a loud and sustained echo, filling the place with sound. It was a compelling place, a strange end to which I'd somehow been invited. Certain places are like that, says Wendell Berry. They offer a sense of meeting, if one can only learn to wait and be patient.[8]

In the center of the space at the end of the canyon lay a large, flat rock. Nearby, a trickle of water seeped out from under the canyon wall, feeding the creek I'd been following. I lay on the rock for a long while, waiting for nothing in particular—watching cliff swallows sweep over the canyon rim above, noticing a hummingbird in the fir tree nearby, being aware of gradually gathering clouds. I'd brought along a pipe and tobacco but had forgotten matches. Yet the tobacco seemed a good gift in itself. Impulsively I threw a pinch of it in each of the four directions, so as to sanctify the place and honor its spirit. At the time the action seemed perfectly natural, not at all an effort to mimic native practice. In its origins, I suspect, ritual is not learned; it is earth-taught.

As I lay in silence, dark, churning clouds began to fill the space of sky framed by the canyon rim above. Then came the first loud crash of thunder, and I knew I was about to be caught by a cloudburst in the middle of the desert. As the initial drops of rain fell, I scrambled up a nearby ledge, looking for shelter, finding the small opening of a cave going into the canyon wall. It wasn't large. I looked carefully to make sure it was empty, then crawled in just as the heavy rains let loose. Soon they were followed by hail the size of quarters—bouncing everywhere, ricocheting off the rocks, dancing in the fierce thunder and lightning. There I lay, under the mountain, looking wide-eyed at this glorious apocalypse, scribbling away in the yellow pad I use for a journal.

Soon sheets of water begin to pour over the top of the canyon rim, loosening the dirt and rocks high above. Then the sound of falling boulders echoed through the canyon like shotgun blasts, crashing right before me onto the path I'd followed an hour or so before. I heard the sound of other rocks falling further down the ravine. Torrents of water flowed wildly in every direction. What was it that had followed me into the remoteness of that box canyon, having stalked me to the very end, hiding now in the cleft of the rock? What had I been suckered into all along in coming to Ghost Ranch?

I learned later that there were Indian petroglyphs scratched on the inside of the cave where I lay. I never saw them, but I knew from the place itself that they must have been pictures of death. There was no doubt that this was a dying place, a place where things necessarily came to an end. That's often the way of the desert. The pictures there in the cave would be ones of a deer stalked by a young brave or a mountain lion. They would tell stories I didn't want to re-member. Pictures of a thirteen-year-old boy whose father had been suddenly and violently killed. A boy who all of his life would seek the lost father. Pictures of that same boy, now in his forties, sitting beside a mother and waiting for her long and painful death to end. A boy whose parents had both died (or were dy-ing) at times in his life when he was struggling most to be born. I knew the pic-tures. But I hadn't known the grieving that had to go with them.

The day before this trip into the canyon, I'd been given a session of shiatzu massage by a woman in our group who was a healer. Shiatzu is a Japanese form of deep massage, based on the idea that painful (and joyous) memories are often retained in particular parts of the body. The human body is seen to offer a mi-cro-geography of past traumas in an individual's experience. Through the proc-ess of deep massage, as one feels his life breath virtually forced out of him, there can be an accompanying release of forgotten pain.

I had experienced this the previous afternoon as the healing woman reached a point in my left hip, pushing a finger deep into my side. It was a place that hurt intensely. But it also released an incredible sobbing that came from some place deeper within me than I knew existed. I had no image of what this grieving was about. At the time, I could only think of the Fisher King in the Grail legend who was also wounded in the thigh. And Jacob . . . who limped away at dawn from his wrestling with the angel, the hollow of his thigh now out of joint. All men, I sus-pect, are wounded in the thigh—at that place where they give life, where they are most vulnerable, where they've failed and been failed by others.

The Unexpected Gifts of Grief

It's only now, as I tell the story, that I realize how the thunder and the cave and the grieving over my father's death (and my mother's dying) were all tied to-gether with something that had been carried in my left side, maybe for years. The healing woman had said the effects of shiatzu might continue for a day or more, that it was not uncommon for people to be deeply touched in the spirit as a result of the fierce and hard touch experienced in their bodies.

When the rain passed and the rock slides ended, I crawled out of the cave. The winds quickly carried the storm clouds away, and before long the sun was out again, shining on a world made perfectly new. Water droplets on every leaf and rock were lit by the sun. The air was clear as crystal, cleansed by rain. Silence had returned.

Then gradually, a trickle of water began to flow over the rim at the canyon's end, cascading a hundred feet down in sunlit brilliance onto the rock where I'd lain before. It grew in strength, becoming a massive waterfall of light-tan waters, fed by arroyos from high above, bringing the runoff of rain from surrounding mesas. These waters of life poured down into the place of death. I stood there watching. Then slowly I walked through the falling water, being soaked in its sand-filled wetness, as a loud, resounding laughter erupted spontaneously from deep inside. This fierce, good laughter came from the same dark place from where the sobbing had come the day before. It echoed down the canyon, summoning everything to life.

What was this place? Everywhere I walked, life burst out of the ground before and behind me. The desert after a hard rain is incredibly alive. Falling water courses over the rocks and fills arroyos. One can practically feel the trees and sage brush gorging themselves with it. I began to walk back down the canyon, following the creek that was now quickly rising, coming to a place I'd passed on the way in, where a side canyon joined the one I'd been walking. The place where the two canyons came together was filled with vegetation, sparkling now with life.

Dark red waters flowed down from the side canyon to join the light-tan waters from the upper creek, flowing side by side, then merging together in some great mystery. The new waters entering the creek were a deep, chocolate red, the runoff of multicolored mesas from above. They formed a menstrual flow, these dark waters, as if the land were cleansing itself of its life-giving blood. Viscous and thick, they poured especially heavy from between two large boulders. I climbed over to the place, cupped my hands, and let the waters fall over my head, rolling down my hair and onto my shoulders. Here, at the place of the joining of the two waters, everything came together.

Up at the end of the box canyon I'd been struck by the masculine power of the place. There the Sky Father had let loose his energy, with a wild display of thunder and lightning. It had been the place of Zeus, of Thor, Yahweh, the Thunderbird. A place of fierceness and death. But this was a different place. Here the waters from above came down to join the waters from below, and all became whole. This was the place of the Earth Mother, life-giving, connecting, sinking deep roots into the anchoredness of the land. It was the place of Demeter, the Old Spider Woman, Mother Guadelupe. A place of birth and nurture.

This place answered the questions posed by the earlier place. How would I live again on the far side of the experience of death, surviving the loss of the father and the mother, discovering a new wildness and rootedness? The answer came in being baptized, first with water and then with blood. Only as I came to terms with the loss of the one, could I deal with the loss of the other. Only then could I be set free to live as the person I'd longed all my life to become.

I had always sought that deep masculine energy of the wildman, who lives his life without being tentative and fearful, who (like Joseph Campbell's hero) loves and risks much for the sake of truth. In my dreams, he often sits by the front window of a village taverna, drinking a glass of *raki* and arm-wrestling one of the young Greek fishermen at the tables, laughing loudly. I watch him at a distance, wishing profoundly that his abandonment were mine. He wanders over, almost drunk now, and leans against the chair where I sit at the corner table, writing on a yellow pad. Always writing on a yellow pad!

"To hell with your fine words, my friend," he says with a smile and an arm on my shoulder. "Come, I buy you some *raki* and deliver you from the dangers of your pen." I smell the sea in his beard. He is Zorba, Neptune, Odysseus, the Fisher King, this man. In my dream, I laugh back. I toss my papers under the table, and with tears running down my face, say, "Yes, father, I've waited for you a long time. Sit and drink. Teach me . . . to dance!"

What comes first in a man's midlife experience may be this baptism in the wild waters of the father, the wildman. Only then can he reaffirm also the mother, being baptized with blood, accepting the feminine energy of the Pacha Mama, the Earth Mother. She is the one who knows her power to create and give birth, to put down roots, to weave the fabric of life into a mystery of interconnectedness. This is a baptism that makes possible a new intimacy. Wholeness will always be found at the middle place, where the two waters join to become one.

In the joy of that afternoon sun, I walked on back down the canyon toward home, stopping to take off my clothes (it just seemed the right thing to do). Walking naked through the land, I turned in slow circles, drinking in the red and orange grandeur of the rocky cliffs around me, all newly washed by rain. In those few moments, I moved through the canyon landscape as one of its details, knowing the land had taught me something I could not name.

Intimacy among Strangers

That place in the high desert country of northern New Mexico has haunted my dreams ever since. [9] It was an uncaring place, with no particular solicitous concern about my well-being. I just happened to be there at a moment of thunderstorm and rain when the desert came suddenly to life, healing everything in its vicinity. A landscape of studied indifference became for a brief span a place that occasioned unsuspecting intimacy. I'd been a stranger there, with whom secrets were momentarily, inexplicably shared.

"There are things so deeply personal," says Richard Rodriguez, "that they can only be revealed to strangers." [10] I sense that truth very poignantly in my sharing of this story, and of others within this book. The fortuitous, casual way by which the desert sometimes shares its secrets suggests something about how we might on occasion reveal our own fragile narratives to others. When spoken into thin air, to no one in particular, deeply personal things acquire a public character that lends them a certain anonymity, and—as a result, perhaps—a greater possibility for healing. Giving voice in the concealment of public speech to what can't be spoken face to face has a way of hiding the speaker, while also inviting his listeners to an engagement that safeguards their own anonymity. This is part of the apophatic hiddenness to which "discourse on the edge" is often drawn.

I'm understandably reluctant to share the intimate story of my parents' deaths. Even though I know there's healing in the telling, especially in the kind of public telling that generally receives and expects no response. It constitutes a "speaking into the night," an abandonment that characterizes some of the best of the desert writers in the apophatic tradition. Frederick Buechner's sharing of the story of his father's death in his book, *Telling Secrets,* exemplifies the extraordinary power of such speech.[11]

I know also that there are rare occurrences in one's life when a window opens, when truth presents itself for a brief moment in all its stark intensity, and despite one's deepest reservations the resulting story simply insists on being told. Sometimes the place alone requires it.

All of this raises the larger question of hiddenness and disclosure that lies at the heart of this book. If its concern is not simply to analyze apophatic spirituality, but also in some way to "model" or "perform" it, then the question of what one says and leaves unsaid becomes critically important. If the desert loves to strip bare, as Jerome liked to argue, to what extent does one go in modeling the vulnerability necessary for a life of desert abandonment? How naked (and clothed) must one be in the effort to describe this mystery? How do any of us, for that matter, speak candidly while trying to honor the privacy and rich ambiguity of the truth we've lived?

One quickly comes to realize that none of these are questions the solitary individual can answer alone. The desert path, for all of its loneliness, is a deeply communal way. This experience of a box canyon behind Ghost Ranch reminds me that I'm inescapably tied to the mothers and fathers who've gone before me. I hear their words still speaking through the sound of my own voice. I'm held accountable by these people, and by the fierce land to which my memory has attached them. They're not only my parents, but Evagrius as well, and Gregory of Nyssa . . . Meister Eckhart and Julian of Norwich, the *Cloud* author, John of the Cross, Thomas Merton. These are teachers who've formed me—keepers of a desert *habitus.* They're the ones who've taught me to trust the night, to love the desert, to long for the One who hides in darkness for the sake of an undeserved love.

Meanwhile, as I wrestle in this community of memory over what may best be said and left unsaid, the desert keeps its own counsel, speaking only in riddles. The box canyon at Ghost Ranch remains dry and speechless, waiting again for rain. The tracks of the deer and a large mountain cat still speak in coded language of what may safely be entertained only in dreams. John Muir, Georgia O'Keeffe, and Ed Abbey continue as wild and enigmatic in death as they were in life.

We all kneel as closely to the ground as we can, with ears alert, listening for something we cannot name. We attend as honestly and faithfully as we're able to those who've gone before us. Only in this way can we discern the differences between what is dying around us and what is trying to be born. "Only then will the wilderness and the dry land be glad, the desert rejoice and blossom; like the crocus it shall blossom abundantly, and rejoice with joy and singing . . ." (Isa. 35:1–2).

· 5 ·

Sinai and Tabor

Mountain Symbolism in the
Christian Tradition

It seems to me that a mountain is an image of the soul as it lifts itself up in contemplation. For in the same manner as the mountain towers above the valleys and lowlands at its foot, so does the soul of [the one] who prays mount into the higher regions up to God. You are the Lord's eagles, who wing your flights high in the ethereal regions. —Theodore of Studios[1]

In the year 383/384 the Spanish nun and inveterate traveler Egeria concluded her famous pilgrimage to the Holy Land. She visited, among other places, two sacred mountains, making her way up the rough, granite slopes of Jebel Mussa in the barren desert of southern Sinai, and subsequently climbing Hār Tavor, the lush, olive-green hill rising out of the plains of central Galilee in the north.[2] By that time, in the late fourth century, these two sites were already associated by tradition with the great events of Moses' encounter with Yahweh in Exodus 24 and Jesus' transfiguration on the mount in Mark 9.[3] According to legend, even Saint Helena, the mother of Emperor Constantine, had been drawn there, building churches in both places.

These two mountains, utterly different in their setting and appearance, have functioned through the centuries in the art of Eastern iconography as mythic opposites. They serve as excellent symbols of apophatic and kataphatic approaches in the history of spirituality, showing how the metaphor of the mountain can be used to speak of God in both constructive and deconstructive ways.

Sinai and Tabor represent two poles of a dialectical tension in biblical theology. The one is a reminder of God's utter freedom and inaccessibility, insisting that in no place are there permanent guarantees of the divine presence.[4] The other is an apocalyptic disclosure of God's glory, localized and made manifest in the messianic character of Jesus.[5]

Sinai is a symbol of the elusive, aniconic quality of the divine being. It can be awesome and frightening. Fierce clouds and flashes of lightning on dark red granite suggest a God untamed by human will. "I had never seen a spot more wild and desolate," biblical geographer Edward Robinson wrote in 1838.[6] Tabor, by contrast, offers a landscape of accessible and gentle beauty. Like a wet, green breast rising out of the Plains of Jezreel, it is bathed in light, covered with woodland trees and wildflowers. In a sense, all icons in Eastern art take their inspiration from the story of the transfiguration. They all seek to incorporate *la lumiere taborique,* allowing the light of the divine presence to be mirrored in the painted icon.[7]

Compared to Sinai's disconcerting darkness, Tabor is light and clarity. The two mountains offer contrasting (but also deeply interconnecting) images of dread and love, *mysterium tremendum* and *fascinans,* masculine and feminine energies that continually feed and challenge each other. These are mountains of the imagination, opposites that attract.[8] In the structural anthropology of Claude Lévi-Strauss, a mythic analysis of the two images in the history of Christian iconography might reveal an effort to reconcile contradictory impulses after the pattern of raw and cooked, moist and burnt, freedom and structure, as these frequently appear in the mythologies of particular cultures.[9]

This chapter will argue that the juxtaposition of these two mountains in icons of the transfiguration serves the purpose in Christian history of reconciling tensions between old covenant and new, Jewish and Christian identities, the experience of finding oneself naked, empty and lost before God on Sinai and the experience of being clothed in light, filled with the image of Christ, and restored to new life on Tabor. Indeed, as one understands how icons are viewed in the Eastern Orthodox tradition, one discovers how this reconciliation of opposites is accomplished also within the viewer's own passage from darkness to light, from fear to love, from loss of self to rebirth of self. The intimate process of viewing the icon offers a participation in the dark cloud on Sinai where one is stripped of all capacity and in the transfiguring light of Tabor where the mystery of one's own deification is disclosed.

Icons of the transfiguration necessarily lead, in Eastern thinking, to this realization of one's own transfiguration. That's why I share in this chapter my particular experience of climbing both of these mountains as well as encountering something of their bewildering mystery. Understanding the nature of mountain iconography demands a personal involvement in the act of perceiving, even to the extent of being changed by what one sees.

The chapter goes on to examine the overlaying of these two mountains in the development of biblical narrative and the later iconographic tradition. As symbols of apophatic and kataphatic modes of understanding, Sinai and Tabor are interpenetrating images, never strictly separated. To characterize them too simplistically as masculine and feminine, dark and light, law and gospel is to miss the interplay of movement constantly going on between them.

Sacred Mountains and the Understanding of Icons in the Eastern Iconographic Tradition

Westerners often have difficulty appreciating the art of icons as well as the personal devotion with which they are held in the Eastern Orthodox tradition. People familiar only with Western art since the Renaissance tend to consider

Eastern icons flat, unimaginative, lacking in depth or perspective. Rightly viewing icons according to Eastern liturgical practice requires an understanding of the theology and aesthetic techniques underlying their artistic form.

This chapter perceives Mount Sinai and Mount Tabor in the highly engaging, sacramental way one learns to read and reverence icons within the Eastern Church. Rooted in the mystery of the incarnation, an icon dares to proclaim the as-yet-unrealized but promised transfigured glory of the entire material world. Because of God having been made flesh in Jesus Christ, humans are able to glimpse the very face of God in matter itself.[10] Mountains, therefore, appear frequently in Eastern iconography as a commonly accepted context for revealed glory, an expected source of reflected light and splendor.[11]

Mountains even play a role in how the icon invites the viewer into the reality of his or her own transfigured humanity. One technique employed for this purpose, for example, is the phenomenon of inverse perspective found in many of the classic Greek and Russian icons. The lines of the painting do not converge at some distant "vanishing point" within the picture's scenic background. Unlike the Western Renaissance tradition, the painting does not draw the viewer's imagination through its frame into the natural world depicted therein. Instead, the lines of perspective (formed by mountains or buildings within the painting) converge at a point several inches in front of the icon's surface (and slightly below it), as if aimed at the heart of the viewer standing in its presence. The supernatural light pictured on the face of the holy person in the painting extends out to embrace the viewer, intimately drawing her into the contemplation of her own transfigured life. "One is left feeling that the beholder is essential to the completion of the icon. The essence of the exercise has been to establish a communion between the event or persons represented in the icon and those who stand before it. . . ."[13]

Stylized mountains depicted in many icons also accomplish this bonding through yet another technique. Slabs of stone stacked in ascending pinnacles and separated from each other by deep crevasses, they bend slowly away from the spectator in the foreground until at the top of the painting they curve back once again toward the viewer as the rock reaches ever higher. The effect of this illusion is to concentrate the light at the icon's center out toward the viewer standing before it.[13] The surrounding mountains function as the concave surface of a large reflecting mirror. This is what desert travelers do, by analogy, in using a curved lens to focus sunlight on dry grass to ignite a fire. In such a way, the spectator himself is virtually "set aflame" by the consuming divine light brought into focus by the icon.

An icon of the transfiguration produced by the Novgorod school in fifteenth-century Russia is one of many providing an example of this curving mountain technique.[15] An illustration of the use of inverse perspective and twisted mountains focusing the divine light on the icon's viewer can be found in a painting of the Holy Trinity composed by this same school of Russian icon painters.[16]

The employment of inverse perspective and the curvature of mountains in an icon of the Holy Trinity, Novgorod school, late fifteenth century.
(Used by permission of the Temple Gallery, London)

At the heart of one's experience of icons in the Orthodox tradition is this entry into transfiguring light on the mountain where Christ appeared with Moses and Elijah. "When the saints contemplate this divine light within themselves," St. Gregory Palamas declared, "they behold the garment of their deification."[17] Here is the deepest mystery that icons of the transfiguration imply: the viewer's own humanity is translated into something never before imagined.

My reflection on the mountains in this chapter, therefore, is an iconographic exercise—standing before them myself, seeing something of my own transfigured possibility within them. The highly personal perspective of the viewer—whether Egeria's or Saint Helena's or my own—is absolutely necessary for grasping the depth of participation the icon requires.

My experience of climbing these two mountains formed the double center of a brief sabbatical in Israel and Egypt several years ago, occurring at a time of deep displacement following my mother's initial bout with cancer. I was drawn there, not only by the research required for this book, but also by the same thirst for place that for centuries has obsessed pilgrims like Egeria. Geography delights the human psyche because of its localization of truth, its way of helping one grasp the abstract by way of the concrete. Biblical scholars have shown how particular places often served as powerful anchors of tradition in the ancient world.[18] Stories of great events in the history of salvation were frequently connected to a given *haftpunkt*, a fixed geographical location that captured the imagination. To know the story was (and is) to desire proximity to the place.

This is what led two of my friends, unknown to each other, to ask me before I left on my trip if I'd bring back a pebble from Mount Sinai (for the one friend) and a small stone from Mount Tabor (for the other). Fascination with the holy mountain as storied place invariably evokes a kinesthetic longing for touch.[19] Given my interest in the two sacred sites, the act of carrying the intentions of others gave the trip an added sense of anticipation. One's involvement in any iconic experience occurs simultaneously on multiple levels.

Sinai, the Mountain of God

The fragments we have of Egeria's travel journal begin with her ascent of Mount Sinai. It was a mountain that left her struggling for words. Having taken the steep path to its summit at 7,497 feet, she wrote to the members of her community back home:

> I want you to be quite clear about these mountains, reverend ladies my sisters, which surrounded us as we stood beside the church looking down from the summit of the mountain in the middle. They had been almost too much for us to climb, and I really do not think I have ever seen any that were higher. . . .[20]

It was a place that impressed her with its aura of lonely majesty. By its remote setting and steep ascent, Sinai is a mountain that seems to forbid entry. Lesley

Hazleton, an Israeli journalist reflecting on her tour of the Sinai, felt that "if I were just to touch any one of those jagged peaks, it would draw blood."[21]

This was my own experience in the grim winter of my pilgrimage. I'd come to Israel anxious to visit Mount Sinai—longing for that mountain, having seen it in my dreams, having read everything I could find about it. Its God-forsaken and treeless wilderness made it, if anything, even more compelling. But getting there would prove far more difficult than I'd imagined. The weather that February was worse than anyone had remembered in years. Severe snowstorms left Jerusalem shrouded in white, broken tree limbs everywhere.

Snowbound in the Holy City, I heard reports from Sinai that the slopes of its highest mountains were a meter deep in snow. The desert tour for which I'd registered was cancelled indefinitely. I'd come so far, it seemed, only to fail at the very end. Sitting in my room at the École Biblique, listening to the sound of thunder breaking over the Judean hills, I knew the loneliness of the solitary pilgrim—stripped of language, bereft of friends, my most carefully laid plans all ruined.

I suspect young writers and graduate students should be warned, as early in their careers as possible, about the topics on which they choose to write. Some can be more dangerous than others. Some have a way of flying back unexpectedly, exploding in one's face. Here I'd wanted to write on the apophatic tradition and its use of fierce nature imagery in the history of spirituality. I'd come to Israel to enter into the experience of abandonment known by desert monks, to know the harshness of an unyielding land. What I'd needed most as an aid in research was a sense of helplessness in the face of a threatening geography.

But when I got the very thing I wanted, I couldn't recognize it as such. I couldn't understand why all my plans were suddenly falling to pieces. Why are we sometimes driven, both intellectually and spiritually, by desires which, when granted, we'd sooner not have received? Ultimately, I had to abandon entirely the idea of traveling to Sinai. Only then did it become a possibility.

A week later, following a sudden change in weather, I was able at the last minute to sign on with another desert trek to the southern Sinai region. Even this surprising good fortune wasn't without its drawbacks, however. I learned on arriving at the travel office that everyone else on the tour spoke only German. They were Austrians, and excellent climbers, but this meant I'd travel largely in my own silence, missing much of the information and camaraderie I might otherwise have gained. My temptation, once again, was to view this as yet another tragedy, simply not able to recognize apophatic gifts for what they were. What could be better, after all, than walking the Sinai in the company of one's own silence?

I should have listened more carefully to John Climacus. On impulse just before leaving home, I'd thrown a copy of his *Ladder of Divine Ascent* into my travel bag. Saint John Climacus had been abbot of the monastery of Saint Catherine's at Mount Sinai in the seventh century. In the Eastern church more people read his book than any other, apart from the Bible. During a long wait at Kennedy Airport on my way to Israel, I'd pulled out the book, beginning my intention of reading a chapter a day over the next thirty days I'd be gone. There in the first few pages, I read these words: "Exile is a separation from everything in order that one may hold on totally to God. It is a chosen route of great grief. . . . A true exile, despite his possession of knowledge, sits like someone of foreign speech among men of other tongues."[22]

During the month I was in Israel and Egypt, I felt often that loneliness of exile, struggling with languages I knew very poorly. Despite the extraordinary kindness of the Dominican fathers at the École Biblique where I stayed in Jerusalem, I sensed keenly the poverty of my wordlessness. Their beautiful French, especially in chanted psalms at Evening Prayer, often passed over my comprehension, leaving me in exile with God alone. My week in the Sinai, among new friends from Austria, was a struggle for understanding in yet another language—stripped of meanings, moving leanly through the desert, always alone.

For six days we hiked the windswept emptiness of the Upper Sinai Massif, making a great loop north through the Wadi er-Raha, to arrive finally in the Valley of Elijah half way up Mount Sinai. The trek with camels took us over high ridges, through narrow canyons. We ate the flatbread of desert wanderers, dipped in couscous and feta cheese. We knew the bleakly beautiful sight of walking the desert by moonlight, sleeping to the sound of a cold and restless wind, finding canteens frozen at dawn.

I'll never forget the gift of a blood-red stone found at sunset on the top of Mount Sinai at the end of the journey. A few of us had made the final ascent that day, after a long forced hike. I sat, tired but unhurried, watching the red sky in the west turn to night. The sun had disappeared behind Jebel Katerina, the mountain of Saint Catherine of Alexandria, after whom the monastery below and my daughter, Kate, are also named. The rocks and small stone church at the top of the mountain were all lit in the alpen glow of evening. A white moon hung suspended in a cornflower sky.

There I found the stone that one of my friends had requested. It was a common pebble, lying on the hard path of discipline and obedience, a path on which he and I had both been launched. I might have expected as much. The stone came, I know, from the hand of Iron John Climacus, that monk of fierce visage and hidden smile, who'd traveled with me all along. His icon of the ladder had inspired monks in the cloister below for centuries. The words were his that I heard on the way back down the mountain in the darkness, as stars came out like fireflies and the world warmed to night: "Keep running, athlete, . . . and do not be afraid."[23]

Sinai was, for me at least, a place of being emptied, a place of dark and difficult beauty. It symbolized the wandering of the children of Israel, the experience of loss and the bread of hardness. The Sinai wilderness is a place far from home, a "no man's land" of fire and smoke. But I loved it . . . in the same way the long-distance runner loves the last mile of the day—spent, beyond exhaustion, running from dusk into a night that refuses, it seems, ever to end.

Like Tabor among the Mountains

Elisaeus, a seventh-century Armenian pilgrim to Mount Tabor, described a very different experience in his effusive effort to recount the splendors of that cone-shaped peak in Galilee. "Concerning the beauty of the mountain and the delightfulness of the spot, if you wish to lend a willing ear I shall briefly describe the appearance of the charming place," he wrote.

> Around it are springing wells of water and many densely planted trees, which blossom from the rain of the clouds and produce all kinds of sweet fruits and delightful scents; there are also vines which give wine worthy for kings to drink.... The path by which the Lord ascended is winding, twisting this way and that; [but] whoever wishes to climb up to pray can easily make the ascent.[24]

If Sinai wins the soul by threat and leanness, Tabor compels by charm. In moving from one mountain to the other, one passes from sandstone desert and smooth-faced granite to bright green mosses under stands of pine, oak, and cypress trees.

A light rain was falling the morning I got off the Arab bus from Tiberias, near the foot of Mount Tabor. In late February spring had already begun in Galilee. Songbirds and the white blossoms of almond trees welcomed the rain. The very shape of the mountain seemed itself to invoke the rites of spring. The name Tabor is thought by some to derive from the Hebrew *tabbur,* meaning "navel."[25] Indeed, the gentle, rounded form of the mountain is similar to the carved stone found at Delphi, where ancient Greeks marked for centuries the navel of the earth. Tabor is a place at the center. Only 1,730 feet high, it appears more imposing than its height suggests, standing alone in the middle of a wide plain north of Megiddo.

Archaeologists have found paleolithic flakes and blades of flint along its slopes, chipped away by Neanderthal hunters.[26] The Canaanites may well have connected the mountain with Asherah, the great mother goddess and wife of El, described in Ugaritic myth.[27] In Jewish history, Tabor is associated with Deborah, the woman of faith and daring who led her people in defeating the captain of the Canaanites and his fearful iron chariots (Judg. 4–5). This mountain is one possessed of an ancient, feminine energy. It is Mother and Sister, one whose strength is bent toward nurture and wholeness.

This was clear to me that morning as I walked alone through the village of Shibli, along the lower slopes of Tabor. Even in the cold rain, *especially* in the rain, this was a place of nourishment, a place to rest and be still. I began looking for the stone I knew belonged to my other friend, whose dream of the transfiguration had long ago connected her to this place. The search took me off the road, into the trees, up grassy slopes, and along goat trails that crisscrossed the mountain. It was good to work my way slowly up the mountain, through the morning mist, toward the beautiful Franciscan church at the top. There, noon Mass was being celebrated for a small group of pilgrims as I arrived.

"Lord, I am not worthy to receive you, but only say the word and I shall be healed." I've always loved those words from the Latin rite, but never so much as on that day at the mount of transfiguration. I wasn't able at the time to receive the body and blood of Christ—being outsider, exile, *protestante.* But after leaving the church, I wandered into the nearby ruins of a Benedictine monastery, and found there the other pebble. It was hidden in tall, wet grass, near a medieval wall. I held it while trying to read the account of the transfiguration from Matthew's gospel. A harsh, cold wind rustled the pages, making them hard to hold. Dark clouds were gathering. I knew that in taking this time alone I was probably also missing a ride back down the mountain with some of those who'd come for Mass.

But the words of the gospel went right through me as I stumbled over the passage. I heard them spoken by God not only to Jesus, but also, it seemed, to me. "You are my son," the voice was saying, "the one I love. I'm pleased with you; I take pleasure in who you are. Listen (and attend carefully) . . . to my glory within you" (Matt. 17:5). There were no lights flashing at the time, no extraordinary vision. God knows, I was half freezing to death. But I couldn't get away from the embarrassed, almost heretical feeling that in all my ordinariness—a foreigner with cold feet and anxiousness about the weather—I was somehow in that moment included in the transfiguring light once revealed in that place. A father was saying words I'd been longing to hear all my life.

While such a reading of the text may seem presumptuous to Western ears, I'd learn later that it follows exactly the Greek fathers' understanding of the transfiguration event. The disciples' vision of Jesus' deified human flesh on Mount Tabor revealed to them not only the glory of God, but also what it means most fully to be human. Part of their amazement at the transfiguration was that, in seeing Jesus, they also saw themselves anew.[28] In beginning to realize that truth for myself, my pilgrimage to two sacred mountains, my search for two stones, had come full circle. The self put into serious question at Sinai was reidentified in a new manner at Tabor. Perhaps it's always the case that "wilderness holds answers to more questions than we yet know how to ask."[29]

A central paradox of the apophatic tradition is that the self once lost in desolate emptiness is subsequently rediscovered (or recreated) through union with God. The new self, no longer bound to the dualism of a human "subject" grasping for a divine "object," exists wholly and intimately in God. The wonder of this transfiguration is profound, as celebrated by mystics in all the Abrahamic faiths. In the Muslim Sufi tradition the tenth-century poet Abu Yazid—briefly experiencing the "passing away" (*fana*) of his acquisitive self—is able to proclaim in the mystical exaltation of this new being, "Glory be to Me! How great is My Majesty!"[30] This is a language of excess toward which the apophatic moment strangely leads. It becomes heresy only if one mistakes its metaphorical intensity for a metaphysical statement of ultimacy.

I myself had come to Israel some weeks before, like Dante entering the dark forest in the midpoint of my years. The trip to Sinai had been, symbolically, one of great anxiety. It had required abandonment—the giving up of language, of security, of all the things on which I'd come to rely. Iron John Climacus had been a demanding mentor, harsh but good. Mount Sinai was, for me, a place of relinquishment, where a dying mother had to be laid to rest, broken relationships reconsidered, a career rethought and a family reclaimed. Its blood-red stone exacted discipline and obedience.

The subsequent trip to Tabor made possible the imagining of new life. There, in the place of birth, a fresh beginning could take form in the wake of brokenness and loss. Words had been spoken and heard there, reaffirming the identity of a son, suggesting wonder. I caught a glimpse of this in the emerald-green grass of the monastery ruins that afternoon. The round, white stone discovered there had a new name written on it, known only to the one who received it (Rev. 2:17). It belonged to my friend, of course, but in another way it also was mine, suggesting commitments of my own, directions I, too, would have to assume. The names written on any of the stones that we recognize as our own are always carved in love.[31]

The wind had grown stronger as I left the grass by the medieval wall and made my way back to the church, now locked and abandoned, all the cars gone. Dark gray clouds were still coming in from the north. Completely alone, I walked the long rows of cypress trees along the path leading from the church to the road, going back down the mountain with two stones in my pocket and a curious, anomalous sense of joy.

An Overlaying of Images

In an effort to convey the mythic meanings of these two sacred mountains, I've joined them by way of a single individual's personal experience. Others' experience of the two places may be very different. Yet the two mountains and the biblical narratives to which they've become attached are often linked in the history of the Christian tradition. From the biblical text itself to the writings of the Greek and Latin fathers and iconic representations in the history of Christian art, Sinai and Tabor are identified as complementary dimensions of a single truth.[32]

The synoptic accounts of the transfiguration are themselves an overlay of the Exodus 24 and 33 passages, juxtaposing the two mountains in such a way as to connect the theophany of Sinai with the glorified Christ revealed on Tabor.[33] In Mark's gospel, like the Exodus narrative, there's an ascent to a high mountain, the covering of the mountain with a great cloud, a voice speaking from heaven, a transfigured appearance, a mention of six days and the making of tabernacles, a partial though profound "seeing" of God, and a subsequent need to "veil" or hide the entire experience. In each case, the central figure takes three friends with him to the mountain—Moses goes with Aaron, Nadab, and Abihu; Jesus with Peter, James, and John.[34] If the parallel experience of Elijah on Horeb/Sinai is brought into the mix, the theophany described in I Kings 19, then the joining of Moses and Elijah with Jesus on Tabor becomes a way of doubly incorporating the mountain of the old covenant into the mountain of the new.[35]

In Eastern icons of the transfiguration the one mountain is continually superimposed over the other. Never bound by any need for topographical accuracy, artistic representations of Sinai and Tabor have traditionally presented each of the mountains as a crest with three different peaks. In pictures of Sinai, Jebel Mussa, the Moses Mountain, is shown in the center, with Mount Horeb (or Zafzafa) and Saint Catherine's Mountain on either side.[36] In iconographical portrayals of Mount Tabor, Jesus stands within a mandorla of light on the middle and taller peak, with Elijah and Moses on lower pinnacles to the right and left.

This became a standard pattern from early Greek mosaics to fifteenth-century icons of the transfiguration by Andrei Rublev and Theophanes the Greek.[37] The trinitarian pattern of three neighboring peaks, crowned with clouds and light, naturally attracted the imagination of Christian artists while also allowing the iconographic fusing of separate revelatory events at Sinai and in Galilee.

This artistic coupling of the two mountains and two events in holy history was expressed beautifully in the sixth century when artists at Mount Sinai created the stunning mosaic of the transfiguration in the apse of the monastery church there. The figures pictured in luminescent stone tied the Sinaitic experience of Moses and Elijah to the disciples' contemplation of Christ's glory on Mount Tabor.[38] The mosaic served as an aid in catechesis for the monks, encouraging them in their own effort to glimpse the light of Christ in the harsh abandonment to which their desert lives had called them. Every attendance at the morning liturgy, as the light came through the eastern windows to illuminate the face of Christ, occasioned a reflection on the meaning of the mountain beneath which they lived.[39]

In this manner, the gospel writers and subsequent iconographers were able to offer Jesus as a new Moses, a fulfillment of promises made at Sinai. By the interweaving of narrative and artistic imagery, they also connected the ineffable experience of "seeing" God on the mountain with the weariness of poor wandering travelers who had passed that way, yearning for the solace of fierce landscapes. The brief ecstasy of perceived glory is framed in each case by the pain of those facing displacement and loss. The narrative in Mark 9, for example, is punctuated by two great announcements of Jesus' rejection and suffering in the chapters immediately preceding and following.

Indeed, every one of the synoptic writers introduces the story of the transfiguration with Jesus' call to take up the cross and follow him. Similarly, they all conclude the story with a summons to silence, to "tell no one." The redactors of the story recognize that the glorious presence of God disclosed in hiddenness will inevitably be scorned and rejected in the public sphere. Glory is inextricably linked to suffering. The road to transfiguration travels the hard, bloodstained path from Egypt toward Golgotha.

In a similar way, the mountain narratives of Moses and Elijah had situated each of them within a context of loneliness and rejection. In going to meet God on the mountain, the one had been scorned by his people, who demanded a golden calf to worship (Ex. 32:1). The other had been threatened by Jezebel, who'd sworn herself to vengeance (I Kings 19:2). In both cases, their "seeing" of God on the mountain was but an interlude in an ongoing struggle, given at a time when the absence of God seemed for them most painfully real.[40] Transfiguration is a hidden, apocalyptic event, offering to those facing anguish a brief glimpse of glory to come.[41] It incorporates a theology of hope into a theology of abandonment and loss.

It is not accidental, therefore, that both mountains are also associated with a challenge to entrenched political power. Lying far from the corridors of influence in Jerusalem (or Egypt, for that matter), they defy the authority of the state, "clashing with every royal religion enamored of image, vision, appearance, structure."[42] Coming to Sinai, Moses had witnessed the overthrow of oppression in Egypt. Elijah came to the mountain fleeing the corrupt regime of Ahab, having just undermined the hegemony of Baal on Mount Carmel.

The mountain of God necessarily brings into question all claims to political power. Its iconographic imagery challenges every human structure. Similarly, at Tabor, the transfiguration reaches beyond the present failure of political justice in Jerusalem to affirm an unrealized future where Christ is king. But the crown cannot yet be claimed. After briefly revealing the justice to come, Jesus sets his face toward Jerusalem, going to his death.[43]

The sacred mountain, from Sinai to Tabor to Zion, is a place where political priorities are realigned.[44] To flee to the mountain is to identify with the marginalized, with those denied access to the empowerment of the state and thus subject to its wrath. Jesus and his disciples may well have contemplated such things as they walked down Tabor on their way back toward Jerusalem.

Central in all of this is the conviction that the sudden, blinding light of divine radiance, as it momentarily appears in human experience, must ever be framed within a context of the utterly mundane, with all the harsh, prosaic discipline it demands. When the desert-mountain tradition does not patently reject ecstatic experience as untrustworthy, it stringently insists that "moments of splendor" serve the purposes of justice and responsibility in the ordinary life. Any fleeting realization of apophatic union with God must re-engage the person on the mountain with the concrete concerns of social and political action.

Origen had been one of the first to use the mountains of Sinai and Tabor as metaphors of the contemplative life, insisting himself that one ascends only by way of *ascesis* (the dogged discipline of the spiritual athlete) to the vision of God.[45] Transfiguring experience is not granted to people as an easy and ready access to glory. Only in going up the mountain, rejecting and being rejected by the world, identifying with those who are most broken, does one encounter the divine refulgence.

This light, seen in the icons of Saint Catherine's Monastery, comes not from beyond human flesh and the suffering to which it is heir, but in and through the experience of pain. The icons convey a profound sense of God's grandeur coming through the broken flesh of Christ and the lives of the saints. Indeed, the church itself, iconographically focused around the joining of Tabor with Sinai, seems to have windows constructed not so much for the purpose of letting light in as for letting out the light of divine splendor.[46]

The desert fathers, gathered in worship at Sinai and reflecting the brightness of Christ in their disciplined lives, would become themselves the finest expression of the distant light of Tabor. I came to recognize this in a brief conversation one morning with Father Elias, a Greek monk in the monastic community there. A simple man in his thirties, with long black hair and bushy beard, he spoke in broken English of his deep love for the *Way of the Pilgrim,* the *Philokalia,* the repetition of the Jesus Prayer—all the traditional disciplines of a hesychast life. His love of prayer was obvious and uncontrived.

Trying to express in an unfamiliar tongue the joy that was his, he closed his eyes, throwing back his head and rapping his forehead with the tips of his fingers. "You come back on the twentieth of July [the feast day of Elijah]," he urged. "Pray that night at the chapel of the prophet and you'll understand what I mean." He knew that Elijah, his namesake, had once heard the silence of God on the mountain above. I smiled, nodding my head and looking over his shoulder at the face of Christ-Pantocrator on the iconostasis nearby. Here was a man who knew something already of the experience of transfiguration.

I fear for good and unpretentious monks like Elias. Their religious life is seriously under threat by hordes of tourists like myself who make their way to Sinai every year. Their solitude is becoming almost impossible. Worse, the Egyptian government keeps reviving plans to enhance the tourist trade still more, talking of luxury hotels in the valley where the children of Israel waited for Moses to return from the mount, even a tram to the top of the peak where a gift shop and restaurant would greet hungry pilgrims.[47] If any iconographic image of Sinai can capture the spiritual poverty of postmodern culture, it's a parking lot and four-star restaurant at the site of the burning bush. Our substitution of consumer tourism for pilgrimage, of canned experience for life-changing risk, is symptomatic of our inability to entertain in any way the reality of our own transfiguration.

Apophatic and Kataphatic Theology

Having seen how the Christian tradition yokes the two mountains of Sinai and Tabor as elusive majesty joined with intimate presence, we can observe also how they suggest an interplay of apophatic and kataphatic motifs in the history of spirituality. These ostensibly inimical traditions are actually interconnecting and mutually correcting realities.[48]

Sinai symbolizes the provocative, aniconic power of the apophatic tradition. Here God is discovered in a sparcity of images, in an absence of the clarity found at Tabor. Elijah meets Yahweh at the cave on Mount Horeb, not in images of earthquake, wind, and fire, but in utter silence—beyond language and understanding. Moses asks to see clearly the face of God but is shown only God's back. Divine accessibility is qualified by an equally zealous concern for divine freedom. The apophatic impulse of Sinai is to empty us of inadequate images, to destroy idolatries, to cut through all false conceptions of the holy. It boldly deconstructs every human attempt to capture and contain a God who dwells in thick darkness.

Tabor, by contrast, symbolizes the iconic, imaginative power of the kataphatic tradition, given to artistic and intellectual expression. There, on the tree-covered slopes overlooking the plains of Galilee, God is found in a sharpness and lucidity of image. The mystery of the incarnation is disclosed in Jesus of Nazareth, his clothes glistening and intensely white. There is no obscurity or confusion about what is seen. The disciples know themselves to have encountered the living God in human flesh. The kataphatic certainty of Tabor allows a brief contemplation of beauty and goodness made one. It naturally lends itself to the painting of icons, to a language of dazzling light, to extravagance of expression.

But these two ways of describing the mystery of God—the way of darkness and the way of light, the ambiguity of silence and the transparency of articulation—can never be separated. There is danger in posing a sharp dichotomy between apophatic and kataphatic approaches, as if the one were superior to the other, as if the higher and purer silence of apophatic mysticism properly took precedence over the concrete concerns of community and speech. These two ways of delineating the image of God must be mutually interconnecting. They require each other.

Some people have described the interrelationship of the two in terms of the Yin-Yang symbol in ancient Taoism; within the dark apophatic there is a small seed of bright clarity and within the light kataphatic lies a tiny germ of impenetrability.[49] Kataphatic expression without the critique of apophatic prophecy becomes dogmatic, abstruse, overly confident in its powers of utterance. Similarly, apophatic criticism, in its rejection of language, its challenge of every conclusion, leads, without a kataphatic willingness to commit itself, to an empty nihilism, never affirming anything.

The interplay of the two motifs is readily apparent in the biblical narratives of the two mountains. On Sinai only Moses finally enters the cloud, speaking to

God. The people remain behind on the plain of er-Raha seeing nothing, eventually complaining to Aaron about God's absence and Moses' delay in returning. Balking at the uncertainty of the divine presence, they want something they can clearly apprehend, a distinct image of God before them. Sustained silence is too much to bear. So they attempt a desperate search for the "false" kataphatic, for an image they can see and touch, a golden calf patterned after the gods they had left behind in Egypt.

When Moses returns, he assails their idolatrous embrace of graven images, reiterating the bold insistence of apophatic prophecy. The calf is destroyed and the idolaters along with it. Yet Moses goes on to redirect the focus of the people's need, pointing them to God's own choice of kataphatic image. The divine *can* be apprehended by tangible and sacramental means. He points to the gold brought with them from Egypt, some of it used in making the calf, showing them how to employ it in constructing the ark of the covenant. God consents to dwell there in the tabernacle in the wilderness, not because the image or the place itself guarantees the divine presence, but because Yahweh chooses to move with God's people, "tenting" among them. Apophatic rebuke thus challenges and refocuses kataphatic commitment.

The same thing happens in reverse on Mount Tabor. There the disciples had been asking Jesus to reveal his glory as coming Messiah. They chafe under his resistance to declare openly before others that hidden truth. Peter rebukes him for predicting instead the suffering and death he must endure (Mark 8:27–33). In what seems to be a sudden reversal of Jesus' reticence to display his grandeur, he takes a handful of disciples up the mountain and shows them a vision of his messianic glory to come. All their kataphatic dreams come true. Everything they had longed for appears in dazzling splendor before them. The mountain is flooded with light.

But their response is no better than that of the people at Sinai. Peter's impulse, like theirs, is to reach for the false kataphatic, wanting to preserve the experience artificially in a monument, building a cluster of shrines to commemorate a lost memory. He longs to sustain this display of mind-boggling power that will forever command the respect of others. Lost on him entirely is the deeper apophatic significance of what had happened on Tabor.[50]

This is the hardest truth for the disciples to bear. Their vision has no permanence. It can not be preserved in stone. Its ultimate fulfillment lies only on the far side of suffering, a suffering which inescapably awaits their Lord—and themselves. The way to glory is unavoidably the way of the cross, the path toward emptiness. In this fashion, therefore, the two poles of apophatic and kataphatic sensitivity continually challenge and renew each other. The one destroys, but only in order to bear new life. The other exults in majesty, but only to recall once again its limits. This is how Sinai and Tabor interact as mythic symbols.

Masculine and Feminine Perceptions of Landscape

If there is danger in separating too neatly these apophatic and kataphatic modes, there is a similar danger in sharply distinguishing masculine and feminine experience in speaking of the two mountains. "Fierce Sinai" and "gentle Tabor" are simplistic labels which the mountains themselves stubbornly refuse to honor. Through the centuries, Mount Tabor has been far more than a sweet-tempered mother. Arabs in the thirteenth century saw it as a place of mystery, remaining untouchable. Thinking themselves unworthy to live there, they designated it the Mountain of God.[51]

On the other hand, fifteenth-century friar Felix Fabri spoke of pilgrims to Mount Sinai filled "with enormous joy and devotion" as they squeezed themselves into the womb-like "cleft in the rock" where Moses had seen God.[52] The two mountains resist easy classification, continually redefining the mutual richness of masculine and feminine experience. Egeria, that intrepid fourth-century nun, climbed and loved them both. Three centuries later, John Climacus refused to speak of the one apart from the other.

This raises a larger question about how men and women perceive landscapes differently and the alleged preferences they have for one over another.[53] The "solace of fierce landscapes," as described in this book, is by no means a matter of masculine interest alone. It is absurd to think that only men exult in threatening terrain while women prefer gentle, pastoral landscapes. Annie Dillard will have none of it. Cutting directly to "the twist and mess" of life, she prefers "its very jaggedness, its random heaps of mountains, its frayed fringes of shore." She is fascinated by "the blue patch where the light doesn't hit," by the shadow places in this world where newly hatched praying mantises devour each other and giant water bugs suck the entrails of pond frogs on Tinker Creek.[54] It is the Creator's wild extravagance in fostering a life given to reproducing and dying by the billions that grips her soul most keenly.

Women naturally delight in wildness, even as men are drawn to gentle images of nature's playfulness. Loren Eiseley's most defining experience of the universe came one morning at dawn as he saw the two sunlit ears of a fox pup above the ruins of an old boat on a remote beach. The wide-eyed, innocent fox, "with a vast and playful humor in his face," held a chicken bone in his paws, inviting the famous anthropologist to play. For all Eiseley might have known, it could have been the same fox the Little Prince met in Antoine de Saint Exupéry's book for children, the fox who wished more than anything else to be tamed by the boy. Eiseley accepted the invitation, tumbling for an ecstatic moment on the sand with a playful fox, knowing himself, if only for an instant, to have "held the universe at bay," to have experienced himself as loved.[55] Masculine and feminine perceptions of landscape, of the world itself, are never easily reduced to simple formulas.

My one friend draws every bit as much energy from Sinai as she does Mount Tabor, and the other friend craves the vitality of Deborah's mountain no less than he does that of Moses. It would be unfair to either mountain, or either friend, to suggest too neat a distinction between the two. Sinai and Tabor, like all multivalent images, are contraries that have a way at times of collapsing into each other.

Sinai rises from out of the desert, where life is frugal and death always near. In the garden of Saint Catherine's Monastery one visits the charnel house, with the skulls and bones of former monks in open view. On the grounds of the monastery in this desolate place, one becomes accustomed to loss. Here Moses splattered his people with blood (Ex. 24:8). The images of Sinai are coarse and lean—stripped clean, like bones in the desert sand. Yet Sinai is also the place where starlight can be most extravagant and silence most compelling. In a scarcity of images, one learns attentiveness to wonder.

Tabor is the mountain of light, taking joy in the greening power of God's spirit, as Hildegard, the twelfth-century Benedictine nun, described its impulse toward growth. This is a mountain that thrives on abundance and redundancy. It supports a plant life of variegated wonder. The apocryphal Gospel of Hebrews connects its summit with the height of mystical insight: "The Holy Spirit, my Mother, came and took me by the hair and carried me to the great Mount Tabor."[56] Here is effulgence, an excess of glory.

Yet Tabor, the generous and yielding, can also be severe. It, too, speaks of limits. This is where Sisera met his end, his head nailed to the ground by a woman sworn to justice. From the mountain's peak one overlooks the war-scarred Megiddo and its valley of the fallen. In a place rich in images, one must choose decisively.

What, finally, is the truth taught by these two mountains, contradictory and complementary as they are? Simply this: that when everything is irretrievably lost, life does not end, but is at a point of new beginnings. "Except a grain of wheat falls into the ground and dies, it remains alone; but if it dies, it bears much fruit" (John 12:24). When language utterly fails, the dumb but patient tongue will someday speak again . . . with golden, winged words, carved in silence.

These mountains are not finished with me yet. They still reverberate in snatches of memory and of dream. They lead necessarily to emptiness and the way of the cross. They demand the questioning of structures, the abandonment of words. But in the final loss of everything that once was sure, there is also the birth of something new. Where relationships had seemed irreparably broken, an unexpected love appears. In the absolutist claims of political power, hope is born for oppressed slaves fresh from Egypt. In the death of rhetoric, the poet is born. In the destruction of idols, the truth is set free. In God's utter absence, when all seems lost, there is movement perceived from the cleft of the rock, and a burst of light beyond all seeing.

Imaginary Mountains,
Invisible Lands

The symbolic and religious significance of mountains is endless. —Mircea Eliade[1]

The fact is, we have different reports of the place from the most trustworthy people. —George MacDonald[2]

The mountain recurred often in his dreams, always the same shape, rising out of the sea in the north to a height that never seemed to end. Cosmas Indicopleustes had never actually seen this great World Mountain, anchoring the earth to its very foundations. He hadn't discovered it on any of the merchant voyages he'd made, some of them reaching as far as India and beyond. But he knew it was there. The sun daily circled its vast conical shape, hiding behind it in darkness each night.[3]

For Cosmas Indicopleustes, a wildly imaginative sixth-century geographer from Alexandria, it was a mountain defined more by a darkness of unknowing than by any charts drawn with sextant, rule or compass. He saw it as an idealized shape of the mountain he knew well, Jebel Mussa in the lower peninsula of the Sinai. He lived in the shadow of that awesome peak, having left his earlier career as a cartographer in the merchant marine to become a monk near the ancient mountain of Moses.

There in the long desert evenings, by an oil lamp in his cell, he'd write of his past travels and draw sketches of the still-greater mountain that transfixed his imagination. Nothing seemed so real as the haunting silhouette of this enormous cosmic peak.

Cosmas Indicopleustes—seasoned sailor, apologist, visionary, and sometime monk—left as his legacy a bizarre piece of scholarship which he titled his *Christian Topography*.[4] Its purpose was to refute the pagan heresy of a round earth, arguing instead for the world as a flat rectangle, modeled after the table of shew-bread in the wilderness tabernacle. He developed a whole cosmology based on the mystical insights of Moses on Mount Sinai.

God had disclosed to Moses on the desert mountain not only the archetypal pattern of the tabernacle but also the whole structure of the universe. For a six-day period, corresponding to the original six days of creation, God had covered Moses with cloud, inscribing on the darkness of his mind the mythic structure of the cosmos. On this holy mountain, itself an archetype of the World Mountain unseen by human eyes, Moses had discovered an interlocking correspondence of spiritual and terrestrial geographies.

Cosmas (his very name echoes his fascination with world order) never tired of illustrating his work with drawings of Moses hidden in the mountain's dark cloud. Everything about the story drove him to near-madness. One imagines him sitting there, near the cleft of the rock where Moses had sat, contemplating from the high slopes of Sinai a Mountain grander than anything his eyes could see.

I know something of the man's obsession, having myself from time to time dreamed of a perfect mountain. Perhaps we all do. I see it always from the same angle, its blue-gray granite shining in the morning sun, every feature glimpsed with perfect clarity through thin, colorless air. It stands alone, jutting into the sky. Majestic and austere, it defies every effort of ascent. More beautiful and real than any mountain I've actually seen, it hangs suspended in my dreams like a New Jerusalem being lowered from heaven.

The Allure of Imaginary Places

This enchantment of the human mind with archetypal landscape forms—with invisible and inaccessible mountains—is a phenomenon as old as myth and persistent as dream.[5] The history of literature, and of religions, is filled with accounts of hidden peaks, unexplored rivers, imaginary deserts, and lost islands that long to make their way onto cartographers' maps, even as bizarre animals of fantasy kept appearing on the edges of ancient charts of the world. We seem to have an insatiable thirst for places that don't exist, for griffins and wondrous dragons prowling the antipodes of a world we hardly recognize. They symbolize states of growth we haven't yet achieved.

Aldo Leopold, the American naturalist, was fascinated by rumors found in seventeenth-century Spanish journals of a great river running east from the Andes, a river without beginning and without end, known as *el Rio de la Madre de Dios,* the River of the Mother of God. Though it appeared on some early maps as a short, heavy line falling into the Amazonian forest, it never was found. He described it as a "perfect symbol of the Unknown Places of the earth," pleading in one of his wilderness essays for the preservation of land that remains undeveloped and even unknown. The human spirit, he thought, requires the existence of, if not accessibility to, places of great imaginative power and mystery.[6]

Religions repeatedly refer to landscapes of the imagination to describe the deepest longings of the human spirit. The maps to such places are always sketched in metaphor, interpreted by wonder.[7] Access is not easy. Barry Lopez speaks of the difficulties involved in reaching a mysterious desert that symbolizes for him what's most worth finding.

> There is, I should warn you, doubt . . . about the directions I will give you here, but they are the very best that can be had. They will not be easy to follow. Where it says left you must go right sometimes. Read south for north sometimes. It depends a little on where you are coming from, but not entirely. I am saying you will have doubts. [But] if you do the best you can you will have no trouble.[8]

In the effort to reach a sacred place, the traveller must be guided by a deep need (whether conscious or unconscious) to reach it.

At his death in 1952, René Daumal, the French poet and orientalist, left an unfinished fantasy novel describing in vivid detail a mountain so high that its summit remained inaccessible. It was invisible under usual circumstances because of a peculiar property of the curvature of space on that part of the globe. Yet it was a real mountain that could be found, though only by those in need. He recounted the events of an extraordinary expedition to this peak undertaken by a group of people "for whom the impossible no longer existed."

Coincidentally, he wrote of this mountain at a time when Everest, the world's highest and still-unclimbed mountain, was very close to being "conquered." After Everest, there would be no more inaccessible places in the world, wholly beyond human control. Yet such places, he knew, were absolutely necessary for the health of the human spirit.[9]

This is why invisible landscapes remain so important in the mythologies of all the great religions. Every twelve years at Allahabad in northern India, a great Hindu pilgrimage called the Triveni is made to the point at which three sacred rivers converge: the Ganges, the Yamuna, and the Saraswati. The third river is the most sacred of all, but it is not found on any map. This is a mythical river, having long ago disappeared from the earth and thought now to flow underground in hidden fields of the spirit.[10]

This imaginary river is sacred to Hindu believers, just as the imaginary Mount Meru is sacred to Buddhists and Mount Kaf to Muslims. Mount Meru, hidden somewhere in the Himalayas, is a mystical mountain eighty thousand miles high, from which all the sacred rivers of the world flow. Mount Kaf is a cosmic mountain rising out of the desert of Iran and serving as the "mother" of every mountain on earth, being connected to them all by subterranean branches and veins. One must walk for four months "in the darkness," in mystical prayer, to reach this magical peak.[11] One must *need* to go there.

As humans, we long for unknown places, affording no entry—approachable only by way of deep need, serendipity, and grace. From the surreal landscapes of Hieronymous Bosch and Ponce de León's fountain of youth to the invisible cities of Italo Calvino, the Western imagination has given birth to abundant geographies of the mind.

Garrison Keillor has described himself as a storyteller "telling lies" about places that don't exist. Yet he views that very act as an exercise in faith. Artfully imagining nonexistent realms expresses a yearning for the Kingdom of God.

> The reason you tell lies about a wonderful place is that you believe that if you get every detail right—absolutely right, and every character in that story has exactly as many hairs on his or her head as he's supposed to have—that if you get it absolutely perfect . . . you will be lifted up out of this life and you will be set down in that wonderful place that you've told lies about. And all your lies become true.[12]

He keeps telling stories with the hope that ultimately he'll be able to live his way into them. That's why we all love tales that give form to a world that is not yet here.

The Cosmic Mountain as Beatific Vision

The inaccessible mountain, stunning in its beauty yet elusive to all approach, is the most prevalent and compelling of all imaginary places recurring in cultural myth and private dream. The image draws its energy from the basic paradox that while the mountain is perceived as an actual physical place existing in the world, under normal circumstances it remains invisible, resistant to every attempt at entry. In Tibetan mythology, this is Shambhala, a hidden paradise that truly exists—somewhere north of Bodhgaya, though no one knows how far.[13] In Western literature it gave rise to the fictional Shangri-La of James Hilton's *Lost Horizon*. In Chinese tradition it is a secluded Taoist palace above six thousand meters in the K'un-lun where the peach tree of longevity grows beside a magic fountain. For Muslims it forms the ancient city of Janaidar rising from the snows of Muztagh Ata north of the Hindu Kush.[14] The image haunts the dreams of people from Egypt to Southeast Asia.

For the myth to have power, the peak must be one that occupies space, even though its position cannot be plotted by azimuth and meridian line. The fabled and elusive Mountains of the Moon, projected by ancient Greek philosophers as located along the upper sources of the Nile, were still sought by African explorers as late as the nineteenth century.[15] René Daumal's inaccessible Mount Analogue, though a creation of his own imagination, was estimated by him (and others) to actually exist in the South Pacific, somewhere between Tasmania and New Zealand. Even Augustine looked vaguely "to the south" for the pear-shaped mountain rising from the sea where angels still guarded the gates of paradise. Though no one could calculate the exact place, he considered it essential that the physical existence of Eden be somehow guaranteed.

The interior truth here is that human beings don't long for another world, far beyond the ordinariness of this one. We long for our own world, perceived in all its hidden grandeur. We sense it to be filled with a glory we could see if only we had the gifts of attentiveness and the proper rituals of entry. The magnificent yet inaccessible mountain is a symbol of our deep longing for the beatific vision. We want to see the ordinariness of our lives transformed into glory, lifted up to clear view on the horizon of our world, like a snow-capped mountain shimmering in the morning sun. The God we seek is always nearer than we suspect.

For the image to work, we must believe that the mountain exists; yet it must remain elusive, yielding to none of our usual means of entry. Not being subject to human control, the cosmic peak stands beyond every exercise of power. One "gets there" only through extremity, by way of abandonment. Mount Meru and Mount Sumeru, mythical mountains traditionally sacred to Hindus and Buddhists, can be perceived only by masters of relinquishment, by those who've released all desire for possession, all efforts to manage and control.

The inaccessible mountain witnesses to human limits. It shares in the mystery that C. S. Lewis once described as Joy, the full and wondrous recognition of the object of one's longing without ever being able to possess it.[16] One's highest joy, strangely enough, may be realized in having one's limits transgressed. It means standing helplessly and with rapt delight in the presence of what is most loved, without being able to lay any claim to it, without any power to make it one's own.

This is the longing for Zion sung in the Hebrew psalms of ascent: "I will lift up my eyes unto the hills from whence comes my help" (Ps. 121:1). The psalmist knows he can place no claim on the Rock of his Salvation. The mountain yields to him only at its own choosing; he can but look upon it with desire. Yet wanting the mountain may be almost as good as having it, since desire itself is the fullest possession we can know on earth.[17] To go up to Jerusalem, to the navel of the earth, atop Mount Zion, is to have one's heart turned with inconsolable yearning toward a still-greater Mountain, to Yahweh who alone is the foundation of Zion. Yahweh is the unseen peak of beauty to which all lesser mountains bear witness.

Each visible (and ordinary) mountain nonetheless remains a door to the invisible. To the eyes of faith, lowly Mount Zion—a mere hillock overshadowed by Mount Scopus and the Mount of Olives nearby—becomes "the fair-crested, utmost peak of Zaphon," taller even than the holy mountain of Baal in Syria, rising over a mile out of the sea (Ps. 48:2).[18] This double vision of the seen and unseen mountain is an exercise in faith, an expression of one's deepest longing.

A Spirituality of Desire

In classic dream interpretation, the mountain symbolizes the dreamer's most profound desire, whether this is perceived as high achievement and ascent to the realm of the spirit or (in Freudian terms) as the mother's breast and the ecstasy of sexual eroticism.[19] The mountain towers on the horizon like an immensity of longing. Far from being something always repressed in the Christian tradition, a "spirituality of desire" (symbolized in the mountain of wistfulness) recurs continually in the writings of the mystics.[20]

Thomas Traherne understood human desire to be the very image of God within us. Saint Bonaventure insisted that only the "man [or woman] of desires" can be disposed to a life of prayer. Julian of Norwich said "there is in God a quality of thirst and longing." Human desire is simply a reflection of that original, irrepressible yearning in Christ. For this reason, Ignatius Loyola never tired of telling people in the *Spiritual Exercises* to "ask God for what they want and desire."[21] The restlessness of the human heart is ever absorbed in a longing that finds rest only in that which transcends all longing.

This is what underlay the craziness of Cosmas Indicopleustes and his desire for what he couldn't see, for what he unquestionably knew to be there—though it always eluded his grasp. I can appreciate this poor man's feverish mind, drawing sketches of his unseen mountain on every loose piece of paper he could find. I myself lie outside in the backyard at night, alone and in silence, as if waiting for a huge mountain to rise over the trees with the moon each evening. I don't know why I've come to "desire" that time alone as much as I do. The mountain never appears. Nothing usually happens, no "religious experience" ever worth reporting. But the sheer delight that's mine each night in that time of utterly thoughtless silence is hard to describe. How do we explain any of the deepest desires that we have?

All I bring to the darkness each night is what the *Cloud* author calls a "naked intent," a wish to be empty and still in the presence of that for which I have no name. The author of the *Cloud* says that if you find this unexplainable desire welling up within you, simply wanting time without speech with one that you love, then you may *have* to start thinking about yourself as a "contemplative."[22] You unavoidably start seeking out people who know more of this simplicity and emptiness, who voluntarily (or involuntarily) practice a life of poverty, stripped of the complicated agendas that bind the rest of us so easily. You discover a stubborn, irrepressible desire for the poor, the marginal, and fugitive as your finest teachers.

What is this desire for a God who remains equally elusive and seductive, this fascination with people like Cosmas Indicopleustes who know the poverty of what can't be possessed? Gregory the Great once said that "wanting" itself is its own reward, even if we never finally acquire what we'd sought to obtain. This sixth-century pope, often described as the Doctor of Desire, argued that "Anyone who wholeheartedly wishes for God, *has* what he longs for, because no one can love God unless he possesses already the one that he loves."[23] The very "desire" is what gives us pleasure, not just its gratification.

Cosmas Indicopleustes must have realized this in his ceaseless yearning for the mountain of his dreams. He looked for the Rock which had followed Israel through the wilderness (I Cor. 10:4), the stone which the builders had rejected, only later to become cornerstone of a temple as yet unrevealed (Matt. 21:42). His wish, above all else, was for Christ, the one who became in his own body the peak of transfiguration.

On lonely nights in the monastery below Mount Sinai, he wrote and dreamed often of the mysterious, magnificent mountain of his longing. After a while, not being able to possess the vision no longer mattered. The unsatisfied desire became itself more desirable than any other satisfaction.[24] So it is with love, especially in loving God. The unseen mountain may be as much as the human heart can hold.

If Gregory of Nyssa was right in his contention that our human longing for God is never exhausted, even in eternity, then eccentric old Indicopleustes still is contemplating his mysterious mountain. He continues even now to draw pictures, to write notes in the margins of his notebook, absorbed in his magnificent obsession. "The true vision of God consists in this," said Gregory, "that the one who looks up to God never ceases in that desire."[25] Gregory's mystical theology was anchored in his notion of *epiktasis,* the yearning for God or "straining forward to what lies ahead" mentioned in Philippians 3:13. In his thinking, the riches of God's incomprehensible being are the subject of continuous discovery without end. Even in the beatific vision, there's only a "satisfied dissatisfaction."

Gregory and Indicopleustes both were fascinated by what Moses had seen on the mountain, by the vision disclosed to him in the cloud of darkness. They longed to love and to be loved by that same mystery. For the rest of their lives, looking up at any mountain, they saw another beyond it, striking them with amazement and joy.

Part III

UNION

Love as the Fruit of Indifference

> For the garden is the only place there is, but
> you will not find it
> Until you have looked for it everywhere
> and found it nowhere that is not a desert.
>
> —W. H. Auden, "For the Time Being"

The deserts are fascinating in their extremes, their contradictions. In the driest of climates are found the most fluid of landscapes, where the wind ripples waves of graceful dunes. Places oppressively hot by day freeze at night. Country lacking water can be scoured by the most violent of floods. Sparse, dull growth erupts in blooms as extravagant and colorful as those of any environment. In an open land, great canyons remain invisible until the visitor is but a few paces away from their edge. —J. A. Kraulis, *Desertlands of America*

The problem today is that there are no deserts, only dude ranches. —Thomas Merton, "Rain and the Rhinoceros"

We have to be in a desert. For he whom we must love is absent. . . . We must be rooted in the absence of a place. —Simone Weil, *Gravity and Grace*

The desert is fertile. —Dom Helder Camara

A land of lost rivers, with little in it to love; yet a land that once visited must be come back to inevitably. —Mary Austin, *The Land of Little Rain*

The experience of emptiness engenders compassion. —Tibetan Buddhist saying

From the point of view of the believer, the purpose of emptiness and desolation is to prepare us for joy and ground us in hope. Unless joy and hope are the goal, the desert becomes a playground for masochists. —Alan W. Jones, *Soul Making: The Desert Way of Spirituality*

The further you go into the desert, the closer you come to God. —Arabic proverb

The desert world accepts my homage with its customary silence. The grand indifference. As any man of sense would want it. If a voice from the clouds suddenly addressed me, speaking my name in trombone tones, or some angel in an aura of blue flame came floating toward me along the canyon rim, I think I would be more embarrassed than frightened—embarrassed by the vulgarity of such display. That is what depresses in the mysticism of Carlos Castañeda and his like: their poverty of imagination. As any honest magician knows, true magic inheres in the ordinary, the commonplace, the everyday, the mystery of the obvious. Only petty minds and trivial souls yearn for supernatural events, incapable of perceiving that everything—everything!—within and around them is pure miracle. —Edward Abbey, *Abbey's Road*

Two weeks before my mother finally died I met with the hospice nurse, signing the necessary papers that signaled the beginning of the end. My mother was placed on "no code." Her body had begun "systems failure," I was told; it would not be long now. There was nothing left to do but to do nothing. In case of emergency, do not break glass, do not dial 911, exert no extraordinary procedures, do nothing. The long and lonely wait on the desert mountain was finally nearing its end.

Over the last few months my mother had begun moving away, spending more and more time in a place distant from the nursing home around her. She'd gone inside. At first I interpreted this as despair, thinking she was retreating from her long and unsuccessful effort at dying. But one day when she was more alert than usual, I asked if she was glad still to be alive—having been through so much, having lasted longer than any of us had ever expected. Her answer surprised me. "Oh, YES!" she cried, with a joy I found astonishing.

For a long time I'd have rated the quality of her life as extremely low. She went nowhere, read nothing, spoke very little, watched no TV, attending only to the endlessly repetitive details of her immediate environment. Yielding to the long, warm silence of half-sleep and half-attentiveness, she accepted the slow passage of time, the routine of eating, sleeping, watching people's movements, waiting for my coming. This was enough. More than enough, apparently. Life itself—unadorned, without artificial stimulation, without the excitement and wonder I imagined necessary for its meaning—life itself was enough. It took me a while to recognize this quiet place to which she was increasingly retreating. Teachers in the apophatic tradition might call it contemplation.

Somewhere along the way of her slow desert pilgrimage, she'd discovered an awakening of desire, a new hunger that gave meaning to her life. It was a subtle thing. Others might have misread it as bore-dom. She had acquired a detached attentiveness to things around her, a simple ability to be present to herself and to God, an indifference to the emotional and intellectual roller coaster on which she'd ridden much of her life. The inadvertent discipline of the nursing home had helped to occasion in my mother's spiritual life something akin to what Buddhists celebrate as *Sunyata* or Emptiness, what Muslim Sufis de-scribe as *fana* or the "passing away" of the self, what in centering prayer is referred to as "just sitting there, doing nothing . . . not even thinking worthwhile thoughts."[1]

This is my reading of her experience, of course. Especially in those final months we communicated largely without language. I don't know ultimately what it was she experienced, if anything at all. The concluding period of her life taught me that the most intimate (and enigmatic) moments of any of our lives are essentially closed to what we call "experience." They can no more be grasped and defined than the desert itself. At the point where the soul confronts its God most nakedly, there's only the meeting of two deserts—one emptiness poured into another.

While there's danger, therefore, in my trying to interpret my mother's experience in a language that wasn't hers, the quiet accept-ance to which she gradually came was unmistakable. Having endured the harsh but purifying experience of the wilderness, having ascended the mountain to await an illumination that comes on the wings of si-lence, my mother seemed to have been invited in those last few months to a third and final stage of union with God. There was noth-ing ecstatic about this experience so far as I could tell. One could hardly even call it an experience. My mother had simply come to a point in her life where it was enough to be present to the moment, be-fore God, no longer needing anything else. She did this without thought or feeling, with only a frail act of the will in finally saying "yes" for the last time in her life.

In the Christian tradition, the third stage of the spiritual life is often symbolized by the cloud, recalling the mist of intimacy through which God spoke to Moses "face to face" on the mountain (Ex. 33:11). The ephemeral shifting of clouds symbolizes the metamorphosis required of broken people who know themselves ignored and emptied yet also unreservedly loved. John Scotus Eriugena spoke of the ascent into a "cloud of contemplation" as the highest theophany possible to hu-man life. Basil the Great looked on the cloud mentioned in I Corin-thians 10:2 as "a shadow of the gift of the Spirit."[2] From Gregory of

Nyssa and Pseudo-Dionysius to Richard of Saint Victor and the *Cloud* author, entry into a bank of high fog has often symbolized the deepest longing of the human soul to be inseparably joined to God.

I've wondered if my mother, during those last few months, had begun to know something of this experience of the cloud. She looked at me often as if through a dark mist on a distant mountain. Her head tilted back, staring into space, she would focus with a quizzical expression on this vaguely familiar person in front of her, trying to remember the connection that once had joined us. She'd forgotten me in her movement through this cloud of quiet contemplation.

"How incredibly sad!" a stranger seeing her in that moment might have remarked. But it wasn't. A new, richer desire (for God) had simply taken the place of an older one (for me); she knew somehow these two desires were distinctly related, but couldn't remember how. But clearly, she was glad to be alive again, having begun this journey inward. While the cloud distanced her from me—with what appeared to be a growing indifference to her surroundings—it also opened her to something I couldn't see, something beyond the mountain, something she clearly recognized as grand.

I'm fascinated by what she sought in those last few months. Three years into the experience of my mother's dying, I finally began to realize how much the process of letting go was also one of being loved. The two things I'd always imagined to be so different were really one. All the griefs of God serve love. Maybe one can grasp this only at the end of a long beginning. In praying through his own experience of facing death by cancer, John Carmody was able to reach the point of proclaiming to God:

> O Felix cancer. If sickness convinces me of your love, makes me a credible witness to your utter goodness, it will be the best part of my life. My wife's love has prepared me for this, but only your palpable coming in the form of this terminal illness has brought my hope to crisis. Thank you, my God. I am not worthy that you should come under my roof, but only say the word and my dying will seem a pure grace.[3]

What allows this prayer to be glorious and not obscene is the mystery that the third section of this book explores.

I realize one must ever be wary of romanticizing illness and death. In looking back on the experience I've shared with my mother, there was nothing "beautiful" in her dying. It smelled of vomit and uncleaned teeth. It was relentlessly monotonous. Yet I have to be honest in sharing the mystery it also occasioned. Susan Sontag speaks eloquently of the risks involved in using illness as a metaphor—whether romantically celebrating tuberculosis as a disease of sensitive artists in the nineteenth century or associating cancer with obscene hopelessness today.[4]

I want to shun every abstraction in presuming to find deep, instructive "meaning" in my mother's death. But I must also recognize and honor the fact that she and I both learned something about love—through the long and torturous experience of her dying—in a way we'd never known before.

"On each of my dyings shed your light and your love," Saint Ignatius Loyola prayed.[5] There are dyings to which one is drawn throughout his life, little dyings rooted in the exercise of abandonment or "indifference." Maybe they prepare us, in their own way, for a love that's never guaranteed. One finds it, if at all, in a final act of relinquishment—beyond all experience, beyond anything yet known.

Transformation at
Upper Moss Creek

Death does not extinguish the light. It puts out the lamp because the dawn has come. —Rabindranath Tagore

This purgative and loving knowledge or divine light we are speaking of has the same effect on a soul that fire has on a log of wood. . . . By heating and enkindling it from without, the fire transforms the wood into itself and makes it as beautiful as it is itself. —John of the Cross[1]

Upper Moss Creek can't be found on any of the usual maps. At the end of an almost impassable road in the Ozark wilderness, hidden among scrub oaks and thickly grown sycamore brush, it seems to resist entry. But I go there from time to time to be healed. My son and I love backpacking up and down that creek. On a warm spring day, we leave our clothes on the rocks and swim in its deeper pools. We've never seen another human being on our trips there. I first camped in its valley one winter, years ago, with an old friend—a grizzled packer and his dog, Finnbar. The dog and my friend's stories of pack trips up the Wind River Range of Wyoming were all that kept me from freezing to death that night. I wasn't conditioned yet to Upper Moss Creek and the sometimes harsh lessons it has to teach.

This creek near the Irish Wilderness of southern Missouri has become sacred to me in ways I never expected. I was there in late winter a few weeks before my mother's death. With things dying all around me at the time, I needed the place more than ever. Two people I loved were making their final joust with cancer. One was my mother, very near the end now. Her body still fought for life, though she was already gone, floating down creeks of her own, back near Poughkeepsie, New York, where she'd grown up as a child along the Hudson River eighty years before. The other person was my friend, a graduate student, also filled with cancer and close to death, grieving over a husband and small child she couldn't imagine leaving behind. In the first case, death was painful but also welcome; in the second, it seemed only painful and obscene. So I went down the creek to let things settle, to listen to the land, to grieve.

Upper Moss Creek is good for that. In the tenth chapter of II Esdras, there's a poignant story about the earth embracing the acute grief of the mothers and those who mourn with them. A woman whose child has died goes out into the dark night to a remote field and pours out her grief, determined to stay there until she dies. The prophet Esdras speaks to her in the depth of her pain, telling her to "ask the earth" what pain is all about. No mother grieves like that mother, says Esdras. The earth weeps for every creature to whom she's given birth, for every creature who returns again to her in death. One doesn't know grief until one knows the depth of the Earth Mother's pain.

This is a strange comfort the prophet offers the woman. Go to the earth, he says, and let your grief be swallowed up in her grief (II Esd. 10:9–11).[2] It was a truth I recognized as I walked the old logging road toward Upper Moss Creek that morning.

Several days before my trip, a late winter storm had dropped twelve inches of snow into the deep gorge through which Upper Moss Creek flows. Warm temperatures and rain followed, filling the creek with the runoff of snow-melt. A torrent of water ten feet deep had come rushing down the gorge toward the St. François River downstream. I walked under debris still lodged in the branches of trees along the creek bank, trying to imagine what it must have been like at the height of the maelstrom.

I don't know why the thought of wild, rushing water gave such comfort on that untroubled winter day. Gary Snyder says nature heals in the same sort of way that dreams and mythic symbols do. "In the shaman's world, wilderness and the unconscious become analogous; he who knows and is at ease in one, will be at home in the other."[3] It was easy enough to feel at home in the unseasonable warmth of that March morning—the sun resting on the pink rhyolite stone of the shut-ins, red-tailed hawks drifting on shifting air currents high above. The debris over my head could speak vaguely to the unresolved torrent of grief within, yet hold it safely beyond the threat of consciousness.

I walked in that slow, ambiguous silence for a mile or more downstream before choosing a place to set up camp. Beside a short stretch of cascading falls, I lay in the sun on a large flat rock, thinking how this place of quiet restfulness must have been a place of chaos and death only a few days earlier. A spider with the same idea was stretched out on a rock nearby, taking delight, it seemed, in the unexpected warmth of the midday sun. Did it need to do that, I wondered? Is sunlight somehow necessary for vitamin production or the activation of internal spider enzymes? Or, perhaps, did the creature, as Jonathan Edwards once observed, take sheer pleasure, as I did, in pausing from its work to bask in the light of a late-morning sun?[4] Whatever its purposes, I had company. For an hour, more or less, we reverenced the light together.

Telling Stories by Firelight

I spent the rest of the day doing nothing—appraising ironwood trees, surveying the shape of passing clouds, taking time to renew my acquaintance with sunlight and running water. Later that evening, after the sun had set and I'd eaten supper, I sat beside a small campfire, noticing a pine tree—about two and a half feet tall—across the fire from me. I hadn't seen it before.

Not usually accustomed to talking to trees, I said hello, feeling a sense of commonality around the fire together. As we sat there, the young tree, almost like a child, seemed to be asking for a story. Fires have a way of suggesting such things. So I told it one. It was a long story, and at times I had to stop to explain things in a way that trees would understand. Storytellers, after all, must adjust their tales to their listeners.

With night coming on, I added another stick to the fire. The wood blazed up, and I suddenly noticed three or four other small pines gathered around us. I could have sworn they hadn't been there earlier when I'd set up camp. I suspect they had moved in closer to be able to hear better. So I continued telling all of them this tale of transformation, a sacred story from the Lakota Sioux about dying and returning to the earth. I told it patiently to these young trees, not realizing at the time the mystery into which I myself was being drawn.

As a storyteller, I don't ever remember listeners as attentive as the ones I had that night. The trees were mesmerized by the tale; I could tell. This was the first time they'd ever heard a story. Few people, if any, venture very far into that wilderness; and the ones that do aren't likely to tell stories to trees. Besides, the truth of the story was something they already knew. These trees understood intimately the reality of death and transformation. They'd just survived a flash flood of raging water. They were growing out of the rotted logs of old pines along the creek bank. Yet even this didn't explain the intensity with which they seemed to be listening to the tale. Something deeper still was drawing them into its mystery as we sat together around the fire.

I suddenly realized what it was—these young trees growing in a remote wilderness area had never before seen flames leaping in the air like fireflies in liquid motion. Over the three or four years of their lives, they'd never witnessed a forest fire. Nor was it likely anyone had ever built a campfire nearby. They were listening to a story of death, with both fascination and terror, as they watched wood burn.

They had never imagined the stuff-of-their-own-being turned into the light and beauty they saw before them, never dreamed of wood disappearing so quickly into a light gray ash. Hearing the story as *they* heard it, I found a whole new way of looking at my mother's dying, as well as my own way of living. The common fear of death that I'd shared with these trees in the back country of Missouri was absorbed into their own wonder at the mystery of transformation. I knew then why I'd been brought there.

Buddhist teachers say that to discover God as "child," recognizing the deep vulnerability and wonder that lies at the heart of the Holy, is one of the highest levels of spiritual encounter. I grasped something of this truth as the coals burned low and the small trees receded back into the shadows that night on Upper Moss Creek.

I don't ever remember sleeping any better or feeling any safer than I did that night alone in the woods. I'd been welcomed. I'd become family. The young trees and I, along with their elders, more distant and still, had been gathered in community around a small fire, sharing a truth that somehow touched us all. The next morning I took a few hours to walk farther down the creek, stopping often, being content to sit for long spells in silence. The thought occurred to me that all the place really needed (if it needed anything at all) was an old man, low in impact on the land and high in the capacity to take delight.

I walked that morning like God in the Garden of Eden, knowing I'd been able to give something back to the place in the process of "telling" the night before. The act of speaking by the fire had been a powerful one. I'd spoken to and for the trees. They'd listened in wonder, hearing a story for the first time in their lives. And I, too, by entering into their hearing of it, had heard its truth more deeply than ever before. That morning I walked as an honored being, welcomed, taking joy in every velvety cluster of green moss, every patch of white lichens tipped in red. The trees might have marveled at my ability to move so easily among them. Maybe they also pitied me for my lack of rootedness. But I walked in their midst with a respect and love I'd never before known in the wilds.

There's a time in every storyteller's life when a threshold is crossed—when he receives a sense of calling, a quiet certainty about one's vocation. Prior to this time he may have called himself a story-collector, a great lover of tales, a person even addicted to narrative, but he'd always shrunk from calling himself a Story-teller. This was because he'd recognized the gift of telling as ultimately the gift of the shaman, the magician and healer, a gift that's never claimed, but only and always "conferred." For years I've told stories in teaching and, from time to time, at storytelling festivals and conferences. But this experience of being heard by a handful of pine trees in an Ozark wilderness finally pushed me over the edge, requiring that I acknowledge—humbly, and with amazement—that I, too, am storyteller. A storyteller is one who watches the stuff-of-his-own-being transformed into wonder through a shared process of listening and dying.

The Deep Mystery of Death

A few weeks after I returned from this trip to Upper Moss Creek, the phone rang at 1:30 in the morning. I was told my mother had just died in her sleep at the nursing home where she'd lived for the last three years. I'd been waiting a long time for that call, but it still came as a shock. I went down alone in the middle of the night to sit by her bed until the car came from the funeral home for her body. It was very quiet that late at night, sitting alone with my mother—like sitting beside a fire that had been burning low for a long time. I felt grief . . . and a fleeting sense of relief. I thought of my friend, the graduate student, who still struggled painfully to live. The deep mystery of death seemed almost right in one respect, yet cruel and unfair in another. I hurt too much at the time to be able to understand any part of it.

I knew only that somewhere along Upper Moss Creek that night a light wind stirred among a few small pine trees. Memory stirred, too, in the sound of water rushing over rocks. What almost seemed like an answer came rumbling back over the long pitch-dark landscape of the Missouri Ozarks, drifting on the night air into the lonely, third-floor room of a nursing home in Saint Louis.

Looking back now, I can see—or sometimes think I can see—that this mystery, like every other, converges finally in the sacredness of place and time. It first took shape in a story at Upper Moss Creek. Within a few weeks it became hauntingly real at the bedside of a dead mother. And then, a week later in early spring, it took yet another twist, disrupting my pain in a turn I still can't fully comprehend. Easter . . . came. Somehow it seemed that resurrection should have made more sense to me than it did at the time. Maybe it will yet. But for now, it's comfort enough that several small pine trees along a distant creek have sufficient wonder to understand.

· 6 ·

Desert Catechesis

The Landscape and Theology of Early Christian Monasticism

Abba Elias was famous for having spent seventy years in the terrible desert of Antinoe. No description can do justice to that rugged desert in the mountain where [he] had his hermitage, never coming down to the inhabited region. The path which one took to go to him was so narrow that those who pressed on could only just follow its track with rough crags towering on either side. —*Historia Monachorum*[1]

A monk out of the desert, said Anthony of Egypt, is like a fish out of water.[2] Early Christian monasticism was so inextricably tied to a particular geographic terrain that the connection between the monk and the desert was never questioned. The choice of vocation and the choice of landscape were almost always one.[3] Jerome accepted this as a given when he described the habitat of the desert fathers and mothers at Wadi Natrun on the borders of the Libyan Desert in Egypt.

> The place is reached by no path, nor is the track shown by any landmarks on earth, but one journeys by the signs and courses of the stars. Water is hard to find. Here abide men perfect in holiness (for so terrible a place can be endured by none save those of absolute resolve and supreme constancy). . . . To this spot they withdraw themselves: for the desert is vast, and the cells are sundered from one another by so wide a space that none is in sight of his neighbour, nor can any voice be heard. One by one they abide in their cells, a mighty silence and a great quiet among them.[4]

A fierce landscape was assumed to be the proper abode of people committed to an austere vocation.

One has to be careful in suggesting a natural love of wildness and wild terrain on the part of the early desert Christians. The Greek patristic view of nature generally preferred the ordered beauty of a "middle landscape," land that had been worked by human hands. Wilderness was more often an object of fear and distrust.[5] Yet the desert, for negative as well as positive reasons, remained the landscape of choice for much of early Christian asceticism. The desert environment played a major role in shaping the character of monastic life.

Peter Brown observes that monasticism in Syria and Egypt assumed different forms because of variations in the desert terrain they occupied. In Egypt one found "true desert," with a rainfall of only 1.1 inches per year. Sheer survival in such a hostile environment required structure, conformity, and adherence to routine. By contrast, in the rugged, mountainous terrain of Syria, milder and less demanding than the Egyptian desert, the ascetic life would be characterized by greater individuality, freedom, the embrace of wildness. Less energy had to be absorbed in the onerous task of staying alive. Hence, Syria was "notoriously the Wild and Woolly West" of early Christian asceticism.[6]

A preference for wild, uneven terrain could be found from time to time, however, even beyond Syria. Gregory of Nazianzus wrote to his friend Basil the Great in 361, complaining in jest about his choice of a site for a desert community in Cappadocia. Basil had praised the place for its remote and beautiful location in a deep canyon, but Gregory's response was probably closer to the truth.

> Everything that is not rock is ravine, everything that is not ravine is brambles, and all that are not brambles are overhanging cliffs. The path climbs up in overhang and is precipitous on all sides; it besets the spirits of the travelers and forces them into acrobatics for their own safety.[7]

The choice of landscape, however perceived, was a deliberate one. While it may appear recklessly wild, even dangerous, to outsiders, for this very reason it fed the spirits of those who had chosen the desert way. Even Basil admitted that it was "a worthy place of exile."

The purpose of this chapter is to examine the reasons for choosing the desert as a favored landscape in the history of early Christian monasticism and to explore the theology of desert experience growing out of that geographical choice. What were the factors involved in choosing a site for a desert monastery? And how did an apophatic theology of abandonment and renunciation, rich in sociopolitical as well as spiritual implications, emerge from such a choice?

Following Peter Brown's broad survey of the desert fathers, a wide swath of early desert asceticism will be considered here, from the eremitic practice of Anthony in third-century Egypt to the highly structured cenobitic life of John Climacus at Mount Sinai in the seventh century.[8] In an impressionistic way, the chapter tries to interweave the insights of cultural geography with patristic scholarship, asking how the experience of desert Christians can be illuminated in new ways by reference to their environment.[9] As an interdisciplinary effort, the chapter attempts to be more exploratory and suggestive than definitive. It seeks to stretch the imagination, encouraging the reader to bring new questions of place and environment to the texts and experience of the early desert Christians. Hopefully, their compelling and rigorous theology can be better appreciated in the process.

Hazard, Prospect, and Refuge in a Desert Landscape

The desert is, to human life, an environment characterized by threat and hazard.[10] It gives no quarter. This was why Edward Abbey loved it so much, because of its utter indifference to human concerns. The desert, whether in the Middle East or the American southwest, readily kills—by its lack of water or the sudden flash floods that fill its arroyos and wadis with the runoff of rare rainfall.

The Wadi Watir, emptying into the Red Sea at Nuweiba, is a huge, dry canyon, with tributaries that drain the western slope of the whole Sinai peninsula. Driving by Land Rover through its miles of dry expanse, one cannot imagine it even being wet. But a few years ago a tour bus with forty people was caught there by rushing torrents of brown water swept down from a rainstorm over twenty miles away. No one survived. The desert is like that. Walking through sandstone slot canyons, where erosion has worn deep and narrow channels into the rock, one sometimes notices a tangle of mud-caked logs wedged between the walls fifty feet overhead.[11] To be caught there, against an angry wall of rushing water, would mean instant death. One moves nervously, with an eye to the gathering of distant clouds, recognizing this as a landscape where wildness rules.

What life there is in the desert is often as bizarre and deadly as the fierce terrain on which it persists. Black and yellow scorpions, bearded vultures, and leopards of the Judean Desert can still be found in the Negev. The caper bush takes root by eating its way into the side of a cliff, secreting a rock-dissolving acid from its roothairs. The acacia tree, from which the Ark of the Covenant was made, is one of the few trees able to thrive in the desert, only because it can sink its roots some hundred feet into the soil. There is an eerie, grotesque quality to the tenacity of desert life. "If one picks up a lizard, it may bleed from the eyes. The whole place seems a bad dream," writes Peter Wild.[12]

Why do people choose to live in such a landscape—poised, as it is, on the edge of nothingness? "Something about the desert inclines all living things to harshness and acerbity," says Ed Abbey.[13] It touches us at our extremities. The desert fathers and mothers chose their barren locale because its values matched their own. They, too, opted to thrive on the boundary where life and death meet, living as simply as possible, with as few words as necessary, separated from the fragile anxieties of the world they had left behind.

Peter Brown has shown how the holy man in late antiquity functioned on the edges of society, serving as mediator of conflict in a Greco-Roman world where classical institutions had been seriously eroded. High taxation, economic insecurity, and friction among local farmers led people increasingly to look to the desert monk for the kind of evenhanded guidance only possible from one wholly disengaged from the world. In a tension-filled society, the ascetic had pulled up stakes and cleared out for the wild country. This very act of radical disengagement or *anachōresis* put him or her in a place of being "dead" to human motivation and rancor, able to adjudicate disputes and offer insights with a clarity found no where else.[14]

The desert provided the necessary platform from which the holy man or woman could objectively assess and mediate tensions emerging in the world from which they had withdrawn. The selection of a site, therefore, had to be far enough from society in order to assure this objectivity, yet close enough to allow access for those seeking counsel. While the proximity of water, the capacity of the soil to support small gardens, and the presence of landforms offering protection from predators were significant, they were no more important than the capacity of the monastery site to symbolize this combination of distance and perceptiveness that the ascetic had to offer. This may suggest an answer to the question of why early Christian monasteries in the Judean Desert were so often built into the tall cliffs of deep ravines, making access difficult while offering a long vista of the surrounding terrain.

British geographer Jay Appleton argues for the attraction of places like this on the basis of his prospect-refuge theory of landscape preference. He says the aesthetic pleasure one takes in a particular environment is often rooted in basic biological needs. Harking back to our paleolithic experience as hunter and hunted, we have a primitive human desire to be situated in a place where we can "see without being seen." Such a site offers both prospect and refuge—an unimpeded opportunity to see, as well as ample opportunity to hide.[15] We naturally delight in tree houses, caves on a high bluff, a room with a view. To seclude oneself in a small, protected place, opening out onto a sweeping panorama of the surrounding area, is a pleasure rooted in the experience of the species.[16]

If, with this in mind, one considers the spatial needs of the ascetic hero in the world of late antiquity, the choice of monastery site begins to make perfect sense. The monk had to be totally separated from society, had to be the "stranger" *par excellence*. Having no place in contemporary culture was crucial to his effectivness. Refuge in the desert, therefore, was mandatory. Yet just as important was an angle from which the world now abandoned could also be viewed in broad perspective. Prospect, too, was required.

One readily discerns this principle at work in the placement of early Christian monasteries in the Judean Desert. The monastery of Mar Sabas is built on the edge of a cliff in the Kidron Valley, the cells of Choziba in the Wadi Qelt seem to hang between earth and sky, the coenobium of Theoctistus lies in "a steep gully in the depths of the Judean Desert."[17] Chariton, the father of Palestinian monasticism, dwelt five miles southeast of Bethlehem in a "hanging cave," accessible only by ladder or rope. In each case the choice of geographical site provided refuge as well as prospect. It offered a way of separating oneself from the surrounding world while gaining a broader perspective on it. Israeli archaeologist Yizhar Hirschfeld confirms that "most monastery sites in the Judean Desert . . . are located in cliff areas or at the tops of high hills."[18]

Open, hazardous terrain has always attracted people for multiple reasons, of course. In the eighteenth century Edmund Burke attributed its appeal to the human fascination with the "sublime." This he defined as an experience of terror entertained within a broader context of safety—something not unlike Rudolf Otto's idea of the Holy, its *mysterium tremendum* qualified by a sense of irresistible *fascinans*. "Whatever is fitted in any sort to excite the ideas of pain, and danger, that is to say, whatever is in any sort terrible . . . is a source of the *sublime;* that is, it is productive of the strongest emotion which the mind is capable of feeling."[19]

Experiencing the terror of the desert under the controlled conditions of monastic life—being close to danger, but not too close—offered early Christian ascetics an ideal setting for reflecting on the sinner's relationship to a God of infinite majesty. The harsh landscape was interpreted within a hermeneutical context of fear tempered by grace. Burke himself was sensitive to how desert landscapes could be read in such a way, arguing that "'beetling cliffs,' chasms, precipices of all sorts, are among the hallmarks of the Sublime."[20] In choosing the precipitous location of his monastery at Annisi in Pontus, for example, Basil the Great spoke of the sublime pleasure he took in gazing on the mountain's impassable wall, which isolated the cloister on either side by deep ravines.[21]

Refuge, prospect, and the hazardous dimension of the sublime may all have been factors in the selection of early Christian monastery sites. These were often locations of harsh and stunning beauty, captivating the imagination by the awesome work of wind and water erosion. They provided many examples of what Appleton refers to as deflected vistas and secondary vantage points offering the promise of indirect prospect.[22] Deflected vistas are able to draw the viewer into a sense of retreating distance, toward a mystery not yet seen. The bending curve of a wadi carries the eye along the smooth wall of its canyon toward yet another undivulged view, not yet in sight. Similarly, secondary vantage points are tall buttes or towering rocks in the distance, from which an even grander panoramic view of the surrounding terrain can be imagined. They irresistibly draw the eye and the mind of the viewer to what lies beyond. A landscape setting, rich in such features, is understandably compelling to the religious imagination.

While Egyptian, Syrian, and Palestinian monasticism (as well as geography) varied tremendously in the world of late antiquity, the placement of early desert monasteries was often influenced by principles such as these. Furthermore, this geographical concept of prospect and refuge found a parallel in the distinctive theology of the desert fathers and mothers.

Reading from the Land a Desert Theology of Death and Rebirth

The power that the ascetic wielded from his or her position on the edge of the wilderness was rooted in a theology of death and rebirth that desert monks read in part from the landscape itself. Their reputation rested on their intimate relationship to God gained through a rigorous renunciation of the world (and their own wills), to the point of having died and been reborn to a new identity in the desert waste.

Anthony, the father of Egyptian monasticism, was once asked how he thought he could live a devout life in the wilds, far from access to holy books. Motioning to the desert itself, he simply answered, "My book is the nature of created things; whenever I want to read the Word of God, it is always there before me."[23] Knowing the physical and the spiritual to be profoundly interwoven, he recognized the desert as his most important teacher.

From the slim text of a desert landscape, he and others like him read a theology of death and resurrection that echoed the refuge-prospect character of their surroundings. The desert was an ideal place for practicing withdrawal from the world (learning to die to its values), and subsequently coming to reevaluate it from a reflective distance (offering insight to those who came seeking help).[24]

The holy man's ability to provide clear, decisive judgments to those who sought him out depended upon his having died already to the anxious thoughts and tensions of the village life they brought with them. To learn this detachment, the desert monks placed themselves under a stringent discipline aimed at destroying all self-illusion and deception. They committed themselves in radical honesty to one of their elders, knowing that nothing was more conducive to personal authenticity than "to sit in subjection to the command of a spiritual father and renounce all their own desires."[25] What the hard-nosed spiritual director would not demand, the desert landscape would.

These "athletes of God" never tired of emphasizing the fact that the desert is, preeminently, a place to die. Anyone retreating to an Egyptian or Judean monastery, hoping to escape the tensions of city life, found little comfort among the likes of an Anthony or Sabas. The desert offered no private therapeutic place for solace and rejuvenation.[26] One was as likely to be carried out feet first as to be restored unchanged to the life one had left. This desert wasteland was "a heap of broken images, where the sun beats, / And the dead tree gives no shelter."[27]

John Climacus advised his novices in the Monastery of Saint Catherine at Mount Sinai to "let the monastery be for you a tomb before the tomb"—a way of dying to the compulsiveness of the ego prior to one's physical death.[28] Saint Anthony of Egypt had literally followed this rule, initiating his life in the desert by entering a sandstone tomb where he slept among the bones of the dead. There he was assaulted by demons that threatened the very foundation of his being.[29] His deepest fears of death were exposed in the desert landscape, suggesting the loss of everything on which his life depended.

Ironically, then, the desert served as a welcoming "refuge" from the self because of the terror of its threatening indifference. The desert constituted a "safe place" to the extent that in its abyss one confronted all the insecurity and powerlessness prerequisite to faith. The desert, in short, became a tomb, a place for the death of the self, for participation in the white martyrdom of the crucifixion of Christ.[30] Its refuge was no refuge at all, only a cleft in the rock from which one awaited God in the abandonment of terror-stricken despair. If the desiccated landscape offered access to the holy, it never did it directly, as if God were found in the mystery of every rocky crag. Access to the holy came only indirectly, through silence, the emptiness of space, and the exacting direction of the spiritual master.

Through this lengthy process of submission—to the mentor and to the desert itself as teacher—the monk gradually came to an abandonment of his will, to a new life in the "emptiness" of Christ. Only then could he recognize the desert as fertile, alive with new possibilities. Only then could he discover an untried freedom, independent of the social and psychological supports of identity still operative in the villages nearby. This freedom gave evidence of the ascetic's power as holy man or woman, legitimating his or her position in the eyes of those who came seeking counsel. The desert monk could arbitrate conflicts over property or land, for example, precisely because he cared so little about what did or did not belong to him. Numerous stories were told of monks who discovered thieves robbing their desert cells, only to help them in loading the donkey with whatever goods they could pack or to run after them on finding something potentially useful they had left behind.[31]

Desert monasticism remained closely connected to the society from which it had separated. The desert Christians were not driven by a simplistic *fuga mundi,* hating the world from which they had fled. Edward Gibbon's caricature of Saint Anthony (a "hideous . . . maniac, without knowledge, without patriotism, without natural affection") was absurd.[32] The desert monks were hardly naive despisers of culture. What they fled with greatest fear was not the external world, but the world they carried inside themselves: an ego-centeredness needing constant approval, driven by compulsive behavior, frantic in its effort to attend to a self-image that always required mending.

The secularity most renounced by desert monks was the tendency they found within themselves to seek the praise of others, being dependent for their well-being on the favorable responses of their milieu.[33] They could exercise their role in a world hungry for spiritual direction only to the extent that they were able to tame their own need for approbation and status.

Ultimately, they chose to live in a desert habitat because they knew how well it teaches, without even trying, the importance of being emptied, the spiritual lessons of kenosis. American naturalist Sigurd Olson said that years of walking through wild country had taught him a great deal about traveling light. Backpackers learn, sometimes the hard way, that simplicity is always a question of knowing what to leave behind. This is a desert truth, translatable to the rest of one's life as well. The spiritual path, as Meister Eckhart observed, has more to do with subtraction than with addition. It is not so much a matter of adding all the active virtues to one's practice of living as of relinquishing everything that can possibly be abandoned. How much can you leave behind? That is the desert's question.

The Desert as a Teacher of Renunciation and Abandonment

One can distinguish three lessons in spiritual renunciation which the desert monks read from (and into) the land on which they lived. A desert vocation involved a dying to language, a dying to oneself, and a dying to one's neighbor. The experience of *eremos*, the Greek word for "desert" from which the word "hermit" also derives, was an experience of desolation, a breakdown of traditional structures thought basic to human life. Linguistic patterns, the identity of the ego, and the expectations of society at large were all subject to review in a desert setting.

The abbas and ammas of the desert spoke often in parable, using as few words as possible, trying always to reach beyond mere signs to the experience of language as creative event. An old man at Scete once said, "The prophets wrote books. Our fathers came after them, and worked much at them, and then their successors memorized them. But this generation has come, and it copies them on papyrus and parchment and leaves them unused on the window-ledge."[34]

The language of the desert was marked by an austere economy, rooted in an oral tradition that valued the concise, the immediate, and the provocative.[35] "Give us a word, Father" was the formula generally used to introduce the *apophthegmata* or "sayings" of the desert monks. Often the response was little more than a single word, a teaching rich in ambiguity and suggestiveness, serving to disturb as frequently as to inspire.

Some of the sayings were able to function like *koans* in the tradition of Zen Buddhism, brief riddles or stories that assaulted the structures of language and meaning, inviting breakthrough to an altogether new way of thinking.[36] "Who will prefer the jingle of jade pendants if once he has heard stone growing in a cliff?" Lao-tzu's compelling question is echoed in the desert thinking of early Christian monks, calling their students (and maybe us as well) to silence, renunciation, and the holy indifference of *apatheia*.

Imagine this exchange in the desert silence. You find yourself alone in a vast and empty terrain, standing before a naked wall of red-hued rock rising hundreds of feet above the canyon floor. Maybe it is the huge stone cliff seen from the chapel windows at Christ in the Desert Monastery in northern New Mexico. The stone never moves as you sit there facing it, but after a while it poses a question. How did the stone face of the canyon cliff change on the day of your divorce, the day your father or mother died, the day you came to admit your dependency on alcohol or drugs?

Surely, it would seem, the whole world must have fallen apart when *your* world collapsed! But the realization dawns (if you stay there long enough, without running) that the stone cliff never changed at all. It remained entirely unmoved. Something continued constant and unbroken throughout the utter depth of your pain. Something stayed there, in all of its majesty . . . for you . . . present, waiting, and still. The landscape's silent immensity—and the God to whom it points—is able to absorb all the grief one can give it.

This is the riddle the desert suggests, inevitably leading those within it to silence. Living in the desert's continual reminder of death and the God met beyond that final mystery, these early monks necessarily learned the value of being still. "The man who is seriously concerned about death reduces the amount of what he has to say, and . . . runs from talkativeness as from a fire."[37]

This sparcity of language had as its chief goal the death of the self, the obsessive ego that thrives in loquacious artificiality. John Climacus spoke of it as "that cur sniffing around the meat market and revelling in the uproar."[38] Renunciation of the self was the second and perhaps central focus of *ascesis,* the spiritual discipline of desert monasticism. This, far more than any mean contempt for society, was what drew people into the wilderness. In the words of Thomas Merton, "What the Fathers sought most of all was their own true self, in Christ. And in order to do this, they had to reject completely the false, formal self, fabricated under social compulsion in 'the world.'"[39]

They knew that only the most unrelenting discipline, echoing the desert's harshness, could deal with the subtle deceptions of the ego. The grand indifference of limestone crags and wormwood served as an effective antidote to all delusions of self-importance. The ancient desert had persisted for eons prior to their coming and would continue long after their death.

The desert remained altogether unmoved by the fact that they had even existed. Desert Christians thrived on the unsolicitous indifference of their environment. As the abbot of Saint Catherine's Monastery put it, "a snake can shed its old skin only if it crawls into a tight hole."[40] There in the desert, one inescapably confronted the threat of nothingness, the loss of all one's activities, distractions, evasions, the exchangeable personas that allow one to retain the semblance of a reputation without confronting one's sin. There in the desert they knew the very scaffolding of their lives to be wholly dismantled.

Games were called for what they were. Utter honesty was demanded by unrelenting spiritual directors, hard as the rock beyond the cloister where they prayed. The unbending John Climacus, for example, insisted on laying bare the pretenses of people in the religious life. He spoke of those who bless silence but cannot stop talking about it; those who fast without drawing attention to themselves but then take pride in such remarkable modesty; those who weep over death and then, with tears still in their eyes, rush off to dinner.[41] Amma Syncletica refused to let anyone deceive herself by imagining that retreat to a desert monastery meant the guarantee of freedom from the world. The hardest world to leave, she knew, is the one within the heart.[42]

In the desert Christians' understanding of renunciation, dying to oneself also meant a dying to one's neighbor. They knew how easy it was to invest oneself in what other people think, measuring oneself by the accomplishments of others, remaining enmeshed in a hopeless pattern of jealousy, subservience, manipulation, and resentment. "To die to one's neighbor is this," said Abba Moses the Black, "to bear your own faults and not to pay attention to anyone else wondering whether they are good or bad."[43] Comparing oneself to others, being concerned about their approval or disapproval, was entirely foreign to the desert way. Watching the sweep of wind over desert sand inevitably gave one practice in studied indifference.

The story is told, in the *apophthegmata,* about a brother who came to Macarius the Egyptian, asking the great abbot of the monastery at Scete how to become holy. The older monk told him to go to the cemetery nearby and to abuse the dead, yelling at them for all he was worth, even throwing stones. The young man thought this strange, but did as he was told and then returned to his teacher. "What did they say to you?" Macarius asked. "Nothing," the brother replied. "Then go back again tomorrow and praise them," answered the abbot, "calling them apostles, saints, and righteous men. Think of every compliment you can."

The young man once more did as he was told, then returned to the cloister, where Macarius asked, "What did they say this time?" "They still didn't answer a word," replied the brother. "Ah, they must, indeed, be holy people," said Abba Macarius. "You insulted them and they did not reply. You praised them and they did not speak. Go and do likewise, my friend, taking no account of either the scorn of men or their praises."[44] This is what it means to learn the dying to neighbor that the desert teaches.

The desert fathers and mothers evince an extraordinary sensitivity to the machinations of the human ego. They knew the futility of "impression management," the effort to nurture one's identity as a reputation in the minds of others. Theirs was an ungullible realism, rooted in an awareness of human sin, that reached beyond the artifice of the false self to an affirmation of new identity and freedom in Christ. Having squarely faced the terrors of death, only then were they free to live in hope, a hope that lay on the other side of abandonment.

Desert Freedom and Affirmation

There are three distinctive dimensions of this hope, lending the desert monks an entirely new prospect on the world they had renounced. They delineate a new way of being human radically in contrast to the values of society at large, in the fourth century as well as today. They include the joyous freedom of the desert eccentric, the power of compassion as the fruit of indifference, and a degree of ecological sensitivity emerging from closeness to the land. These would become definitive marks of the desert Christian, modeling an earthy freedom and joy and love of justice seldom discovered in the history of spirituality.

The Freedom of the Desert Eccentric

Francis de Sales once remarked that "a sad saint is a sorry sort of saint," under-standing playfulness to be an intrinsic dimension of the holy life. He would have found much in which to delight in the playful eccentricity of the early desert monks. Among them the Pauline tradition of the holy fool was fully developed (see I Cor. 2:6–13; 4:10).[45] These were men and women delivered from the bond-age of having to take themselves too seriously. Unlike ourselves, they were not trapped on what Hugo Rahner has described as "the hopelessly wrong road of idiotic earnestness."[46] A sense of earthy ordinariness and light, self-effacing hu-mor pervades many of the stories of the desert mothers and fathers.

They found it easy to laugh at themselves. This is especially apparent in the way they dealt with "spiritual groupies," those people coming into the desert as sightseers in holiness, looking for reputed celebrities in the religious life. Such people were invariably disappointed. Hoping to find examples of extraordinary virtue, they were confounded by ordinariness more often than not.

A magistrate once came into the desert looking for Abba Moses, asking the first person he met where he could find this prodigiously devout human being. The man told him, "Don't waste your time. Abba Moses is a heretic and a fraud. He's not any of the things people say that he is." The magistrate marched back to the city with his newfound truth, eager to despoil the reputation of the alleged holy man. Someone asked him who it was he had talked to in the desert waste, inquiring if by any chance it had been a tall black man. "Well, . . . yes," answered the magistrate. "Ah," the person told him, "that was Abba Moses himself. You met the saint at his best. He'd never make anything of his own sanctity."[47]

Similarly, Abba Macarius never responded to those who spoke to him in rev-erent tones of praise and respect. But he always listened intently to anyone who talked harshly, rebuking him for his early days in the desert when he stole niter and resold it to the other camel drivers.[48] Abba Simon, when warned that ad-mirers were coming into the desert to seek his blessing, would invariably sit in front of his cell, stuffing himself with bread and cheese, or climb a nearby palm tree, polishing its branches for all he was worth. The visitors would then look down with disdain on the glutton gorging himself with food, or gaze up at the fool hanging unceremoniously from the tree, and wonder where the great Abba Simon had gone.[49]

There is a refreshing, ludic quality to the lives of the early desert Christians. They anticipated the dictum of Thomas Aquinas that "unmitigated seriousness betokens a lack of virtue."[50] The stories told of Saint Menas in the western Egyp-tian desert even border on the risqué. When a woman unable to speak and a crippled man came separately to the desert saint, asking for healing, he told the disabled man to crawl into bed that night with the speechless woman. "Don't be afraid, "he said, "but fasten your lips to the dumb woman's. Then get into bed with her and you will be cured." Bewildered by such a highly unusual command, the paralytic nonetheless did as he was told. Dragging himself to the woman's bed that night, he bent down and fastened his mouth to hers. When he did so, she screamed at the top of her voice and he, fearing he would be caught, ran away in terror, both of them—in the process—being miraculously cured of their ailments.[51]

The story smacks too much of bedouin humor to be historically authentic, but it speaks nonetheless to something important. A frank and earthbound realism often marked the asceticism of the desert Christians, keen observers of human nature that they were. Their playful disregard for the proprieties of society grew directly out of their desert experience of *apophasis* and loss.[52] Having taken "refuge" in the wilderness, as a place occasioning the death of the self, they gained an entirely new "prospect" on the world they left behind. Only those having sustained the terrors of the cross can understand the raucous laughter of resurrection. Only the ones who have died completely to the expectations of the world are free to be truly eccentric, off-center by every standard of the majority.

The monks gave high value to the desert because of the freedom it offered. One of the brothers tried to console Abba Sisoes, old and in poor health, grieving at no longer being able to live in the wilds. "Abba, why do you grieve? What would you do in the desert, now that you are old?" The old man answered, with sorrow in his voice, "What are you saying to me, Ammoun? Was not the mere liberty of my soul enough for me in the desert?"[53] In the place where he had learned to die, he had learned also to live. That was why he loved it. It is a central paradox of desert experience that only that which dies can live again. The fundamental rule of the divine game is this: "He who loses, wins."[54] The carefree playfulness and freedom of God are mysteries entered only on the far side of darkness and death.

The Power of Compassion as the Fruit of Indifference

A second dimension of the new life discovered in and through the desert experience of loss is an entirely new possibility for compassion and justice. The desert monks learned that love thrives on the distance made possible by solitude. The same distance from enmeshment with others that gives rise to the laughter of freedom can also make possible a new compassion-as-justice. Only those who have died to others can be of service to them. Only when we have ceased to need people—desperately, neurotically need them—are we concretely able to love. This was how Peter Brown interpreted the dynamic freedom of the holy man in the fourth and fifth centuries. "His powers and his prestige came from acting out, heroically, before a society enmeshed in oppressive obligations and abrasive relationships, the role of the utterly self-dependent, autarkic man."[55]

The discipline of solitude gave the monastic desert dwellers an altogether new center from which to view the world. They were no longer centered out there in the endless expectations of others, but inside the hidden desert of the heart, in God's presence found in the silence of one's cell. Drawing on the wellsprings of holy indifference, they no longer needed others to manufacture a sense of inner well-being, to secure an identity. Relationships did not have to be marked by manipulation and neurotic need. Genuine love is ultimately impossible apart from such indifference. Without it, the sinful self remains *incurvatus se,* as Luther insisted, curved in upon itself in hopeless self-preoccupation. Only the solitary, therefore, can truly care for all the right reasons, because he or she has ceased to care for all the wrong reasons.

Abba Pambo spoke of this rock-hard indifference as the chief goal of monastic discipline. "A man who lives with a companion ought to be like a stone pillar," he said, "hurt him, and he does not get angry, praise him, and he is not puffed up."[56] While this may sound like a coldly Stoic disengagement from all human interaction, it is, in fact, the only basis on which *agape* becomes possible. True love, a love that is unacquisitive and free, cannot exist when the person loved is being used as an object for the satisfaction of another's needs. To love, in the sense of *agape,* is to treat the other person not with any preference for one's own good but as an equal—indeed, as one's own self.

Thomas Merton explained the desert Christians' conception of love as a matter of taking one's neighbor as one's other self. "Love means an interior and spiritual identification with one's brother, so that he is not regarded as an 'object' to 'which' one 'does good.' We have to *become,* in some sense, the person we love. And this involves a kind of death of our own being, our own self."[57]

"I die daily," said Abba Anthony.[58] But his *memento mori* was no maudlin fixation on death. It was a matter of being emptied and revivified every moment in the freedom of the desert Christ. Only in that way was he able truly to love.

In love such as this, all judgment is suspended. One gives the other person every benefit of the doubt, even as he or she would wish to be considered in return. "The monk must die to his neighbor and never judge him at all, in any way whatever," insisted Abba Moses.[59] John Climacus warned the brothers, "Do not condemn. Not even if your very eyes are seeing something, for they may be deceived."[60] Unconditional acceptance of this sort is possible only for people who, renouncing all comparisons of themselves with others, have nothing invested in the failure of their peers.

Admittedly this idea of compassion as the fruit of indifference may be difficult to grasp in contemporary culture. Popular conceptions of love are often limited to sentimental feelings and delusions of self-denying grandeur. As a result, we often fail to recognize the extent to which all this disguises a highly manipulative bid for our own self-aggrandizement.[61] We are entirely too needy—too anxious about the fragility of our own self-worth—to be free to love. We have missed the desert truth that, ironically, only those who no longer care can be truly loving. Love at its best, is wholly disinterested, "a harsh and dreadful thing."

The broader political implications of this truth were not lost on the authorities in the early years of the Christian empire. The desert monks, unlike others in society, were free to love at great risk. It was no wonder that prelates and emperors continually sought to curry the favor of these desert athletes, recognizing the intense political danger of a people who had nothing whatever to lose. The *apophthegmata* of the desert Christians are filled with references to magistrates and their difficulties in dealing with the freedom of the desert ascetics. These were a people who, having chosen to live in the wilds, wanted nothing; hence they could not be coopted or threatened. Having metaphorically died to the world and all its seductions, they were far less subject to outside pressures of status, power, money, and knowledge.[62]

> They were in a certain sense "anarchists," and it will do no harm to think of them in that light. They were men who did not believe in letting themselves be passively guided and ruled by a decadent state, and who believed that there was a way of getting along without slavish dependence on accepted, conventional values.[63]

Abba Poemen refused to bend to a magistrate's will, even when his sister's son was thrown into prison because of his resistance.[64] Abba Ammonathas had to deal with a troubling magistrate who tried to levy an unfair tax upon the brothers of his community.[65] Abba Arsenius sent away a public official who had told him he had inherited a great sum from a recently deceased senator in his family. "I was dead long before this senator," proclaimed Arsenius, and returned the will to him, accepting nothing.[66] The solitary can be a person of deep compassion and justice because he or she cannot be coerced by ordinary systems of power.

Indeed, because of their freedom, the desert monks themselves could be perceived as a threat to those remaining anxiously dependent on the approbation of society. In our own time Desmond Tutu has observed that if governments knew the danger of apophatic prayer they would ban it immediately. No threat is as dangerous as the power of a people radically set free from the value structures of their world.[67]

A New Harmony with the Land

A third and last dimension of the new prospect occasioned by a desert refuge takes us back to the landscape itself. While the wilderness symbolized for the desert Christians a sense of spiritual disintegration and loss, it also came to symbolize for them the beauty and interrelatedness of life. These were people who lived for years in the closest symbiotic relationship with the land.

The typical desert monk dwelt in a hut of stones covered with branches from a nearby oasis. Inside was a reed mat for a bed, a jar of water in which palm leaves and fibers were soaked for making mats and weaving ropes, a sheepskin for the cold of night, a handful of dried peas or lentils waiting to be steeped. Perhaps also, as Helen Waddell observes, a jar of wine for visitors, brackish water for oneself.[68] They lived simply, with a necessary appreciation for the desert habitat which was theirs, eating edible wild plants and cultivating others.[69] "If it is true that the Greek fathers displayed deep interest in the natural world, it is equally true that they enjoyed it."[70]

Unfortunately, the stereotype of the nature-hating monk has persisted through the centuries, despite evidence to the contrary. Roderick Nash, in his otherwise excellent study of American wilderness, comments on the history of the perception of wild terrain in Western civilization. "On the whole," he says, "monks regarded wilderness as having value only for escaping corrupt society."[71] From the early years of the Christian desert experience to Benedict, Bernard of Clairvaux, and Hildegard of Bingen, this was rarely the case.

The truth is that many of the early ascetics came to appreciate and explore the desert, valuing it for its own austere grandeur. Admittedly, those who most idealized the desert in late antiquity were people who never lived in it. The ones who knew it firsthand were most inclined to speak of its terrors.[72] Yet the anonymous author of the *Historia Monachorum* described Macarius of Alexandria as "a lover beyond all other men of the desert," one who "had explored its ultimate and inaccessible wastes" far beyond the borders of Scete.[73]

Similarly, Abba Anthony was accustomed to fasting until the ninth hour each day, when, usually alone, but sometimes taking with him one of the brothers, he would "go out for a walk in the desert and explore the country," walking until sunset.[74] Drawn by rock formations, golden thistles, and thornbush, he passed over the land in the methodical motion of prayer. The unremitting doggedness of it all was absolutely compelling to him. "Life is gaunt and spare in the desert," writes Ed Abbey, "that's what old time desert rats like best about it. They feel they cannot breathe properly without at least a cubic mile of unshared space about them."[75]

The various sources for the study of early Christian monasticism, from Palladius' *Lausiac History* to the sayings of the fathers and mothers themselves, all substantiate a picture of the desert monks as subsistence gardeners, living close to the land. Athanasius, in his *Life of Anthony*, described the small garden worked by the Egyptian saint in his hermitage at his "inner mountain" east of the Nile. On one occasion, some wild asses, coming to the area for water, began to trample the new plants he had set out. He caught one of the animals, holding it gently around the neck, and firmly scolded the lot of them for bringing harm to him when he had done nothing to hurt them. Athanasius observed that never again did the animals step on the good monk's vegetables.[76]

Susan Power Bratton, in a study of the ecological sensitivity of early Christian ascetics, argues that the typical desert monk was portrayed as a "new Adam," living in reciprocity with the created world around him.[77] Abba Theon often walked at night in the wilderness "with a great troop of desert beasts" following along behind. "The tracks of gazelle and goat . . . were thick about his cell" where he drew water and let them drink from his cup.[78] Abba Macarius was nursed to strength by a wild antelope and later returned the favor by healing the blind pup of a hyena.[79] John Climacus knew a monk who reared a leopard by hand. Pachomius spoke of being carried across a river on the backs of crocodiles.

In desert iconography, lions became special companions of the monks. Paul the Hermit, one of the earliest of the fathers, was so beloved by desert lions that two of them came at his death to bury him with honor.[80] These were stories serving a hagiographic purpose, of course. They do not allow us to read an ecological sophistication into the thinking of fourth- and fifth-century monks. Nonetheless, an intimate identification with nature did become one of the hallmarks of early monastic life.

The desert fathers and mothers were by no means despisers of the created world, as if they had turned their gaze exclusively to the concerns of heaven. For them, heaven itself must have been a vast expanse of dry land, teeming with indefatigable life. In coming to the wilderness they had sought refuge in a remote and hostile setting where death stalks all that lives. But they soon found that their refuge also occasioned for them a new prospect, a new way of seeing and appreciating life.

As strange as it sounds, given the austere, threatening quality of the monks' life in the wilderness, what the desert finally taught them was love. There in the wilds, they could be ignored enough, invited outside of themselves enough, to love and to be loved in a way that met the deepest social needs of the tension-filled world of late antiquity. Loving God, loving other people, loving the created world in which they were placed—this was the grand and hoped-for conclusion of *apatheia,* that sublime indifference which ever ended in love. The athletes of God understood the movement from desert austerity to desert compassion as perfectly natural, an altogether appropriate reading of Christian theology from the lay of the land.

This theme is well expressed in the story of Abba Abraham, a Syriac desert father known for his great holiness and austere living, but also for his love. When his married brother died in a distant city, leaving a seven-year-old daughter with no one to care for her, he took her in, letting her stay in the outer room of his cell. Her name was Mary, and through the years she grew into a beautiful and devout young woman, the image of her uncle.

But one day a false and wicked hermit passed through the desert where they lived. Captured by Mary's beauty, he determined to have her at any cost. He caught her by surprise one afternoon while her uncle was away, raped her, and left her alone in the desert in complete despair. Mary, a young woman of tender conscience, blamed herself for what had happened. Tortured by guilt and shame, she punished herself by going to live in a brothel in a distant city.

On returning, Abba Abraham looked everywhere for his missing niece. Finally, two years later he learned what had happened and where she was. With a father's love he went to find her, putting aside his monk's habit, dressing in a military uniform, pulling a great hat down over his ears. He borrowed a horse and set off toward the city. When he found the tavern where she lived, he said to the innkeeper, "They tell me, friend, that you have a fine wench here. I'd like to have a look at her, if you would." Then he sat down and ordered a drink. Mary came in, not recognizing her uncle. "Innkeeper," he cried, "make us a good supper, because I plan to make merry with this lass. Aye," he added, "I've come a long way for the love of Mary." Then this man who had eaten only bread and water for forty years of his life, ate meat for all he was worth—all for the love of a lost niece.

After supper, Mary took him to her room. As the two of them were alone for the first time, she bent down to take off his shoes, still not knowing who he was. Out of deep grief, her uncle spoke yet again, saying, "Aye, I've come a long way for the love of Mary!" Suddenly she recognized him, falling at his feet in tears as she realized how much her uncle must have loved her. Abba Abraham, known for his austere and holy life, would never have done such things had he not loved and forgiven her everything. And if her uncle could love and forgive to such an extent, then how much more, she thought, could she expect of God.

That day she left the brothel, returning with her uncle to their desert cell where she lived out a life of great holiness. In years to come many people would be healed through her prayers. Eventually she would come down to us, in the calendar of saints, as Saint Mary the Harlot—one who, like her uncle, loved much because she had been emptied of much.[81]

Such is the desert way. The fathers and mothers of early Christian asceticism learned to risk everything for the sake of compassion because they already had lost everything in the harsh renunciation demanded by desert life. Their unrelenting theology of the cross brought them to love by way of death. This, in the end, was the compelling truth they read from the fierce desert landscape in which they lived.

Desert Terror and the Playfulness of God

There comes a moment when the children who have been playing at burglars hush suddenly: was that a *real* footstep in the hall? There comes a moment when people who have been dabbling in religion . . . suddenly draw back. Supposing we really found Him? We never meant it to come to *that!* Worse still, supposing He had found us?" —C. S. Lewis[1]

As the office of love is to wound, that it may enkindle with love and cause delight, so . . . these wounds are the playing of God. —John of the Cross[2]

We set up camp on the southern edge of Urraca Mesa after the storm clouds had broken that afternoon. It was our second day on the trail at Philmont Scout Ranch in the Sangre de Cristo Mountains of northern New Mexico. My son and I had come with other members of our scout troop to spend ten days in the back country, walking some seventy miles through the high desert of the Jicarilla Apache. We hadn't yet learned to move as a team. Our heads hurt from the recent change in altitude. Boots still weren't broken in. And we'd yet to cross Urraca Mesa.

We'd heard tales about the place—this mesa in the shape of a skull, with its stories of strange lights and campers who'd long ago disappeared. At sunset we laughed as we took the trail across the mesa to a campfire at the ranger base on the other side. But around the fire our lightheartedness began to disappear. Maybe it was the Apache ghost stories that began to play on our minds. As far back as the Anasazi, we were told, this mesa had been recognized as a foreboding place, a point of entry to the underworld. Maybe it was the thick clouds that swept in, covering the moon as we started back across the ridge in the dark. Maybe that night we simply wanted to believe the tales, to play with thoughts of terror as children in the dark are prone to do.

Whatever it was, the tall firs seemed strangely mysterious, menacing us on either side of the trail as we began the return to camp.

Flashlights kept failing. The trail played tricks on us, never looking familiar, continually doubling back on itself. We stopped more and more frequently to count off, making sure all fourteen of us were still together. No one was laughing anymore. Only as we finally reached the mesa's southern edge once again did the landscape suddenly open before us. The moon came out from behind dark clouds, the path toward camp became perfectly clear, we moved with the ease and joy of those who know themselves accepted by the land. We came to feel that night as if we'd passed some test, moving from threat into love. We knew somehow that nothing else would frighten us over the next eight days on the trail.

It isn't accidental that the threat of terror is incorporated into so much of children's play. As children (and adults), we work through our deepest fears of not being loved in the process of imagining ourselves abandoned, deceived, or hopelessly lost. I've seen it happen again and again in lonely stretches of back country. Only as we "play" at being lost do we most assuredly come to know ourselves as found.

Such is the insistence of the *ludus amoris* tradition that flourished in medieval and Renaissance literature, making its way into the writings of Julian of Norwich and the author of *The Cloud of Unknowing*.[3] God plays, we're told, in an often disconcerting way, provoking a mock fear that's suddenly overcome in unanticipated joy. Like a mother playfully hiding from her child or a lover playing hard to get, God hides from those God loves, occasionally playing rough for love's sake. The purpose of God's apparent absence, of God's hiding, is to deepen in the lover a longing for the one loved, to enhance the joy experienced when fear dissolves and the separated are rejoined.

This is the experience of the bride in the Song of Songs as she awaits with fearful anticipation the coming of her love in the dark of night, only to open the door and discover that he's disappeared (Song of Songs 5:4–6) It's what the disciples encounter on the Emmaus road as Jesus hides his identity so as to sharpen within them their longing for his words. Only later do they remember how their "hearts burned within them" as he expounded the scriptures along the way (Luke 24:32). Love becomes most apparent in the process of its being lost.

This is a difficult truth that desert and mountain paths readily teach. Hosea evokes, in his own tragic experience of unrequited love, Israel's memory of walking hand-in-hand with Yahweh like young lovers in the cool desert evening (Hos. 2:14–15). The desert is the place where God hides, where love at times seems almost cruel, but it's also the place where deepest intimacy and trust are learned. There in the long, haunting stretches of the Sinai, the people of God discover how often desert terror gives way to desert love. In the wilderness the people of Israel experienced, more than they might have liked, the rough play of God's deep longing for them.

There's a playfulness in hiding (and pretending to be lost) as well as a good-natured gruffness (breaking always into merriment) that are integral to the finest aspects of children's play. They're intrinsic also to the experience of desert and mountain terrain. Moreover, they express themselves in the often fierce and tender character of our most privileged meetings with God. Two reflections on children's play and the sometimes truculent character of God's love may suggest the intimacy to which we're invited in the untoward desert moments of our lives.

A Hidden and Playful God

Truly, thou art a God who hidest thyself. —Isa. 45:15

My children are long past the age of taking delight in childhood games, but I remember hours in years past playing hide-and-seek together, even though it was a game they never quite learned to play according to the rules. In fact, I used to worry about my son. For years I couldn't get him to understand that he shouldn't yell "ready" when he'd found a good hiding place; that only gave it away. He was missing the whole point of the game, I explained. One wants to hide well! Only later did I come to realize that from his perspective, I had missed the whole point of the game. The most fun comes, of course, in being found! Meister Eckhart expressed this mystery well when he said that "God is like a person who clears his throat while hiding and so gives himself away." Even God—perhaps especially God—discovers the highest joy in hiding only so as to be found.

This simple truth reveals a fault that cuts through much of our mistaken thinking about God as *Deus absconditus.* Too often we associate the "hiddenness of God" with a fearful sense of obscurity, inaccessibility, remoteness—as if the divine inscrutability were an end in itself. We lose the playfulness involved in this truth. Looking upon God's act of masking or veiling as a means of protecting the divine majesty from prying human eyes, or as a way of protecting us from a grandeur too terrifying to perceive, we forget that God's hiding is rooted first of all in divine compassion. God hides not only to protect, but also to draw us to herself in love.

God's elusiveness serves her longing for relationship. Hiding, therefore, can become an act of playful teasing—a blithe form of seduction, God's way of inviting us to the place of surprised encounter. God simply can't resist clearing her throat, calling "ready," so as to bring us more quickly to herself. God as *Deus absconditus* is never far removed from God as *Deus ludens,* a God revealed in playfulness.[4]

Alan Watts develops this theme in a radical way—perhaps excessively blurring the distinction between the divine teaser and those who are teased—yet he rightly captures God's playful purpose in the divine game of hide-and-seek. He suggests that since

> there is nothing outside of God, he has no one but himself to play with. But he gets over this difficulty by pretending that he is not himself. . . . He pretends that he is you and I and all the people of the world, all the animals, all the plants, all

the rocks, and all the stars. . . . Now when God [does this], he does it so well that it takes him a long time to remember where and how he hid himself. But that's the whole fun of it. . . . He doesn't want to find himself too quickly, for that would spoil the game. That is why it is so difficult for you and me to find out that we are God in disguise, pretending not to be himself.[5]

While this explanation may be inadequate as a thoroughgoing account of God's relationship to the world, it echoes the playful language of mystical insight, not at all unlike the language of Meister Eckhart or Saint John of the Cross. God disguises himself, hiding in a manger, his majesty veiled upon a cross, so that we might irresistibly be drawn to a grace far closer than we ever imagined.

The Jewish tradition tells a story about the first Lubavitcher rebbe, Schneur Zalman, the founder of one of the most vital of today's Hasidic communities. His young son once came running to him, crying inconsolably. Between huge sobs, he managed to say, "Father, I've been playing hide-and-seek with the other children. It came my turn to hide, but after I found a good place, I sat there in the woods for hours waiting for the others to find me. No one ever yelled into the woods to tell me to come out. They just left me there alone." His father put his arms around the child and held him close, rocking him back and forth. "Ah, my son," he said, "that's how it is with God, too. God is always hiding, hoping that people will come to look for him. But no one wants to play. He's always left alone, wanting to be found, hoping someone will come. But crying because no one seeks him out."[6]

What is this mystery of God's great compassion, wanting so much to draw us to God? Like others, I too often shrink back in fear. I'm reluctant to embrace a God of hidden majesty. Yet I'm surprised again and again to find myself sought out more lovingly than I ever dared to hope by what I first had feared. Francis Thompson discovered the playful, grand conclusion to his own lifelong flight from God in being found by that from which he'd fled. At the end of his great poem on being sought by a love too fierce to withstand for long, he speaks with incredulous joy:

> Halts by me that footfall;
> Is my gloom, after all
> Shade of His hand, outstretched caressingly?
> "Ah, fondest, blindest, weakest,
> I am He Whom thou seekest!
> Thou dravest love from thee, who dravest Me."[7]

For him, it was as if Christ, the Hound of Heaven, had finally shouted out in reckless abandon, "Olly, olly, oxen free!" and the hiders had come from behind every bush and nearby tree, running safely home to outstretched arms. This, at last, is the meaning of God as *Deus absconditus*, the truth which Luther found so important in his own theology of a gracious God.[8]

When my daughter was very young, one of her favorite tricks in playing hide-and-seek was to pretend that she had run away to hide, and then to come sneaking back beside me while I was still counting—my eyes shut tight. She breathed as silently as she could, standing inches away, hoping I couldn't hear. Then she'd take the greatest delight in reaching out to touch home base as soon as I opened my eyes and began to search for someone who'd never even left. She was cheating, of course, and though I don't know why, I always let her get away with it. Was it because I longed so much for those few moments when we stood close together, pretending not to hear or be heard, caught up in a game that for an instant dissolved the distance between parent and child, that set us free to touch and seek and find each other? It was a simple, almost negligible act of grace, my not letting on that I knew she was there. Yet I suspect that in that one act my child may have mirrored God for me better than in any other way I've known.

Still to this day, it seems, God is for me a seven-year-old daughter, slipping back across the grass, holding her breath in check, wanting once again to surprise me with a presence closer than I ever expected. "Truly, thou art a God who hidest thyself," the prophet once declared (Isa. 45:15). A playfulness as well as a dark mystery lies richly intertwined in that grand and complex truth.

God Plays Rough for Love's Sake

In the middle of all my troubles, you roll me over with rollicking delight.
—Psalm 94:19

The great English medievalist and raconteur T. H. White recalls a wonderful and touching story from his youth. It captures that essential ambiguity which forms the delight as well as the sometimes unsettling character of play. He remembers one year when he had turned six or seven:

> My father made me a wooden castle big enough to get into, and he fixed real pistol barrels beneath its battlements to fire a salute on my birthday, but made me sit in front the first night—that deep Indian night—to receive the salute, and I, believing I was to be shot, cried.[9]

I understand painfully well the child's response. How many times have I, too, misinterpreted the ambiguity of play, thinking myself to be shot when the parent all along had meant only deliberate delight? It's a danger that ever lies near the heart of playfulness at its best. In moments of unanticipated jest, I'm never quite certain whether I'm being threatened or toyed with most affectionately. Particularly this is the case with respect to God. It's a truth learned well by all the desert saints that God plays rough before breaking into laughter.

The sort of play which has always charmed me most is that which explores the uneven edge between syrupy compassion and a fierce, lean roughness. Such play is full of risk. It entertains the possibility of being misunderstood because of the greater yield that comes in being lightly touched by love. At those moments when I'm most fraught with vulnerability, I find myself also most open to unexpected grace. It happened to my son once when he was eight years old; he thought he was being scolded for hitting a ball into the neighbor's yard. But the neighbor's scowl suddenly broke into a huge, engaging grin, the ball came bounding back over the fence, and John knew himself to be loved when he'd expected only scorn.

Admittedly, there's a fine distinction here. The best humor, it seems, often harbors a dimension of menace, assuming at times the very aspect of evil. The highest form of play is one that dares to toy with deepest fears. It entertains the dragon's threat so as finally to see the dragon face defeat. That's something that play less given to boldness can never quite obtain. The soft and harmless play we often prefer may be too gentle, too careful not to give offense, too cloying and sweet. It lacks ambiguity altogether, occasioning no surprise, promising no danger, bringing no reward. Only a bold and rowdy playfulness can draw the whole of what I am to the God who toys with death for the sake of stubborn love.

Yet I'm not always able to grasp that truth. My problem is one of limited imagination. Like most of us, I simply can't believe that God's love is actually as exuberant and playful as it is. Grace slips by us all, misconstrued as harshness. If the psalmist is right—that Yahweh's festive gaiety is somehow to be discerned in the midst of our own troubled fears—then the truth is lost on us much of the time. Why is it always easier to anticipate God's wrath than to perceive God's joy? Ever expecting to be shot, we're invariably dumbfounded by a grace we can't conceive.

Martin Luther once spoke of his experience as a young student in Magdeburg, singing in the streets with another youngster, hoping for small gifts of money or food. A huge man suddenly came running out from a nearby house, waving sausages in the air and yelling at them in noisy jest, "What are you boys up to with such a racket?" The man grinned as he spoke, yet the boys weren't sure how to respond. They wanted the sausages, but in fearful confusion they bolted at last and ran. Luther later asked in his *Tabletalk* if the story wasn't typical of our response to God and God's grace. Like the man frantically waving sausages, he said, God holds out Jesus Christ to us, not seeking to frighten but to draw us to himself. Yet we're afraid. We can't imagine such forgiveness. We run the other way, certain that God is angry with us, tragically misinterpreting God's play.[10]

When we finally do begin to understand this business about the playfulness of God, when we decide not to run the other way, we discover that God invites us to playfulness in return. If God plays rough for the sake of deeper love, it's also true that God takes delight in reciprocal boldness. Thérèse of Lisieux, for example, could speak of virtually wrapping God around her finger with respect to her habit of sometimes falling asleep during prayer, a habit her sisters in the religious life found disconcerting. She knew that God was a sucker for "little nothings" like herself who frequently fall asleep in their fathers' arms. Far from expecting any punishment, therefore, she knew that her "weakness" was the very thing that bound God to her, allowing her to "hold him prisoner" for the sake of love.[11]

There's a hardy and playful banter with God that one finds at times among the saints. Teresa of Avila once talked back when God was playing unusually rough with her, saying, "If this is how you treat your friends, I know why you have so many enemies!" This bold and playful rejoinder to God is one that pushes the outer edges of God's covenant with God's people. Its goal is intimacy, a deeper relationship with God made possible by the mutual acceptance of play. It's even more prevalent in Judaism, where it takes the form of a particular kind of prayer known as *chutzpa k'lapei shemaya*, a boldness with regard to heaven.[12]

In the rabbinical tradition it is said that Moses once took God to task for using inconsistent pronouns in speaking of the people of Israel. In Exodus 3:10 Yahweh had said, "Come, I will send you to Pharoah that you may bring forth *my people,* the Israelites, out of Egypt." But after Israel's sin with the golden calf, God said to Moses, "Go down, for *your people,* whom *you* have brought up out of the land of Egypt, have corrupted themselves" (Exod. 32:7). Moses then cried out in protest, saying, "Wait a minute, God. You can't call them *your* people when they're good and my people when they're bad. Whether good or bad, they're still *your* people!" The rabbis, of course, knew that God broke into laughter at that moment, unable to resist the prayerful teasing of someone he loved.

An extraordinary access to the inner life of God is offered in such experiences of playfulness. Because of God's incalculable love, it is God's nature to be helpless before those who bank most fully on that love. That is why the Baal Shem Tov once playfully spoke of God being guarded in a great palace, protected from those who might lay bold claims to his graciousness. Tall walls keep out their prayers because God is wholly unable to resist those who come with intense and loving playfulness. Guards have to protect the king from his own excessive compassion; otherwise he'd give the whole kingdom away to such people if he could.

Therefore, the guards freely admit those casual petitioners who bring only matters of shallow inconsequence. They know the king will pay them no mind. But they watch most carefully for those who come in the agony of prayer or the joyousness of play, because the king is perfectly helpless before them. Those who come with a bold and loving eagerness are the ones who gain access to the deepest heart of God.

God plays rough before breaking into laughter. In all my questions about this strange, compelling truth—in all my doubts about the ambiguity of what God often allows—what I find myself longing for most is not a well-formulated theodicy. I wouldn't be satisfied with answers to the problem of evil even if I had them. What I desire most of all is the assurance of God's love, the echo of God's laughter breaking over me in waves of playfulness that won't let me go. In playing with God, none of us ever mind losing, so long as we know ourselves to be loved. In her book of poems, *The Awful Rowing toward God,* Anne Sexton offers a poignant picture of herself as having pulled at last with blistered hands and salt-caked face to the island called God. There she and God squat on the rocks by the sea and play—can it be true?—a game of poker.

> He calls me.
> I win because I hold a royal straight flush.
> He wins because He holds five aces.
> A wild card had been announced
> but I had not heard it
> being in such a state of awe
> when He took out the cards and dealt.
> As he plunks down His five aces
> and I sit grinning at my royal flush,
> He starts to laugh,
> and laughter rolling like a hoop out of His mouth
> and into mine,
> and such laughter that He doubles right over me
> laughing a Rejoice-Chorus at our two triumphs.[13]

The laughter of being beaten by God, trumped by the high card always up God's sleeve, is a joy known only to those who've entered the game and discovered losing to be yet another form of being loved. Simone Weil was surely right when she asked, "Isn't it the greatest possible disaster, when you are wrestling with God, not to be beaten?" God's invitation to the spiritual life is a call to the high-risk venture of being loved more fiercely than we ever might have dreamed. It's an invitation to embrace the ambiguity of play. Admittedly, I'm sometimes frightened when confronted by a God who plays rough, but then slowly the laughter begins to well, God's arms open wide, and suddenly I know myself to have been loved all along. The two of us roll together in helpless laughter, shrieking a wondrously wild Rejoice-Chorus at our mutual triumphs.

It's the laughter of the magpie, this wild and astounding desert laughter, noisily sung even today on the slopes of Urraca Mesa. *Urraca* is the Spanish word for magpie. Spanish settlers, and the Apaches before them spoke of this black-feathered bird of prey as a messenger of the devil, a trickster, one who plunders the nests of others. The magpie they knew to be a symbol of death as well as new life. It delights in small, bright objects; it even is capable of echoing human speech. *Uracca,* the magpie, possesses the power of mediating between worlds, occasioning fear as well as joy. In the canyons of New Mexico, it dwells in the place where dread often yields to love.

On that lonely night as our scout troop made its hair-raising and tenuous way back across the mesa, at the moment when the moon broke through the clouds and we knew ourselves at last to be headed home, I heard its cry. It was a raucous laughter breaking with the playfulness of God through the dry and brittle heart of desert fear. It was the voice of the trickster and gambler, the con man and thief who robs us of what we never really needed, only to leave us with an emptiness we'd come eventually to recognize as gift. "Sing for joy, O heavens, and exult, O earth; break forth, O mountains, into singing! For the Lord has comforted his people and taken pity on those he has afflicted" (Isa. 49:13).

· 7 ·

Attentiveness, Indifference, and Love

The Countercultural Spirituality of the Desert Christians

The finest quality of this stone, these plants and animals, this desert landscape is the indifference manifest to our presence, our absence, our coming, our staying or our going. Whether we live or die is a matter of absolutely no concern whatsoever to the desert. —Edward Abbey[1]

Desert *apatheia* has a daughter whose name is love. —Evagrius of Pontus[2]

In December 1935 Antoine de Saint-Exupéry, on a mail flight between Paris and Saigon, crashed in the Libyan Desert west of the Nile. It was in the same place the desert fathers and mothers of the fourth century had withdrawn to seek the face of God in a landscape of emptiness. Saint-Exupéry's story of survival, in his now classic book *Wind, Sand and Stars,* evokes the same desert discipline practiced by those who had preceded him there centuries earlier.[3] No one lives for long in the desert without acquiring its crusty virtues of attentiveness and indifference. It was only because of these that Saint-Exupéry survived.

Over a period of three days he walked 124 miles without water through desert sands, stumbling at last, half dead, into the path of a remote bedouin caravan. He had been told that no one could survive more than nineteen hours in the desert without water. The eyes then filled with a ghostly light, and death soon followed. What saved him were two things. First, he was meticulously observant of his surroundings, noticing an unusual northeast wind, full of moisture, retarding the dehydration of his body and bringing a light dew he could collect on parachute silk. Second, he remained stubbornly indifferent to the panic, pain, and despair which preyed on his mind. Learning to be fiercely attentive, he learned also not to care—to ignore everything unnecessary, everything unrelated to the primary task of staying alive.

When he was found at last by the bedouins, he looked like some desert rat, crazed and blistered. Unable to raise any saliva, his lips had sealed together with a kind of glue. His tongue felt as if it were made of plaster of Paris. There was a rasping in his throat, a horrible taste in his mouth. In the last hours he had waited for the telltale cough to begin, the throat to close up, the shining spots to appear before his eyes, spots that would soon change to flames, and then the end. This, he had learned from others, was the pattern of desert death he could expect as his own.

Having once known the desert in a way as intimate as this, Antoine de Saint-Exupéry could never again succumb to the naiveté of desert romanticism. Those of us whom the desert has never touched find it much easier to imagine only the beauty and glory of desert spirituality, thumbing our way through old copies of *Arizona Highways* and dreaming of desert retreats. We suppose arid and empty terrain to be naturally solicitous of our human need for contemplation. But the stark, unsettling truth is that the desert doesn't give a damn. Its capacity for indifference seems almost infinite. It was precisely this sense of danger and disregard that fed the spiritual vigor of early desert monasticism.

There is an unsolicitous and ungenteel quality about the desert Christians that makes them especially attractive in our current climate of sentimentalized, "feel good" spirituality. The spiritual life extolled in popular religious circles today is eminently unexceptionable, generically inoffensive, and (almost without exception) culturally correct. We too often substitute amiability for friendship, agreeableness for dialogue, pleasantry for compassion. The acrid smell of the desert is lost.

By contrast, one has to consider the surly, discourteous piety of the desert fathers and mothers. They were "resident aliens" in a world that fostered gentility and comfort. They simply did not fit. As Bruce Berger observes, "the desert notoriously harbors the loner, the misfit, the only child."[4] It attracts a people who are downwardly mobile, often cantankerous, ill at ease in polite society. Shun the city and all of its niceties, growled Jerome from his desert lair. His Christianity required the harsh solace of open spaces.

The desert has always been the abode of dingbats, visionaries, and half-crazed fools. It invites departure from every form of civility. "Never forget," warns one contemporary desert writer, "that it was in the Mojave that the first claimed UFO sightings took place, and the pioneer conversations with little green men from Venus. In a landscape where nothing officially exists (otherwise it would not be 'desert'), absolutely anything becomes thinkable, and may consequently happen."[5] The desert, as a place where one expects nothing, becomes the source of the hauntingly unexpected: this unpredictability formed the robust spirituality of the desert monks.

Not surprisingly, their God was no different from their place. Theirs was not, as John Crowe Ransom once described, a "God without thunder," having been thoroughly housebroken and made presentable to the cultural elite of their day.[6] Their God remained mystery—feared certainly, and much loved, but never understood. They would have agreed entirely with John Muir's assessment that in God's wildness lies the hope of the world.[7] They were quick to recognize "the wildness of God" as a theological category too often ignored by the rest of the church.

Agrupnia and *Apatheia*

The threat of desert landscape—from its grudging stinginess with water to its poisonous lizards and waiting vultures—has a way of eliciting the sharp, lean qualities of attentiveness and indifference. Both are desert virtues, honed by exposure to the elements. The one is necessary for survival. No one lasts in the desert without constant attentiveness to exterior and interior landscapes alike. One must keep an eye out for landmarks, the position of the sun in the sky, tracks in the sand, threatening clouds. But equally important is staying attuned to one's inner condition—the progress of fatigue, the irritation of blisters, the forgetfulness to which the mind is prone, the slow rise of panic at the fear of being lost. The desert fathers and mothers spoke of this attentiveness as *agrupnia,* the spiritual discipline of "wakefulness."[8]

The other virtue of "indifference" is the more slowly learned attitude of abandonment that grows from prolonged desert experience.[9] It means learning to ignore the things that are not important, being able—as one prepares for desert travel—to know what to leave behind. It, too, is directed toward interior as well as exterior landscapes. One must learn to accept the empty silence, to ignore sun and heat, to be untroubled by the scarcity of food—by the sparseness of everything other than space. Yet even more important, this indifference must be aimed inwardly at the self. It means not taking the ego too seriously, being able to watch one's compulsive needs wilt under the discipline of inattention. The desert invites an ignoring of the ego, its separation from the inner audience to which it continually plays for sympathy and admiration. The desert fathers and mothers spoke of this indifference as *apatheia,* the spiritual discipline of "detachment" or "dispassion," the practice of apathy with respect to matters of unimportance.

"Indifference" is offered here as an intentionally provocative translation of the term, understood after the pattern of Ignatius Loyola's "active indifference." It does not suggest a blasé attitude of uncaring disinterest so much as the rigorous ordering of one's desires, a reducing of everything to the demanding measure of God's will.[10] In discerning the will of God on any given matter, Ignatius insisted that one must "become like balance scales that are evenly weighted on both sides," not pushing down one way or the other, simply resting there, waiting indifferently.[11] Only in such a detached way can the ego be still enough to hear the voice of God.

Attentiveness and indifference are, respectively, the constructive and deconstructive poles of the spiritual life. They tell us when to pay attention and when to let go, what to concentrate on and what to ignore, how to survive and how to abandon everything that is not necessary. T. S. Eliot, in his poem "Ash Wednesday," prayed for both: "Teach us to care and not to care."[12] John Climacus, the crusty old abbot of the monastery at Mount Sinai, understood these virtues as two of the most important rungs of his *Ladder of Divine Ascent.*[13]

They stand in paradoxical relation to each other, these two disciplines of the spirit: how to pay attention and how not to pay attention (and when to apply which of the two standards). Nothing else is more important or more difficult in one's faltering practice of a life of prayer.

Learning to Pay Attention

The Talmudic sage Rabbah bar Bar Hana, traveling in the wilderness of Sinai in the third century, spoke of meeting an old Arab merchant who, "by taking up sand and smelling it," could tell how far he was from the nearest water. The rabbi tested him with sand that was eight parasangs (about thirty-two miles) away from the nearest oasis, then again with sand that was three parasangs away. In each case, even when the rabbi tried to fool him with sand substituted from another place, the old Arab proved infallible in his sense of smell.[14]

People who dwell in wilderness, living close to the land, often evince powers of attentiveness that seem magical by comparison to others. But the only difference is one of discipline. Most of us have little experience in paying careful attention to anything. We marvel at a naturalist such as Louis Agassiz of Harvard, who once said he had spent the summer traveling, only to get halfway across his back yard. We cannot imagine spending that much time on that narrow a field of attention.

That's why the life of the monk seems so utterly foreign, even frightening. Our conditioning as members of a consumer society prevents us from abandoning hope that, with sufficient planning, we might yet be able to see and do everything. To move slowly and deliberately through the world, attending to one thing at a time, strikes us as radically subversive, even un-American. We cringe from the idea of relinquishing, in any moment, all but one of the infinite possibilities offered us by our culture. Plagued by a highly diffused attention, we give ourselves to everything lightly. That is our poverty. In saying yes to everything, we attend to nothing. One only can love what one stops to observe. "Nothing is more essential to prayer," said Evagrius, "than attentiveness."[15]

The desert, as a lean and arid landscape having few distractions, is a place that can teach us this truth well. With its uncluttered horizon, its tendency toward simplicity and repetition, it offers little to the eye and provides great clarity in what it offers. Stars, for example, are far more brilliant in its dry, night air, stripped of humidity, than anywhere else. The desert serves as an optimal place for sharpening one's skills at paying attention. Survival demands it. The five senses are heightened by wilderness experience and apophatic prayer alike. Disciplined familiarity with emptiness is an exercise the desert teaches equally well to body and soul.

But there are never, of course, any guarantees. The desert occasions no simplistic environmental determinism: entering a dry and barren terrain does not automatically assure one of deep spiritual insight. People go to Las Vegas and

Reno every day, finding in the desert absolutely nothing. The place may invite them to a deeper reflection on the nature of the "nothing" they have found, but few people pause long enough to listen on their way out of town.

The desert fathers and mothers, by contrast, took all the time necessary to attend to the desert's subtle, taciturn wisdom. Abba Moses praised the barren landscape of the wilderness at Scete because it had nothing whatever to offer. Its very lack of fruitfulness meant that men and women would not be distracted by thoughts of cultivation, production, yield per acre.[16] Its yield had to be measured in the increase of emptiness and abandonment, the slow growth of attentiveness. The discipline of the desert was gradually acquired in the methodical weaving of palm fronds into mats and baskets, the practice of long exposure to desert loneliness, the reduction of everything in one's life to a radical simplicity. Growth in the spiritual life came to be measured in microparameters, in how much could be given up, how much one could be emptied.

Tom Brown, author of *The Tracker* and *The Search,* sees this process of emptying as part of one's learning to pay attention in wilderness settings. He teaches wilderness-survival and nature-observation skills in the Pine Barrens of New Jersey. On entering the desert, he knows, one must learn to be quiet enough to distinguish disturbances in the surrounding landscape from those within the soul, to distinguish between exterior and interior deserts.[17] Otherwise we recklessly charge into the wilderness, imagining ourselves being followed on unfamiliar trails, jumping at startling sounds, projecting an inner turmoil onto the outer world. One's internal baggage makes true attentiveness impossible.

Saint-Exupéry speaks of waiting one night for a late flight to depart from a remote landing field in the Sahara. Feeling vaguely uneasy as he walked out into the desert air, he heard dragonflies striking their wings against an oil lamp nearby. It was a sound that vaguely disturbed him, though he did not know why. The unsettling feeling required a sorting of inner and outer landscapes, checking the one against the other.

Back home in France, the flight of moths around a candle flame at night would have been perfectly common, provoking no particular interest. But in the desert the sudden presence of insects meant something entirely different. Swept hundreds of miles from their inland oases, the dragonflies were clear signs of impending danger. A savage sandstorm was on its way, sweeping every living thing before it.

Saint-Exupéry was grateful for the warning that had come, but was moved even more by the powerful experience of having been attentive in an unfamiliar environment, having been able to distinguish the mystery of the land from the mystery of himself. "What filled me with a barbaric joy was that I had understood a murmured monosyllable of this secret language, had sniffed the air and known what was coming, like one of those primitive men to whom the future is revealed in such faint rustlings; it was that I had been able to read the anger of the desert in the beating wings of a dragonfly."[18]

Desert attentiveness of this sort is not easily acquired, as people from Anthony of Egypt to Mary Austin and Edward Abbey have learned. The desert Christians sought it carefully in the pattern of prayer they adopted for themselves, paying meticulous, repetitive attention to the subtle presence of God in a sparse and meager landscape. They shared the hard-won wisdom of such desert naturalists as Joseph Wood Krutch, who never tired of attending to the ordinary. "In nature," he said, "one never really sees a thing for the first time until one has seen it for the fiftieth."[19]

The practice of paying attention is the rarest of gifts because it depends upon the harshest of disciplines. So uncommon is it for us to grasp the beauty and mystery of ordinary things that, when we finally do so, it often brings us to the verge of tears.[20] Appalled by our own poverty, we awake in wonder to a splendor of which we had never dreamed.

Ignoring What Doesn't Matter

But the compelling mystery of the desert is even more pronounced in what it is able to ignore. One easily becomes lost, physically as well as figuratively, in its vast indifference, in the great emptiness to which it bears witness. The desert is a place fraught with the danger of disappearance. Its ability to absorb people into the terrifying nothingness of its boundless space is legendary.

The *Lady Be Good*, a bomber attached to the Allied forces in North Africa during the Second World War, took off on its first combat mission in 1943. Within hours, all radio contact was lost and the plane disappeared, apparently swallowed up by the desert's vast expanse. Seventeen years later the plane was found in the sands of the Libyan Desert, perfectly preserved, offering no clue to what might have gone wrong.[21]

The desert is often like that. It cares little. Stories are repeated in desert towns of the American southwest about people who have vanished into thin air, their tracks fading away in some remote canyon, never to be seen again. The desert, apparently, simply consumed them. Such was the case of Everett Ruess, a desert enthusiast whose love of Zion National Park took him often into the wilds of the Escalante River system in southern Utah. On one of those trips, in 1934, he disappeared. His boots were later found, but nothing else. There were no signs of animal attack or foul play, only an inscription on the doorway of an Anasazi ruin nearby, in his handwriting, of the words "Nemo 1934." *Nemo*, in Latin, means "no one."[22]

What (or who) was it that Everett Ruess encountered in the awesome nothingness of the Escalante wilderness? What terrifying and yet joyous freedom is discovered in the desert's enormous capacity for indifference? These are questions posed by the desert's grand disinterest in all the affairs that preoccupy our attention. The desert scoffs at much that we hold dear.

This harsh virtue of desert indifference seems to conflict with its opposite impulse of careful attentiveness, the one taking away what the other gives. Actually the two principles operate very much in tandem. Indifference serves as a corrective lens, indicating what does and does not deserve attention. It provides the negation that gives meaning and direction to the broad field of one's concentration. If focusing one's attention is half of the desert art of contemplation, the other half is a matter of knowing when and how to withhold it.

For the early fathers and mothers, the immensity of the desert's indifference, suggesting for them the even greater immensity of God, offered great clarity about what did and did not matter, about what they would attend to and what they would ignore. In the calm, critical judgment of divine insouciance, bold decisions could be made about how the community of faith would conduct itself in the world.

To use the provocative language of Stanley Hauerwas and William Willimon, the desert Christians understood the church as an alien community no longer caught up in the anxious, self-interested preservation of the world-as-it-is. Their practice of indifference to the dominant social values of their age, exercised from the desert's edge, stood in stark contrast to the accommodating spirit of post-Constantinian, urban Christianity. Indeed, they understood their "oddness" to be an essential part of their faithfulness to Christ and the new community being formed in their midst.[23]

The indifference practiced by this desert colony of believers took shape in response to the social and political preoccupations of a compulsive world. In their reading of the gospel, they knew that a person's worth could never be measured by reference to any contemporary cult of success. The esteem with which they were held by others remained a matter of utter inconsequence.[24] They came to regard glib praise as swift cause for distrust. When an angel of light appeared to one of the brothers, saying, "I am Gabriel and I've been sent to you [above all the other monks]," the brother knew immediately that it was the devil. He replied with artless candor, "I'm sorry. There must be some mistake. Gabriel would never appear to the likes of me."[25]

Becoming equally indifferent to the praise and blame of the world was one of the primary goals of spiritual discipline in the desert. Learning not to care was a matter of utmost importance. Yet the desert masters were careful to distinguish between "true" and "false" indifference. True indifference was a fruit of contemplation, a direct result of disciplined attentiveness. The "no" of desert *apatheia* could emerge only out of deep certainty about the "yes" of the gospel. Detachment from the world and its values required informed, deliberate choices about what does and does not matter in light of Jesus and the inbreaking of his kingdom. True indifference is rooted in a very conscious caring.

False indifference, by contrast, was seen as an easy, casual matter of choosing haphazardly by neglect. It dissolved very readily into the worst of the seven deadly sins—sloth or *accidie,* the lazy sullenness and despairing indiscipline of not caring about anything. Maurice Sendak whimsically satirizes this vice in his tiny cautionary tale for children entitled *Pierre*. There the constant refrain of his young protagonist is "I don't care." All threats are empty, all promises void for children like Pierre who live beyond hope. In the desert experience of the early Christians, such was the temptation of despair that often struck at noon, with the sun high overhead, the heat oppressive, mind and body giving in to the weary, monotonous passing of time.

False indifference is the scourge of domesticated Christianity, tired and worn out, readily accommodating itself to its culture, bowing to the social pressures of the status quo. It remains so tame as to fear nothing so much as the disdain of sophisticated unbelief. This is the indifference that allows the church to abandon its call to radical obedience to Christ in the world. It becomes the driving force behind every injustice, allowing dominant cultural forms to remain unchallenged by people too indifferent to care.

But indifference properly understood can become a source of profoundly liberating power. Adopted as a discipline of ignoring what is not important, in light of the truth of the gospel, it becomes a countercultural influence of great significance. People who pay attention to what matters most in their lives, and who learn to ignore everything else, assume a freedom that is highly creative as well as potentially dangerous in contemporary society. Having abandoned everything of insignificance, they have nothing to lose. Apart from being faithful to their God, they no longer care what happens to them.[26]

Were Christians (and others) to practice this stubborn desert discipline today, they would find a freedom that is refreshing and contagious to some, but also threatening and intolerable to others. Unjust societal structures and people addicted to power will not tolerate being ignored. They are profoundly threatened by those not subject to their influence, those no longer playing by the accepted rules. To cease to be driven by the fear of what other people think is to become a threat to the world as we know it. Only at great personal risk does one become indifferent to the accepted standards and expectations of the dominant culture.

Yet the people willing to assume this risk, the ones who find the center of their existence outside the cultural milieu, are those who model for us today the vitality of Christian faith. A marginal character in William Golding's novel *The Paper Men* seems strangely unaffected by everyone else's compulsive craving for attention and success. "The things you could see that woman had no need of," an acquaintance cries out in astonishment and envy.[27] Such a declaration may be the highest praise possible in a commodity culture like our own. But it was common reality among desert Christians. People in the fourth century were dumbfounded by all the things of which the monks seemed to have no need.

The Moral Equivalent of Desert

Where, then, does one go to learn such freedom? Can the gruff virtues of the desert be cultivated in contemporary urban life? Is physical proximity to an arid landscape necessary for the practice of desert spirituality? The answer is both yes and no. Clearly the desert as desert teaches attentiveness and indifference with great finesse. For some of us there is no substitute for physical wilderness. Nothing is able to take the place of periodic forays into the land of little rain. The desert feeds something that is fragile but insistent in the modern soul.

Even for those who never enter the land of cholla and creosote bush, the mere existence of wilderness is important. "We simply need that wild country available to us," Wallace Stegner argued, "even if we never do more than drive to its edge and look in." The desert answers to deep needs of the human spirit. Something in us requires its presence.[28]

But the practice of Christian discipline has never been limited to specific physical environments. The truth of the desert fathers and mothers has to be transferable, able also to be lived out in the canyons of our great cities, where steel and glass cliffs of mirrored indifference border the street corners of lonely anonymity at Madison and State, Fifth Avenue and 57th Street.

Where, in the modern landscape of our lives, do we find the moral equivalent of desert? What are the places in our experience where desert abandonment is forced on us with the threatening insistence of fierce geographical terrain? In what hazardous contexts does an alien community of faith struggle even now to survive?

All of us know desert Christians who have never been to Egypt, never wandered the dry arroyos of southern Utah. But they have been no strangers to the most terrifying of desert landscapes. They have known intimately the parched and cracked land of an AIDS hospice, the steep cliffs beyond the waiting room of radiation oncology. Through their struggle with cancer and AIDS, they have acquired much of the attentiveness, explored many of the deep caves of indifference mapped out by desert Christians centuries before them.

We know others who have frequented the bombed-out wastelands of the projects in inner-city neighborhoods, people who have trod the high country of abuse, poverty, or prejudice, dealing with levels of indifference for which we have no language. They dwell in the harsh desert of addiction and mental illness, knowing the sustained pain of unemployment, divorce, physical disability. The possibilities of desert experience in contemporary life are more varied than we can imagine.

Certainly a distinction has to be drawn here between voluntary and involuntary desert experience, between those who intentionally embrace the vulnerability of self-emptying and those inadvertently thrust into the dark night of body and soul. A crucial question of our time is how to provoke people into practicing the former while identifying in solidarity with those suffering the latter. In early monastic practice, the desert served a double function of comforting the afflicted as well as afflicting the comfortable.

The desert as metaphor is that uncharted terrain beyond the edges of the seemingly secure and structured world in which we take such confidence, a world of affluence and order we cannot imagine ever ending. Yet it does. And at the point where the world begins to crack, where brokenness and disorientation suddenly overtake us, there we step into the wide, silent plains of a desert we had never known existed.

We cross its sands—unwelcomed, stripped of influence and reputation, the desert caring nothing for the worries and warped sense of self-importance dragged along behind us. There in the desert everything is lost. Absolutely everything. The extent of its unrelenting indifference is devastating. This awareness, at first, is terrifying. But if we stay long enough, resisting the blind panic that gnaws at our minds, we discover, beyond hope and all caring, that "in the end we're saved by the things that ignore us." The deepest mystery of love is never realized apart from the experience of having nothing to offer in return. Only there does love reveal itself in unaccountable wonder.[29]

In that place we discover ourselves no longer alone. In the wilderness, we meet other wizened souls who have weathered sun and heat, all of them healed of the same wound. There is a wildness in their eyes. They hardly give a damn for things they used to find so terribly important. Scarcely fit for polite company, they nonetheless love with a fierceness echoing the land through which they have passed. Like Abba Simeon and Amma Syncletica, theirs is a harsh love, pure as it is lean. The desert has taught them well. They are what the church has been summoned to be, a community of broken people, painfully honest, undomesticated, rid of the pretense and suffocating niceness to which "religion" is so often prone. They love, inexplicably and unflinchingly, because of having been so loved themselves.

The desert, unquestionably, is a hard schoolmaster. Its discipline is harsh and unrelenting. Mark Twain proclaimed in *Roughing It,* his own ornery account of desert survival, "Prov'dence don't fire no blank ca'tridges, boys."[30] All games in the desert are played for keeps. D. H. Lawrence described the arid terrain of New Mexico as a place of "splendid silent terror."[31] Hundreds of nineteenth-century travelers succumbed to the heat and rattlesnakes along a thirsty stretch of land known as *el Camino del Diablo* on the southern Arizona border.

The desert kills. But it also gives life—robust and insistent life. Nothing is more beautiful than the red splash of desert sky after a late-afternoon storm, no flower more lovely than the cactus bloom that opens but once a year. In the desert a landscape of terror becomes also a land of allure and love. Even in its darkest mysteries the desert reveals its beauty. The sacred datura, or moon-flower, blooms only at night, its white, trumpet-shaped flowers as rich in ghostly dreams as they are in fragrance. "All things excellent," recalls Edward Abbey, "are as difficult as they are rare."[32]

Through all its stern lessons in attentiveness and indifference, the desert points to a beauty and wholeness found only on the far side of emptiness. In desert wildness we meet an untamed God who upsets every expectation, destroys all order as we have known it. Our plane crashes in the desert and burns. Everything is lost. Death, most likely, is nineteen hours away. Never have we been so alone or so empty. But in the clarity of that moment, in the reckless wilderness beyond all hope, we are somehow met, inexplicably and without reason. We discover something worth paying attention to, something more beautiful than we had ever imagined in all of our lives. We realize how very little everything else matters by comparison. In our absolute nothingness, we are loved unreservedly by a God on whom we have no claim.

"Teach us to care and not to care," the "Ash Wednesday" prayer intones. Nothing else seems quite so important for those who have been to the desert and back. Attentiveness and indifference form the foundation of the desert discipline by which their lives continue to make sense in a world increasingly desperate for meaning.

Agape as the Fruit of Attentiveness and Indifference

This marriage of attentiveness and indifference gives birth at last to desert love. Such is the inevitable fruit of *agrupnia* and *apatheia,* the flowering of *agape.* Evagrius affirmed this from his fourth-century habitat in the desert west of the Nile when he claimed that desert *apatheia* has a daughter whose name is love. She is a full-blooded and lovely child, this one, a desert gift awakened by attentiveness and purified through the long exercise of holy indifference.

It was love more than anything else that drew the Egyptian fathers and mothers to the trackless desert beyond the Nile. They knew that scarcity and dry land awaken desire. Longing is the first product of desert experience. In the heat of the Egyptian sun, love bursts into flame as desire and is banked by discipline into a slow and steady burn.

Desiccated terrain, by its physical character, automatically sharpens the senses, makes the body alert, arouses want. Desire is born in the desert of biological necessity as an instrument of adaptivity. Environmental psychologist Stephen Kaplan observes that potentially dangerous environments strike us inherently with a sense of fascination. They get our attention, involuntarily, as a function of our evolutionary instinct for survival.[33]

A parched and dangerous terrain—where nothing lives without extraordinary adaptation, where kangaroo rats survive by recycling their own urine—enthralls the imagination. A threatening environment demands the most careful scrutiny of creatures like ourselves, whose survival depends upon wit more than speed. The desert awakening of desire, therefore, compensates for what we lack biologically in mechanisms of flight and defense.

In seducing the senses, the desert stirs inevitably the appetites of love. Lawrence Durrell described Alexandria, the dust-red city along the delta of the Nile, as a "great winepress of love." He wrote of its "dry, palpitant air, harsh with static electricity, inflaming the body through its light clothing. The flesh coming alive, trying the bars of its prison."[34] He understood how passion is kindled in desert heat, its "light filtered through the essence of lemons." In the wilds of North Africa, absence is ever the mother of desire.

The desert Christians were fully aware of this propensity of a dry and thirsty land to stir the human passions. Accounts of their lives are filled with temptation narratives. Far from being a place of escape and freedom from conflict, the desert became a battleground. They recognized how the mind reaches distractedly for everything they had abandoned at the desert's edge. Their senses sharpened by the desert's minimalist vision, they recall in exquisite detail the loveliness of all they had relinquished in coming. The desert makes it easy to yield to the seduction of the mirage, building cities of memory on the sands of nothing.

Their temptation accounts describe the bewitching desert woman or man who tantalizes the imagination, fixing all that is broken in oneself, mending the ego with fawning attention and esteem, satisfying every physical and emotional need. These temptations may appear as apparitions of beautiful women, sometimes as flattering disciples or ingratiating admirers. In a fifteenth-century engraving by Pinturicchio, the Italian Renaissance artist, Saint Anthony and Saint Paul of Thebes are pictured together against a rocky Egyptian landscape. Behind them are the demons that assail them in the form of beguiling women and obsequious men, protégés that make up the entourage of the desert masters.[35]

The winsomeness of this lithe desert image is irresistible, a figure promising to fulfill every newly awakened longing. Perhaps you meet her in the high desert country, a mirage walking alone at dusk. It is a dream to which you readily succumb. Your paths cross unexpectedly. She is stunning, seen at a distance, the late-afternoon sun shining in her hair. You recognize her, having known this person in half-forgotten dreams. She is the inner projection of everything you have ever longed for, a specter of infinite diversity on whom you have played out fantasies all your life. She delights in your every word, mirroring every interest that is yours, living only for you.[36] There in the desert she is more compelling than anywhere you have ever seen her before.

But this personification of desire is an illusion, a mere projection of one's ego, offering the alluring and twisted seduction of self-love. The desert echoes back to us our own emptiness, our longing to be made complete, to move with confidence and self-poise through an unfriendly world. So we fabricate an imaginary being who is able to fulfill us, to lend us the illusion of our own growth toward wholeness, without any of the risk and loss that the desert demands.

The seductive strength of this image is rooted far more in a craving for power than in the appeal of sexual fantasies. The desert fathers realized that their most dangerous temptation had nothing to do with women. It was rather the appeal to the ego posed by Pinturicchio's fawning admirers. Devoted students, ever anx-

The Meeting Between St. Anthony and St. Paul, fresco by Pinturicchio
(Bernardino de Betto), ca. 1493, Appartamenti Borgia. *(Used by permission
of the Monumenti Musei e Gallerie Pontificie, Vatican)*

ious to praise, are the teacher's greatest danger. They bind him to an idealized image of his own spiritual accomplishments. The temptation is to use the infatu-
ating semblance of the "other" to obtain a fullness of self, the flattering of the ego.

Genuine wholeness in the spiritual life is much harder to obtain. It requires
unflinchingly facing one's own hollowness. The harshness of the desert exacts a
stripping away of every chimera and self-delusion for the sake of what is real.
"Delight in the truth," exhorts Donald Nicholl. "Truth tastes better with each illusion that evaporates."[37]

John Cassian identified very clearly the games people play in managing the
impressions they make on others. The demon of self-esteem often leads us to
imagine our playing to a roomful of spectators.

> When it cannot seduce a man with extravagant clothes, it tries to tempt him by
> means of shabby ones. When it cannot flatter him with honour, it inflates him by
> causing him to endure what seems to be dishonour. When it cannot persuade

him to feel proud of his display of eloquence, it entices him through silence into thinking he has achieved stillness.[38]

"Don't do anything with a view to being praised by other people," Cassian charged. "'The Lord has scattered the bones of those anxious to please men.' (Ps. 53:5)."[39] Desire, he knew, must be purged of all self-absorption and illusion.

Monologia: The Transformation of Desire into Love

But the desire itself is a gift.[40] Having learned in the desert to quell the temptations of undisciplined longings, Saint Anthony knew how deeply the desire for God could be felt. "The soul is overcome by a desire for divine and future realities," he proclaimed.[41] One can hardly imagine the power of that longing for God that desert thirst and desert discipline make possible.

Saint Nonnus, the fourth-century bishop of Edessa, said meeting God could be like falling in love on a starlit Syrian night. When tried in the crucible of desert conditioning, God's love became wondrous beyond words. Nonnus found it similar to his encounter with Pelagia, a woman converted to Christianity because of the pure delight he took in her loveliness. He saw reflected in her the beauty of all created things, even his own soul.[42]

On first meeting her in the streets of Antioch, "the most blessed Nonnus did long and most intently regard her," asking his fellow bishops as she passed by, "Did not the sight of her great beauty delight you?" The other bishops, not trained in the same desert simplicity as Nonnus, were embarrassed by his guileless honesty, "turning away their heads in silence." They had seen in her only an object of seduction, tempting them to the satisfaction of their own hidden needs. But Nonnus had seen in her the God he desired above everything else, reflected in the perfect splendor of her (and his own) created being.

Longing for God is the highest desire to which the desert gives birth. "Lucky the man," wrote John Climacus from his monastery at Sinai, "who loves and longs for God as a smitten lover does for his beloved."[43] This is the desire of a "stag, enflamed by love, as if struck by an arrow." It is the "inebriation of the soul."[44] Only in the desert is such longing made perfect. Brought to careful focus by the exercise of attentiveness and winnowed by indifference, the monk becomes a lover of God *par excellence.*

But how does this happen? If the desert, in its bleak emptiness, gives rise to frenzied desire, how is this desire made pure, stripped of its illusions, and reconsecrated as love? If wild terrain initially evokes a nervous attentiveness, rooted in one's anxious need for survival, how is this attentiveness slowly transformed into the calm and undistracted watchfulness of the desert saints? The answer, as Evagrius knew, lies in the exercise of *apatheia* as the mother of *agape*. Indifference, aimed at one's exercise of desert attentiveness, turns frantic desire into focused love.

The early desert fathers and mothers accomplished this task by incorporating into their discipline the very qualities of simplicity and redundancy that characterized their environment. Attending over and over to the same repetitive detail with unblinking watchfulness became the highest aim of desert prayer. Only as one's attention was narrowly focused—by means of a simple, repetitive prayer, by the monotonous motion of the hands in weaving—could one learn gradually to be fully present, without distraction, in any given moment to whatever presents itself. This, and this only, is the final meaning of love.

As Francis de Sales would later insist, "Contemplation is simply the mind's loving, unmixed, permanent attention to the things of God."[45] From his monastery in the Sinai Desert, Saint Hesychios the Priest defined attentiveness as "the heart's stillness, unbroken by any thought."[46]

These desert teachers never tired of emphasizing the need to focus one's attention. To this end, Abba Lucius urged the constant repetition of the first verse of Psalm 50, "Have mercy upon me, O God, according to thy great mercy."[47] John Cassian preferred Psalm 70:1 ("Come to my help, O God; Lord, hurry to my rescue"), asking what could be more perfect than to latch onto God by means of a brief phrase.[48] John Climacus claimed that even a single word was enough.

> Try not to talk excessively in your prayer, in case your mind is distracted by the search for words. *One word* from the publican sufficed to placate God, and a single utterance saved the thief. Talkative prayer frequently distracts the mind and deludes it, whereas brevity [*monologia*] makes for concentration.[49]

This practice of *monologia,* the prayer of a single word, became the basis of the Jesus Prayer as it developed in Eastern monastic life and was later incorporated in the teachings of the *Philokalia.*[50] It would evolve into the repetition of the phrase "Lord Jesus Christ, have mercy on me," but it could also refer simply to the continued reiteration of the name "Jesus" alone. This practice emerged as the foremost desert technique for abandoning all the restless thoughts and desires that preoccupy the frantic mind. In its metaphorical act of putting one foot in front of another, doggedly making one's way across the sands, the stubborn, methodical practice of prayer assumed the characteristics of desert survival. "What saves a man is to take a step," Saint-Exupéry affirmed. "Then another. It is always the same step, but you have to take it."[51]

Repeated over and over again, the simple prayer has an effect of silencing the anxious ego, with all its wearying demands for attention, for intellectual certainty and the comforting assurances of home.[52] Thoughts and fantasies are released. The mind is pulled down into the heart and allowed to glimpse for the first time the simple, inconstruable beauty of everything around it. The desert comes alive; simplicities take on a whole new life. One begins to hear all that had been drowned out by the noise of the ego, how much one's fretful anxiety had limited one's capacity to love. At this crucial moment, the desert teachers explain, something astonishing occurs. "The ego becomes interested in its own destruction."[53] This happens as one acquires a taste for silence, and for love, in the quiet exercise of attentiveness.

The prayer of repetition serves to whet the appetite of the soul, stilling the fretful mind, offering an ever-clearer perception of what is desired most, the untamed and fiercely loving God of the desert. But even as this desire is heightened, the actual possibility of its being fulfilled is diminished.

The desert makes it very plain that a God of awesome and elusive grandeur cannot be had. The God of wilderness lies beyond human control, beyond acquisition. Yet the desert lover continues to beat on the distant heart of God with the slow, repetitive word of his prayer. The word or phrase is transformed into an arrow of steel, says Carlo Carretto, and it beats again and again against God's thick cloud of unknowing. The fourteenth-century mystic who first employed this image knew the subtle truth that God longs to be feverishly sought, hiding from those God cherishes so as to quicken desire into a deep, long-suffering love.[54]

There is a sweetness, therefore, in every bitter exercise of the discipline. We are never so close to the one we love as when we relinquish our anxious grasp of her or him. C. S. Lewis argued that love is most fully realized "when what you most desire is out of reach." It is love's unattainability that draws us inexorably to it. Nothing is so unattainable as God, nothing more out of reach. Yet nothing evokes our love more strongly. God is the elusive one, at the heart of our very being, who promises to give according to our capacity to release. As Saint-Exupéry observed, "the Love of the Sahara, like love itself, is born of a face perceived and never really seen."[55] We love and are loved by God in the act of relinquishing every guarantee of love. The wild and joyous freedom that comes rumbling up from the depths of the soul in that moment remains an utter mystery, the dark and inexplicable mystery of love.

Contemplating One's Neighbor: Attentiveness Distributed

Finally, this desert practice of focused attention in prayer radically alters one's relationships with others. When the ego embraces indifference and the heart exercises attentiveness, we become, for the first time, truly available to others. Openness to the person before us, in all of his or her otherness, suddenly becomes possible. "Attention consists of suspending our thought, leaving it detached, empty . . . ready to receive in its naked truth the object that is to penetrate it."[56] As Simone Weil insisted, true attentiveness leaves itself perpetually open to surprise.

To love someone is to grant him or her the gift of one's pure and undivided attention, without preconceived expectations of what the other person needs, what we imagine to be best in the situation, what particular results we want to engineer. This is a love finally purged of the ego's calculating desires, a love without strings. It contemplates other people with the same wonder it has found in contemplating God. The choice is simple, as Alan Jones contends: "'We either contemplate or we exploit.' We either see things and persons with reverence and awe, and therefore treat them as genuinely other than ourselves; or we appropriate them, and manipulate them for our own purposes."[57]

Love as distributed attentiveness is the only form that justice can take in a world of people aching for attention. Contemplative prayer must be fulfilled in the loving contemplation of one's neighbor. To suggest otherwise is to misunderstand entirely the teachings of the desert masters.

Simone Weil learned this from her experience with oppressed factory workers in Paris, with poor miners and vine-workers in southern France. "Those who are unhappy," she said, "have no need for anything in this world but people capable of giving them their attention. The capacity to give one's attention to a sufferer is a very rare and difficult thing; it is almost a miracle; it is a miracle."[58] Remaining indifferent to every predetermined program for "helping the poor" and, instead, being altogether present to the person before us—*this* is the desert practice of love as justice. "It is the recognition that the sufferer exists, not only as a unit in a collection, or a specimen from the social category labeled 'unfortunate,' but as a man, exactly like us."[59]

Only to the extent that attentiveness (or contemplation) remains concrete and specific can it also be true. A brother once asked an older monk in a desert community, "Which is holier, someone who leads a solitary life for six days a week, giving himself much pain, or another who simply takes care of the sick?" The old man smiled and replied, "Even if the one who withdraws for six days were to hang himself up by his nostrils, he could not equal the one who serves the sick." Self-denial never substitutes for love.[60]

This is a theme that echoes repeatedly throughout the sayings of the desert Christians. To attend to the poor is to contemplate the mystery of God's presence in the world. Paying attention (both to God and to each other) is all that ever really matters. One of the Egyptian fathers, seeking a sign of divine approval for his long years of monastic devotion, was told that his sanctity was nothing compared to that of a common grocer in a nearby town. On going to study this man very carefully, the monk found him occupied with his vegetables amid the noise and hurry of the city streets, attentive to the needs of all those coming to him. Even as night came on, with the people growing rowdy, singing loudly in the streets, the man stayed at his task, helping latecomers with their needs.

In exasperation the monk finally blurted out, "How can you ever pray with noise like this?" The grocer looked around, feeling compassion for the people that made up his ordinary life, and answered very simply. "I tell myself they're all going to the kingdom," he said. "They're concentrating with single-minded attention on what they do, singing songs with all the joy they can muster. See how they prepare for the kingdom of God without even knowing it! How can I do less myself than to praise in silence the God they inadvertently celebrate in song?" That night the old monk walked slowly back to his cell, knowing himself to have received—from a grocer, no less—an important lesson in the craft of desert attentiveness.⁶¹ Contemplative prayer can be practiced only where people grant each other the gift of their attention.

Conclusion

"The essence of the spirituality of the desert," Benedicta Ward explains, was something "not taught but caught; it was a whole way of life."⁶² Through its discipline, men and women learned to balance attentiveness and indifference in a way that made possible the transformation of desire into love. Their deepest insights were shared as longings rather than ideas. They recognized the beginning point in the spiritual life as always an exercise in wanting. "The high road and the nearest way to heaven is measured not by yards but by desires," said the author of *The Cloud of Unknowing*.⁶³ The early monks knew that the desert taught desire as nothing else could.

Antoine de Saint-Exupéry, in his own North African desert reflections, spoke of the passionate attentiveness he found among the Moors. Desert life had bred in these sun-scorched bedouins a lean sense of hunger, an awareness that the niggardly God of the desert is never given to excess or waste, a conviction that "want" is always the desert norm. The French pilots, in their idle hours at Cape Juby, would sometimes try to "tame the Moors," taking them up for rides in their planes, sharing the riches of *la vie supérieur française*. But the Africans remained stubbornly contemptuous of European displays of power, even when three of them were taken to Paris and shown the Eiffel Tower, huge locomotives, and steamships on the Seine.⁶⁴

The marvels of technology did nothing to impress the Arabs. They wept, however, at the sight of trees. These Arab bedouins had never seen a waterfall, a river, a rose. The only natural world they had ever known was flagrantly stingy with its gifts. Years of desert attentiveness had trained them to expect only shortfall and subtlety. Back home, where water was precious, they might walk for days on end in search of a tiny spring, maybe a handful of palms. So when they stood in a high alpine meadow beside an enormous waterfall in the French Alps, its water roaring out of the mountain in a huge braided column, they had no way of comprehending such lavishness.

> They stood in silence. Mute, solemn . . . gazing at the unfolding of a ceremonial mystery. That which came roaring out of the belly of the mountain was life itself, was the life-blood of man. The flow of a single second would have resuscitated whole caravans that, mad with thirst, had pressed on into the eternity of salt lakes and mirages. Here God was manifesting Himself: It would not do to turn one's back on Him.⁶⁵

They refused to leave, adamantly declaring to their French guide that honor required their waiting . . . waiting for the end. Knowing the water could not last much longer, they awaited the moment "when God would grow weary of His madness," when this wild extravagance would suddenly and finally exhaust itself. Resolutely they stood their ground. "But, you see," the guide at last proclaimed, realizing how absurdly unintelligible his words must seem to such men, "this water has been running here for a thousand years!"

Having known the depths of desert thirst, these men could scarcely fathom a surging torrent of water, rushing forever from the rock. Nothing had prepared them for it—other than desire itself. Their hearts set aflame by longing, they had learned through the years an indifference to everything less than love. *Apatheia* had taught them that purity of heart is to will one thing. Hence, they could fiercely say no to locomotives and Gallic conquerors of the sky. But they must stand in silent awe before a raging cataract, beholding in wet-eyed wonder the unwearying madness of their God.

Perhaps this is where we all eventually stand, held attentive by what we cannot understand but vehemently love. The heart trained in poverty lives perpetually in hope of wonder.

Scratchings on the Wall
of a Desert Cell

I have often said that the sole cause of man's unhappiness is that he does not know how to stay quietly in his room. —Blaise Pascal[1]

For many of the earliest monks, stability of place was the primary condition for all else—"stay in your cell, and your cell will teach you everything." "Let your imagination think what it likes only do not let your body leave the cell." —Rowan Williams[2]

I sit on the porch of a bunkhouse up the mesa from Ghost Ranch, looking across the valley toward Pedernal, that forever-blue mountain with its squared top of chiseled flint. The screen door to my room swings open and shut behind me with a sudden gust of air. Night is coming on. A hard wind sweeping across the valley brings tales of witches from this place once called *el Rancho de los Brujos.* I hear cries of La Llorona, the weeping mother who has slain her children, secrets that resist being told.

I've come to northern New Mexico once again to share in a seminar on what the desert means, as well as to ask the landscape how at last to finish—how to bring this book, and this season of my life, to a final conclusion. A lonely desert cell is an appropriate place for such a task. Accompanied by an untoward night wind, its bodeful mystery keeping one close to home, it gives me time to assess what has been lost, what also has been found, and how much of the story can be told.

My mother's room in the nursing home where she spent her last three years became her own desert cell. Neither of us would have imagined this happening when she first moved in. On that dreadful morning it seemed, as all cells do at first, only a prison. But as months moved into years, it became apparent that her growth toward quiet attentiveness, and even a new capacity to love, somehow emerged as a consequence of accepting the room. Michael Ventura speaks of "the gift of the room" as the most important discipline in any creative work. To be a writer, an artist, a monk creating praise out of the stuff of his own being, one has to be able to endure staying alone in a room. Unless one has this "talent of the room," all one's other talents may be worthless.[3]

My mother's experience of this truth has been so persuasive that I'm no longer sure I want to be protected from a nursing home room of my own some day. I have no illusions about the pain and loneliness of the place, the boredom, the indignities sometimes heaped upon the aged by poorly paid and indifferent staff, the endless smell of urine. I know full well that my mother would have moved if she'd had any other choice, that others on her floor bitterly resented the place until the day they died, never accepting "the gift of the room." The cell in itself carries absolutely no guarantee of healing. But the powers of acceptance discovered by the human spirit are sometimes amazing. To freely choose what one cannot change may be the highest exercise of the will, and its deepest freedom.

My mother's acceptance of the cell gave her, for the first time in her life, a quiet space for the healing of memories. She was able to pour a lifetime of anxieties and compulsions into that suffocatingly quiet room. It received everything. As a place she could not leave, it became ironically a source of the highest freedom she ever attained.

In all of the great traditions that practice silence, the body is recognized as the spirit's most effective teacher. Let the imagination roar, but keep the body still, they urge. Despite one's inability to control one's thoughts or remain attentive at prayer, if the body is stationary, all is not lost. In Soto Zen, the secret of meditation is a matter of *zazen,* sitting perfectly still. The practice of *salat* or ritual prayer in Islam involves staying within the two-and-a-half-by-four-foot perimeter of the prayer rug on which one kneels. Assuming the lotus position in Hindu yoga, dovening in place during Jewish prayer, resolutely staying in one's desert cell—all these are expressions of the same principle: contain the body in order to release the soul.

So I sit here, in the straight-backed chair outside my cell, resisting the impulse to hike toward Chimney Rock in the ominously gathering sunset, to chat with others over coffee down at the dining hall, to squeeze anything else into the more-than-sufficient hurriedness of this day. I listen to the night wind, letting the woeful tales borne upon it work their way more deeply into the silence. I think of other cells in other places.

Without ever leaving her room, my mother traveled everywhere in the last few years of her life. As her body remained still, her mind learned to release its overzealous control of all the stories she'd lived. Boundaries were dissolved between past and present, living and remembered places, hallucinations that operated as sickness and also as cure. Often the stories we most need to recover surface only as the body comes to a reluctant stop. "Let your imagination think what it likes, only do not let your body leave the cell." My mother explored the outer reaches of this discipline in ways I'm not yet able to understand.

Her fantasies grieved me at first. It seemed sad that she retreated so often into an escape from reality. But I came to recognize her fictions as far more than a mere avoidance mechanism. They provided also a way of recovering the most penetrating and healing narratives of her life, becoming deeply curative, for myself as well as for her. For years on end, in her restless activity, she'd run from these truths, just as I, too, had resisted the stillness of the body, always running, lest stories from which I'd fled so long might finally track me down. All of us are pursued by such demons, the desert fathers insisted.[4]

Fantasy and the Healing of Memories

My mother was on a train one day when I came to visit her in the nursing home. When I gave her the ice cream cone I'd brought, she abruptly warned me that the train was apt to start up at any time. "What train?" I asked, caught off guard. "The one I'm *on!*" she declared, with her usual inability to suffer fools. My mother was a woman who had survived six husbands and untold tragedies. Cantankerousness was one of the desert virtues she had acquired early.

"Where are you going on the train?" I asked, intrigued by the travel imagery that so often marked her dreams. I knew I should feel sorry for her, lamenting the sad loneliness of an old woman's mind in a deserted nursing home. But frankly I felt more fascination than sadness. There was nothing pathetic about this woman before me. She was riding the rails that afternoon, "on the road," as footloose as Jack Kerouac. Tooling through the high desert toward Santa Fe in an open box car, her hair in the wind, sucking up the miles—I didn't feel an ounce of pity for her.

"I don't know," she answered my question with half a smile. "They don't tell you much here." "They" were the managers of my mother's heavily institutionalized world. Nurses, controllers, the runners of things. Difficult people you gotta live with, from her point of view. "They rob you blind, if you let 'em," she'd say, though without rancor. My mother was a lover of the art of complaint, but she knew also how to forgive.

In the reverie that her fantasy invited, I thought of trips we'd taken together as a family through the years. "Remember when I was seven and we took the train to New York City to see Aunt Adelaide?" "Of course," she smiled, nodding her head enthusiastically. We had ridden the Atlantic Coast Line Railroad, making our way up the eastern seaboard. Day running into night, it had been to me like traveling the Orient Express from Paris to Istanbul. It was my first trip on a train, a journey forever imprinted on a seven-year-old mind.

By now I'd started to take notes, thinking there might be something worth remembering in all of this. "You keepin' track of the mileage?" she asked. "Yeah," I nodded, staying with the game, scribbling on the back of an old envelope. "How do you know how many miles you've gone?" she asked curiously, as she got near the bottom of her cone. "You count the telephone poles," I responded, searching for an answer to a fair question. "One every three hundred feet. Add 'em up and you know how far you've gone." She shook her head knowingly. It made good sense to her, too. One of those little-scraps-of-useful-information you immediately recognize as valid.

In the shared solitariness of her cell that afternoon, I entered the fantasy, and I, too, found it healing. I realized how much I'd become a participant in her whole experience there. I, too, had been drawn into the discipline of the cell, required to abandon my restlessness, to let old memories surface in the brackish-water ponds of the mind. Healing comes in the body's quietness, as the imagination is allowed to play out its fantasies without judgment or regret. So long as the body can move, the mind is never forced to count its losses or embrace its greatest joys. Until one accepts the inescapability of the cell, it is forever easier to run.

My mother's desert experience has allowed me, even required me, to accept repressed and forgotten fantasies of my own. Sharing in her slow, increasingly honest movement toward death has made possible a deeper understanding of the loss of my father as well. His death, when I was thirteen, forced from me a childhood I would never finish. I was too young, and too frightened at the time, to be healed. My life ever since has been an effort to understand, or (more truthfully) to deny, that pivotal event.

Sitting here in the darkening, blood-red landscape that bewitched the imagination of Georgia O'Keeffe, I watch menacingly purple clouds from the west pushing the night closer. It raises in me a sense of uneasiness, the memory of dreams I'd rather forget. Ancient cries of desert Penitentes, the prayers of Mother Guadalupe, the bleeding body of her Son still crucified on *bultos* and *retablos* across this land—all these are carried on the wind. Last night in my cell I was aware of a dark, dreadful thing lurking on the floor beside my bunk. Fearing it would take me if I didn't grasp it first, I reached down in my dream and seized this Protean beast, holding on for dear life as it went through all its horrible changes. Yet just before I woke at dawn, it became a child—something not to be feared at all, only to be loved.

The Search for the Lost Father

What haunting yet hopeful stories does this desert night carry on its wind? It stirs the memory of tales often repeated beside my mother's bed in the nursing home, the familiar story, for example, of my parents having met in upstate New York at the end of the Depression. They were no longer young, having both been married twice before. But even when love should have known better, they gave themselves to hope. Leaving Poughkeepsie to start a new life, they traveled south in a Model-A Ford with fifteen dollars in their pocket. They stopped in Washington, D.C., went into the rotunda of the Capitol, and there said their vows to one another. It was shortly thereafter that my life began. Going on to Florida, they worked at odd jobs, dancing with despair, slowly building a small frame house with their own hands, laughing like Abraham and Sarah with the son of their old age.

My life, as the story later was told, began in hope and seemed forever charmed, at least until the phone rang one early Thursday morning and the world came abruptly to an end. My father, we were told, had been shot, his body found in a teller's cage at the bank where he worked as a guard. The story is shrouded with shame, mystery, the sense of betrayal that comes with disclosing family secrets. Perhaps if it can be told at all, it's only on a stormy New Mexican night like this, with dark shapes flying on the wind. Only as Ishmael can I tell the tale, only as the last surviving member of the family, the only one left to be hurt in the telling.

We never learned the details of my father's death, whether it was suicide or murder. Two days before he died, he had discovered money that had been missing in the bank. Investigations had been launched. Either my father had known too much and was killed by those who sought his silence or he'd been implicated in some way and had taken his own life. I would never know whether my father was a hero or something far less, but the coroner's report would leave me with the four most anguish-filled words of my entire life: "self-inflicted gunshot wound." My father had not simply died; he apparently had left.

It has taken me forty years to write those words. Through forty years of silence I've waited, like Telemachus, for the lost father, for the one who would return with arms thrown open to his son, with stories of sacrifice and bravery, a robbery interrupted, honor preserved and love proclaimed. I have longed, like every son, for Ulysses.

What I haven't known, through all these years, is how to grieve. If it was murder that took my father, then my grief was necessarily displaced by fear. I, too, could be snatched by the same terror that seized him. But if it was suicide that ended his life, then grief was stifled by guilt; I kept wondering what I hadn't done to keep my father from despair. For years I've been robbed even of the right to anger. How can one rage at his father's murderers without also pursuing them to justice, demanding answers to questions he was too afraid to ask? And how can one rage at the father for taking his life—compounding the sin of filial disobedience with the desecration of the father's name—if he never did this thing? What, one asks of the harsh, nocturnal wind, is the shape of grief for those long deprived of lamentation and complaint? What caldron awaits the outpouring of their bile?

Only in the dark New Mexican night can the son rage and remember and cry his own despair, lamenting the father who left—or was taken—for whatever reason, he will never learn. The secrets, if they were known, have now all died with the mother. He can only mourn with her, with Rachel, with Llorona, for their children, because he was one of them, long ago abandoned and left for dead. To the father he can cry into the whirlwind, "Where were you when I needed you most, when at thirteen I wanted a father as never before?" And to the mother he whispers after the words now lost on the night, "Why did the depths of your grief have to make you so deaf to my own?"

It is safe to ask such questions of the night. The wind scatters the short-lived words over distant mesas. The land can bear them. Here the earth has shared in crucifixion and is unafraid of death. The blood of Christ (*el sangre de Cristo*) flows from snow-capped mountains through the arteries of small rivers and *acequias,* washing away unmentionable sins, restoring life to the land. All deaths can be borne here, dissolved into the death of death in the death of Christ. They are taken finally to the cross, to the *bulto* with the bleeding knees, the bloody brow of the grief-filled Jesus, where all deaths are absorbed at last into love.

This is a truth, I realize now, that I've known even longer than my father's death. This sanguine landscape points to an earlier place in my childhood where God's strange love and the threat of death first met. I think I fell in love with God for the first time at the age of ten. In the early 1950s, my parents had begun attending a small Bible church that opened down the street from where we lived in central Florida. There I learned, with childlike horror and awe, the story of Jesus and the agony of his death. Transfixed by an exquisite tale of blood and pain— with the teacher suggesting that all of it was borne for *me*—I answered my first call to become a writer, starting a book of my own. Scrawled in King James English on a spiral tablet, it told the story of the cross, joining the awfulness of death with the mystery of God's indecipherable love. For years I would try to recover, in all the subsequent dyings of my life, the irretrievable wonder of that original grace.

In the months after my mother's death, I found among her things some of the yellowed pages of that long-ago unfinished work. I recalled the naive amazement with which I'd penned those words, blurring on the page as I wrote them. Words of being unaccountably loved, even unto death . . . even unto startling, violent death.

But it was a truth for a long time lost on the child of innocence who, when his father died, began collecting deaths the way other children collected stamps or coins: a teacher taken by cancer, a friend at school who committed suicide, an assassinated president. I was an only child, and with my mother hospitalized by the trauma of my father's death, I had to be strong (she said) for both of us. For years I held at arm's length this mystery of death and loss, viewing it with avid fascination, but always safely, from a distance.

The death of the father had left within me a yawning, empty place, something no amount of approval ever seemed able to fill. My temptation was to seek out substitute fathers everywhere, trying to be the perfect son, the ideal student, the one so anxious to please—as if to guarantee that no one would ever abandon this child again. Yet the compulsive need to be nice, to avoid every possibility of rejection, becomes itself dangerous and seductive. "Being nice" as a way of acquiring love is often not very nice at all.

The desperate need to be loved can keep one from love itself. True intimacy is only possible where emptiness is accepted as gift, where people don't use one another to try to fill (and to fix) each other's hollowness. Yet neither do they leave. Intimacy is participation in each other's unalterable emptiness, the sharing of a vulnerability that grows even deeper in being shared. If the desert has taught me anything, it's that love can only blossom in abandonment.

Only now, as the father—and the mother—are irretrievably gone, as the son retraces the path of his long search for the blessing of the firstborn son, does he find it possible (because now also necessary) to release these anxious dependencies of the past. Without parents, without anyone left to mend him, he's cast into this desert night, thrown on its darkened God as if nothing else were left. Maybe this desolate, desert God is the one he'd sought all along in the endless quest for a lost father.

A Lonely Cell in Jerusalem

This relentless New Mexican wind, still undiminished by the dark of night, takes me back to yet another cell on that other night in the distant city of Jerusalem several years ago. The aching memory of insufficiency and loss known to me as Jerusalem forms a coarse thread woven through the whole of this narrative. I remember that night sitting in my room at the *Ancien Couvent* of the École Biblique, watching the snow beat wildly against a lone cypress tree beyond the window. The fierce February storm had struck the Holy City, confining everyone to their rooms. A single candle burned in the monastery niche I'd been given. Scattered papers lay on a small desk by the bed. An apple, a flashlight, the open pages of a hand-written journal. I had nowhere to go, no distractions from the flickering shadows of a night wind in another land.

Having come to Israel on sabbatical to engage in desert research, I'd been launched on pilgrimage, recognizing (as every pilgrim must) the need to put one's life in order. If the pilgrimage is true, there's ever the possibility of one's not returning. Such fears are easily exaggerated, of course; fears always are. But they seemed real enough that night. Going alone, for an entire month, without the necessary languages, without friends, with people at home wondering why it was necessary to go at all, entering a place I'd never been—all this was fraught with anxiety. It was more desert than I'd bargained for.

Unable to sleep that night, I worried about all I'd left behind: a mother who was dying, a wife and children who grieved the distance that divided us, a career that had absorbed too much of my attention for far too long. For several days I'd feared not being adequate for the mountain climbing and long desert trek that lay ahead. Stumbling through the sublimely flowing French of the Psalter at Evening Prayer, I'd stared at my plate during meals, embarrassed by how little of the conversation I could follow. I'd felt keenly the loss of language, the comforting illusion of competence that it brings. A gaping hollowness filled me with a growing sense of dread. I'd been launched on a journey into loneliness, in the city a medieval poet once described as a golden basin filled with scorpions.

Word had come that very morning that even the trip to Sinai was cancelled, the last of my dreams for the sabbatical shattered. Everything had been lost, or so it seemed—the pilgrimage, the languages, the father and mother, the research and the career, the family I'd left behind. But most of all that night, in its expanding multiplication of apophatic loss, the long-term, unresolved fears of a father's violent death came slinking back, reawakened by the awareness of how little control I'd ever had over anything in my life.

That February night these were the real, if overdramatized, fears that filled the cold and lonely cell from which I could not run. "Make your cell a desert of its own," Abba Macarius had said.[5] He knew that one's room must become a crypt, a tomb, a chrysalis from which the larva of a new being may painfully and gradually emerge. Only in its tight cocoon does the caterpillar dream of change, in the place from which it cannot flee.

The cell, on that stormy night in Jerusalem, became for me a desert. Sometimes, it seems, one has to make the mistake of camping in a narrow wadi, an arroyo in the dry desert waste, not paying sufficient attention to the sound of distant thunder, not listening to the torrent of water that for years may have been sweeping down from dark canyons above.

Sometimes one needs only the cell, in a far and distant place, to concentrate all of these remembered fears. They come tumbling down in a seething wall of brown and foaming waves, the thick smell of dust and carrion pushed before the angry flow. A pale figure on a frothing horse rides this wave, slaughtering everything in its path, leaving no survivors. The figure is the terror of death one might have fled for years. In its shadow, one knows that the night of the dead (*la noche de la muerte*) has arrived.

Grandiose as this may sound, these moments in our lives of decisive—if entirely symbolic—confrontation with death may hold more terror and yield more deliverance than any of the tangible, immediate experiences we have of death itself. We're most free to "practice" at death—coming to terms with our deepest fears of it—in metaphorical situations where secondary terrors substitute for the real thing. That's why the cell functions so powerfully as the metaphorical equivalent of the tomb.

It was curious, for example, to experience myself that night as "dead" . . . lying on the wet sand of the arroyo after the deluge had passed, beyond tears, beyond caring, only slightly aware of the murmuring, sucking silence filling the desert in the middle of the half-spent night. There in the deep silence of a monastery cell, past memory, and even hope, nothing remained. All was lost, or so it seemed. No one was left to measure the interminable silence of the night. No residual self, no "me" to be aware any longer of being aware.

In that brief apophatic moment one comes as close to knowing death as it may be possible in life. It is strangely absent of any further terror, any thought or feeling of any sort. It simply is. One can't predict in that moment what will happen next, but we have it on good report (from those who've certainly been there) that in the emptiness, a single, fragile word is often whispered just before the dawn. The word is "love." It may have been spoken at previous times in a person's life, but only now is it heard, in the darkest hollow of the night, in a silence sufficient for its hearing. Only love can pierce the stillness left in the horseman's deathly wake. Only love dispels death's fear. It rises wet with Christ from his baptism in the night, and summons the dead to life on the cold, damp grave of all that had been lost.

In that tenuous moment, in the monastery cell, I heard that word and was offered back my life, for whatever inexplicable reason, I do not know. Who can ever say why one is loved? But I was told that I would live again, beyond the father's death and mother's dying, beyond every inflated fear of emptiness, inadequacy, and even love itself. As the lost child had written so many years before in the book of his becoming, "I am crucified with Christ . . . nevertheless I live."

This is a truth taught by the experience of the night: that the dead are no longer bound by fear. They confront no greater threat than that through which they've passed already. Having once faced death, with all its terrors, one cannot die again.

I find very compelling this bold, free company of those with nothing left to fear. No longer starved for the approval of others, they thrive on risk and hunger for love. They constitute a brother- and sisterhood of those who, having died, now live again to walk in undaunted freedom beyond the desert and the grave. They accompany others along the way they've come, returning to that terror of death throughout their lives. This is how they grow toward wholeness, submitting every subsequent fear to the death of fear in their memory of the cross.

It's from within this freedom that I, too, can speak at last to the father who left so many years ago. It isn't unusual for fathers to make poor choices at times in their lives. A deep fear of confrontation and rejection keeps them from life itself, shunning the ordinary, demanding details of relationship. "Leaving" is always easier. I know the temptation.

But I know, too, how much my father wished it might have been otherwise in his own experience. And I'm the one now free to choose something different . . . for both of us. I'm able to call out to him on the night wind still blowing across these plains: "You and I will no longer bypass the desert for the sake of an easier route to Canaan. I will affirm the struggle to sustain ordinariness that you abandoned so long ago. We will choose—you and I—the long and harder path of attention to detail and commitment to relationship. We will leave no more." Intuitively I know my father's deep pleasure in hearing those words. They represent a choice to live, not by what he might have feared throughout his life, but by what he most desired. What greater hope does a parent ever have for his child than to see the faults they'd come to share eventually transformed into something altogether new?

Stories Carried on the Wind

By now the wind has nearly spent itself outside my desert cell. Clouds have broken. Antares appears, the brightest star in the summer sky. This flaming super giant, seven hundred times the size of our own sun, lies at the heart of Scorpio, a vast constellation spread across the southern horizon. Strange that a deadly creature would possess such beauty at its core. Yet this was the mystery I'd discovered in Jerusalem. A golden basin full of scorpions had also promised life.

There is a healing that's only possible in the darkest hour of the night, when death and loveliness walk hand in hand. The old *curanderas,* or healing women, in this region have known for centuries that certain curative herbs can only be harvested by the light of the moon. In this landscape of blue cornmeal, red chiles tied in long, thick *ristras,* and the white brilliance of *la luna,* many things are healing. But they often require the night to release the life they have to share.

Their healing is carried on the wind, in the *cuentos,* the half-remembered stories that sweep through canyons and up high mesas as the night descends. They make their way through old screen doors and cracks in the walls of lonely desert cells. Some are tales from which we may have fled for nearly all our lives. Others are fantasies that help us through the night. But each of these *cuentos* must be heard in solitude, in the curative silence of the room, at the place from which it's impossible any more to run. This is what my mother taught me about the sanctity and the inescapability of the cell.

"You take care," I said to her, that afternoon I'd found her on the train. "Have a good ride. The ticket is paid for all the way through." She smiled slightly as I prepared to leave. Something in me wanted to stay on board myself that afternoon—in a seat by the window, riding the New York Special, churning up the miles of the Atlantic Coast Line Railroad, moving toward a tomorrow that never comes . . . and always comes. I wanted to stay there beside my mother, listening to the droning sound of clinkers on the rail bed, counting telephone poles, watching people moving up and down the car. I wanted to ride forever, from the palmettos of north Florida to the tidewaters of Virginia, into the darkening night. Through deep tunnels under rivers of mystery, on my way to the Great City. To a morning that would dawn with huge skyscrapers and new adventure.

I wanted more than anything to escape into her fantasy, to recover the childhood I'd never been able to finish. But the story to which I was called to be faithful was a different one from hers. I had a family to love and promises to keep, new risks that I had to assume. Having made a choice of my own for intimacy and freedom in a cell one stormy night, I was required to travel alone this time. Love demanded accepting the emptiness from which I'd never again be able to flee.

"Are we traveling yet?" my mother asked me as I left. "We're traveling," I replied, with a smile and a kiss on her forehead. "You rest for now. I'll see you soon." I walked to the door without looking back. It was my mother's last train ride. She was taking the train home . . . up to New York, to Poughkeepsie, to where she'd grown up as a child. She went there to heal old wounds she'd been carrying for many years. She wouldn't return. For a long while, I listened to the engine pulling out of the station and I didn't feel sorry for either one of us. We were both launched on pilgrimage.

Conclusion

Rediscovering Christ
in the Desert

People who have not been in Narnia sometimes think that a thing cannot be good and terrible at the same time.

The Lion was coming on, always singing, with a slow, heavy pace. . . . Though its soft pads made no noise, you could feel the earth shake beneath their weight. . . . The children could not move. They were not even quite sure that they wanted to. The Lion paid no attention to them. . . . It passed by them so close that they could have touched its mane. They were terribly afraid it would turn and look at them, yet in some queer way they wished it would. —C. S. Lewis[1]

There is an unaccountable solace that fierce landscapes offer to the soul. They heal, as well as mirror, the brokenness we find within. Moving apprehensively into the desert's emptiness, up the mountain's height, you discover in wild terrain a metaphor of your deepest fears. If the danger is sufficient, you experience a loss of competence, a crisis of knowing that brings you to the end of yourself, to the only true place where God is met.

Beyond language, beyond human control, beyond all that is safe, one encounters a great beast prowling the edges of uncertainty. Lesser fears, in the presence of this beast, give way to a still greater fear whose other name is love. Scenery alone cannot accomplish this swift undoing of the soul. Wilderness simply occasions the vulnerability necessary for trust. But if you risk your life to the feral mystery glimpsed in the Lion's face, to what is first perceived with dread, you find that some things can indeed be good and terrible at the same time.

The threat of exposure to wilderness, a painful upheaval in one's personal life, the nakedness of prayer—all of these invite a similar danger. To meet one's God in the forfeiture of language is to ascend with fear and trembling the distant desert mountain of the soul. Apophatic spirituality naturally returns again and again to the suggestive image of Sinai. There, in flashes of lightning on red granite, Moses watches for God in the cleft of the rock, his mind stripped of images and his tongue rendered mute.

In its rebuke of glib theologizing, the *via negativa* longs for an intimacy with God that lies beyond human speech. It recognizes God's deepest vulnerability at the point of God's own agonizing loss of the Word, in the abandonment of the cross. Only in coming to Golgotha (or the Stone Table on the fields of Narnia) where everything is lost, does one experience the mystery of God as the slain Lion of the tribe of Judah. There God also loses everything, though willingly for the sake of love.

This search for a broken Christ in the fields of emptiness is what has driven me in this work. Permission to write on desert and mountain spirituality has to come from the landscape itself, from one's inadequate exercise of prayer and the experience of death at close range. What little expertise I can offer to legitimate these words lies less in the training of a scholar than in the perseverance of the *compañero,* one who has traveled with another through dangerous territory.

With this in mind I returned once again to the desert at the very end of my work, searching for a clue to an as-yet unanswered question. All along I'd been familiar with the hard fact of desert apprehensiveness, learning only with difficulty how the mystery of compassion grows out of indifference. I realized the order had to follow this pattern: until we've known fear, love remains a gift unrecognized and unclaimed. But I didn't understand how one makes this movement from desert harshness to desert love, if and when it occurs.

Naturally there are no guarantees that it ever happens. Some people die in the desert. Others flee as quickly as possible before it can affect them in any serious way. Only a few remain long enough to discover a hard-headed, unromanticized compassion, stripped of the sentimentalism that too often substitutes for love. They are the ones who manage to sustain the terrible and the good, without compromising either one.

Disillusionment and the Reading of Wilderness Landscapes

Wanting to understand how this mystery is still lived out in the desert practice of religious life, I went to the Monastery of Christ in the Desert, a small Benedictine abbey in northern New Mexico. Fifteen miles from the nearest phone down a winding dirt road that's treacherous at best, I quickly understood why these monks had chosen such a remote, secluded place to practice the silence described in chapter six of Benedict's Rule. I went there with the hope of bringing this project to a close, asking how terror and mercy come to be mixed in the desolate beauty of raw land.

There's more than a little seductiveness in the imagined splendor of a retreat at a desert monastery. One easily fancies himself going into the desert the way Thomas Merton did, having spat on Albuquerque and tromped on Santa Fe, headed for the wilderness with John of the Cross in one pocket and Charles de Foucauld in another, holding the Bible open at the Apocalypse. I went with high expectations, as I do on every retreat, always anticipating magic. Happily, it never happens. I'm left instead with something far better, a quiet reminder of ordinariness. But as usual on that first day of retreat, I marched into the wilderness, hungry once again for a stunning "desert experience" of my own.

I suppose I expected a morose company of reclusive desert monks, hardened by the landscape, knowing more of harsh ascetic discipline than of love. Old stereotypes don't die easily. But I found, instead, a community of ordinary people for whom the harsh desert had sometimes blossomed like a rose, for whom threatening mountains could seem to skip like rams. Laughter was, if anything, more common there than holiness. I was curious as to what discipline had made this possible, how they took notice of the Lion Aslan in a landscape that, to others, remained an empty, howling wilderness. If desert terrain is read in multiple ways, why do some people find strange comfort where others discover only desolation?

I found part of my answer in the liturgical life of the congregation there at Christ in the Desert. Liturgy has constituted the heart of desert communities throughout their history. The discipline of the Liturgy of the Hours, with its seven offices punctuating the day, serves continually as a refracting lens for reading the surrounding landscape, bringing to it a particular interpretative focus.

The liturgy demands a constant symbolic participation in the death and resurrection of Christ, inviting those present to recognize in everything about them a corresponding movement from abandonment to hope. Similarly, the daily repetition of the psalms, with all their psychological and liturgical diversity, underscores the twofold desert experience of anguished lament and joyful praise. As a result, dark, ruddy sandstone insistently proclaims the blood of Christ while hawks beyond the river sing the triumph of his baptism. Liturgy and landscape become separate readings of a single mystery.[2]

Evagrius observed in fourth-century Egypt that the desert is full of these two things, Mother *Apatheia* and Daughter *Agape,* the bane of indifference and the allurement of love. Everything in the desert ignores us, wholly unimpressed by any of our credentials. But everything in the desert is also thirsting and longing, aching for water, for sun and for life, including even us in its fervid desire.[3] The desert liturgy gives vivid expression to each of these realities, beginning with loss and plodding slowly toward hope.

My desire in going to the monastery was to realize for myself the symbolic power of both poles of the dialectic. Already familiar with the reality of desert threat, enough things in my life having prepared me for relinquishment, I hadn't yet been able to grasp the full conundrum of desert promise. I didn't know how love comes to life in the dry chaparral of indifference. I couldn't understand what allowed some people to discern the tracks of a lion beneath scrub oak trees while others saw nothing. I longed to be able to pierce to the heart of this great mystery in a dramatic desert encounter suddenly making everything clear. But count on the desert to welsh on every naive expectation of this sort. Even the hawk doesn't bet on his next meal.

My time there offered a confirmation (and also an undoing) of everything I'd learned about the solace of fierce landscapes. It occasioned a new confrontation with the land itself, a deeper appreciation of silence, and a richer insight into the "world-constructing" power of the liturgy. These three dimensions of my experience at Christ in the Desert finally provide a way of summarizing the essential argument of this book. They show how a threatening geography suggests the thoroughgoing emptiness necessary for apophatic prayer.

Ultimately, failure was the most valuable truth the desert monastery had to teach me. Disillusionment marks every new beginning in the spiritual life. I went there with the intent of imitating monastic practices of asceticism and prayer, of achieving (within the span of eight short days, no less) a grandly self-authenticating desert experience. It's the perennial temptation of the acquisitive self, trying to "cultivate pseudo-experiences" that will fill an inner void so as to make even emptiness itself an "object of experience."[4] We never tire of the effort to manipulate and possess idealized states of consciousness. Many people would rather have an "experience" of God than God himself.[5]

The masters of prayer in the apophatic tradition described throughout this book, however, insist that in the practice of silence ultimately there's no experience of God to be had. One finds in rushing to a desert monastery that there's nothing to "get" in that fervent quest for a canned mystical encounter. As the Cloud author resolutely affirmed, one finally has to be content with a naked God, having nothing to offer, completely unattached from all of God's gifts.[6] In entering the cloud of unknowing, there is nothing to be experienced, proved, felt, thought, acquired, or achieved. One loves God there for God's sake alone, not for anything that's gotten in return, not even an alleged experience of the holy.

Sometimes the gifts may be thrown in later as an afterthought; God has a way of doing that. But the gifts—the benefits of silence, the comforts of prayer, any sense of the divine presence—can never be sought as an end in themselves. You have to give up everything, the desert demands, every comforting assurance of passage through the wilderness. "The land of the spirit," John of the Cross stubbornly declared, "is a land without ways."[7]

Meeting Love in the Most Unlikely Places

My initial experience at Christ in the Desert near Abiquiu was one of disconcerting uneasiness. Standing at the end of the long, desolate road to the monastery, I waved goodbye to the friend who had dropped me off late that afternoon. The sun was setting on tall sandstone cliffs, a light wind moved through the juniper trees nearby, water in the river flowed silent and dark. There was a deep stillness to the place that I found inexplicably disturbing. With no one else around, I located my room in the guest house down the canyon from the chapel.

There in the cell, I stretched out on my sleeping bag and surveyed the tiny room. There was a small table to pray at, a kerosene lamp for light, a pot-bellied stove with a few sticks of piñon pine. But otherwise only an enormous, unnerving silence. I felt loneliness crawling onto my chest like a heavy cat. The sound of nothingness was penetrating, interrupted only by the sudden, haunting cry of a coyote somewhere off in the distance. I wondered if I was really prepared for this. Having considered myself something of a contemplative, I found the silence so devastating I wasn't sure I could endure an entire week of it.

This is characteristically the first impression the desert makes upon us. Put on edge by its wildness, we initially miss its beauty. Its vast sense of absence and anomie is disquieting. We feel physically threatened. In the process, however, we're opened to a great truth, that we often end up loving what we first approach with fear.

Allurement—that careful and passionate fixing of our attention, drawing us often to love—can be triggered by an experience of being unstrung, made very observant, mindful of things we might not otherwise notice because now our safety depends upon it. The desert teaches us to watch for mercy in the least likely places. Evagrius observed that "the Physician of souls heals by abandoning us," or so it often seems.[8] The desert becomes a good place for distinguishing between what is indeed a threat and what is actually another way of being loved.

Unfriendly terrain forces us beyond our popular conceptions of love as predictably sweet and warmly accepting. Much of the kindest love we know, we first were tempted to read as rejection. Think of the friends who are extremely blunt and outspoken, even caustic at times. On our first meeting we were most likely put off by their gruffness. Yet the hint of a smile or wink of an eye allowed us to recognize their brusque persona as hiding a fierce, unyielding love. These are people not afraid to speak the truth when loyalty demands it. On the Enneagram scale they're classified as "eights," often scorned by others as being far too direct.[9] Theirs is a desert love, exercised without apology or restraint. Only slowly do we appreciate their honesty. They invite us to a hard-nosed intimacy about which our culture knows very little.

Amma Syncletica of Egypt warned her disciples not to wear their saintliness on their sleeves. Don't try to manage first impressions, she urged. Don't be afraid if your gifts remain hidden, if people don't immediately recognize your worth. "Just as a treasure that is exposed loses its value, so a virtue which is known vanishes."[10] The desert itself teaches you not always to trust what you think you may be seeing. The deepest caring often initially disguises itself as indifference.

Syncletica was typical of those plainspoken desert Christians whose lives had been intimately shaped by harsh terrain. She and other desert women like her remind us that a rustic desert-mountain spirituality is the comfortable domain of women as well as men. It has nothing to do with *machismo*, the supposed male delight in abrasiveness and violence. To learn indifference to how one's worth is measured in the world is simply to be wise (and candid) as a desert snake while harmless as a dove. Women, as I've argued already, are drawn to the solace (and disregardfulness) of fierce landscapes every bit as much as men. Indeed, as the lives of Amma Syncletica, Georgia O'Keeffe, and Clarissa Pinkola Estés seem to suggest, they may be even more likely to embrace this fierce desert honesty.

One of the most moving books I've read in the process of this work has been Terry Tempest Williams's *Refuge,* an account of her mother's death by cancer and her own search for healing in the severe beauty of Utah's Great Salt Lake. Standing in the throbbing silence of the Great Basin Desert, exposed and alone, she finds it strange how "deserts turn us into believers," how "wilderness courts our souls." The loss of her mother and her thirst for refuge in wildness makes her sister to me, sharing a common loneliness. She reminds me of a truth I'd sometimes rather forget: "Without a mother, one no longer has the luxury of being a child."[11]

Women are inexorably drawn to all that is untamed in nature (and in themselves). Annie Dillard stares into the eyes of a weasel near Tinker Creek, fascinated by its feral tenaciousness, and remarks that, "I [too] could very calmly go wild."[12] Wilderness has never been solely a male preserve.

I'm awed by my spiritual director, a religious of the Sacred Heart in her seventies who thrives on all things Celtic and wild. Visiting the blustery emptiness of the Shetland and Orkney Islands in northern Scotland several years ago, she found them as irresistable as they were inhospitable. It was a landscape empty of everything but sea, stone, and sky. Because of high winds and rocky soil, practically nothing grows there. She could speak of something almost ontological in the vast openness of the place, its utter absence of boundaries. It was all too much, she exclaimed. Yet at the same time it spoke to something deep within her. Standing beside ancient stone rings on those barren isles in the far North Sea, in the very moment of being undone she knew herself also to be fiercely loved.

My experience at Christ in the Desert was not unlike hers. That first night at the monastery I went to bed while it was still light, knowing I had to be up early if I was to make it to chapel for Vigils. I lay there, listening to the wind howl as night came on. The desert was dark, cold, and moonless. Unable to sleep, I pulled the sleeping bag around me and waited out the night. When three-thirty finally arrived, I pulled on clothes in the cold morning air and walked outside with a small flashlight. It was pitch black. Still completely alone, I nervously felt my way up the canyon toward the chapel.

But as I stopped to lie down on a large rock and look up into the night sky, my uneasiness suddenly dissolved. I was home. The sky was lit with thousands of stars, stars I immediately recognized from my backyard in Saint Louis where I pray every night. Leo the Lion, Bootes the Ox-Driver, Hercules with his arms upraised—they were all there, stretched out across the heavens. A place without comfort or familiarity suddenly revealed itself as home.

My practice of watching the night each evening in Saint Louis as I give the day back to God isn't nearly as romantic as it may sound. It's a time remarkably free of rhapsody; nothing ever happens there. To the surprise of both of us, a raccoon reached out to touch my foot on his way across the grass the other night. But most of the time it's a place to think and to do nothing, a fine context for the practice of apophatic prayer.

What a monastery does best, perhaps, is to connect a person with his life of prayer back home. It was a brilliant skyscape of shared stars that made the connection for me that first night at Christ in the Desert. Being reminded of the liturgical pattern of my own routine at home made possible a "seeing of the Lion" in the vast expanse of the southern sky. There he lay as usual, Leo stretched out on all fours, the sickle-shaped pattern of stars forming his head and mane shining brightly in the night.

Without realizing it, I'd been made participant, in a small way, with the ancient tradition of desert monks at Scete in Egypt. They, too, knew the power of the night. They, too, found their way back home through the desert by following stars.

This mystery of encountering love through a landscape we first had learned to fear is sometimes a poignant metaphor of one's relationship to God. Put off by what strikes us as God's harsh majesty, we can't imagine being loved by what first had wholly disarmed us. Stripped of all efforts to manipulate and control, we're left without any ground for laying claim to God. If we're found (and loved) in the dead of the desert night, it's only by a God who instead lays claim to us.

The Power of Silence To Connect and Heal

Fierce landscapes offer a strange solace, yet they require a silence and solitude necessary for entry, as well as a discipline (or *habitus*) capable of disclosing meaning. A second theme recurring in the book and rediscovered in my stay at a desert monastery is the mystery of silence in the apophatic tradition.

The desert's profound exterior silence invites one to an unnerving, interior silence for which one is usually ill-prepared. Yet the fruit of this silence is a vulnerability absolutely essential to the spiritual life. Actual entry into a desert geography isn't necessary for acquiring the nakedness of word and thought that desert teachers of prayer advise. In my own case, it was a mother's terrifying silence of memory, brought on by Alzheimer's disease, that echoed my utter inability to change any of the things happening to either of us. It was a silence symptomatic of a general loss of control to which I had to consent.

This is what desert Christians cultivated in their practice of apophatic prayer, in the exercise of the *monologia,* the prayer of a single word used to still the heart. Each of these silences carries its own misgiving. Each points to unforeseen possibilities in the exhaustion of language. My own participation in the silence of a Benedictine abbey helped illuminate this discipline of the emptiness of words in new and unexpected ways.

A typical day in the monastery begins at four o'clock in the morning with Vigils in a dark chapel lit by candles. It ends liturgically with Compline at seven-thirty in the evening. That's when the Great Silence begins, when all talk is suspended until the next morning. It's a time to listen to geese singing alleluias on the river while walking back to one's room, time to watch the shadows rise on the huge cliff behind the chapel as the sun slowly sets. It's a magical time of the day, when light is most delicate, when sage brush (back-lit by the sun) glows like a burning bush. The silence is almost palpable.

An economy of language was generally characteristic of this remote desert community, something I observed through the rest of the day as well. Contrary to what I might have imagined, however, the practice of stillness didn't separate people as isolated individuals so much as it drew them together in a shared unity with the landscape itself. Seven times a day the community gathered in the chapel to break its silence, to chant psalms and pray, speaking in a voice common also to cholla and sage, river and rock. This intimate connectedness of the whole of creation was continually reemphasized. The psalms saw to that.

As other guests arrived later in the week, I was curious to notice how we related to each other in this common observance of silence. Not knowing one another's names or places or jobs—any of the things we normally use to pigeonhole (and to dismiss) each other in our minds—we were surrounded by a shroud of silence that seemed on the surface to shut each other out. We smiled and nodded in passing, but refrained from the small talk and niceties ordinarily expected in polite society. As a result, something unusual began to occur. Instead of ignoring these people, I found myself oddly caring about them, valuing their presence without even knowing their names. I started praying for them during the offices, looking forward to their being present even when nothing apparent passed between us. I'd never related to other people in such a way, connected by nothing more than a deliberate silence.

A few days later I "met" and at the same time said goodbye to Sharon and Nanette, two women who had been there for several days already. We mentioned how strange it seemed that despite (or, more properly, because of) the shared silence, we'd come so quickly to appreciate each other. Ignoring the other person on the surface level of genteel exchanges and public personas allowed us to "see" each other more deeply as human persons alone. I began to wonder if it's only the people from whom we come to expect nothing that we're ever able to perceive in all their uniquely created splendor.

There's a danger here of romanticizing monastic silence. I was admittedly a sucker for it, coming in search of some profoundly moving "desert experience of God," wanting as a Protestant to probe the mystery of Benedictine life. I imagined that if I did everything right, paying attention to every single detail, I'd find hidden somewhere in the practice of desert prayer the key to what I'd been seeking all along.

What I discovered at this desert monastery was a deeply caring community of radically diverse people joined together by the silence I found so remarkable. I remember one particular evening at dinner. A tape of music was playing while we ate, as usual, without speaking. I didn't know at the time that it was Maria Callas singing various arias from Puccini operas, but I was captivated by the sound. Leaning over to Brother Aelred sitting next to me, I asked in a whisper if he recognized the music. He's a former construction worker, a man of wonderful earthiness and simplicity. Rolling his eyes with a smile, he said he had no idea, adding that he preferred Miles Davis and a little New Orleans jazz.

The music had made me particularly curious, because I'd also noticed, across the room, Brother Tomás, a man of Mexican descent who sat with his eyes closed, his head tilted back and a seraphic smile on his face. He was perfectly absorbed in the beauty of that voice. He could have been drifting on light New Mexican clouds crossing the mountains in the late afternoon sun. I thought to myself, if these two men could live in the same community and delight so much in each other's differences, then what does shared silence have to teach me about love?

The silence was compelling, but disconcerting, too. I realized how much one afternoon as I sat alone in a corner of the chapel, beside a large *retablo* of Mother Guadalupe. Carved by one of the artists in the community, she wears a red dress under a dark-blue cape studded with stars. Rays of yellow light radiate from her body. Her face is unconventionally beautiful, with the hollow cheeks, aquiline nose, and tanned skin of a Latin American Indian woman. One recognizes in her the Mother of God to whom one might pour out all one's grief, knowing it to be absorbed in her own far deeper sorrow.

Sitting beside her in silence for a long time that afternoon reminded me of the hours spent at my mother's bedside in the nursing home. It wasn't necessary, in either case, to say anything to each other. The silence itself held something between us that words couldn't bear. Moreover, the sad eyes of this Mother kept taking me to the *bulto* of her crucified Son nearby. It was to him that she pointed, laying her grief at the foot of the cross. "Speak to the mother; she knows about death," Hindu believers say of the goddess Kali.[13] It was a truth I recognized that afternoon as I sat beside this woman of the desert. She taught me, through her anguish and through her silence, the desert shape of an unexpected love.

Yet again, there was nothing to be "gotten" in all of this, no "Hispanic-Catholic experience" suddenly captured by a spiritually bereft Protestant on retreat. There were no roses in December, no voices for Juan Diego, no particular sense of presence. It was simply good to sit in silence beside this woman, doing nothing, thinking nothing, in the same dull emptiness with which I'd often sat by my mother in the nursing home.

I need to be careful in describing the silence, the nothingness, to which I've been drawn in the writing of this book. Despite my temptations to the contrary, it hasn't been an effort to duplicate some stylized spiritual experience of emptiness described by Thomas Merton or any other desert hero. It hasn't been a search for some meditative technique to be used in acquiring the Gnostic self-awareness that Harold Bloom has characterized as the quintessential "American

Religion."[14] It isn't anything to be realized by effort, by a special *gnōsis,* by arcane exercises in *imitatio sancti.*

Nor, on the other hand, is it a celebration of the empty void as an end in itself, reaching for some Neoplatonic sense of being "alone with the Alone." The Christian practice of desert prayer, at its best, has no interest whatever in fleeing material things in order to ascend mystically to the sublime darkness of the immaterial. The concrete reality of the fierce landscape makes that as difficult as possible. What distinguishes the Christian exercise of silence in prayer is the "naked intent" of the person who, while empty of thoughts, nonetheless reaches blindly for the God that cannot be seen or even named. What keeps contemplative prayer from becoming privatized, disembodied, and free-floating is its anchorage in the repetition of the psalms, *lectio divina,* the sacramentality of the Mass, and the stabilizing influence of community.

What the desert teaches is a radical letting-go of the thinking-experiencing-managing self, so as to be content with God alone, a God without adjectives, without comforting signs of presence, so that at last one learns truly to delight in *nothing.* This nothing may be ultimately disclosed by the Christian *habitus* as "Something," as the Holy Trinity hidden in light inaccessible from every effort to grasp its mystery. But the naming of the mystery is no longer an anxious concern of those who've been to the desert. Naming implies a control that the wilderness no longer allows.

Liturgy and the Reaffirmation of Ordinariness

If the reading of solace from multicolored canyon walls requires a deep silence, it also obviously demands an interpretative discipline able to reveal the power of landscape as metaphor. I've argued that a carefully formed *habitus* offers the vision necessary for discerning the deepest meanings of one's habitat. Landscape is always constructed, a lively work of the imagination. It reveals its secrets to those who are attentive, who see with the eyes of a tradition molded by the land itself.

It's the liturgy that plays this role in a desert monastery. It opens the members of the community to the surrounding terrain in a way that reinterprets their mutual existence. "The world is remade each time the liturgy is reenacted," Walter Brueggemann argues in his study of ancient Israel's worship.[15] The earth is restored to all its ordinariness and wonder through the constant repetition of the psalms. The night sky declares anew the glory of God as Psalm 19:1–4 gives voice to the landscape. Human creatures respond by assuming their own role in the liturgical act of reestablishing the earth. Clouds are reset above the mountains, streams are sent down once again from the hills, young lions are set free to roar, humans are charged with singing the beauty of it all (Ps. 104). The liturgy, in short, invites everything in the landscape to reaffirm its contribution to the whole, in a celebration of embodiment as a sacrament of the living God.[16]

Liturgy is inevitably the life-coursing blood of a monastery. I worked hard

The chapel at Christ in the Desert Abbey, Abiquiu, New Mexico.
(*Photograph by author*)

during those first few days at Christ in the Desert, learning the rhythm of the liturgy, trying to feel natural in the texture and movement of monastic prayer. I loved the chanting of the psalms. I'd wake up in the middle of the night still hearing the melody, remembering the faint, pungent smell of incense. By my third day there, in fact, I started to think I'd gotten the whole thing down fairly well—knowing when to stand and to sit, how to bow properly for the doxology, which responses to use. Not bad, I thought, for a stiff Presbyterian. What's more, I hadn't missed a single office. I'd been the only guest to get up for Vigils every morning! I'd pulled off almost perfectly this task of pretending to be a desert monk.

But no sooner had I become a little familiar with the liturgy, priding myself on doing it so well, than it began to seem, after all, a very dull and ordinary thing. I couldn't imagine doing this day in and day out for the rest of my life. The genius of the liturgy, though I hadn't yet learned it at the time, is its ability to anchor the ordinary in the psalms' repetitive process of continually reconstituting the world, and us within it.

Too many people (including myself) are given to highly romantic ideas about the character of religious life in the desert, imagining how wonderful it must be to live amidst silent beauty, praying always in the presence of God. But even in my limited experience of a desert monastery, I found it a very ordinary and *un-romantic* place. At four o'clock in the morning a cold wind is blowing down the canyon. People in the chapel are coughing their way through the psalms, trying to clear their throats without having had their first cup of coffee. The monks are passing gas (like everyone else) because of all the beans and tortillas eaten at dinner the night before. Brother Aelred, as Hebdomadary (leader for the week), is helplessly breaking down as his gravelly voice tries to reach those impossible high notes, while Brother Pachomius is laughing into his hand, thinking how silly the whole thing must sound. That's pretty much the ordinary day-to-day experience of monastic life.

The liturgy is hard work, a matter of constant repetition, seemingly dull and boring. But the desert teachers have always said that if you give yourself to the recurrent ordinariness of prayer, if you don't fight it—letting all your scattered, anxious thoughts pull you this way and that—your mind will gradually be taken down into the heart. Distractions can be released. The ceaseless regularity of the liturgy works on those distractions with a stubborn indifference, so that the mind is silenced and the heart made able to love.

I found this true even of the manual labor that forms an extension of the liturgy in Benedictine experience. For four hours each morning I took part in a work detail, helping to dig a four-foot-deep ditch from the refectory down to the pump house at the river. It was hot and monotonous work, but I loved the company of the other men. We talked more while we worked than at any other time of the day. Maintaining a slow and steady pace, we watched for blisters that might form, kept an eye out for rattlesnakes in the grass nearby, stayed attentive to the sun. It was a wonderful rhythm of ordinariness, the work inviting us to forget ourselves, paying attention to the goodness of each moment with its possibilities for relating to each other and being connected to the land. It provided yet another example of faithful, repetitive indifference to distractions giving quiet birth to compassion.

The desert is a place for learning to lower one's expectations almost to the point of absurdity, being content increasingly with less and less, giving up living ambitiously for lofty "ends" of any sort. One discovers there the importance of the simplest of "means," ignoring everything else that doesn't serve the ordinary.

That's how one comes, at last, to find strange comfort in the desert waste, only by embracing indifference, learning to delight in nothing so much as simplicity. Solace lies at the still point of emptiness—beyond hope, beyond proof, beyond consolation. Deliberately aiming the exercise of indifference (*apatheia*) at oneself, one releases little by little the anxious thoughts of the distracted ego. The false self is gradually starved by inattention. One learns also to be indifferent to others, ignoring surface impressions so as to open oneself to radically different people on the clean, level ground of an unspoken humanity. No longer driven by short-lived feelings of sympathy or pity, one consistently, doggedly works for justice without thought of reward.

Ultimately one becomes indifferent even to God, remaining blithely uncon-
cerned about particular answers to prayer, about anything one might previously
have wanted to "get" from God. One waits, instead, in curiosity to see what
comes in the dark uncertainty of the night, content simply with God alone.
Prayer becomes less a matter of petition than of relationship. Moving beyond
the objectifying of one's self, one's neighbor, one's God, the wilderness traveler
arrives at that lonely desert place where love is now possible because it finally is
wholly free, released of every frantic need to exploit and possess.

Miracles are Nothing

If my week at Christ in the Desert had begun with anxiousness and fear, it
threatened to end in the same way. From the beginning I hadn't been sure about
how I'd get back to the airport for the flight home. My hope had been to find a
ride with one of the other guests, at least to the end of the road. From there, I
figured, I could hitchhike down to Santa Fe where I'd catch the bus to Albuquerque. It took several days to find someone who could give me a ride, but
soon everything was arranged. I felt relieved—at least until storm clouds began
gathering later in the week.

By early evening of the day before we were scheduled to leave, the sky turned
black, huge thunderheads approaching from the south. The driver who'd promised me a ride came running in, explaining that she was sorry but she couldn't
risk waiting until the next day. She had to leave right away lest the rains come
and her car get stuck on the road, missing a meeting she absolutely had to attend
the next morning. By that time it was too late for me to pack and leave with her,
so I stood there waving goodbye, suddenly without a way home, wondering
what I'd do next. I was tempted (as always) to panic. Yet I knew I'd been taken
care of all week long and if worst came to worse, I could walk out.

In the end, that's what happened. Early the next morning after Vigils, while it
was still dark, I picked up my backpack (full of a few icons, dirty clothes, a couple of Power Bars and a liter of water) and started down that thirteen-mile road.
I'd picked up some garbage bags to cover my gear if the rains came. I'd even
strapped to my pack the skull and horns of an old dead cow I'd dug up in the
ditch during the week, taking it home as a Georgia O'Keeffe kind of memento.

After the first hour of walking, as dawn came and the sun rose, there wasn't a
cloud in the sky. The rain had missed us altogether. I walked the Chama River
Canyon Wilderness and it was beautiful beyond words. There were multicolored
mesas in the distance, rapids singing in the river, jays and nutcrackers chirping
everywhere. "And also with you," I'd call back to them every now and then, continuing my participation in the liturgy, walking like Adam through Eden on the
day after creation.

Having taken the risk of being content with nothing, with a naked God
stripped of all gifts, I'd fully expected a long walk in soaking rain. Whatever hap-

pened would have been all right; it didn't matter. But oddly enough, in that utter indifference to need, God had thrown the gifts in anyway (at least this time), as a gesture of wild and unnecessary extravagance.

Four hours later I made it to the highway, just as the last of my water gave out. But by that time, I was home free, or so I thought. All I needed was a ride to Santa Fe. While I hadn't done any hitchhiking since college, I didn't expect any problem. Surely every other pickup truck on the highway would offer a ride to a harmless fool fresh from the wilderness. But none did. This bearded, middle-aged man with a dead cow scull on his back must have looked suspicious.

Walking down Highway 84 toward Santa Fe, I began slowly yielding to panic, wondering how I'd ever get to the bus in time to make it to the airport in Albuquerque. At the last minute, just as hope seemed once again entirely lost, I was able to catch a ride with someone from Ghost Ranch making a hurried trip into Santa Fe. She got me to the bus stop five minutes before my bus left for the airport.

The whole day—the whole week, it seemed—had been charmed. All along I'd been asked only to trust, with a rugged and disciplined indifference, and God's response had been to occasion wildly unpredictable love in every way possible. Indeed, as I boarded the bus, headed at last toward home, a woman passed me on the sidewalk nearby wearing a T-shirt that read, "*Milagros son nada!*" (Miracles are nothing!). In a world remade each day by the mystery of the liturgy, in a magical desert land regarded traditionally as *la tierra encantada*, who knows what might happen next? The miraculous becomes wholly ordinary where the ordinary itself is recognized as holy.

What, finally, is this mystery that *apatheia* has a daughter named *agape*, that desert harshness can yield so readily to desert love? The desert and mountain terrain surrounding Christ in the Desert is a "land of enchantment," constantly eliciting desire. Even God is enchanted by it. I discovered there the astounding depth of God's own desire, even for me. The Grail translation of the psalms speaks of God's "desiring our beauty" as much as the beauty of any such magical terrain. There I'm loved unaccountably, by the Christ in the Desert who had sought me out for so long.

Sometimes in my dreams I'm still there, looking out across the desert in the quiet of the evening after Compline as the sun begins to set. All the fierce places surround me there in the Chama River wilderness. I'm at Sinai again, atop Urraca Mesa, trapped in Box Canyon behind Ghost Ranch. I'm back at my cell in Jerusalem, by my mother's bed in the nursing home. The lost and dying ones are all there beside me, in the place where fear is born. Yet the fear is overwhelmed by a desire for the One whose shadow has also passed that way. It's the shadow of the Lion by whom I've been loved, the One to whom the father's death and the mother's dying have been pointing me all along. What, finally, have I learned in this prolonged desert sojourn? That it's only in the empty place, in the place where everything appears to die—there in the place of the Lion, that any of us are ever loved . . . and set free to love as well.

Centuries ago, in a desert community of monks—or so the story goes—the brothers chose one of their number to go each day to a distant town to beg. It was always hot as he returned home after long hours of abuse in the city, bringing whatever food or money he'd been able to beg. But day after day in the late afternoon sun he recrossed the desert with joy, never complaining. God marveled at the old monk's faithfulness and, in response, created every evening there in the desert a well of cold water to refresh him on his way back across the sand.

The monk was profoundly grateful for the gift, but returned even greater glory to God by choosing not to receive it. Thinking himself unworthy of miracles, he always passed by the well, stopping only to express his thankfulness and joy. Later each night as he lay down to sleep, he'd look up through the small window of his cell to see a single bright star in the sky, knowing God had placed it there just for him. He slept with the greatest peace.

And so the man counted out the years of his life. Eventually the brothers chose a younger man to go along with him, to learn the work he soon would no longer be able to perform. The two of them set off for the city on their first day together. The young monk found it hard persisting in begging, accepting abuse from the people, and especially enduring the heat returning across the desert in the afternoon sun. But when he saw the well of cold water, something he hadn't noticed on the trip earlier that morning, he quickly ran to it and drank deeply with the greatest appreciation.

Meanwhile, the old monk was torn. If he refused to drink as usual—and told the young monk why—the young man would feel ashamed of his own impulsiveness, not having been as devout as the revered older brother. But then again, if he drank, he wouldn't be offering back the same gift to God he'd been able to give with joy all these years. Finally he thought of the young monk and ran to drink with him . . . to the glory of God.

The rest of their way back home that evening, the old brother was a little more silent than usual. He feared that maybe he'd disappointed God by what he'd done, by drinking the water. But as he lay down to sleep that night, looking up through the small window of his cell, he saw the whole sky lit with stars just for him. The joy was too much to contain. They found him dead the next morning. He'd slept with the greatest peace. And if they'd been able to see the words that last fell from his lips, they might have found the words from Hosea that love is always better than sacrifice.

How much can you give up? the desert asks. And how much can you love? Only in offering the severest answers to these two questions does one ever discover, at last, the solace of fierce landscapes.

Epilogue

The desert demands the last word—even though it remains a silent place of forbidding mystery, absorbing the sound of all other voices in its fierce terrain. A group of white settlers learned this the hard way in the fall of 1849 as they set out from the Utah Territory toward gold fields in the San Joaquin Valley of California. They called themselves the Sand Walking Company, based upon their mispronunciation of the destination toward which they traveled. Taking a "shortcut" recommended to them by the leader of a passing pack train, they headed into a 140 mile-long stretch of desert waste known to us today as Death Valley. It was a tragic mistake.

Nothing grows there, even today, except for a little cactus and mesquite, some salt grass and iodine bush. It has places with strange names such as Badwater and Furnace Creek, Funeral Mountains and Devil's Cornfield. At 280 feet below sea level, Badwater is the lowest point in the western hemisphere. Temperatures of 134 degrees Fahrenheit have been measured there on a shaded platform five feet above the ground. On the floor of the desert itself, temperatures have been read as high as 201 degrees Fahrenheit. That's eleven degrees short of the boiling point for water. Does it take much more, I wonder, for blood to boil?

It's a bizarre, unearthly place, this Death Valley. At Badwater the silence is so intense it drives people crazy. The only unnerving sound is the occasional snapping and cracking of tiny ionization explosions on the salt flats nearby. Visitors describe it as a landscape from hell. South of Ubehebe Crater there's a wide stretch of dried mud where "moving rocks" are still found today. These are several-hundred-pound blocks of limestone that have been slowly pushed along the desert floor by gusts of wind one hundred miles an hour or more. There are tracks eight hundred feet long in the dried mud behind them. How does one define such a place? What is this desert, this uncanny terrain that threatens so readily to undo us?

Throughout this book, the desert has functioned as a kind of Greek Chorus, never speaking but always present, offering its own critique of everything else that's said, silently deconstructing every naive and romantic notion. The desert is where one confronts one's inevitable loss of control, the inadequacy of language, the spectre of one's own demise.

Where, then, does one look for the moral and social equivalent of desert in our world today? Not only in a geography where rain is scarce and people few, but also in the deserted, abandoned centers of our major cities—the fearful places avoided as much as possible by those of us who can afford to live elsewhere. There and in nursing homes or hospices, deserted places where emptiness and death can't be denied as easily as they are in bustling centers of activity and power. These are the deserts to which we're invited to attend.

One such place lies not far from the midtown university where I work. On the northside of Saint Louis, near Karen House (the Catholic Worker community), there's a vast urban wilderness, the site of the old Pruitt-Igoe housing development, a colossal blunder in urban planning that was blown up in the 1970s. Practically nothing lives there now. It's a desolate neighborhood where torn-down houses have never been rebuilt, where poor families fear for their children's safety. But the Catholic Workers remain there. Like the Little Brothers and Sisters of Jesus, who look to Charles de Foucauld as the desert founder of their rugged style of life, they find in the city the clearest spiritual equivalent of the desert in our time.

There isn't anything romantic about Karen House. It's a desert place for desert people—like the waiting room of radiation oncology, the nursing home where I still visit my mother's friends, the AIDS hospice nearby. People there are accustomed to risk, vulnerability, brokenness. But in a place where God often seems absent, they discover something liberating and free, something they cannot name but would never want to lose. These are the desert fathers and mothers I count as my teachers today. They're as spirited and life-giving as the Abba Anthonys and Amma Syncleticas of centuries past.

The desert has to lead us, at last, from aloneness with God (in a moment of great and silent emptiness) to community with others, from the loss of the fragile self to the discovery of a new identity binding us to the world. The apophatic moment, if genuine, must ever result in a recommitment to speech and engagement, a renewal of kataphatic energy. Desert attentiveness and desert indifference lead necessarily to desert love.

In the fall of 1849 twenty-seven wagons started into that long desert valley east of the Sierra Nevada. Only one of them came out. A survivor of that misguided party spoke of the dreadful sameness of the terrain, the awfulness of the Panamint Mountains, remembering only "hunger and thirst and an awful silence."[1] Two months later, as the only surviving wagon topped the westernmost crest of the distant mountains, one of the settlers looked back on the place that had nearly claimed them all and said, "Goodbye, Death Valley." That's how the site received its name.

But there's another name the Spanish used to describe this God-forsaken land. They referred to it as *la Palma de la Mano de Dios,* the very palm of God's hand. I think now, at the end of this long season of my life, that I finally understand why.

Notes

LIST OF ABBREVIATIONS

AP-alph   *Apophthegmata Patrum*, The Sayings of the Fathers. Greek alphabetical collection, Jean Baptiste Cotelier, ed. *Ecclesiae Graecae monumenta*, I, Paris: Muguet, 1677. Reprinted in J. P. Migne. PG 65:72–440; Supplemented by Jean-Claude Guy in *Recherches sur la tradition Grecque des Apophthegmata Patrum*. Subsidia Hagiographica 36. Brussels: Société des Bollandistes, 1962.

AP-anon   *Apophthegmata Patrum*, The Sayings of the Fathers. Greek anonymous collection. F. Nau, ed., "Historie des solitaires égyptiens (MS Coislin 126, fol. 158f.)." Nos. 133–369. *Revue d'Orient Chrétien* 13 (1908):47–57, 266–83; 14 (1909):357–79; 17 (1912):204–11, 294–301; 18 (1913): 137–40.

Cloud   *The Cloud of Unknowing*, ed. James Walsh (New York: Paulist Press), 1981.

DictSp   *Dictionnaire de Spiritualité, Ascétique et Mystique: Doctrine et Histoire*, ed. Marcel Viller (Paris: Beauchesne, 1937–95), 17 vols.

DkNight   John of the Cross, *The Dark Night*, in The *Collected Works of St. John of the Cross*, trans Kieran Kavanaugh and Otilio Rodriguez (Washington, D.C.: Institute of Carmelite Studies, 1979), pp. 291–389.

GregMos   Gregory of Nyssa, *The Life of Moses*, in *Gregory Nyssa: The Life of Moses*, trans. Abraham J. Malherbe and Everett Ferguson (New York: Paulist Press, 1978).

Ladder   John Climacus, *The Ladder of Divine Ascent*, in *John Climacus: The Ladder of Divine Ascent*, trans. Colm Luibheid and Norman Russell (New York: Paulist Press, 1982).

Philok   *The Philokalia*, ed. G. E. H. Palmer, Philip Sherrard, and Kallistos Ware (London: Faber & Faber, 1979), 3 vols.

PG   *Patres Graeci*, the Fathers, Doctors and Ecclesiastical Writings of the Greek Church. Jacques Paul Migne, ed., *Patrologiae Cursus Completus: Series Graeca* (Paris: Migne, 1857–1866), 161 vols.

PL   *Patres Latini*, the Fathers, Doctors and Ecclesiastical Writings of the Latin Church. Jacques Paul Migne, ed., *Patrologiae Cursus Completus: Series Latina* (Paris: Migne, 1844–1890), 221 vols.

Introduction

1. Tim Vivian, "Mountain and Desert: The Geographies of Early Coptic Monasticism," *Coptic Church Review* 12:1 (Spring 1991), p. 15.

2. Henry David Thoreau, *Walden* (New York: Holt, Rinehart & Winston, 1963), p. 265.

3. The word *apophatic* appears among Greek writers in late antiquity who speak of that which is "apart from" (or incapable of) expression in theological discourse.

4. The contradictory notion of "aniconic images" suggests the deconstructive role played by certain symbols that are used simultaneously to question as well as to depict what they represent. It is a visual equivalent of the effort of the poet and mystic in "unsaying" through words what has already been put into language.

5. Michael Sells, in his study of the apophatic tradition, *Mystical Languages of Unsaying* (Chicago: University of Chicago Press, 1994), reserves the term *apophasis* "for those writings in which unnameability is not only asserted but performed." Such writings involve a "performative intensity" in which language is repeatedly turned back on itself, unsaying what has been said and then negating the negation (p. 3). On the subject of "apophatic fusion," see pp. 113–14.

6. Ibid., p. 10.

7. Dorothy Sölle sees nothing unusual in this at all, arguing to the contrary that "I consider the separation of the personal from the professional, of one's own experience from reflections that then vaunt themselves as 'scientific' philosophical-theological thought, to be a fatal male invention, the overcoming of which is a task for any serious theology that intends to be a theology of both women and men." *The Window of Vulnerability* (Minneapolis: Fortress Press, 1990), p. 35.

8. Mark Noll, Robert Orsi, Albert Raboteau, and Karen McCarthy Brown discussed this question in a session, The Author's Voice and the Study of North American Religion, at the meetings of the American Academy of Religion, November 20, 1995. An example of the kind of scholarship I am trying to emulate here is Robert Orsi's "'Mildred, is it fun to be a cripple?': The Culture of Suffering in Mid-Twentieth-Century American Catholicism," *South Atlantic Quarterly* 93:3 (Summer 1994), pp. 547–90.

9. Walter Brueggemann, "Texts That Linger, Words That Explode," a lecture in the Frontiers in Biblical Scholarship series, given at the meetings of the Society of Biblical Literature in Philadelphia, November 19, 1995.

10. Richly provocative comparisons to Christian apophatic thought can be found in Hindu notions of Brahman as *nirguna* (without attributes), the infinite emptiness of the void in Hui Neng's Ch'an Buddhism, the *sunyata* of Zen, and the *fana* of the Sufi tradition. Thomas Merton began exploring many of these connections in the last decade of his life. See John F. Teahan, "A Dark and Empty Way: Thomas Merton and the Apophatic Tradition," *Journal of Religion* 58 (1978), pp. 279–87. John B. Cobb, Jr. asks if a God void of substantiality and form, beyond definition, can be recognized in the West, in his "Buddhist Emptiness and the Christian God," *Journal of the American Academy of Religion* 45:1 (March 1977), pp. 11–25.

11. See Jon Sobrino, "The 'Doctrinal Authority' of the People of God in Latin America," in *The Teaching Authority of the Believers*, ed. Johannes-Baptist Metz and Edward Schillebeeckx (Edinburgh: T. & T. Clark, 1985), pp. 54–62.

12. Literary theorist Julia Kristeva uses the term "intertextuality" to refer to the different codes, discourses, or voices that traverse a given text, opening it to a greater play of semiosis. See *Encyclopedia of Contemporary Literary Theory*, ed. Irena R. Makaryk (Toronto: University of Toronto Press, 1993), pp. 568–72.

CHAPTER 1 · Connecting Spirituality and the Environment

1. Jon D. Levenson, *Sinai and Zion: An Entry Into the Jewish Bible* (Minneapolis: Winston Press, 1985), p. 116.

2. Bruce Chatwin, *The Songlines* (New York: Viking, 1987), pp. 2, 11–14. See Graeme Ferguson and John Chryssavgis, eds., *The Desert is Alive: Dimensions of Australian Spirituality* (Melbourne: Joint Board of Education, 1990).

3. Chatwin, *The Songlines*, pp. 291–92.

4. Cultural geographer John B. Jackson argues that "dwelling" in a place (as opposed to simply occupying its space) inevitably involves a participation in its customary behavior, its *habitude* or *Gewohnheit. Discovering the Vernacular Landscape* (New Haven, Conn.: Yale University Press, 1984), p. 91.

5. The impulse of modernity has been to emphasize the universal rather than the vernacular, the anonymous instead of the personal, the freedom of uninterrupted space as opposed to the particularity of place. See J. Nicholas Entriken, "Place, Region, and Modernity," and David Ley, "Modernism, Post-Modernism and the Struggle for Place," both in *The Power of Place: Bringing Together Geographical and Sociological Imaginations,* ed. John A. Agnew and James S. Duncan (Boston: Unwin Hyman, 1989), pp. 30–65.

6. This is the definition of *habitus* offered in the article "Habitude et Habitus" in DictSp, vol. VII, p. 2. French Sociologist Pierre Bourdieu speaks of a community's *habitus* as the way by which accepted models of behavior are unconsciously imbibed from one generation to the next. A *habitus* "ensures the active presence of past experiences which . . . tend to guarantee the 'correctness' of practices and their constancy over time, more reliably than all formal rules and explicit norms." Pierre Bourdieu, *The Logic of Practice* (Stanford, Calif.: Stanford University Press, 1990), p. 54.

7. Michael Ondaatje, *The English Patient* (New York: Vintage Books, 1992), p. 155.

8. Denys Turner, *The Darkness of God: Negativity in Christian Mysticism* (Cambridge: Cambridge University Press, 1995), pp. 11–18.

9. On Performance Theory and the nature of asceticism, see Richard Valantasis, "A Theory of the Social Function of Asceticism," in *Asceticism,* ed. Vincent Wimbus and Richard Valantasis (New York: Oxford University Press, 1995), pp. 544–52.

10. John Cassian, *Conferences,* 1.15, in *John Cassian: Conferences,* ed. Colm Luibheid (New York: Paulist Press, 1985), p. 50.

11. Evagrius, *Chapters on Prayer,* 67, in Evagrius Ponticos, *The Praktikos; Chapters on Prayer,* trans. John Eudes Bamberger (Spencer, Mass.: Cistercian Publications, 1970), p. 66.

12. See Bernard McGinn, "Ocean and Desert as Symbols of Mystical Absorption in the Christian Tradition," *Journal of Religion* 74:2 (April 1994), pp. 155–81.

13. Eriugena refers to "the desert of the divine nature" in his *Commentary on the Gospel of John,* associating the word *eremos* with the notion of "inexpressible height" as well as desert barrenness. God is, for him, a Desert Mountain removed from all things, yet through whom all things are made. McGinn, "Ocean and Desert," p. 162 n.23. Similarly, Eckhart describes God as a "marvelous desert" and a "mountain" which the intellect must ascend. See his *Granum Sinapis, IV,* in M. O'C. Walshe, ed. *Meister Eckhart: Sermons and Treatises* (London: Watkins, 1979), vol. I, pp. xxviii–xxxi.

14. "The great danger," Dom John Chapman wrote, "is that people love God for His gifts, and are always on the look out for them, and think all is lost when they have a little aridity; it is hard for them to learn to love aridity, to desire nothing so much as to be perennially dissatisfied with themselves, and full of an entirely vague and unsatisfactory longing for something unknown and unknowable." Roger Hudleston, ed., *The Spiritual Letters of Dom John Chapman*

(New York: Sheed & Ward, 1935), p. 125. John of the Cross also affirmed that it is a mistake "to desire to feel God and taste him as if he were comprehensible and accessible." DkNight, I, 6, 5, pp. 308–309.

15. See Hans Bayer, "Vita in deserto: Kassians Askese der Einode und die mittelalterliche Frauenmystik," *Zeitschrift für Kirchengeschichte* 98:1 (1987), pp. 15–20, and McGinn, "Ocean and Desert," pp. 160–61.

16. Evagrius, *Chapters on Prayer,* 71, p. 66–67.

17. Roberta Bondi speaks of the importance that the Desert Christians attributed to the self and its abandonment of needs for approval in chapter four of her book, *To Pray and to Love: Conversations on Prayer with the Early Church* (Minneapolis: Fortress Press, 1988).

18. Meister Eckhart insisted that "People must be so empty of all things and all works, whether inward or outward, that they can become a proper home for God. . . ." German Sermon 52, in *Meister Eckhart: A Modern Translation,* ed. Raymond Blakney (New York: Harper & Brothers, 1941), p. 230. Marguerite Porete spoke boldly of Mary Magdalene going willingly into the desert to be "annihilated," even "ravished" by the love of God in the mystery of divine union. Ellen Babinski, trans., *Marguerite Porete: The Mirror of Simple Souls* (New York: Paulist Press, 1993), 93: 8–13, p. 168. These are familiar images in the apophatic tradition for describing that "loss of self" which is sought in being joined to God (or, as Augustine might have preferred, the *return* to self, where God is found to have been waiting all along at the center of one's being). Augustine said to God, "You were within me and I was outside myself; it was there that I sought you." *Confessions,* X, 27, 38. See James J. O'Donnell, ed. *Augustine: Confessions* (Oxford: Clarendon Press, 1992), vol. I, p. 134.

19. See Bondi, *To Pray and to Love,* p. 78.

20. Donald W. Mitchell, *Spirituality and Emptiness: The Dynamics of Spiritual Life in Buddhism and Christianity* (New York: Paulist Press, 1991), p. 140. There are important differences, as well as similarities, between the conception of the self in the desert tradition of Christian spirituality and the Buddhist embrace of the void (sunyatta) or the Hindu hope of dissolving the individual self (*atman*) into the Brahman of ultimate reality.

21. John Cassian, in his *Conferences* (X.10), spoke of being taught this pattern of prayer by Abba Isaac in the Egyptian desert. Saint Hesychios of Sinai later taught the "single-phrased Jesus Prayer" in his ninth-century work *On Watchfulness and Holiness,* 174, in Philok, vol. I, p. 193. [The *Philokalia* is a collection of ancient Greek texts—many of them from the desert fathers—compiled in the eighteenth century.] The fourteenth-century *Cloud of Unknowing* similarly emphasized the use of "a little word" in prayer. See Cloud, chaps. VII and XXXVII, pp. 133–34, 192.

22. See Turner, *The Darkness of God,* pp. 258–59. Seventeenth-century Jesuit writer Jean-Pierre de Caussade warned of being "enslaved by devotional practices," stressing utter abandonment to God in the exercise of prayer. See his *Abandonment to Divine Providence,* discussed in Simon Tugwell's *Ways of Imperfection* (Springfield, Ill: Templegate Publishers, 1985), pp. 208–18.

23. See Turner, *The Darkness of God,* pp. 250, 210.

24. Louis Dupre and James A. Wiseman, eds., *From Light: An Anthology of Christian Mysticism* (New York: Paulist Press, 1988), p. 23.

25. Recent books that tend to approach landscape in this way include Natasha Peterson's *Sacred Sites: A Traveler's Guide to North America's Most Powerful, Mystical Landmarks* (Chicago: Contemporary Books, 1988) and Cynthia Corbett's *Power Trips: Journeys to Sacred Sites as a Way of Transformation* (Santa Fe, N.M.: Timewindow Publications, 1988).

26. Arthur Conan Doyle, "Silver Blaze," in "Memoirs of Sherlock Holmes," found in *The Complete Sherlock Holmes* (Garden City, N.Y.: Doubleday & Company, 1927), p. 347.

27. Philosophers have often attributed cultural mores and ideas to the ineluctable influence of climate and geography—as if landscape inexorably molds the human spirit. Hippocrates asked why those dwelling in cold districts were naturally courageous, while the inhabitants of warm regions were more cowardly. Montesquieu argued that warm climates invariably produce passionate natures, cold climates yield bodily strength and endurance, and temperate climates result in intellectual superiority. See Clarence J. Glacken, *Traces on the Rhodian Shore* (Berkeley: University of California Press, 1967), pp. 81, 87.

28. Ellen Churchill Semple, *Influences of Geographic Environment* (New York: Henry Holt & Co., 1911), p. 1. More recently, Japanese geographer Watsuji Tetsuro has delineated three different personality and cultural types based on their differing sources in climate and geography. See Watsuji Tetsuro, *Climate and Culture: A Philosophical Study* (Japan: Hokuseido Press, 1961).

29. Semple, *Influences*, p. 1.

30. Ernest Renan, *Histoire du peuple d'Israel* (Paris: Calmann-Levy, 1887).

31. Walter Kaufmann says, "The desert makes for simplicity and a sense for the sublime. It is not pretty, not lovely, not charming, but vast and powerful. This does not mean that monotheism would naturally come to anyone who spent some time in the desert, but the desert provides an environment in which the austere doctrine of the One God gains some reinforcement from experience." *Religions in Four Dimensions* (New York: Reader's Digest Press, 1976), p. 374.

32. Chatwin, *The Songlines*, p. 199.

33. Ibid.

34. R. J. Johnston, *On Human Geography* (Oxford: Basil Blackwell, 1986), p. 54.

35. D. H. Lawrence, "The Spirit of Place," in *The Symbolic Meaning*, ed. Armin Arnold (New York: Viking Press, l964), pp. 15–31.

36. Tony Hillerman, *People of Darkness* (New York: Harper & Row, 1980), p. 81.

37. See G. Clarke Chapman, "Crime and Blessing in Tony Hillerman's Fiction," *The Christian Century*, 13 November 1991, pp. 1063–65.

38. See Simon Schama, *Landscape and Memory* (New York: Alfred A. Knopf, 1995) and Peirce F. Lewis, "Axioms for Reading in the Landscape," in *The Interpretation of Ordinary Landscapes*, ed. D. W. Meinig (New York: Oxford University Press, 1979), pp. 11–32.

39. See Arthur de Bles, *How to Distinguish the Saints in Art* (New York: Art Culture Publications, 1925), pp. 115–17; Ann Brownell Jameson, *Sacred and Legendary Art* (New York: AMS Press, 1970), vol. II, pp. 749–54; and Nancy Bell, *Lives and Legends of the Great Hermits and Fathers of the Church* (London: George Bell & Sons, 1902), p. 7f.

40. In the field of environmental psychology, this interpretative process is studied under the rubric of cognitive mapping. See Gary W. Evans, "Environmental Cognition," *Psychological Bulletin* 88:2 (1980), pp. 259–87.

41. Douglas Burton-Christie's *The Word in the Desert: Scripture and the Quest for Holiness in Early Christian Monasticism* (New York: Oxford University Press, 1992) asks about the hermeneutical process by which the desert fathers understood the truth they served, vis-à-vis the setting in which they lived (pp. 3–32).

42. Deborah Tall, *From Where We Stand: Recovering a Sense of Place* (New York: Alfred A. Knopf, 1993), pp. 212–13. "Metaphor negates even as it carries us into new understanding," she adds. "Because every act of depiction is inevitably interpretation, to turn the land into an emblem feels suspiciously like appropriating it."

43. Ralph Waldo Emerson, "Nature," IV, 2, in *The Collected Works of Ralph Waldo Emerson*, ed. Robert E. Spiller (Cambridge, Mass.: The Belknap Press of Harvard University Press, 1971), vol. I, p. 18.

44. See Rowland A. Sherrill, "American Sacred Space and the Contest of History," in *American Sacred Space,* ed. David Chidester and Edward T. Linenthal (Bloomington: Indiana University Press, 1995), p. 324f. Sharing something of Sherrill's concern about this propensity, I still have to emphasize the importance of interiority, of why and how sacred places appeal to people in particular ways.

45. Tall, *From Where We Stand,* p. 215.

46. On the question of the researcher's role in balancing critical distance and personal participation in the study of Christian spirituality, see Belden C. Lane, "Galesville and Sinai: The Researcher as Participant in the Study of Spirituality" and Douglas Burton-Christie, "The Cost of Interpretation: Sacred Texts and Ascetic Practice in Desert Spirituality," both in *Christian Spirituality Bulletin* 2:1 (Spring 1994), pp. 18–25.

47. Hans-Georg Gadamer speaks of a "fusion of horizons" necessarily occurring in the process of interpretation, whereby the limited horizons of text and interpreter are fused in a common experience of meaning. See *Truth and Method* (New York: Seabury Press, 1975), pp. 273f. and Bernard Lonergan, *Method in Theology* (New York: Seabury Press, 1972), pp. 235–37.

48. Joseph Wood Krutch, *The Desert Year* (New York: William Sloane Associates, 1952), p. 171.

49. Philip Sheldrake, *Spirituality and History* (New York: Crossroad, 1992), pp. 94–96. See his recent work, *Living Between Worlds: Place and Journey in Celtic Spirituality* (New York: Cowley, 1995). In "Spirituality and History: Keeping the Conversation Going," *Christian Spirituality Bulletin* I:1 (Spring 1993), he argues that "our understanding of the spatio-temporal, or 'place' and 'placedness,' is crucial to the ways we formulate and live our spiritualities" (p. 8).

50. Keith H. Basso, *Wisdom Sits in Places: Landscape and Language among the Western Apache* (Albuquerque: University of New Mexico Press, 1996).

51. Derwas Chitty, *The Desert a City: An Introduction to the Study of Egyptian and Palestinian Monasticism under the Christian Empire* (Oxford: Başil Blackwell, 1966); Alan Jones, *Soul Making: The Desert Way of Spirituality* (San Francisco: Harper & Row, 1985); Henri Nouwen, *The Way of the Heart: Desert Spirituality and Contemporary Ministry* (New York: Seabury Press, 1981).

52. Douglas Burton-Christie, "A Feeling for the Natural World: Spirituality and the Heart in Contemporary Nature Writing," *Continuum* 2:2–3 (Spring 1992), pp. 154–80, and "Mapping the Sacred Landscape: Spirituality and the Contemporary Literature of Nature," *Horizons* 21:1 (Spring 1994), pp. 22–47.

53. Terry Tempest Williams, *Refuge: An Unnatural History of Family and Place* (New York: Pantheon Books, 1991) and Kathleen Norris, *Dakota: A Spiritual Geography* (New York: Ticknor & Fields, 1993).

54. Sandra Schneiders, "Spirituality in the Academy," *Theological Studies* 50:4 (December 1989), p. 695. David Tracy argues in *The Analogical Imagination* (New York: Crossroad, 1981) that "there is never an authentic disclosure of truth which is not also transformative" (p. 78).

55. A story told by Aytana Ben-Shimon, guide for the Society for the Protection of Nature in Israel, the Sinai desert, 1989.

56. Homeopathic treatment in psychotherapy, as contrasted with allopathic, "goes with the symptom," offering the problem back to the client in a way that shows its necessity, even its value, in the client's experience. One too often runs away from the very thing that is able to give life. The desert may be the last place a person in grief may want to go, but paradoxically it might be the most helpful. See Thomas Moore, *The Care of the Soul* (New York: HarperCollins, 1992), pp. 6–10.

57. James A. Nash, *Loving Nature: Ecological Integrity and Christian Responsibility* (Nashville, Tenn.: Abingdon Press, 1991), p. 115.

58. T. E. Lawrence, *Seven Pillars of Wisdom* (Garden City, N.Y.: Garden City Publishing Co., 1938), pp. 29, 41.

59. Adapted from Idries Shah, ed., *Tales of the Dervishes* (New York: E. P. Dutton & Co., 1969), pp. 23–24.

PART I · Purgation

Emptiness in a Geography of Abandonment

1. See Kenneth Leech, *Experiencing God: Theology as Spirituality* (San Francisco: Harper, 1985), pp. 336–37.

2. Bernard of Clairvaux, "Sermons on the Song of Songs," 3–4, in *Bernard of Clairvaux: Selected Works,* ed. G. R. Evans (New York: Paulist Press, 1987), pp. 222–25.

MYTHIC LANDSCAPE · Grace and the Grotesque

Reflections on a Spirituality of Brokenness

1. Philip Thomson, *The Grotesque* (London: Methuen & Co., 1972), p. 18.

2. Sally Fitzgerald, ed. *The Habit of Being: Letters of Flannery O'Connor* (New York: Farrar, Straus, Giroux, 1979), p. 163.

3. See John Saward, *Perfect Fools: Folly for Christ's Sake in Catholic and Orthodox Spirituality* (Oxford: Oxford University Press, 1980).

4. Wolfgang Kayser, *The Grotesque in Art and Literature* (Bloomington: Indiana University Press, 1963), p. 188f.

5. Flannery O'Connor, *Mystery and Manners* (New York: Farrar, Straus, Giroux, 1969), p. 112.

6. Joseph Zornado describes the mystery of unknowing to which the reader is taken in O'Connor's fiction in his article "Negative Writings: Flannery O'Connor, Apophatic Thought, and Christian Criticism," *Christianity and Literature* 42:1 (Autumn l992), pp. 117–40.

7. O'Connor, *Mystery and Manners,* p. 44.

8. Diane Arbus, *Diane Arbus* (New York: Museum of Modern Art, 1972), p. 3.

9. Simone de Beauvoir, *A Very Easy Death* (New York: Pantheon, 1965), p.78.

10. Jean Vanier suggests that "some people can only talk with their bodies; only from there do true words flow. Sometimes it is because they cannot speak, but also it may be because they have lost trust in words." *The Broken Body* (Toronto: Anglican Book Centre, 1988), p. 81.

11. Michael Downey, *A Blessed Weakness: The Spirit of Jean Vanier and l'Arche* (San Francisco: Harper & Row, 1986), p. 87.

12. Ibid., p. 118.

13. O'Connor, *Mystery and Manners,* p. 34.

14. Laura Gilpin, "The Two-Headed Calf," in *The Hocus-Pocus of the Universe* (New York: Doubleday & Company, 1977).

CHAPTER 2 · Places on the Edge

Wild Terrain and the Spiritual Life

1. Kathleen Norris, *Dakota: A Spiritual Geography* (New York: Ticknor & Fields, 1993), p. 157.

2. Lawrence Kushner, *Honey from the Rock: Ten Gates of Jewish Mysticism* (New York: Harper & Row, 1977), p. 54.

3. Martin E. Marty, *A Cry of Absence* (San Francisco: Harper & Row, 1993), pp. 1–21. Karl Rahner has also spoken of a "wintery spirituality," one more "closely allied to the torment of atheists" as opposed to a lighter, more enthusiastic spirituality, with its "almost naive immediacy to God." Karl Rahner, *Faith in a Wintry Season: Conversations and Interviews with Karl Rahner in the Last Years of his Life,* ed. Paul Imhof and Hubert Biallowons (New York: Crossroad, 1990), p. 35.

4. See Aelred Cody, "What the Desert Meant in Ancient Israel," *Studia Missionalia* 28 (1979), pp. 33–37.

5. Philip Sheldrake discusses the significance of edge places and boundaries in his book *Living Between Worlds: Place and Journey in Celtic Spirituality* (Boston: Cowley Publications, 1995), pp. 46–57, 81.

6. Thoreau, *Walden* (New York: Holt, Rinehart & Winston, 1963), p. 265. David Tracy insists that there is "a limit-character to all religious experience and language." See *The Analogical Imagination* (New York: Crossroad, 1981), p. 160.

7. Victor Turner studies the function of religious pilgrimage in occasioning liminal experience, seeing the ritual movement from a mundane center to a sacred periphery to offer release from ordinary cultural structures, a preference for simplicity in dress and behavior, a new sense of marginal community or *communitas,* an experience of ordeal, and a reflection on the meaning of basic religious and cultural values. See Victor Turner and Edith Turner, *Image and Pilgrimage in Christian Culture* (New York: Columbia University Press, 1978), pp. 34–35. Mountain and desert pilgrimages considered by the Turners include Croagh Patrick in Ireland and Mount Kailas in Tibet, as well as the *hajj* to Mecca and the shrine of Nuestra Senora de los Remedios in Mexico.

8. Jerome, Letter to Heliodorus, 3, in *Sancti Eusebii Hieronymi Epistulae: Epistula XIV: Ad Heliodorum Monachum,* ed. Isidorus Hilberg, Corpus Scriptorum Esslesiasticorum Latinorum, vol. LIV (Vindobonae: F. Tempsky, 1910), p. 45.

9. Uwe George, *In the Deserts of This Earth* (New York: Harcourt, Brace, Jovanovich, 1977), p. 10. See "Desert" in *A Glossary of Geographical Terms,* ed. Dudley Stamp (New York: John Wiley & Sons, Inc., 1966), pp. 153–54.

10. Larry W. Price, *Mountains and Man: A Study of Process and Environment* (Berkeley: University of California Press, 1981), pp. 1–3.

11. Roderick Peattie, *Mountain Geography* (Cambridge, Mass.: Harvard University Press, 1936), pp. 3–4.

12. Dolores LaChappelle describes the fascination with sacred mountains in East and West, including stories of the "Spectre of the Brocken," in her book *Earth Wisdom* (Silverton, Colo.: Finn Hill Arts, 1978), pp. 10–53.

13. James Dickey, *Deliverance* (Boston: Houghton, Mifflin, 1970).

14. Robert L. Cohn's chapter on "Liminality in the Wilderness," in *The Shape of Sacred Space: Four Biblical Studies* (Chico, Calif.: Scholars Press, 1981), pp. 7–23.

15. Denis Wood describes the beginnings of environmental psychology as a discipline in his article "I Don't Feel That about Environmental Psychology Today, but I Want To," *Journal of Environmental Psychology* 7 (1987), pp. 417–23. Howard F. Stein says that "psychogeography, the psychoanalytic study of spatial representation, is an approach that may help unravel why *who one is* comes to be experienced as indistinguishable from *where one is,* and in turn where and who others are perceived to be in relation to one's own [identity and place]." *Developmental Time, Cultural Space: Studies in Psychogeography* (Norman: University of Oklahoma Press, 1987), p. 15.

16. James T. Lester, "Wrestling with the Self on Mount Everest," *Journal of Humanistic Psychology* 23:2 (Spring 1983), p. 37. See Maurice Herzog's account of a similar experience on the French ascent of the first eight-thousand-meter mountain ever climbed, in *Annapurna* (New York: E. P. Dutton, 1953), p. 206.

17. Simon Schama surveys the different ways that mountains have transfixed the Western imagination, from Saussure's confession of intense human frailty atop Mount Blanc to Ruskin's mystical celebration of mountain beauty. *Landscape and Memory* (New York: Alfred A. Knopf, 1995), pp. 383–513.

18. "Rather than conquer the mountain, the climber vanquishes himself, much as a hermit or yogi overcomes the enemy of his own pride and arrogance on the way to attaining his goal of self-transcendence," says Edwin Bernbaum, speaking of the spiritual dimensions of mountaineering in *Sacred Mountains of the World* (San Francisco: Sierra Club Books, 1990), p. 238. Frederick Sontag relates mountain climbing to spirituality in "The Climb toward God," *Word & World* XI:1 (Winter 1991), pp. 79–83.

19. William R. Catton, Jr., "The Quest for Uncertainty," in *Humanscape: Environments for People,* ed. Stephen Kaplan and Rachel Kaplan (North Scituate, Mass.: Duxbury Press, 1978), pp. 112–15.

20. Richard G. Mitchell, *Mountain Experience: The Psychology and Sociology of Adventure* (Chicago: University of Chicago Press, 1983), pp. 153–69.

21. Victor and Edith Turner argue this in *Image and Pilgrimage,* p. 254. See Mihaly Csikszentmihalyi, *Flow: The Psychology of Optimal Experience* (New York: Harper & Row, 1990).

22. Environmental psychologist Peter Suedfeld argues that in situations of restricted environmental stimulation (REST)—such as one might experience in desert settings—"information from the ambient world is greatly attenuated and attention is refocused to residual and endogenous stimuli." The reduction in external sensation leads to a much deeper internal sensitivity. See Peter Seudfeld, *Restricted Environmental Stimulation: Research and Clinical Applications* (New York: John Wiley, 1980).

23. Researcher Peter Hackett at the University of Alaska studies changes in the human mind and body that occur above five-thousand-feet, from a lower level of oxygen in the blood and increase in the alkalinity of the body to decreased sensitivity in the eye. Quoted in Winifred Gallagher, *The Power of Place* (New York: Poseidon Press, 1993), p. 69. With respect to the effects of extreme desert conditions, Gallagher observes, "In some parts of the world, wind is among the variables thought to intensify the aggravating effects of heat. When the hot, dry Sharav blows across the Middle East, for example, some judges regard impulsive crimes more leniently." One form of desert-related hysteria, sometimes leading to murder or suicide, is called *cafard* by the French Foreign Legion (pp. 64, 146).

24. Stein, *Developmental Time,* p. 15.

25. Charles A. Lindbergh, *The Spirit of St. Louis* (New York: Charles Scribner's Sons, 1953), pp. 388–90.

26. See Peter Suedfeld and Jane S. P. Mocellin, "The 'Sensed Presence' in Unusual Environments," *Environment and Behavior* 19:1 (January 1987), pp. 33–52.

27. His imagination was captured, for example, by the notion of the ascent of Mount Carmel. He even drew sketches of the mountain as a peak symbolic of movements in the spiritual life. But he never actually travelled to the mountain overlooking modern Haifa in northern Israel. See *The Collected Works of St. John of the Cross,* trans, Kieran Kavanaugh and Otiolio Rodriquez (Washington, D.C.: Institute of Carmelite Studies Publications, 1979), pp. 66–67.

28. James Hillman, "Peaks and Vales: The Soul/Spirit Distinction as Basis for the Differences between Psychotherapy and Spiritual Discipline," in *Puer Papers,* ed. Cynthia Giles (Irving, Tex.: Spring Publications, 1979), pp. 54–74.

29. David M. Knight does make a distinction between mountain spirituality (the *via positiva*) as it pertains to the quest for meaningful, transcendent experience and desert spirituality (the *via negativa*) which remains a matter of stubborn commitment to God, apart from any rewarding sense of fulfillment. "Desert Spirituality: An Answer to Massah and Meribah," *Studies in Formative Spirituality* I:2 (May 1980), pp. 181–92.

30. See Abraham Maslow, *Toward a Psychology of Being* (Princeton, N.J.: D. Van Nostrand Co., 1962), pp. 67–96.

31. William Theodore, ed. *The Manyoshu: The Nippon Gakujutsu Shinkokai Translation of One Thousand Poems* (New York: Columbia University Press, 1969), p. 215.

32. Thomas Moore, *Care of the Soul* (New York: HarperCollins, 1992), p. 203.

33. In his celebration of "soulfulness," Moore tends to dismiss traditional "spirituality" because of its ties to theological reflection and institutional religion. He assumes rather naively that spiritual experience can readily be separated from questions of morality, the development of doctrine, and the exercise of power and authority in given communities. See Thomas Moore, "The Soul's Religion," *Parabola* XXI:2 (Summer 1996), pp. 18–22.

34. Exod. 15:22–19:1.

35. John of the Cross, DkNight, II.17.6 and *The Ascent of Mount Carmel,* I.5.6–7, in Kavanaugh and Rodriquez, ed. *Collected Works of St. John of the Cross,* pp. 370, 83.

36. M. Streck, "Kaf," in *Encyclopedia of Islam,* ed. E. van Donzel, B. Lewis, and Ch. Pellat (Leiden: E. J. Brill, 1978), pp. 400–402.

37. Marjorie Hope Nicholson, *Mountain Gloom and Mountain Glory: The Development of the Aesthetics of the Infinite* (New York: W. W. Norton & Co., 1963). See Price, *Mountains and Men,* pp. 6–23.

38. See "Literary Attitudes toward Mountains," in *Dictionary of the History of Ideas,* ed. Philip P. Wiener (New York: Charles Scribner's, 1973), vol. III, pp. 253–54. Curiously, John Calvin, who spent years in the Swiss Alps, indicated in his map of paradise in the Geneva Bible of 1560 that the original creation did include mountains.

39. Roderick Nash asserts that desert wilderness in Western thought is "instinctively understood as something alien to man." *Wilderness and the American Mind* (New Haven, Conn.: Yale University Press, 1982), p. 8. See "Desierto," in *Diccionario de los Símbolos,* ed. Jean Chevalier (Barcelona: Editorial Herder, l986), pp. 410–11.

40. See "Desert," in J. E. Cirlot, *Dictionary of Symbols* (New York: Philosophical Library, 1971), p. 79. On demons in the desert, see Isa. 13:21f. 34:14; and George H. Williams, *Wilderness and Paradise in Christian Thought* (New York: Harper & Brothers, 1962), pp. 12–15.

41. Williams, *Wilderness and Paradise,* pp. 28–46. See John L. McKenzie, "Into the Desert," *The Way* 1:1 (1961), pp. 27–39.

42. Clarissa Pinkola Estés, *Women Who Run with the Wolves* (New York: Ballantine Books, 1992), p. 85.

43. Gary Snyder, *The Practice of the Wild* (San Francisco: North Point Press, 1990), p. 22.

44. Ulrich Mauser argues that "the wilderness period was the decisive phase in Israel's primeval history." *Christ in the Wilderness: The Wilderness Theme in the Second Gospel and its Basis in the Biblical Tradition* (Naperville, Ill.: Alec R. Allenson, 1963), p. 17. See G. I. Davies, *The Way of the Wilderness: A Geographical Study of the Wilderness Itineraries in the Old Testament* (New York: Cambridge University Press, 1979); George W. Coats, *Rebellion in the Wilderness: The Murmuring Motif in the Wilderness Traditions of the Old Testament* (Nashville, Tenn.: Abingdon Press, 1968); Augustine Stock, *The Way in the Wilderness: Exodus, Wilderness and Moses Themes in Old Testament and New* (Collegeville, Minn.: Liturgical Press, 1969); and A. Haldar, *The Notion of the Desert in Sumero-Accadian and West-Semitic Religions* (Uppsala: Lundequistska bokhandeln, 1950).

45. Morris S. Seale argues that the Hebrew scriptures must be understood over against the nomadic background of a desert people. When ancient Jews confessed that "a wild and wandering Aramaean was my father," they acknowledged their untamed, nomadic origins. See *The Desert Bible: Nomadic Tribal Culture and Old Testament Interpretation* (London: Weidenfeld and Nicholson, 1974), pp. 2–4.

46. Adin Steinsaltz, *The Long Shorter Way: Discourses on Chasidic Thought* (Northvale, N.J.: Jason Aronson, 1988), p. xivf.

47. The experience of ancient Israel in the wilderness is understood in various ways, even in the biblical record. For some interpreters the period of the Sinai trek is remembered as a golden age in Israel's history, offering a "desert ideal" when God and God's people were closest. Others look back on the same time as one of punishment and failure. See Shemaryahu Talmon, "The 'Desert Motif' in the Bible and in Qumran Literature," in *Biblical Motifs: Origins and Transformations,* ed. Alexander Altmann (Cambridge, Mass.: Harvard University Press, 1966), pp. 31f. and Michael V. Fox, "Jeremiah 2:2 and the 'Desert Ideal,'" *Catholic Biblical Quarterly* XXXV:4 (October 1973), pp. 441–50.

48. The Hebrew word for wilderness, *midbar,* is derived from the root *dbr,* meaning "to drive out." It is, by definition, a place beyond the boundaries. For this reason, "the desert stories of Exodus and Numbers almost always combine two elements: danger and divine help." Mauser, *Christ in the Wilderness,* p. 21. See Talmon, "The 'Desert Motif,'" p. 40.

49. Vincent Taylor, *The Gospel According to St. Mark* (New York: St. Martin's Press, 1966), p. 163.

50. Mauser, *Christ in the Wilderness,* pp. 96–102.

51. Elizabeth S. Malbon, *Narrative Space and Mythic Meaning in Mark* (San Francisco: Harper & Row, 1986), pp. 102–3. On the geographical tension in Mark between Galilee and Jerusalem, see Willi Marxsen, *Mark the Evangelist: Studies on the Redaction History of the Gospel* (Nashville, Tenn.: Abingdon Press, 1969), pp. 54–116.

52. See Mark 1:45; 6:30–44; 8:1–10.

53. Christian Bonnet observes how the desert, since early Judaism, has been a place prone to the development of messianic and revolutionary movements. See "Le désert: Sa signification dans l'Evangile de Marc," *Hokhma* 13 (1980), p. 22.

54. Terence L. Donaldson, *Jesus on the Mountain: A Study in Matthean Theology* (Sheffield, Eng.: JSOT Press, 1985).

55. See R. J. Clifford, *The Cosmic Mountain in Canaan and the Old Testament* (Cambridge, Mass.: Harvard University Press, 1972) and H. G. Quaritch Wales, *The Mountain of God: A Study in Early Religion and Kingship* (London: Bernard Quaritch, 1953).

56. Robert L. Cohn, "Mountains in the Biblical Cosmos," in *The Shape of Sacred Space,* p. 26.

57. David Sperling compares Hebrew attitudes toward sacred mountains to the Syrian view of Mount Zaphon as divine in his article "Mount, Mountain," in *Interpreter's Dictionary of the Bible,* ed. Keith Crim (Nashville, Tenn.: Abingdon Press, 1976), supp. vol., pp. 608–09.

58. The association of fire with mountain theophany recurs frequently in the Hebrew Bible, seen in the burning bush at Horeb (Exod. 3:1–2), with Moses on Sinai (Exod. 24:17; Deut. 4:11–12), with Elijah at Horeb (I Kings 19:12), etc.

59. The argument here is dependent upon Malbon's *Narrative Space and Mythic Meaning in Mark,* pp. 26–30.

60. Robert G. Bratcher and Eugene A. Nida suggest that the word *anagkadzo* ("force" or "compel") clearly implies unwillingness on the part of the disciples. See *A Translator's Handbook on the Gospel of Mark* (Leiden: E. J. Brill, 1961), p. 211.

61. Marcus Borg emphasizes the "boundary shattering" character of Jesus' message and activity in his book *Meeting Jesus Again for the First Time: The Historical Jesus and the Heart of Contemporary Faith* (San Francisco: Harper, 1994).

62. John of the Cross, *The Ascent of Mount Carmel,* III, 39–42, in Kavanaugh and Rodriguez, ed. *Collected Works,* pp. 282–86.

63. Such symbolic landscapes, in Eastern spirituality, can readily be seen in the Japanese gardens of Zen monasteries. Sparse beds of raked gravel suggest the desert emptiness to which the monks aspire. Grottoes, garden tombs, and outdoor stations of the cross often serve a similar purpose in Western monastic practice.

64. See Burton-Christie, *The Word in the Desert,* pp. 7–15. A popular history of Western

spirituality, drawing on this motif, can be found in Thomas M. Gannon and George W. Traub, *The Desert and the City* (New York: Macmillan, 1969).

65. See Spiro Kostof, *Caves of God: The Monastic Environment of Byzantine Cappadocia* (Cambridge, Mass.: M.I.T. Press, 1972).

66. Writing from his desert retreat, Basil proclaimed, "I am living . . . in the wilderness wherein the Lord dwelt. . . . Here is Christ, the lover of the wilderness." Roy J. Deferrari, trans., *The Letters of Saint Basil* (Cambridge, Mass.: Harvard University Press, 1960), XLIII, p. 261.

67. Conference 3.1, in *John Cassian: Conferences.* ed. Colm Luibheid (New York: Paulist Press, 1985), pp. 82, 196.

68. Conference 18.15, in ibid., pp. 199, 201.

69. See Timothy Fry, ed., *The Rule of St. Benedict* (Collegeville, Minn.: Liturgical Press, 1981), pp. 3–64. Jacques Le Goff shows how deserted islands came to serve as a monastic substitute for desert terrain in Western Europe in "The Wilderness in the Medieval West," in *The Medieval Imagination,* trans. Arthur Goldhammer (Chicago: University of Chicago Press, 1988), pp. 50–51.

70. See Duncan Fisher, "Liminality: The Vocation of the Church (The Desert Image in Early Medieval Monasticism)," *Cistercian Studies* XXV:3 (1990), pp. 198–207.

71. Bruno taught that "following [Jesus'] example, we must also become our true selves in the desert, ridding ourselves of every impediment in order that we may give ourselves to God joyfully and become his children." *The Wound of Love: A Carthusian Miscellany* (Kalamazoo, Mich.: Cistercian Publications, 1994), p. 102. See Cyprian Marie Boutrais, *The History of the Great Chartreuse* (London: Burns, Oates & Wasbourne, 1934).

72. *Correspondence of Thomas Gray,* quoted in Schama, *Landscape and Memory,* pp. 448–49. Schama adds that Gray celebrated these mountains as "a chastiser of human vanity, the natural saboteur of those who, literally, got above themselves" (p. 459).

73. William of Saint-Thierry, *Golden Letter to the Brethren of Mount Dieu,* I, 1, in *The Works of William of St. Thierry,* ed. M. Basil Pennington (Spencer, Mass.: Cistercian Publications, 1971), vol. IV, p. 9.

74. While Benedicta Ward admits that "it is tempting to see the flight of the early Cistercians as a repetition of the life and ideals of the Desert Fathers in the fourth century," she argues that first generation Cistercians were actually following the rule of Saint Benedict more than the light of Eastern monasticism. Desert interpretation emerged later, among second-generation writers such as William and Bernard. See Benedicta Ward, "The Desert Myth," in *Signs and Wonders: Saints, Miracles and Prayers from the Fourth Century to the Fourteenth* (Hampshire, Eng.: Variorum, 1992), pp. 183–99.

75. Bernard of Clairvaux, "Description of the Position and Site of the Abbey of Clairvaux," in *The Life and Work of Saint Bernard, Abbot of Clairvaux,* ed. Dom James Mabillon (London: John Hodges, 1889), vol. II, pp. 460–67. See James Cotton Morison, *The Life and Times of Saint Bernard* (London: Chapman and Hall, 1863), p. 28.

76. Thomas Merton, "The Primitive Carmelite Ideal," in *Disputed Questions* (New York: Farrar, Straus, & Giroux, 1960), p. 245.

77. Hadewijch of Brabant, Poems in Couplets, 13; Poems in Stanzas, 14, in *Beguine Spirituality: Mystical Writings of Mechthild of Magdeburg, Beatrice of Nazareth, and Hadewijch of Brabant,* ed. Fiona Bowie (New York: Crossroad, 1990), pp. 101, 118. Cf. Columba Hart, ed., *Hadewijch: The Complete Works* (London: SPCK, 1981), p. 282.

78. Poems in Stanzas, 22, in Bowie, *Beguine Spirituality,* p. 121.

79. John Ruusbroec, The Spiritual Espousals, I, in *John Ruusbroec: The Spiritual Espousals and Other Works,* trans. James A. Wiseman (New York: Paulist Press, 1985), p. 78.

80. Charles Lepet, *Two Dancers in the Desert: The Life of Charles de Foucauld* (Maryknoll,

N. Y.: Orbis Books, 1983), p. 108. See Charles de Foucauld, *Meditations of a Hermit* (London: Burns & Oates, 1981).

81. Carlo Carretto, *Letters from the Desert* (Maryknoll, N.Y.: Orbis Books, 1972), p. 73. In a similar way, Catherine de Hueck Doherty has drawn from her roots in Russian Orthodox spirituality to emphasize the importance of a *poustinia*, a lonely, silent place for prayer—taken from the Russian word for "desert." See *Poustinia: Christian Spirituality of the East for Western Man* (Notre Dame, Ind.: Ave Maria Press, 1975), p. 30.

82. Carretto, *Letters from the Desert,* p. 35.

83. Thomas Merton, "Wilderness and Paradise: Two Recent Studies," *Cistercian Studies* 2:1 (1967), p. 84.

84. Merton's distinction of the true and false self will be examined more fully in subsequent chapters. D. W. Winnicott discusses this division of the personality into true and false selves from a psychoanalytic perspective in "Ego Distortion in Terms of True and False Self," in *The Maturational Processes and the Facilitating Environment* (New York: International Universities Press, 1965).

85. Thomas Merton, *The Wisdom of the Desert* (New York: New Directions, 1960), pp. 5–7. See Raymond Bailey's discussion of the desert in Merton's thought in his book, *Thomas Merton on Mysticism* (Garden City, N.Y.: Doubleday & Company, 1974), pp. 53–79.

86. Williams, *Wilderness and Paradise,* pp. 50–57.

87. Francis received the stigmata at the end of his life on the summit of La Verna, having been told in prayer that the huge crevices in the rocky terrain around him had been opened at the time of Christ's death, when the rocks of Calvary themselves were rent. See Omer Englebert, *Saint Francis of Assisi: A Biography* (Chicago: Franciscan Herald Press, 1965), pp. 305–06.

88. Mechthild of Magdeburg, "The Wilderness has Twelve Things," in Bowie, *Beguine Spirituality,* p. 63.

89. David Douglas, *Wilderness Sojourn: Notes in the Desert Silence* (San Francisco: Harper & Row, 1987), p. 4.

MYTHIC LANDSCAPE · Fierce Back-Country
and the Indifference of God

1. Yi-Fu Tuan, "Attitudes toward Environment: Themes and Approaches," in *Environmental Perception and Behavior,* ed. David Lowenthal (Chicago: University of Chicago, 1967), p. 11.

2. John Updike, *A Month of Sundays* (New York: A. A. Knopf, 1975), pp. 13, 25.

3. Andrew Harvey, *A Journey in Ladakh* (New York: Houghton Mifflin, 1983), p. 93.

4. Detlef Ingo Lauf, *Tibetan Sacred Art: The Heritage of Tantra* (Boston: Shambhala Publications, 1976), p. 171.

5. John Calvin, *Institutes of the Christian Religion,* ed. John T. McNeill (Philadelphia: Westminster Press, 1960), Book I.V.6, vol. I, pp. 56–58.

6. See Jonathan Edwards, "Personal Narrative of 1740," in *Jonathan Edwards: Representative Selections,* ed. Clarence H. Faust and Thomas H. Johnson (New York: Hill & Wang, 1962), pp. 57–72.

7. Ernst Troeltsch, *The Social Teachings of the Christian Churches* (New York: Macmillan, 1931), vol. 2, pp. 583–89. See Sacvan Bercovitch, *The Puritan Origins of the American Self* (New Haven, Conn.: Yale University Press, 1975).

8. Anthony DeMello, *One Minute Wisdom* (New York: Doubleday, 1988), p. 91.

9. Meinrad Craighead, *The Mother's Songs: Images of God the Mother* (New York: Paulist Press, 1986), p. 67.

10. Francis de Sales, *Treatise on the Love of God,* book IX, chapter 4, trans. Henry Benedict Mackey (Westminster, Md.: Newman Book Shop, 1942), p. 374.

11. Edward Abbey, *The Journey Home* (New York: E. P. Dutton, 1977), pp. 21–22.

12. Charles Bowden, *Desierto: Memories of the Future* (New York: W. W. Norton, 1991), pp. 159–60.

13. Francis Thompson, "The Hound of Heaven," in *The Hound of Heaven*, ed. Michael A. Kelly (Philadelphia: Peter Reilly, 1916), pp. 23–31.

CHAPTER 3 · Prayer Without Language in the Mystical Tradition
Knowing God as "Inaccessible Mountain"—"Marvelous Desert"

1. Gregory of Nyssa, *Contra Eunomium*, xii, in PG:45.1108C.

2. J. Quint, ed., *Meister Eckhart: Deutsche Predigten und Traktate* (München: C. Hanser, 1977), pp. 229–30.

3. Karl Barth, *Evangelical Theology* (London: Fontana Library, 1965), p. 15. Barth spoke of theology as "necessarily the logic of wonders." "In theological wonder," he adds, "it is a sheer impossibility that [the theologian] might one day finish his lessons, that the uncommon might become common, that the new might appear old and familiar, that the strange might ever become thoroughly domesticated" (p. 63).

4. A comprehensive history of the apophatic tradition has yet to be written, but two recent studies begin to address that need. Denys Turner's *The Darkness of God: Negativity in Christian Mysticism* (Cambridge: Cambridge University Press, 1995) traces the dominant metaphors of the cave and the mountain (interiority and ascent) in the Neoplatonic Christian tradition, from Pseudo-Dionysius to John of the Cross. Michael Sells, in his book *Mystical Languages of Unsaying* (Chicago: University of Chicago Press, 1994), explores apophatic language in writers such as Plotinus and Ibn Arabi, Marguerite Porete, and Meister Eckhart. Bernard McGinn's multivolume work, *The Presence of God: A History of Western Christian Mysticism* (New York: Crossroad, 1991–1995), will—when finished—go a long way toward providing a history of the Christian fascination with God's absence, as well as presence.

Other studies can be found in Verna Harrison, "The Relationship between Apophatic and Kataphatic Theology," *Pro Ecclesia* IV:3 (Summer 1995), pp. 318–32; Harvey D. Egan, "Christian Apophatic and Kataphatic Mysticisms," *Theological Studies* 39:3 (September 1978), pp. 399–426; Mary Gerhart, "The Word Image Opposition: The Apophatic/Cataphatic and the Iconic/Aniconic Tensions in Spirituality," in Ann W. Astell, *Divine Representations: Postmodernism & Spirituality* (New York: Paulist Press, 1994), pp. 63–79; A. H. Armstrong, "Negative Theology," in *Plotinian and Christian Studies* (London: Variorum Reprints, 1979); and John P. Kenney, "The Critical Value of Negative Theology," *Harvard Theological Review* 86:4 (October 1993), pp. 439–53.

See Alain Gouhier's article "Neant," in DictSp, vol. XI, pp. 64–80; Veselin Kesich's article "Via Negativa" in *The Encyclopedia of Religion*, ed. Mircea Eliade (New York: Macmillan, 1978), vol. 15, pp. 252–54; R. B. Williams, "The Via Negativa and the Foundations of Theology," in *New Studies in Theology*, Stephen Sykes and Derek Holmes, ed. (London: Gerald Duckworth, 1980), pp. 95–117; Charles Journet, *The Dark Knowledge of God* (London: Sheed & Ward, 1948); Henri de Lubac, "The Ineffable God," in *The Discovery of God* (New York: P. J. Kenedy, 1960); Marguerite Harl, "Le Langage de l'Experience Religieuse chez les Pères Grecs," in *Rivista di Storia e Letterature Religiosa* XIII:1 (1977), pp. 5–34; and Ralph Harper, *The Path of Darkness* (Cleveland, Ohio: Case Western Reserve University Press, 1968).

5. The root *phasis*, meaning "form" or "shape," can refer to the form taken by any particular image or speech. Michael Sells, in *Mystical Languages of Unsaying*, translates *apophasis* and *kataphasis* as an "un-saying" or "speaking-away," as opposed to a "saying with" (pp. 2–3).

6. This is how the *via negativa* was definitively stated by the Fourth Lateran Council (1215).

See H. Denzinger and A. Schonmetzer, *Enchiridion Symbolorum, Definitionum et Declarationum de Rebus Fidei et Morum* (New York: Herder, 1974), p. 806.

7. Harvey Egan, "Negative Way," *New Dictionary of Catholic Spirituality* (Collegeville, Minn.: Liturgical Press, 1993), p. 700.

8. I once read in the works of Simone Weil that "two prisoners whose cells adjoin communicate with each other by knocking on the wall. The wall is the thing which separates them but is also their means of communication. It is the same with us and God. Every separation is a link." *Gravity and Grace* (London: Routledge & Kegan Paul, 1963), p. 132.

9. Vincent Gillespie and Maggie Ross, "The Apophatic Image: The Poetics of Effacement in Julian of Norwich," in *The Medieval Mystical Tradition in England,* Exeter Symposium V, ed. Marion Glasscoe (Exeter, Eng.: University of Exeter Press, 1992), p. 53. As John of the Cross observed, "God commanded that the ark of the Covenant be empty and hollow [Ex 27:8] to remind the soul how void of all things God wishes it to be if it is to serve as His worthy dwelling." *Ascent of Mount Carmel,* I, V, 7, in *The Collected Works of St. John of the Cross,* trans. Kieran Kavanaugh and Otilio Rodriguez (Washington, D.C.: Institute of Carmelite Studies, 1979), p. 84.

10. See Bernard McGinn, *The Foundations of Mysticism* (New York: Crossroad, 1991), pp. 44–61; A. H. Armstrong, "Apophatic-Kataphatic Tensions in Religious Thought from the Third to the Sixth Century A.D.," in *From Augustine to Eriugena: Essays on Neoplatonism and Christianity in Honor of John O'Meara,* ed. F. X. Martin (Washington, D.C.: Catholic University of America Press, 1991), pp. 12–21; and Stephen Gersh, *From Iamblichus to Eriugena: An Investigation of the Pre-History and Evolution of the Pseudo-Dionysian Tradition* (Leiden: E. J. Brill, 1978).

11. Eunomius of Constantinople (335–394 C.E.) maintained that "it is unworthy of a Christian to profess the impossibility of knowing the Divine nature and the manner in which the Son is generated." James Hastings, ed. *Encyclopedia of Religion and Ethics* (New York: Charles Scribner's Sons, 1911), vol. V, p. 576. Gregory of Nyssa countered that "the divine being, such as it is essentially, is beyond the reach of the curiosity that would try to comprehend it." *Contra Eunomium,* II, in PG:45.463D–572A. Cf. Lucas F. Mateo-Seco and Juna L. Bastero, ed., *El "Contra Eunomium I" en la Produccion Literaria de Gregorio de Nisa* (Pamplona: Ediciones Universidad de Navarra, 1988), pp. 66–73, 124–29.

12. See Gregory of Nyssa, GregMos, II, 46. I deal with Gregory's reaction to Eunomius in more detail in chapter 4.

13. Evagrius, *Chapters on Prayer,* ch. 11, in trans. John Eudes Bamberger, *The Praktikos; Chapters on Prayer* (Spencer, Mass.: Cistercian Publications, 1970), p. 57.

14. The mention of Abba Pambo is from AP-anon, in PL:73.961C. See Owen Chadwick, ed. *Western Asceticism* (Philadelphia: Westminster Press, 1958), Section XV.42, pp. 165–66. The story of Abba Agathon is from the AP-alph, Agathon, 15, in PG:65.113B.

15. Pseudo-Dionysius, *The Mystical Theology,* III, in *Pseudo-Dionysius: The Complete Works,* trans. Colm Luibheid (New York: Paulist Press, 1987), p. 139.

16. Ibid., I, 3, pp. 136–37.

17. See Kallistos Ware's article "God Hidden and Revealed: The Apophatic Way and the Essence-Energies Distinction," *Eastern Churches Review* VII:3 (1975), pp. 125–36. In later Judaism, God's place (*maqōm*), as well as God's wisdom (*sophia*) and light (*shekinah*), had come to be emphasized as ways of making more accessible a God of absolute transcendence. This would be echoed in Christian efforts to balance the place and placelessness of God. See Belden C. Lane, "Landscape and Spirituality: A Tension Between Place and Placelessness in Christian Thought," *The Way Supplement* 73 (Spring 1992), pp. 4–13.

18. Philo of Alexandria, *Life of Moses,* II, xiv, 70, in *The Works of Philo,* trans. C. D. Yonge (Peabody, Mass.: Hendrickson Publishers, 1993), p. 497.

19. Maximus, *The Church's Mystagogy*, ch. 1, in *Maximus Confessor: Selected Writings*, ed. George C. Berthold (New York: Paulist Press, 1985), p. 186.

20 See Ian Ramsey, *Religious Language* (New York: Macmillan, 1957); Frederick Ferre, *Language, Logic and God* (Westport, Conn.: Greenwood, 1961); Robert W. Funk, *Language, Hermeneutic, and the Word of God* (New York: Harper, 1966); David Tracy, *The Analogical Imagination* (New York: Crossroad, 1981); and Kevin Hart, *The Trespass of the Sign: Deconstruction, Theology and Philosophy* (Cambridge: Cambridge University Press, 1989), pp. 173–206.

21. Karl Rahner, "The Hiddenness of God," *Theological Investigations* (New York: Seabury Press, 1979), vol. XVI, pp. 227–43; William H. Shannon, *Thomas Merton's Dark Path: The Inner Experience of a Contemplative* (New York: Farrar, Straus, Giroux, 1981); Vladimir Lossky, *The Mystical Theology of the Eastern Church* (London: James Clarke & Co., 1957), ch. 2; Bernard McGinn, *The Foundations of Mysticism* (New York: Crossroad, 1991).

22. See Donald W. Mitchell, *Spirituality and Emptiness: The Dynamics of Spiritual Life in Buddhism and Christianity* (New York: Paulist Press, 1991). Pope Paul VI called the Cistercians to Rome in 1971, asking them (in light of the popularity of Eastern meditation in the 1960s) to make available to the Catholic laity the riches of Western Christianity's own contemplative tradition. Basil Pennington, "Centering Prayer and the Friends," in *Spirituality in Ecumenical Perspective*, ed. E. Glenn Hinson (Louisville, Ky.: Westminster/John Knox, 1993), p. 129.

23. See Thomas Keating, *One Mind, One Heart* (New York: Continuum, 1995), and M. Basil Pennington, *Centering Prayer* (Garden City, N.Y.: Image Books, 1982).

24. Pennington, *Centering Prayer*, pp. 111f. Guigo II, a twelfth-century Carthusian, offered a classic formulation of this fourfold *spirituale exercitium* in his *Ladder of Monks*. See Simon Tugwell, *Ways of Imperfection* (Springfield, Ill.: Templegate Publishers, 1985), pp. 93–124.

25. Jarsolav Pelikan, *The Melody of Theology* (Cambridge, Mass.: Harvard University Press, 1988), p. 7.

26. Augustine, *Sermo* 52, C. vi, n. 16, in PL:38.360. One is tempted to compare Augustine's words to the Heart Sutra in Buddhism, as it expresses the deepest Buddhist wisdom by negating fundamental Buddhist teachings.

27. Gillespie and Ross, "The Apophatic Image," pp. 65, 75.

28. Julian of Norwich, *Revelations of Divine Love*, Long Text, ch. 18, par. 4, in *Julian of Norwich: Showings*, ed. Edmund Colledge and James Walsh (New York: Paulist Press, 1978), p. 211.

29. Ibid., ch. 5, par. 2–4.

30. Ibid., ch. 11, par. 1. Andrew Lough speaks of Julian's desert imagery in his book, *The Wilderness of God* (London: Darton, Longman, & Todd, 1991), pp. 75–76.

31. Colledge and Walsch, *Julian*, ch. 51, par. 10.

32. Ibid., ch. 6. Julian is not, however, a purely apophatic theologian, extolling an unknown God. She insists repeatedly that "God wille be knawwen."

33. Sam Keen, *To A Dancing God* (New York: Harper & Row, 1970), p. 44.

34. As Denys Turner defines it, the apophatic is "the linguistic strategy of somehow showing by means of language that which lies beyond language." Turner, *The Darkness of God*, p. 34.

35. John Chrysostom insists that God is known only as God comes down in condescension and accommodates himself to human weakness. *On the Incomprehensible Nature of God*, trans. Paul W. Harkins (Washington, D.C.: Catholic University of America Press, 1984), pp. 122–23.

36. Pseudo-Dionysius, *The Mystical Theology*, I (997B), in *Pseudo-Dionysius: The Complete Works*, trans. Colm Luibheid (New York: Paulist Press, 1987), p. 135. Denys Turner distinguishes two approaches in the apophatic tradition—"the route of the breakdown of discourse through its own excess of affirmations" (as in Bonaventure or Julian of Norwich) and "the route of the hierarchical ascent of denials" (seen in the predominantly negative imagery of Eckhart and the Cloud author). Turner, *The Darkness of God*, p. 257.

37. German Sermon 52, in *Meister Eckhart: A Modern Translation*, ed. Raymond Blakney (New York: Harper & Brothers, 1941), p. 231. Eckhart insists that "He . . . who is to be poor in spirit must be poor of all his own knowledge, so that he knows nothing of God, or creatures, or of himself" (p. 230).

38. Maurice O'C. Walshe, trans., *Meister Eckhart: Sermons and Treatises* (London: Watkins, 1979), vol. II, p. 105.

39. Following Oliver Davies, Denys Turner urges that Eckhart's rhetoric in his vernacular sermons provided a "poetization" of language never meant to be read as precise doctrinal statement. Turner, *The Darkness of God*, p. 149.

40. German Sermon 12, in *Meister Eckhart: Teacher and Preacher*, ed. Bernard McGinn (New York: Paulist Press, 1986), p. 270. See Alois Maria Haas, "Schools of Late Medieval Mysticism," in *Christian Spirituality: High Middle Ages and Reformation*, ed. Jill Raitt (New York: Crossroad, 1989), p. 148.

41. See Cheslyn Jones, Geoffrey Wainwright, and Edward Yarnold, eds., *The Study of Spirituality* (New York: Oxford University Press, 1986), p. 317.

42. German Sermon 10, in McGinn, *Meister Eckhart*, p. 265.

43. *Granum Sinapis*, IV, as translated in Bernard McGinn, "Meister Eckhart and the Desert: Reflections on the *Granum Sinapis*," an unpublished paper kindly shared by the author. McGinn traces historically the image of the desert as a symbol of God's inaccessible nature in his "Ocean and Desert as Symbols of Mystical Absorption," *Journal of Religion* 74:2 (April 1994), pp. 155–81.

44. Jones, Wainwright, and Yarnold, *The Study of Spirituality*, p. 318.

45. Louis Dupré discusses the influence of Plotinus on negative theology in *The Other Dimension: a Search for the Meaning of Religious Attitudes* (New York: Doubleday & Co., 1972), pp. 506–23. Cf. McGinn, *The Foundations of Mysticism*, pp. 158ff.

46. Jaroslav Pelikan sees Maximus, as an interpreter of Pseudo-Dionysius, to have "turned apophatic theology and spirituality around . . . back to a concentration on the person of Jesus Christ." Berthold, *Maximus Confessor*, p. 9.

47. Morton Kelsey cautions people against the potential dangers of this in *The Other Side of Silence: A Guide to Christian Meditation* (New York: Paulist Press, 1976), pp. 89, 134–36, 156.

48. Dorothee Sölle, in her book *Suffering* (London: DLT, 1977), insists that "the desire to be in God's image without attaining Christ's image is a desire for immediacy, which wants everything without detour and without self-actualization, a narcissistic desire of the ego to settle down in God, immortal and almighty, that doesn't find it necessary 'to let its life be crucified' and to experience the night of pain" (p. 131).

49. The repetition of a "little word" in the exercise of contemplative prayer appeared as early as Evagrius and John Cassian in the history of Christian prayer. See also Cloud, ch. VII, p. 134.

50. Frederick Franck offers an important caution here about not being too quick to "destroy the self" before we have recognized its validity. "Glib talk about the necessity of 'killing the ego' is to be distrusted. The development of ego is an indispensable phase of the human voyage. To 'kill it' before it has matured, is as questionable an operation as any other abortion." *A Little Compendium on That Which Matters* (New York: St. Martin's Press, 1993), p. 18.

51. Cloud, ch. XXXIV, pp. 185–86.

52. The language of the *Cloud* is the northeast Midland dialect used by Chaucer; an English Carthusian house is known to have been established in Nottinghamshire by the middle of the fourteenth century. See Cloud, introduction by James Walsh, p. 8.

53. Cloud, ch. LXXI, pp. 258–59.

54. Ibid., ch. VI, p. 131. The same author writes in another work, *The Book of Privy Counselling* (A Letter of Private Direction), ch. 8, in *The Pursuit of Wisdom and Other Works by the Au-*

thor of the Cloud of Unknowing, ed. James A. Walsh (New York: Paulist Press, 1988), that "this is the true condition of a perfect lover, only and utterly to spoil himself of himself for that thing that he loveth . . . and that not only for a time, but endlessly to be enwrapped therein in full and final forgetting of himself."

55. Cloud, ch. V, pp. 128–29. Richard of Saint Victor had also spoken of a cloud of forgetfulness, used "to hide from the mind the awareness of whatever lies at hand." *Benjamin Major: The Mystical Ark*, V, 2, in *The Twelve Patriarchs, The Mystical Ark, Book Three of the Trinity*, trans. Grover A. Zinn (New York: Paulist Press, 1979), pp. 310–12.

56. Cloud, ch. XLVI, p. 209. Thomas Merton observes that "the root of false mysticism is the yearning to 'have experiences'" in his foreword to William Johnston's *The Mysticism of the Cloud of Unknowing* (Saint Meinrad, Ind.: Abbey Press, 1975), p. ix.

57. Bonaventure, *Journey of the Mind to God*, ch. 7, in Ewert Cousins, trans. *The Soul's Journey into God* (New York: Paulist Press, 1978). Cf. Pseudo-Dionysius, *The Divine Names*, ch. II, in Luibheid, *Pseudo-Dionysius*, pp. 58–67.

58. Maggie Ross tries to describe the apophatic experience in *The Fountain and the Furnace: The Way of Tears and Fire* (New York: Paulist Press, 1987). "With many of the saints their histories say that their intellect was snatched while they were standing in prayer," she says of Issac the Syrian (p. 270).

59. See Thomas Merton, *New Seeds of Contemplation* (New York: New Directions, 1961), pp. 21–46, and Shannnon, *Thomas Merton's Dark Path*, p. 81.

60. Alice Gardner, *Studies in John the Scot* (New York: Oxford University Press, 1900), p. 28.

61. Berthold, *Maximus Confessor*, p. 215 n.4.

62. Cloud, ch. VI, p. 130. Or, as Hugh of Saint Victor said before him, "Love knocks and enters, but knowledge stands without."

63. Thomas Merton, *Ascent to Truth* (New York: Harcourt, Brace, 1951), p. 295.

64. Teresa of Avila, his spiritual director and colleague in Carmelite reform, expressed this well in her *Way of Perfection*, XII, in *The Collected Works of St. Teresa of Avila*, trans. Kieran Kavanaugh and Otilio Rodriguez (Washington, D.C.: Institute of Carmelite Studies, 1980), pp. 81–85. Cf. John of the Cross, *The Ascent of Mount Carmel*, I, 1, 4, in *The Collected Works of St. John of the Cross*, trans. Kieran Kavanaugh and Otilio Rodriguez (Washington, D.C.: Institute of Carmelite Studies, 1979), p. 74.

65. John of the Cross, DkNight, I, 12, 6, p. 323. John's personal love of desert terrain is revealed in a letter of August 19, 1591 during a brief stay in "the desert of La Penuela," where he says "the vastness of the desert is a great help to the soul and body, although the soul fares very poorly. The Lord must be desiring that it have its spiritual desert." Kavanaugh and Rodriguez, *Collected Works of St. John of the Cross*, p. 704.

66. DkNight, II, 17, 6, p. 370. This, he says, is also why Jesus chose solitary places for prayer, "such as the mountains that are elevated above the earth and usually barren of the objects that would provide sensitive recreation." *The Ascent of Mount Carmel*, III, 39, 2, in Kavanaugh and Rodriguez, *The Collected Works of St. John of the Cross*, p. 283.

67. DkNight, Stanzas of the Soul, pp. 295–96. Cf. *Poems of St. John of the Cross*, trans., John F. Nims (Chicago: University of Chicago Press, 1979), p. 19. The imagery here is that of the lover in the Song of Songs who comes in the night, a theme echoed as well in the Greek myth of Cupid and Psyche.

68. John of the Cross, *The Ascent of Mount Carmel*, his drawing of the mount, in Kavanaugh and Rodriguez, *The Collected Works of St. John of the Cross*, pp. 66–67.

69. John Ruusbroec, *The Spiritual Espousals*, II, 4, C, in James A. Wiseman, ed., *John Ruusbroec: The Spiritual Espousals and Other Works* (New York: Paulist Press, 1985), p. 133.

70. Thomas Merton, *Eighteen Poems* (New York: New Directions, 1985). Cf. Douglas Bur-

ton-Christie, "Rediscovering Love's World: Thomas Merton's Love Poems and the Language of Ecstasy," *Cross Currents* XXXIX:1 (Spring 1989), p. 73.

71. Columba Hart, ed., *Hadewijch: The Complete Works* (London: SPCK, 1981), p. 239.

72. John of the Cross, *Sayings,* 57, in Kavanaugh and Rodriguez, *The Collected Works of St. John of the Cross,* p. 672. Cf. Jones, Wainwright, and Yarnold, *The Study of Spirituality,* pp. 365–76.

73. Thomas Merton, "The Inner Experience," a manuscript left unfinished at his death, pp. 19–20, 104–6, quoted in Shannon, *Thomas Merton's Dark Path,* pp. 121–22, 131. "Mere withdrawal, without the return to freedom in action, would lead to a static and death-like inertia," Merton added.

74. Translated by Matthew Fox, *Meditations with Meister Eckhart* (Santa Fe, N.M.: Bear & Co., 1983), p. 120.

75. Cloud, ch. XXIV, p. 170.

76. Meister Eckhart, *German Sermon 39,* in McGinn, *Meister Eckhart: Teacher and Preacher,* pp. 296–97.

77. Ibid.

78. Thérèse of Lisieux spoke of her littleness, her being a mere "nothing," as the sole basis for her claim upon God. Cf. Tugwell, *Ways of Imperfection,* pp. 219–32.

79. Thomas Merton, letter to James Forest, February 21, 1966, in *The Hidden Ground of Love,* ed. William H. Shannon (New York: Farrar, Straus, Giroux, 1985), p. 294.

80. Thomas Merton, *Seeds of Contemplation* (New York: New Directions, 1949), p. 153.

81. Raymond Bailey, *Thomas Merton on Mysticism* (Garden City, N.Y.: Doubleday, 1975), p. 54. See Merton's poem, "Macarius the Younger" in Thomas Merton, *The Collected Poems of Thomas Merton* (New York: New Directions, 1977), pp. 319–20.

82. Thomas Merton, *Contemplation in a World of Action* (Garden City, N.Y.: Doubleday, 1973), p. 186. See John F. Teahan, "A Dark and Empty Way: Merton and the Apophatic Tradition," *Journal of Religion* 58 (1978), pp. 263–87.

83. Evagrius, *Gnostikos,* ch. 27, in *Évagre le Pontique: Le Gnostique,* ed. Antoine Guillaumont and Claire Guilllaumont, vol. 356 of *Sources Chrétiennes* (Paris: Les Editions du Cerf, 1989), pp. 133–34. See McGinn, *The Foundations of Mysticism,* p. 155.

84. Simone Weil, quoted in Harper, *The Path of Darkness,* p. 63.

85. William Johnston, S.J., "The Experience of God in Christian Apophatic Mysticism," in *God: The Contemporary Discussion,* ed. Frederick Sontag and Darrol Bryant (New York: Rose of Sharon Press, 1982), p. 365.

86. Merton, *The Ascent to Truth,* p. 94.

87. Maggie Ross, "The Human Experience of God at Turning Points: A Theological Expose of Spiritual Counterfeits," unpublished, p. 7. Cf. Her article on "Apophatic Prayer as a Theological Model," *Journal of Literature & Theology* 7:4 (December 1993), pp. 325–53.

88. Art Spiegelman, *Maus, Book II: A Survivor's Tale* (New York: Pantheon, 1991).

89. Pseudo-Dionysius the Areopagite, *On the Divine Names and the Mystical Theology,* trans. C. E. Holt (London: SPCK, 1957), p. 191.

MYTHIC LANDSCAPE · Stalking the Snow Leopard
A Reflection on Work

1. Donald Hall, *Life Work* (Boston: Beacon Press, 1993), p. 54.

2. Peter Matthiessen, *The Snow Leopard* (New York: Viking Press, 1978).

3. William Least Heat Moon, *Blue Highways* (Boston: Little, Brown, & Co., 1982), p. 211.

4. Cotton Mather, *A Christian at His Calling: Two Brief Discourses* (Boston: B. Green & J. Allen, for S. Sewall, 1701), pp. 37–38.

5. Simone Weil, *Waiting for God* (New York: Harper & Row, 1973), pp. 105–16.

6. "Nothing," said Evagrius, "is more essential to prayer than attentiveness." *On Prayer*, 149, in Philok, I, p. 71. "Unawareness is the root of all evil," added another of the desert fathers. AP-Anon. See Simon Tugwell, *Ways of Imperfection* (Springfield, Ill.: Templegate Publishers, 1985), p. 16.

7. Matthiessen, *Snow Leopard*, p. 257.

8. Ursula LeGuin, *The Farthest Shore* (New York: Athenaeum, 1972), p. 43.

9. Wendell Berry, *Collected Poems* (San Francisco: North Point Press, 1985), p. 140.

PART II · Illumination
Waiting in a Silence Beyond Language

1. Linda Imm Marconi, "Child's World," unpublished poem (1993).

2. The cosmic play of Vishnu precipitates pain as well as joy, but in its bliss transcends them both. See Heinrich Zimmer, *Philosophies of India* (New York: Pantheon Books, 1951), p. 571.

MYTHIC LANDSCAPE · Dragons of the Ordinary
The Discomfort of Common Grace

1. C. S. Lewis, "The Alliterative Metre," in *Selected Literary Essays*, ed. Walter Hooper (London: Cambridge University Press, 1969), p. 18.

2. Adapted from the children's book by Jay Williams, *Everyone Knows What a Dragon Looks Like* (New York: Four Winds Press, 1976).

3. See Otto Nagel, *Käthe Kollwitz* (Greenwich, Conn.: New York Graphic Society, Ltd., 1971), plates 146 and 148.

4. Quoted in Jane Yolen's *Touch Magic: Fantasy, Faerie and Folklore in the Literature of Childhood* (New York: Philomel Books, 1981), p. 55.

5. See Cristiano Grottanelli, "Dragons," in *Encyclopedia of Religion*, ed. Mircea Eliade (New York: Macmillan, 1987), vol. 2, pp. 431–36.

6. *Luther's Works*, ed. Jaroslav Pelikan (Saint Louis: Concordia Publishing House, 1964), vol. 4: Lectures on Genesis, ch. 21–25, pp. 115–17.

7. Pierre Teilhard de Chardin, *Letters to Two Friends, 1926–1952* (New York: New American Library, 1968), pp. 156–57.

8. C. S. Lewis, *The Lion, the Witch, and the Wardrobe* (Harmondsworth, Eng.: Penguin Books, 1959), p. 75.

CHAPTER 4 · The Sinai Image in the History of Western Monotheism

1. Jon D. Levenson, *Sinai and Zion* (Minneapolis: Winston Press, 1985), p. 15.

2. Ludwig Wittgenstein, *Tractatus Logico-Philosophicus*, trans. C. K. Ogden (London: Kegan Paul Trench Trubner & Co., 1922), thesis 7.

3. A recent study of Mount Sinai—including geographical, historical, biblical, and ethnographic perspectives—can be found in Joseph J. Hobbes, *Mount Sinai* (Austin: University of Texas Press, 1995).

4. Three main theories have been offered in the effort to locate the site of the original Mount Sinai. John Bright, in his *History of Israel* (Philadelphia: Westminster Press, 1981), is content to accept the traditional view supporting Jebel Mussa, where the mother of Constantine had a church built in the fourth century commemorating the site of the burning bush (p. 114). Paul Maiberger offers an interesting new argument for this in his *Topographische and historische Untersuchungen zum Sinaiproblem. Orbis Biblicus et Orientalis*, vol. 54, (Freiburg: Universitätsverlag, 1984).

A second opinion, urged by Martin Noth in his *History of Israel* (New York: Harper & Row, 1960), insists that Mount Sinai must have been a volcano, probably located in northern Arabia (pp. 128–32). Jean Koenig describes the black lava crags there as fitting the biblical description of a fierce landscape in a desert of darkness. "Le Sinai montagne de feu dans un désert de ténèbres," *Revue de l'Histoire des Religions* 167 (1965), pp. 131–55. See also Jean Koenig, "Le probleme de la localisation du Sinai," *Acta Orientalia Belgica: Correspondance d'Orient* 10 (1966), pp. 113–23. Yet a third approach would locate Mount Sinai in the northern Sinai peninsula or close to the Negev. Italian archaeologist Emmanuel Anati, for example, argues inconclusively for Har Karkom, between Eilat and Beer Sheva, as the original Mount Sinai. See Anati, *Har Karkom: The Mountain of God* (New York: Rizzoli International, 1986). From the perspective of mythic symbolism, any of these geographic possibilities is sufficiently desolate to evoke the kind of response found in the history and lore of Sinai through the centuries.

5. Barry Lopez, *Arctic Dreams: Imagination and Desire in a Northern Landscape* (New York: Scribner, 1986); John Van Dyke, *The Desert* (New York: Charles Scribner's Sons, 1901). One of the first Americans to appreciate desert terrain, Van Dyke was a precursor of later writers such as Edward Abbey.

6. Thoreau, *Walden* (New York: Holt, Rinehart & Winston, 1963), p. 265. Thoreau's climbing of Mount Katahdin in 1846 was for him a deeply unsettling and disturbing experience of threatening wilderness. On the mountain, he declared, "Some part of the beholder, even some vital part, seems to escape through the loose grating of his ribs as he ascends. He is more alone than you can imagine. There is less of substantial thought and fair understanding in him than in the plains where men inhabit . . . Vast, Titanic, inhuman Nature has got him at disadvantage, caught him alone. . . ." *The Maine Woods* (New York: Penguin Books, 1988), p. 85.

7. Gregory of Nyssa, *Commentary on the Canticle,* Homily 11, in Jean Danielou, *From Glory to Glory: Texts from Gregory of Nyssa's Mystical Writings* (Crestwood, N.Y.: St. Vladimir's Seminary Press, 1995), p. 247. See PG:44.1001.

8. Barry Lopez speaks of Beautyway in discussing the relationship of internal and external landscapes in his essay "Landscape and Narrative" in *Crossing Open Ground* (New York: Charles Scribner's Sons, 1988), pp. 61–71.

9. Robert R. Desjarlais, "Healing through Images: The Magical Flight and Healing Geography of Nepali Shamans," *Ethos* 17:3 (September 1989), pp. 289–307.

10. Rainer Marie Rilke, *Duino Elegies,* trans. David Young (New York: W. W. Norton & Co., 1978), First Elegy, p. 19. Cf. Yi-Fu Tuan's contrast of the frightening character of impersonal, indifferent, and uncharted "space" with the comfort, familiarity and particularity of "place," in *Space and Place: The Perspective of Experience* (Minneapolis: University of Minnesota Press, 1977), p. 54.

11. See Jennifer Westwood, *The Atlas of Mysterious Places* (New York: Weidenfeld & Nicholson, 1987), pp. 198–209.

12. W. Y. Evans-Wentz, *Cuchama and Sacred Mountains* (Chicago: Swallow Press, 1981), pp. 41–45. Cf. Kiyohiko Munakata, *Sacred Mountains in Chinese Art* (Urbana: University of Illinois Press, 1991).

13. See Turner, *The Darkness of God: Negativity in Christian Mysticism* (Cambridge: Cambridge University Press), p. 37. Paul Ricoeur speaks of this "tensional" character of metaphorical truth in *The Rule of Metaphor* (Toronto: University of Toronto Press, 1975), pp. 255–56. On the role of metaphor in religious language generally, see John Dominic Crossan, *The Dark Interval: Towards a Theology of Story* (Allen, Tex.: Argus Communications, 1975), and Sallie McFague, *Metaphorical Theology: Models of God in Religious Language* (Philadelphia: Fortress, 1982).

14. See Ernst Fuchs, *Studies of the Historical Jesus* (London: SCM, 1964), pp. 210ff.

15. A blind man once told William James that "he thought few seeing people could enjoy the view from a mountain top more than he." *Principles of Psychology* (New York: Henry Holt, 1918), vol. 10, pp. 203–4.

16. Matsuo Basho, *The Narrow Road to the North and Other Travel Sketches*, trans. Nobuyuki Yuasa (New York: Penguin Books, 1966), p. 125.

17. The psychological affect of mountains upon people is examined by Richard G. Mitchell, Jr. in *Mountain Experience: The Psychology and Sociology of Adventure* (Chicago: University of Chicago Press, 1983).

18. Nicholson, *Mountain Gloom and Mountain Glory* (New York: W. W. Norton, 1963), pp. 67ff.

19. Friedrich Nietzsche, *Thus Spoke Zarathustra*, trans. R.J. Hollingdale (Baltimore: Penguin Books, 1961), p. 174.

20. Al-Ghazzali, *Mishkat Al-Anwar*, quoted in Heinz Skrobucha, *Sinai* (London: Oxford University Press, 1966), p. 2.

21. See F. C. Bauerschmidt, "Doing Theology in Light of Divine Aniconicity," *St. Luke's Journal of Theology* 29:2 (1986), pp. 117–35.

22. An apophatic sensitivity could be found earlier in the prophetic and wisdom traditions of Israel, as well as in Neoplatonic writers from Plotinus to Proclus. See Samuel L. Terrien, *The Elusive Presence* (San Francisco Harper & Row, 1978), and R. T. Wallis, "The Spiritual Importance of Not Knowing," in *Classical Mediterranean Spirituality*, ed. A. H. Armstrong (New York: Crossroad, 1986), pp. 460–80.

23. Arianism emerged in the early fourth century as a Christological heresy, with Arius of Alexandria (c. 250–336) declaring that Jesus, as a created being, could not have shared the same essence (*ousia*) as God the Father. He rejected the Trinity, therefore, as a denial of the essential simplicity and unity of the Godhead. Eunomius had been a disciple of Aetius, the founder of the Anomoean branch of the Arian heresy. His *Apology*, written about 360, was answered shortly thereafter by Basil the Great in his *Adversus Eunomium*. Gregory of Nyssa, Basil's brother, continued the controversy after his death. See Ronald E. Heine, *Perfection in the Virtuous Life: A Study of the Relationship Between Edification and Polemical Theology in Gregory of Nyssa's De Vita Moysis* (Cambridge, Mass.: Philadelphia Patristic Foundation, 1975), pp. 127–58.

24. Eunomius, Fragment ii, in *Eunomius: The Extant Works*, trans. Richard P. Vaggione (Oxford: Clarendon Press, 1987), pp. 178–79. Cf. Paul W. Harkins, trans. *St. John Chrysostom On the Incomprehensible Nature of God*, vol. 72 of *The Fathers of the Church* (Washington, D.C.: Catholic University of America Press, 1984), p. 23.

25. A new English translation of Gregory's *Contra Eunomium*, with articles discussing its historical and theological context, is found in *El "Contra Eunomium I" en la Produccion Literaria de Gregorio de Nisa*, ed. Lucas F. Mateo-Seco and Juna L. Bastero (Pamplona: Ediciones Universidad de Navarra, 1988). The homilies of John Chrysostom are translated in Harkins, *St. John Chrysostom on the Incomprehensible Nature of God*.

26. Chrysostom, *On the Incomprehensible Nature of God*, Homily I, 36, in Harkins, *St. John Chrysostom*, p. 66.

27. Ibid., Homily I, 24, p. 60.. Ocean and desert images are often used interchangeably to suggest the vastness of the divine being. See Bernard McGinn, "Ocean and Desert as Symbols of Mystical Absorption," *Journal of Religion* 74:2 (April 1994), pp. 155–81. Columbanus, a sixth-century Celtic Christian, argued that the "knowledge of the Trinity is properly likened to the depths of the sea.... If then a man wishes to know the deepest ocean of divine understanding, let him first (if he is able) scan that visible sea, and the less he finds himself to understand of those creatures which lurk beneath the waves, the more let him realize that he can know less of

the depths of its Creator." G.S.M. Walker, ed., *Sancti Columbani Opera* (Dublin: Dublin Institute of Advanced Studies, 1970), Sermon I, p. 65.

28. Chrysostom, *On the Incomprehensible Nature of God*, Homily II, 22, in Harkins, *St. John Chrysostom*, pp. 79–80.

29. Rudolf Otto, *The Idea of the Holy* (New York: Oxford University Press, 1958), p. 184.

30. See Heine, *Perfection in the Virtuous Life*, pp. 127–58.

31. See Philo, *Life of Moses* II, xiv, 70, in *The Works of Philo*, trans. C. D. Yonge (Peabody, Mass.: Hendrickson Publishers, 1993), p. 497; Clement of Alexandria, *The Miscellanies*, II, 2, 5–6, in *Clement of Alexandria: Stromateis, Books One to Three*, trans. John Ferguson, vol. 85 of *The Fathers of the Church* (Washington, D.C.: Catholic University of America Press, 1991), pp. 160–161; and Origen, *Contra Celsus*, VI, 17, in *Origen: Contra Celsum*, trans. Henry Chadwick (Cambridge: Cambridge University Press, 1980), pp. 330–31.

32. GregMos, III, 158, p. 93.

33. Ibid., II, 46, p. 43.

34. Basil the Great, in his *Hexaemeron*, Homily 9, 3–5, made use of desert imagery in pointing to the unexplainable mysteries of nature that leave the mind in uncomprehending dread. He spoke of horrible things such as serpents eating through their mother's womb in their eagerness to be born, or of the arcane life of desert ants. "Not only is the essence of God unknowable in theory," he insists, "but the essence of even such a tiny creature as the ant is unknowable as well." Robert W. Thomson, ed., *The Syriac Version of the Hexaemeron by Basil of Caesarea* (Lovanni: In Aedibus Peeters, 1995), pp. 159–74.

35. As Gregory puts it: "This is what I think the soul experiences when it goes beyond its footing in material things, in its quest for that which has no dimension and which exists for all eternity." *Commentary on Ecclesiastes*, Sermon 7, in PG:44.729D–732A. See *From Glory to Glory: Texts from Gregory of Nyssa's Mystical Writings*, ed. Jean Danielou (Crestwood, N.Y.: St. Vladimir's Seminary Press, 1979), p. 42.

Gregory uses the same cliff metaphor in his *Commentary on the Beatitudes*, sermon 6, where he says: "Along the sea-coast you may often see mountains facing the sea, sheer and steep from top to bottom, while a projection at the top forms a cliff overhanging the depths. Now if someone suddenly looked down from such a cliff to the depths below he would become dizzy. So too is my soul seized with dizziness. . . . This then is the steep and sheer rock that Moses taught us was inaccessible, so that our minds can in no way approach it." PG:44.1264C, in Danielou, *From Glory to Glory*, pp. 42–43.

36. Gregory of Nyssa, *Commentary on the Canticle*, Homily 11, in PG:44.1001B. See Danielou, *From Glory to Glory*, pp. 247–48. Cf. Louis Bouyer, *The Spirituality of the New Testament and the Fathers* (New York: Desclée Co., 1960), p. 363.

37. See Jean Danielou, "Mystique de la Tenebre chez Gregoire de Nysse," DictSp, vol. II, pp. 1872–85.

38. "Never to reach satiety [*koros*] of desiring is truly to see God," said Gregory. GregMos, II, 239, p. 141. This grace-filled "straining towards God" is later emphasized by the author of *The Cloud of Unknowing* in his "naked intent toward God."

39. *Commentary on the Canticle*, Homily 11, in PG:44.1000C–1004C. See Danielou, *From Glory to Glory*, pp. 246–50; GregMos, II, 163.

40. Pseudo-Dionysius the Areopagite, *The Mystical Theology*, I, 1, in Luibheid, *Pseudo-Dionysius*, p. 136.

41. For a discussion of Dionysius' affirmation and negation of a Neoplatonic hierarchy of being, see Turner, *The Darkness of God*, pp. 19–49.

42. Maximus the Confessor, *Chapters on Knowledge*, I, 82–83, in *Maximus Confessor: Selected Writings*, ed. George C. Berthold (New York: Paulist Press, 1985), pp. 143–44.

43. Richard of Saint Victor, *Benjamin Major: The Mystical Ark*, XXII, in *The Twelve Patriarchs, The Mystical Ark, Book Three of the Trinity*, trans. Grover A. Zinn (New York: Paulist Press, 1979), p. 303.

44. Richard of Saint Victor, *Mystical Notes on the Psalms*, Psalms CIII and CXIII, in *Richard of Saint-Victor: Selected Writings on Contemplation*, ed. Clare Kirchberger (New York: Harper & Brothers, 1957), pp. 240–42. John of the Cross carried this imagery further, contrasting the mountain (or "morning") knowledge of God, gained through contemplation, with the hill (or "evening") knowledge of God deduced from God's creatures and works. *Spiritual Canticle*, Stanza 36, 6, in *The Collected Works of St. John of the Cross*, trans. Kieran Kavanaugh and Otilio Rodriguez (Washington, D.C.: Institute of Carmelite Studies, 1979), p. 547.

45. Meister Eckhart, German Sermon 15, in *Meister Eckhart: The Essential Sermons, Commentaries, Treatises and Defense*, trans. Edmund Colledge and Bernard McGinn (New York: Paulist Press, 1981), p. 192. John of the Cross similarly insisted that Elijah on Mount Horeb "covered his face (blinded his intellect) in the presence of God," knowing that "everything the intellect can understand, the will experience, and the imagination picture" would be inadequate in grasping God. *Ascent of Mount Carmel*, II, 8, 4–5, in Kavanaugh and Rodriguez, *The Collected Works of St. John of the Cross*, p. 127.

46. *The Book of Privy Counselling* (A Letter of Private Direction), II, in *The Pursuit of Wisdom and Other Works by the Author of the Cloud of Unknowing*, ed. James A. Walsh (New York: Paulist Press, 1988), p. 222.

47. GregMos, II, 249–54, pp. 118–20.

48. William of Saint-Thierry, *On Contemplating God*, III, in *The Works of William of St. Thierry*, ed. M. Basil Pennington (Spencer, Mass.: Cistercian Publications, 1971), vol. I, p. 38. "O Lord, my soul is as waterless ground in your sight, unwatered and untrodden," William wrote in *Meditation* 2:6, "I appear before you in your holy place, that I may see your power and your glory."

49. John Ruusbroec, *The Sparkling Stone*, II, section f, in *John Ruusbroec: The Spiritual Espousals*, ed. James A. Wiseman (New York: Paulist Press, 1985), pp. 180–81. (italics mine).

50. Maximus, *Chapters on Knowledge*, I, 84 and II, 13–14, in Berthold, *Maximus Confessor*, pp. 144, 150.

51. John Climacus, Ladder, introduction by Kallistos Ware, pp. 1–2.

52. Maggie Ross, American solitary sister at Christ Church, Oxford, in a lecture on Julian of Norwich at Saint Louis University, April 22, 1992.

53. Turner, *The Darkness of God*, pp. 20.

54. John Levenson, *Sinai and Zion*, pp. 16–21.

55. *Mekilta Wa-Yassa* 1, 44b, in *The Legends of the Jews*, trans. Louis Ginzberg, (Philadelphia: Jewish Publication Society of America, 1911), vol. III, p. 37.

56. Daniel Matt, ed., *Zohar: The Book of Enlightenment* (New York: Paulist Press, 1983), p. 123.

57. *Shabbat* 88b, 89a, in Ginzburg, *Legends*, vol. III, pp. 112–14.

58. *Targum* and *Tosefta Targum* Jud. 5.5, in Ginzberg, *Legends*, vol. III, p. 83. Cf. Joshua Schwartz, "Sinai in Jewish Thought and Tradition," *Immanuel: A Bulletin of Religious Thought and Research in Israel* 13 (Fall 1981), p. 10.

59. *Pesikta Rabbati* 21, 99b–100a, in Ginzberg, *Legends*, pp. 91, 97.

60. *Melkilta RS* 100, in Ginzberg, *Legends*, vol III, pp. 92–93. See the *Quran*, sura 7:170.

61. The bold use of nature imagery to suggest the presence and mystery of God is not uncommon in the Jewish tradition, despite traditional scholarship's tendency to minimize ancient Israel's attentiveness to nature. See Theodore Hiebert, *The Yahwist's Landscape: Nature and Religion in Early Israel* (New York: Oxford University Press, 1996), pp. 107–11. In a shocking case of metonymy found in the Talmud, for example, the oral tradition proclaims that

"Moses received Torah from Sinai," from the very mountain itself. The rabbis later have to explain how the mountain here stands for "Him who revealed Himself at Sinai." *Pirke Aboth,* ch. 1, in *The Mishnah,* trans. Herbert Danby (London: Oxford University Press, 1933), pp. 446–47.

62. Turner, *The Darkness of God,* pp. 22–23.

63. *Quran,* sura 95:1–2 and sura 52:1.

64. *The Tales of the Prophets of al-Kisa'i,* trans. W. M. Thackston (Boston: Twayne Publishers, 1978), p. 237.

65. Ibid., p. 235.

66. *The Mathnawi of Jalalu'ddin Rumi,* trans. Reynold Nicholson (Cambridge: E.J.W. Gibb Memorial, 1934), pp. 393–94. See G. John Renard, Jr., "Flight of the Royal Falcons: The Prophetology of Jalal ad-Din Rumi," (dissertation, Harvard University, 1978), pp. 118–19.

67. Accounts of pilgrimage to Sinai range from Helena, the mother of Constantine, and Egeria, the fourth-century Spanish nun, to the Dominican Felix Fabri in the fifteenth century, Friedrich von Tischendorf, the nineteenth-century "discoverer" of *Codex Sinaiticus,* and Henry Emerson Fosdick, Baptist minister of Riverside Church in New York.

68. Richard Pococke's *Description of the East,* published in 1734, offered to pilgrims a series of detailed sketches of the various sacred sites on and near Mount Sinai. See Heinz Skrobucha, *Sinai* (London: Oxford University Press, 1966), pp. 83–85. Felix Fabri, in the fifteenth century, spoke of being taken by the monks of Sinai to see "the place where the earth opened to swallow up Korah, Dathan, and Abiram (Num. 16); the hole in the rock, which Aaron used as a mould when he cast the golden calf; the place where the same Aaron watched the people dancing, while Moses was coming down from the Mount . . ." etc. Skrobucha, *Sinai,* p. 82

69. "For most Jews, it is not the mountain but the message which is important; the mountain should remain *terra incognita,* unlocated, unlocatable in no man's land," says Joseph J. Hobbes in *Mount Sinai,* p. 33. Cf. Daniel Jeremy Silver, *Images of Moses* (New York: Basic Books, 1982), pp. 161–65.

70. See Skrobucha, *Sinai,* pp. 53–62.

71. Jonathan Z. Smith observes that pilgrimage sites in Jerusalem did not come to be defined until the fourth century, in the era following Constantine's conversion. He analyzes the creation of new ritual sites that serve the later complex elaboration of imperial-Christian ritual in his book, *To Take Place: Toward Theory in Ritual* (Chicago: University of Chicago Press, 1987), pp. 74–95.

72. Procopius, *Buildings,* V.viii.I,4–9, in Procopius, *History of the Wars, Secret History, and Buildings,* trans. Averil Cameron (New York: Washington Square Press, 1967). See John Galey, *Sinai and the Monastery of St. Catherine* (Givatayim, Israel: Massada Publishing Ltd., 1980), pp. 50–51.

MYTHIC LANDSCAPE · Encounter at Ghost Ranch

1. Georgia O'Keeffe, "About Painting Desert Bones," in *Georgia O'Keeffe: Paintings—1943* (New York: An American Place, 1944), quoted in Charles Eldredge, *Georgia O'Keeffe* (New York: Harry N. Abrams, Inc., 1991), p. 119.

2. Georgia O'Keeffe, *Catalogue of the 14th Annual Exhibition of Paintings with Some Recent O'Keeffe Letters* (New York: An American Place, 1937), quoted in Roxana Robinson, *Georgia O'Keeffe: A Life* (New York: Harper & Row, 1989), p. 420.

3. Ghost Ranch, near Abiquiu, New Mexico, is a national conference center of the Presbyterian Church (USA). The area, with its compelling rock formations and mesas, was once known by Hispanic peoples as *El Rancho de los Brujos,* the ranch of the witches. Georgia O'Keeffe purchased eight acres of land there in 1940, living in an old adobe house under the shadow of Chimney Rock.

4. Barry Lopez, *Desert Notes* (New York: Avon Books, 1981), p. xi.

5. See Robert Bly, *Iron John: A Book about Men* (Reading, Mass.: Addison-Wesley, 1990), and Clarissa Pinkola Estés, *Women Who Run with the Wolves* (New York: Ballantine Books, 1995).

6. Edward Abbey is best known for his book *Desert Solitaire* (New York: McGraw Hill, 1968) and his novels about the Monkey Wrench Gang, a group of anarchists and Green activists who defend the southwestern landscape from the onslaught of developers. See *The Best of Edward Abbey,* ed. Edward Abbey (San Francisco: Sierra Club Books, 1984).

7. Gary Snyder, *The Practice of the Wild* (San Francisco: North Point Press, 1990), p. 23.

8. Wendell Berry, *Recollected Essays, 1965–1980* (San Francisco: North Point Press, 1981), pp. 230–44.

9. A particularly compelling dream that I had shortly after returning from this trip to Ghost Ranch is related in the original form of this narrative as published in *Spirituality Today* 43:2 (Summer 1991), pp. 170–72.

10. Richard Rodriguez, *Hunger of Memory* (Boston: David R. Godine, 1981), p. 185.

11. Frederick Buechner, *Telling Secrets* (San Francisco: Harper Collins), 1991), pp. 7–10.

CHAPTER 5 · Sinai and Tabor
Mountain Symbolism in the Christian Tradition

1. Theodore of Studios, writing in the year 815 to monks who had fled from persecution to the recesses of the mountains. Quoted in Skrobucha, *Sinai* (London: Oxford University Press, 1966), p. 2.

2. See Valerius' letter, "To the Monks of Vierzo in Praise of the Most Blessed Egeria," published in *Egeria's Travels,* trans. John Wilkinson (London: SPCK, 1971), pp. 175–76. Egeria was fascinated by holy mountains, climbing many of them, including Mounts Nebo, Faran, Eremus, Carmel, and Hermon. The sequence in which she visited these peaks is not entirely clear (pp. 27–29).

3. As early as 327 Empress Helena, the mother of Constantine, made a pilgrimage to the alleged site of the burning bush at the foot of Jebel Mussa and ordered a church to be built there in honor of the Virgin Mary. By the time Justinian had a fortress and new church erected there for the monastic community in 557, the identification of Mount Sinai with this peak was firmly established. Nicephorus Callixtus claimed that Saint Helena had also built a church on Mount Tabor in the year 326, making an interesting connection of the mother of Constantine with both mountains. See Leonid Ouspensky and Vladimir Lossky, *The Meaning of Icons* (Boston: Boston Book & Art Shop, 1969), p. 211.

The earliest reference to Tabor as the Mount of Transfiguration appears in the third-century Gospel of Hebrews, as quoted by Origen. See Pierre Maraval, "La Transfiguration au Mont Tabor?" in *Le Monde de la Bible* 23 (February–March 1982), pp. 24–26, and Julius Boehmer, "Der Gottesberg Tabor," *Biblische Zeitschrift* XXIII (1935–36), pp. 333–41.

4. Levenson, in *Sinai and Zion* (Minneapolis: Winston Press, 1985), describes Mount Sinai as exemplifying the uncontrollable and unpredictable quality of God's choice of place (pp. 15–23).

5. The transfiguration narrative and its connection with Mount Tabor is carefully examined in Maria Teresa Petrozzi's *Il Monte Tabor e Dintorni* (Jerusalem: Franciscan Printing Press, 1976).

6. Edward Robinson, *Biblical Researches in Palestine, Mount Sinai and Arabia Petraea* (Boston: Crocker and Brewster, 1841), vol. I, p. 131.

7. Oliver Clement, "L'Icone de la Transfiguration," *Le Monde de la Bible* 23 (February–March 1982), pp. 44–46.

8. Richard of Saint Victor (d. 1173) spoke of Tabor and Sinai in his major works on *The*

Twelve Patriarchs and *The Mystical Ark,* using the biblical experiences occurring there to describe various stages of contemplation. See *Benjamin Minor: The Twelve Patriarchs,* ch. LXXV–LXXXIII, in *The Twelve Patriarchs, The Mystical Ark, Book Three of the Trinity,* trans. Grover A. Zinn (New York: Paulist Press, 1979), pp. 132–142.

9. Claude Lévi-Strauss, *Structural Anthropology* (New York: Basic Books, 1963). For Lévi-Strauss, myth characteristically serves the purpose of harmonizing conflicting tensions within a culture.

10. See Ambrosios Giakalis, *Images of the Divine: The Theology of Icons at the Seventh Ecumenical Council* (Leiden: E.J. Brill, 1994), pp. 65–70, for a discussion of the deification (*theosis*) of matter in the Eastern Orthodox tradition.

11. Even when the light appears as a ray of darkness, as on Mount Sinai, it is a supernatural light that the icon emits through its "window on eternity." See Gennadios Limouris, ed., *Icons: Windows on Eternity; Theology and Spirituality in Colour* (Geneva: WCC Publications, 1990), and John J. Yiannias, "The Transfiguration of Nature in the Byzantine Iconographic Tradition," *Epiphany* 10 (1990), pp. 37–45.

12. Limouris, *Icons,* pp. 104–5, 196–98. One finds an example of reversed perspective in Andrei Rublev's famous icon of the Holy Trinity, painted in fifteenth-century Russia. The lines of the floor and furniture at the bottom of the picture, if extended out, would converge at the height of the viewer's chest.

13. John Baggley, *Doors of Perception: Icons and Their Spiritual Significance* (Crestwood, N.Y.: St. Vladimir's Seminary Press, 1988), pp. 80–81.

14. Reflecting on the sense of dynamic space revealed in icons of this sort, Egon Sendler suggests that "the spherical space moves out toward the spectator and shines its light on him like a headlight." *The Icon: Image of the Invisible; Elements of Theology, Aesthetics, & Technique* (Redondo Beach, Calif.: Oakwood Publications, 1988), p. 139.

15. See Sendler, *The Icon,* pl. 27, pp. 172–73. This same icon places Christ within a mandorla of three concentric circles representing the magnificence of the divine light. Each circle becomes increasingly darker as it moves toward the center of the divine being, suggesting the influence of the "theology of darkness" found in Gregory of Nyssa and Pseudo-Dionysius.

16. See Baggley, *Doors of Perception,* pp. 112–13.

17. Gregory of Palamas, *Triads,* I, 5, in *Gregory Palamas: The Triads,* ed. John Meyendorff (New York: Paulist Press, 1983), p. 33. A discussion of Tabor's light became the focus of theological debate between Gregory and Barlaam of Calabria in the hesychast controversy of the fourteenth century. Barlaam opposed on rationalist grounds the idea that the disciples on Mount Tabor or the hesychast fathers on Mount Athos could arrive at a vision of the Divine Light, seeing that light for himself as nothing more than a symbol. By contrast, Gregory insisted that Tabor's uncreated light discloses the energies of the divine nature in a way that transforms one's entire being.

Reflecting on the development of icons in this period, Leonid Ouspensky observes, "It is precisely at this time that representations of the Transfiguration became widely spread in sacred art, as an expression of the hesychast doctrine on the light of Tabor." *Theology of the Icon* (Crestwood, N.Y.: St. Vladimir's Seminary Press, 1992), vol. II, p. 240 n.24.

18. Martin Noth uses the word *Orbgebundenheit* (or "earth-boundedness") in speaking of the tenacity with which biblical traditions adhere to particular places. The cultic tradition associated with Jacob, for example, was closely bound to the tree shrine at Shechem. See Martin Noth, *A History of Pentateuchal Traditions* (Englewood Cliffs, N.J.: Prentice-Hall, 1972), pp. 79–87. John Bright offers a critique of this emphasis on place in his *Early Israel in Recent History Writing* (London: SCM, 1956), pp. 45ff. and 101ff.

19. Naaman of Syria indicates this same impulse in II Kings 5:17 when he asks Elisha for two

mule-loads of earth so that in the future he might offer sacrifice to Yahweh on the very land in which he'd been healed. (In sharing this story I realize that I run the danger of encouraging the taking of stones from sacred sites, an act that is spiritually and ecologically reprehensible.)

20. *Egeria's Travels*, p. 95.

21. Lesley Hazleton, *Where Mountains Roar: A Personal Report from the Sinai and Negev Desert* (New York: Penguin, 1980), p. 27.

22. Ladder, Step 3: On Exile, pp. 85, 87.

23. Ibid., Step 4: On Obedience, p. 120.

24. R. W. Thomson, "A Seventh-Century Armenian Pilgrim on Mount Tabor," *Journal of Theological Studies* New Series XVIII (1967), p. 30. Arculf, the bishop of Gaul, also traveled to Tabor about the year 700, speaking of its "remarkably round shape, covered in an extraordinary manner with grass and flowers." See Thomas Wright, ed., *Early Travels in Palestine* (New York: Ktav, 1968), p. 9.

25. D. Winton Thomas, "Mount Tabor: The Meaning of the Name," *Vetus Testamentum* I (1951), pp. 229–30. Cf. Levenson, *Sinai and Zion*, p. 115.

26. Eugene D. Stocton, "Prehistory of Mount Tabor," *Liber Annuus* XV (1964–65), pp. 131–36.

27. See Otto Eissfeldt, "Der Gott des Tabor und seine Verbreitung," *Archiv für Religionswissenschaft* 31 (1934), pp. 14–41, and Petrozzi, *Il Monte Tabor e Dintorni*, pp. 125–29. The most important sacred mountain in Canaanite mythology was Mount Zaphon in present-day Syria, the dwelling place of Baal-Hadad, the Syrian storm-god. See R. E. Clements, *God and Temple* (Oxford: Basil Blackwell, 1965), pp. 1–15.

28. Summarizing John of Damascus and Gregory Palamas, John A. McGuckin says, "When the disciple comes before the mystery of the Transfiguration he sees an image of his true face that he has known but long since forgotten." *The Transfiguration of Christ in Scripture and Tradition* (Lewiston, N.Y.: Edwin Mellen Press, 1986), p. 142; pp. 117–19. George Habra suggests that both Christ and the apostles were transfigured in the experience at Tabor. From one perspective "the transfiguration is that of the disciples themselves, consisting in a certain mystical perception of the divinity of Christ coming through the veil of the flesh." *La Transfiguration selon les Pères Grecs* (Paris: Editions S.O.S., 1973), p. 47.

29. Ansel Adams and Nancy Newhall, *This Is the American Earth* (San Francisco: Sierra Club, 1960), p. 62.

30. See Malise Ruthven, *Islam in the World* (New York: Oxford University Press, 1984), pp. 234–35. While there are important differences between Sufi and Christian mysticism, Teresa of Avila can argue in a similar way that the soul in its most interior chamber occupies the same ground as the divine being. *The Interior Castle*, VII, 2, 4, in *The Collected Works of St. Teresa of Avila*, trans. Kieran Kavanaugh and Otilio Rodriguez (Washington, D.C.: Institute of Carmelite Studies, 1980), p. 434. Catherine of Genoa insists that, "once stripped of all its imperfections, the soul rests in God, with no characteristics of its own, since its purification is the stripping away of the lower self in us. Our being is then God." *Catherine of Genoa: Purgation and Purgatory, The Spiritual Dialogue*, trans. Serge Hughes (London: SPCK, 1979), p. 80.

31. Joachim of Fiore spent the Lenten season of 1157 or 1158 praying on Mount Tabor. In his *Expositio in Apocalypsim*, fol. 39r, he too spoke of receiving a "fullness of knowledge" at the end of his stay on the mountain. See *Joachim of Fiore: Expositio in Apocalypsim*, ed. Edward Burger (Toronto: Pontifical Institute of Medieval Studies, 1986), p. 49.

32. Irenaeus could describe the glimpsing of God face to face on Tabor as an act of "God's making good his ancient promise" to Moses, who had seen only God's back from the cleft of the rock on Sinai (Exod. 32:20–22). *Against Heresies*, 4.20.9, in *The Writings of Irenaeus*, trans.

Alexander Roberts and James Donaldson, vol. V of the *Ante-Nicene Christian Library* (Edinburgh: T. & T. Clark, 1868), p. 446.

33. B. D. Chilton argues that "the relationship between the Sinai scene and the Transfiguration appears to have been fully appreciated by all three synoptic evangelists." "The Transfiguration: Dominical Assurance and Apostolic Vision," *New Testament Studies* 27:1 (October 1980), p. 121. Listing parallels between Exodus 24 and Mark 9, he describes the latter as a Tabernacles Haggada, "a visionary representation of the Sinai motif" (p. 122, 124).

34. See Terence Donaldson, *Jesus on the Mountain* (Sheffield, Eng.: JSOT Press, 1985), pp. 142–43 and Ulrich Mauser, *Christ in the Wilderness* (Naperville, Ill.: A. R. Allenson, 1963), pp. 111–16.

35. "Sinai," "Horeb," and "the mountain of God" seem to be used interchangeably in the Exodus narrative. "Sinai" is normally the preference of the Yahwist and Priestly writers; "Horeb" is more characteristic of the Elohist. See Th. Booij, "Mountain and Theophany in the Sinai Narrative," *Biblica* 65:1 (1984), p. 6. At times Horeb has been identified with Mount Zafzafa, immediately behind Saint Catherine's monastery, standing next to Jebel Mussa.

36. See Skrobucha, *Sinai*, p. 72.

37. See Baggley, *Doors of Perception*, pp. 136–37.

38. For a fine description of the architecture and mosaics of the monastery katholikon see George H. Forsyth and Kurt Weitzmann, *The Monastery of Saint Catherine at Mount Sinai* (Ann Arbor: University of Michigan, 1976).

39. Athanasios Paliouras notes that the focus of the mosaic "has been par excellence the favorite subject of the monks who aspire to holiness, to become worthy of contemplating and viewing God's ineffable glory, the increate Taborian light." *The Monastery of St. Catherine on Mount Sinai* (Glyka Nera Attikis: E. Tzaferi, 1985), p. 27.

40. See Margaret Pamment, "Moses and Elijah in the Story of the Transfiguration," *Expository Times* 92 (1980–81), pp. 338–39.

41. The hidden, apophatic character of the transfiguration was emphasized by Maximus the Confessor, who spoke of the disciples being "brought up to the glory of the only begotten Son of the Father, 'full of grace and truth,' by means of an apophatic theological gnosis that sings of him as wholly uncontained." *Ambiguorum Liber*, PG:91.1125–8, quoted in McGuckin, *The Transfiguration of Christ*, p. 199.

42. See Walter Brueggemann, "The Crisis and Promise of Presence in Israel," *Horizons in Biblical Theology* 1 (1979), p. 60.

43. "Having preached to his disciples the imminent inbreaking of the glorious Kingdom, his eventual coronation was in reality a far cry from his disciples' expectations. He was given a crown of thorns not gold, and his death took place to the sounds of mocking hilarity rather than reverential hymns." McGuckin, *The Transfiguration of Christ*, p. 139.

44. On the role of the New Year's liturgy on Mount Zion in calling into question the power of the king and reaffirming the kingship of Yahweh, see Walter Brueggemann, *Israel's Praise* (Philadelphia: Fortress Press, 1988), pp. 55–87.

45. Origen, *Commentary on Matthew*, XII. 36–43. See *Der Kommentar zum Evangelium nach Mattaus, X–XVII*, trans. Hermann J. Vogt (Stuttgart: Hiersemann, 1983).

46. Jonathan Z. Smith, discussing the nature of sacred space, speaks of light in this way with respect to the architectural design of the temple in Jerusalem. In a mythic sense, the notion may be true of all sacred buildings. *Map is Not Territory* (Leiden: E. J. Brill, 1978), p. 116.

47. Joseph J. Hobbes discusses "the new golden calf" of big-money tourism in *Mount Sinai* (Austin: University of Texas Press, 1995), pp. 261–305.

48. Mary Gerhart warns against viewing the apophatic and kataphatic as opposite energies,

seeing them rather as interrelating moments in the spiritual life. "The Word Image Opposition: The Apophatic-Cataphatic and the Iconic-Aniconic Tensions in Spirituality," in *Divine Representations: Postmodernism and Spirituality,* ed. Ann W. Astell (New York: Paulist Press, 1994), pp. 63–79.

49. Others understand the apophatic as a movement from us to God, while the kataphatic is a movement from God to us. I am indebted to my colleague Renee Bennett for these reflections.

50. McGuckin notes how important this theme became in Eastern theology. "From the earliest writings on the subject we find the Fathers stressing the Transfiguration as proclaiming the hiddenness of God as much as being a revelation." *The Transfiguration of Christ,* pp. 100–101.

51. Jean M. Briand, "Le mont Thabor—son histoire, ses eglises," *La Terre Sainte* 6 (November–December 1990), p. 270.

52. H. F. M. Prescott, *Once to Sinai: The Further Pilgrimage of Friar Felix Fabri* (New York: Macmillan, 1958), pp. 86–87.

53. Annette Kolodny, in her books *The Lay of the Land* and *The Land Before Her* (Chapel Hill: University of North Carolina Press, 1975 and 1984), compares mythic interpretations of American landscape as offered by men and women respectively. Cf. Carolyn Merchant's *The Death of Nature: Women, Ecology, and the Scientific Revolution* (San Francisco: Harper, 1988).

54. Annie Dillard, *Pilgrim at Tinker Creek* (New York: Harper's, 1974), pp. 132, 69, 55–56, 5–6. See Eugene H. Peterson, "Annie Dillard: With Her Eyes Open," *Theology Today* XLIII:2 (July 1986), pp. 178–91.

55. Loren Eiseley, *The Star Thrower* (New York: Times Books, 1978), pp. 60–65. See Antoine de Saint Exupéry, *The Little Prince* (New York: Harcourt, Brace, Jovanovich, 1971), pp. 78–88.

56. Quoted in Maraval, "La Transfiguration au Mont Tabor?" p. 25.

MYTHIC LANDSCAPE · **Imaginary Mountains, Invisible Lands**

1. Mircea Eliade, *Patterns in Comparative Religion* (New York: New American Library, 1974), p. 99.

2. George MacDonald, *At the Back of the Northwind* (Ann Arbor, Mich.: University Microfilms, 1966), p. 113.

3. Similarly, in Buddhist mythology the sun circled around the invisible Mount Meru; in Muslim mythology the sun hid daily behind the Peak of Hara on Mount Kaf, also present but unseen. Bernbaum, *Sacred Mountains of the World* (San Francisco: Sierra Club Books, 1990), p. 91.

4. For the Greek text and a French translation (including sketches of the great World Mountain and Mount Sinai), see Wanda Wolska-Conus, ed., *Cosmas Indicopleustes: Topographie Chrétienne,* Vols. 141 and 159 of *Sources Chrétiennes* (Paris: Les Éditions du Cerf, 1968, 1970). A partial English translation can be found in J. W. McCrindle, *The Christian Topography of Cosmas, an Egyptian Monk* (London: The Hakluyt Society, 1897). An introduction to the Greek text is also available in E. O. Winstedt, ed., *The Christian Topography of Cosmas Indicopleustes* (London: Cambridge University Press, 1909).

5. See Belden C. Lane, "Fantasy and the Geography of Faith," *Theology Today* L:3 (October 1993), pp. 397–408.

6. Susan Flader and J. Baird Callicott, eds., *The River of the Mother of God and Other Essays by Aldo Leopold* (Madison: University of Wisconsin Press, 1991), pp. 123–27.

7. See Phillip C. Muehrcke and Juliana O. Muehrcke, "Maps in Literature," *The Geographical Review* LXIV:3 (July 1974), p. 319.

8. Barry Lopez, *Desert Notes* (New York: Avon Books, 1976), p. 75.

9. René Daumal, *Mount Analogue,* trans. Roger Shattuck (Baltimore: Penguin Books, 1974).

10. Cf. Tony Heiderer, "Sacred Space, Sacred Time," *National Geographic* 177:5 (May 1990), pp. 106–17.

11. Cf. Henry Corbin, *Spiritual Body and Celestial Earth* (Princeton, N.J.: Princeton University Press, 1977), pp. 74–75.

12. Garrison Keillor, *The Prairie Home Companion,* National Public Radio broadcast, August 4, 1989.

13. Arthur and Jo Schwartz, "The Land of Snow Ridges: A Conversation with Thubten Jigme Norbu," *Parabola* XIII:4 (November 1988), p. 7.

14. Bernbaum, *Sacred Mountains,* pp. 42–55.

15. Ibid., p. 130.

16. C. S. Lewis, *Surprised by Joy* (New York: Harcourt Brace & Co., 1956). pp. 17–18.

17. Ibid., p. 166.

18. See Levenson, *Sinai and Zion* (Minneapolis: Winston Press, 1985), p. 175.

19. Cf. J. E. Cirlot, *A Dictionary of Symbols* (New York: Philosophical Library, 1971), pp. 219–21, and Emil A. Gutheil, *Handbook of Dream Analysis* (New York: Liveright, 1951), pp. 153–54. In the ancient world, Artemidorus saw mountains in one's dreams as signifying sorrows, fears, and disturbances, adding that "it is always better to pass through these regions, find the roads in them, descend from these places onto the plains, and to awaken from one's sleep when one no longer remains in them." This combination of longing and dread within a single dream symbol makes it especially appropriate in speaking of the numenous. Robert J. White, ed., *The Interpretation of Dreams: Oneirocritica by Artemidorus* (Park Ridge, N.J.: Noyes Press, 1975), Book II, 28. p. 108.

20. Philip Sheldrake demonstrates this very effectively in *Befriending Our Desires* (Notre Dame, Ind.: Ave Maria Press, 1994).

21. Thomas Traherne, *Centuries,* 1.44, in *Poems, Centuries, and Thanksgivings,* ed. Anne Ridler (London: Oxford University Press, 1966); Bonaventure, *Itinerarium,* Prologue, 3, in *The Soul's Journey into God,* trans. Ewert Cousins (New York: Paulist Press, 1978); Julian of Norwich, *Revelations of Divine Love,* ch. 31, in *Julian of Norwich: Showings,* ed. Edmund Colledge and James Walsh (New York: Paulist Press, 1978); Ignatius of Loyola, *Spiritual Exercises,* para. 48, *The Spiritual Exercises of St. Ignatius,* ed. David L. Fleming (Saint Louis, Mo.: Institute of Jesuit Sources, 1978).

22. In *The Book of Privy Counseling* (A Letter of Private Direction), section XII, there is a wonderful passage about how one knows whether he or she is called to the practice of contemplative prayer. See *The Pursuit of Wisdom and Other Works by the Author of the Cloud of Unknowing,* ed. James A. Walsh (New York: Paulist Press, 1988), pp. 242–46.

23. Gregory the Great, Homily 36.1–2 and 30.1–2, PL:76.1266A, 1220C, in *Be Friends of God: Spiritual Reading from Gregory the Great,* trans. John Leinenweber, (Cambridge, Mass.: Cowley Publications, 1990), pp. 15, 145.

24. Lewis, *Surprised by Joy,* p. 18.

25. GregMos, II, 233, p. 115.

PART III · Union
Love as the Fruit of Indifference

1. M. Basil Pennington, *Centering Prayer* (Garden City, N.Y.: Image Books, 1982), p. 19. This practice of attentiveness in contemplative prayer is what Jacob Needleman regards as essential to the recovery of spirituality in *Lost Christianity* (Rockport, Mass.: Element, Inc., 1993).

2. See Deirdre Carabine, "Eriugena's Use of the Symbolism of Light, Cloud, and Darkness in the *Periphyseon,*" in *Eriugena: East & West,* ed. Bernard McGinn and Willemien Otten (Notre Dame, Ind.: University of Notre Dame Press, 1991), pp. 141–52, and Michael Haykin, "'In the Cloud and in the Sea': Basil of Caesarea and the Exegesis of I Cor. 10:2," *Vigiliae Christianae* 40 (1986), pp. 135–44.

3. John Carmody, *Cancer and Faith* (Mystic, Conn.: Twenty-Third Publications, 1994), p. 24.

4. Susan Sontag, *Illness as Metaphor* (New York: Farrar, Straus & Giroux, 1978). Sontag wrote this book, in part, as a way of dealing with her own experience of cancer.

5. The *Anima Christi* prayer at the opening of the Spiritual Exercises. See *The Spiritual Exercises of St. Ignatius,* ed. David L. Fleming (Saint Louis, Mo.: Institute of Jesuit Sources, 1978), p. 3.

MYTHIC LANDSCAPE · Transformation at Upper Moss Creek

1. DkNight, II, 10, 1, p. 350.

2. See Belden C. Lane, "Mother Earth as Metaphor: A Healing Pattern of Grieving and Giving Birth," *Horizons* 21:1 (Spring 1994), pp. 7–21.

3. Gary Snyder, *The Old Ways* (San Francisco: City Lights Books, 1977), p. 12.

4. "Of all insects," Edwards proclaimed, "no one is more wonderful than the spider—especially in respect to their sagacity and admirable way of working." Wallace E. Anderson, ed., *Works of Jonathan Edwards: Scientific and Philosophical Writings,* vol. 6 (New Haven, Conn.: Yale University Press, 1980), pp. 154–58. Unfortunately, Edwards is remembered only for the spider imagery of "Sinners in the Hands of an Angry God." See Clyde A. Holbrook, *Jonathan Edwards, the Valley and Nature* (Lewisburg, Penn.: Bucknell University Press, 1987), pp. 25–26.

CHAPTER 6 · Desert Catechesis
The Landscape and Theology of Early Christian Monasticism

1. *Historia Monachorum,* XII, in PL:21.432B. Cf. Tim Vivian, "Mountain and Desert: The Geographies of Early Coptic Monasticism," *Coptic Church Review* 12:1 (Spring 1991), p. 16.

2. AP-alph, Anthony, 10, in PG:65.77C. English translations of the apophthegmata of the desert fathers and mothers offered here are indebted to Benedicta Ward's *The Sayings of the Desert Fathers: The Alphabetical Collection* (London: A. R. Mowbray & Co., 1975). For a good introduction to early Christian monasticism, see Derwas J. Chitty, *The Desert a City: An Introduction to the Study of Egyptian and Palestinian Monasticism* (Oxford: Basil Blackwell, 1966).

3. "For the early monks," writes Tim Vivian, "spirit and place are not separate realities; they give meaning to each other and to the life of prayer a person lives in the presence of God." "Mountain and Desert," p. 15.

4. *Historia Monachorum,* XXIX, in PL:21.453C. Cf. James Wellard, *Desert Pilgrimage* (London: Hutchinson & Co., 1970), p. 18. Jerome's romantic description of withdrawal or *anachoresis* among the desert Christians may be less than completely accurate, as suggested in James E. Goehring's "The World Engaged: The Social and Economic World of Early Egyptian Monasticism," in *Gnosticism and the Early Christian World* (Sonoma, Calif.: Polebridge Press, 1990), pp. 134–44.

5. "Natural beauty is often praised by the Greek fathers, but it is almost invariably farmland, parkland, cultivated land." David S. Wallace-Hadrill, *The Greek Patristic View of Nature* (New York: Barnes & Noble, 1968), p. 90. Leo Marx defines a "middle landscape" as that preferred ground between wilderness and the city, so often celebrated in the history of Western thought. See Marx, *The Machine in the Garden* (London: Oxford University Press, 1964).

6. Peter Brown, *Society and the Holy in Late Antiquity* (Berkeley: University of California Press, 1982), p. 109–12. See also Brown, *The World of Late Antiquity* (New York: Harcourt, Brace, Jovanovich, 1971), pp. 96–112.

7. Gregory of Nazianzus, Letter 4 to Basil, in *The Fathers Speak: St. Basil the Great, St. Gregory of Nazianzus, St. Gregory of Nyssa,* ed. George A. Barrois (Crestwood, N.Y.: St. Vladimir's Seminary Press, 1986), p. 19.

8. Peter Brown, "The Desert Fathers: Anthony to John Climacus," in *The Body and Society* (New York: Columbia University Press, 1988), pp. 213–40.

9. Presuppositions for the task of joining the study of geography and spirituality are spelled out in my earlier work, *Landscapes of the Sacred: Geography and Narrative in American Spirituality* (New York: Paulist Press, 1988).

10. For a geographical study of human response to hazardous environments, see Thomas R. Herzog, "A Cognitive Analysis of Preference for Natural Environments: Mountains, Canyons, and Deserts," *Landscape Journal* 6 (1987), pp. 140–52. See also Ian Burton, Robert Kates, and Gilbert White, *The Environment as Hazard* (New York: Oxford University Press, 1978), and Yi-Fu Tuan, *Landscapes of Fear* (New York: Pantheon Books, 1979).

11. Desert photographer J. A. Kraulis describes the mysterious appeal of such canyons in his *Desertlands of America* (New York: Gallery Books, 1988). "The interiors of these slots are among the most extraordinary places in the desert. The constricted walls block out the sky. Indirect light bounces around the swirled stone chambers, as sound echoes do, creating unexpected effects" (p. 42).

12. Peter Wild, ed., *The Desert Reader* (Salt Lake City: University of Utah Press, 1991), p. 1.

13. Edward Abbey, *The Journey Home* (New York: Dutton, 1977), p. 14.

14. Cf. Peter Brown, "The Holy Man in Late Antiquity," in *Society and the Holy in Late Antiquity*, pp. 130–152; and "From the Heavens to the Desert: Anthony and Pachomius," in *The Making of Late Antiquity* (Cambridge, Mass.: Harvard University Press, 1978), pp. 81–101.

15. Jay Appleton, *The Experience of Landscape* (London: John Wiley & Sons, 1975), p. 73. Edward O. Wilson similarly observes the preference early humans had for a savanna-like environment offering protection as well as open space. In such a setting, "cliffs, hillocks, and ridges were the vantage points from which to make a still more distant surveillance, while their overhangs and caves served as natural shelters at night." *Biophilia* (Cambridge, Mass.: Harvard University Press, 1984), p. 110.

16. Tony Hiss uses the Appleton thesis to suggest approaches to the urban planning of parks and neighborhoods in *The Experience of Place* (New York: Alfred A. Knopf, 1990), p. 41f.

17. Yizhar Hirschfeld, "List of the Byzantine Monasteries in the Judean Desert," in *Christian Archaeology in the Holy Land: New Discoveries*, ed. G. C. Bottini, L. Di Segni, and E. Alliata (Jerusalem: Franciscan Printing Press, 1990), p. 12. See also J. Patrich, "The Cells (*Ta Kellia*) of Choziba, Wadi El-Qilt," in the same volume, pp. 205–26; and Hirschfeld's *The Judean Desert Monasteries in the Byzantine Period* (New Haven, Conn.: Yale University Press, 1992).

18. Hirschfeld, "List of the Byzantine Monasteries," p. 3. In the Egyptian desert, toward the Red Sea, Anthony lived for the last forty years of his life at his "inner mountain," a rocky crag with a cave at the top, reached by way of a dizzying spiral climb.

19. Edmund Burke, *Philosophical Enquiry into the Origin of Our Ideas of the Sublime and the Beautiful* (1757), James T. Boulton, ed. (London: Routledge & Kegan Paul, 1958), p. 39.

20. Ibid., p. 99.

21. Barrois, *The Fathers Speak*, p. 16.

22. Appleton, *The Experience of Landscape*, pp. 90–93.

23. Evagrius Ponticus, *Capita Practica ad Anatolium*, 92, in PG:40.1249B. See *Évagre le Pontique: Traité Pratique ou Le Moine*, trans. Antoine Guillaumont and Claire Guillaumont, vol. 171 of *Sources Chrétiennes* (Paris: Les Éditions du Cerf, 1971), vol. II, pp. 693–695.

24. Martha Robbins discusses the pattern of death and resurrection in Jungian terms in her article, "The Desert-Mountain Experience: The Two Faces of Encounter with God," *Journal of Pastoral Care* XXXV:1 (March 1981), pp. 18–35.

25. Joseph of Thebes, 1, in PG:65.241C. See Columba Stewart, "Radical Honesty about the Self: The Practice of the Desert Fathers," *Sobornost* 12:1 (1990), pp. 25–39.

26. See Henri Nouwen, *The Way of the Heart: Desert Spirituality and Contemporary Ministry* (New York: Seabury Press, 1981), p. 27.

27. "The Waste Land" (1922), in T. S. Eliot, *The Complete Poems and Plays, 1909–1950* (New York: Harcourt, Brace & World, Inc., 1971), p. 38.

28. Ladder, Step 4, p. 113.

29. Athanasius, *The Life of Anthony*, par. 8, trans. Robert C. Gregg (New York: Paulist Press, 1980), pp. 37–39. The image of the desert as a place of threatening demons can be traced from the temptation narratives in the synoptic gospels, through the desert literature since Athanasius' *Life of Anthony* and its vivid portrayal in the history of Christian art (from early Eastern iconography to Matthias Grünewald).

30. The white, or bloodless, martyrdom of desert discipline came, in the fourth century, to replace the red martyrdom of persecution experienced by the church prior to the advent of Constantine as emperor in 313.

31. AP-alph, Macarius the Great, 18, 40, in PG:65.269BC; and AP-anon, in F. Nau, *Revue de l'Orient Chrétien* 8 (1913), pp. 137–38. See Benedicta Ward, *The Wisdom of the Desert Fathers* (Oxford: SLG Press, 1975), p. 55.

32. W. E. H. Lecky, *History of European Morals* (New York: D. Appleton, 1895), vol. II, p. 107. See Edward Gibbon, *The Decline and Fall of the Roman Empire* (New York: Modern Library, 1932), vol. II, pp. 3ff.

33. See Nouwen, *The Way of the Heart*, p. 22.

34. AP-anon, in PL:73.933A. See *Western Asceticism*, ed. Owen Chadwick (Philadelphia: Westminster Press, 1958), Section XI.114, p. 131. Thomas Merton points to the linguistic irony found in the story of Abba Serapion, who sold his last book, a copy of the gospels, to provide food for the hungry. In the process, he sold "the very words which told him to sell all and give to the poor." Thomas Merton, *The Wisdom of the Desert* (New York: New Directions, 1960), p. 19.

35. Douglas Burton-Christie stresses the oral character of the sayings of the desert fathers, drawing on the work of Walter Ong. *The Word in the Desert: Scripture and the Quest for Holiness in Early Christian Monasticism* (New York: Oxford University Press, 1992), pp. 115–29.

36. Take, for example, the old man of Thebes who gave a piece of dry wood to Abba John the Dwarf, telling him to "Water it every day with a bottle of water, until it bears fruit." Abba John did so, and within three years the dry wood blossomed into life. AP-alph, John the Dwarf, 1, in PG:65.204D.

37. John Climacus, Ladder, Step 11, p. 159. Abba Arsenius insisted, "I have often repented of having spoken, but never of having remained silent." Quoted in Nouwen, *The Way of the Heart*, p. 43.

38. Ladder, Step 1, p. 75.

39. Merton, *Wisdom of the Desert*, pp. 5–6. Merton concluded that "the hermit had to be a man mature in faith, humble and detached from himself to a degree that is altogether terrible" (p. 7).

40. Ladder, Summary of all Preceding Steps, p. 257.

41. Ibid., Steps 18, 22, pp. 192, 202.

42. "It is possible," she said, "to be a solitary in one's mind while living in a crowd, and it is possible for one who is a solitary to live in the crowd of his own thoughts." Jean-Claude Guy, *Recherches sur la Tradition Grecque des Apophthegmata Patrum* (Brussels: Société des Bollandistes, 1962), p. 34. See Josep Soler, "Les Mères du désert et la maternité spirituelle," *Collectanea Cisterciensia* 48:3 (1986), pp. 235–50.

43. AP-alph, Moses, 7, in PG:65.289C. As Thomas Merton said of the desert Christians, "The opinions of others had ceased, for them, to be matters of importance." *Wisdom of the Desert*, p. 10.

44. AP-alph, Macarius the Great, 23, in PG:65.272C.

45. See Belden C. Lane, "The Spirituality and Politics of Holy Folly," *The Christian Century* (15 December 1982), pp. 1281–86, and "Merton as Zen Clown," *Theology Today* XLVI:3 (October 1989), pp. 256–68.

46. Hugo Rahner, *Man at Play* (New York: Herder & Herder, 1972), p. 3.

47. AP-alph, Moses, 8, in PG:65.285B.

48. AP-alph, Macarius the Great, 31, in PG:65.273D.

49. AP-alph, Simon, 1, 2, in PG:65.412D.

50. Thomas Aquinas, *Commentary on the Nicomachean Ethics,* IV, 16, 853f, trans. C. I. Litzinger (Chicago: Henry Regnery Co., 1964), vol. I, p. 368. Cf. Rahner, *Man at Play,* p. 2.

51. *Analecta Bollandiana,* ed. Hippolytus Delehaye (Brussels: Société des Bollandistes, 1910), vol. XXIX, pp. 117ff. See James Wellard, *Desert Pilgrimage,* pp. 145–46. Though Saint Menas has been decanonized by the Bollandist fathers, he is still held in high regard among Coptic Christians.

52. It is not inappropriate that figures in the apophatic tradition, such as Gregory of Nazianzus, Maximus the Confessor, and even Thérèse of Lisieux, have been foremost in the development of a Christian theology of playfulness. Rahner observes, "When God himself breaks into our apparently closed order of play, something occurs that is completely beyond the power of any human words to express." *Man at Play,* p. 47.

53. AP-alph, Sisoes, 26, in PG:65.400D–401A.

54. Rahner, *Man at Play,* p. 56.

55. Brown, "From the Heavens to the Desert," p. 86. As much as the emptying of the self is emphasized throughout the apophatic tradition, the goal of spiritual attainment is not to become a "void" or nonentity, but rather to realize a new, free self, prompting confidence and love, always inseparable from Christ.

56. Guy, *Recherches sur la Tradition Grecque,* p. 30. Abba Poemen also urged those who teach to do so with the indifference of *apatheia,* being disengaged from how they may be perceived by others. AP-alph, Poemen, 127, in PG:65.353D.

57. Merton, *Wisdom of the Desert,* p. 18 (italics added).

58. Athanasius, *Life of Anthony,* par. 19, p. 45.

59. AP-alph, Moses, 14, in PG:65.288B.

60. Ladder, Step 10, p. 157.

61. M. Scott Peck, in *The Road Less Traveled* (New York: Simon and Schuster, 1978), rejects the popular notion of love as an emotion that accompanies the experience of cathecting, of incorporating into ourselves an object that is useful.

62. Edward Gibbon expressed a truth deeper than he knew when he said, "The peace of the Eastern church was invaded by a swarm of fanatics, *incapable of fear,* or reason, or humanity; and *the Imperial troops acknowledged without shame, that they were much less apprehensive of an encounter with the fiercest barbarians." Decline and Fall,* vol. II, p. 9 (italics added).

63. Merton, *Wisdom of the Desert,* p. 5. Power of any sort was suspect, even that of the ordained clergy. Pachomius, like many other early monks, took a dim view of the priesthood, seeing ordination as "the beginning of the thought of love of command." See Derwas Chitty, *The Desert a City,* p. 23.

64. AP-alph, Poemen, 5, in PG:65.320B.

65. AP-alph, Ammonathas, 1, in PG:65.136D–137A.

66. AP-alph, Arsenius, 29, in PG:65.97C.

67. I am indebted for much of this argument to Sister Maggie Ross, a contemporary solitary at Christ Church, Oxford, who witnesses in her own life and writings to this ancient desert truth. See "Apophatic Prayer as a Theological Model," *Literature and Theology* 7 (December 1993), pp. 325–53.

68. Helen Waddell, *The Desert Fathers* (Ann Arbor: University of Michigan Press, 1966), pp. 60–61.

69. Yizhar Hirschfeld speaks of their gathering salt bush, caper, and manonthion or tumble thistle, the leaves of which are fried with onions and spices and eaten by bedouins still today. "Edible Wild Plants: The Secret Diet of Monks in the Judean Desert," *Israel Land and Nature* 16:1 (Fall 1990), pp. 25–28. Whatever they ate, the desert monks were known for their longevity. Abba Cyriac of Chariton died at the age of 107; John Hesychastes at Mar Saba was 104.

70. Wallace-Hadrill, *Greek Patristic View of Nature,* p. 80.

71. Roderick Nash, *Wilderness and the American Mind* (New Haven, Conn.: Yale University Press, 1982), p. 18.

72. Antoine Guillaumont contrasts the idealized conception of desert landscape found among Hellenistic writers in general with the more sober, even demonic description of the desert provided by Egyptians who actually lived there. Guillaumont, "La conception du desert chez les moines d'Egypt," in *Aux origines du monachisme chrétien* (Begrolles-en-Mauges: Abbaye de Bellefontaine, 1979), pp. 69–87.

73. *Historia Monachorum,* xxix, in PL:21.453A. See Waddell, *The Desert Fathers,* p. 56.

74. AP-alph, Anthony, 34, in PG:65.85D.

75. Edward Abbey, *Beyond the Wall: Essays from the Outside* (New York: Holt, Rinehart & Winston, 1984), p. 86.

76. Athansius, *Life of Anthony,* par. 50, p. 69.

77. Susan Power Bratton, "The Original Desert Solitaire: Early Christian Monasticism and Wilderness," *Environmental Ethics* 10:1 (Spring 1988), pp. 31–53.

78. *Historia Monachorum,* vi, in PL: 21.410B. See Waddell, *The Desert Fathers,* p. 46.

79. Palladius, *The Lausiac History,* trans. Robert T. Meyer, in *Ancient Christian Writers,* ed. Johannes Quasten, Walter Burghardt, and Thomas C. Lawler, vol. 34 (Westminster, Md: Newman Press, 1965), pp. 61, 66. Many such tales in the hagicgraphy of the desert fathers would subsequently be incorporated into the literature of the Celtic saints and Francis of Assisi. See Edward A. Armstrong, *Saint Francis: Nature Mystic; The Derivation and Significance of the Nature Stories in the Franciscan Legend* (Berkeley: University of California Press, 1973).

80. John Climacus, Ladder, Step 7; Helen Waddell, *Beasts and Saints* (London: Constable & Co., 1949), pp. 17–23; and Jerome, *The Life of St. Paul the First Hermit,* in PL:23.27C. See also Waddell, *The Desert Fathers,* p. 38.

81. Ephraem of Edessa, *The Life of St. Mary the Harlot,* in PL:53.651–60. See also Waddell, *The Desert Fathers,* p. 189f. Mary's experience of abuse, shared in the desert tradition from the perspective of a male relative, obviously raises important questions for the modern reader. I recognize the danger of using her story without attending to the insights of a critical, feminist hermeneutic.

MYTHIC LANDSCAPE · Desert Terror and the Playfulness of God

1. C. S. Lewis, *Miracles* (London: Collins, 1947), p. 98.

2. John of the Cross, *The Living Flame of Love,* Stanza I, 8, in *The Collected Works of St. John of the Cross,* trans. Kieran Kavanaugh and Otilio Rodriguez (Washington, D.C.: Institute of Carmelite Studies, 1979), p. 582.

3. Julian of Norwich speaks of "our heavenly Mother Jesus" playing with us—allowing us to fall and be distressed in various ways so that we might behave like a child running quickly to its mother. *Julian of Norwich: Showings,* ed. Edmund Colledge and James Walsh (New York: Paulist Press, 1978), Long Text, ch. 61, pp. 300–301. The *Cloud* author similarly invites his reader to "play a sort of game" with God, "as though you did not wish him to know how you desire to see him and have him or experience him." This, it would seem, is a way of bringing God run-

ning to us in playful longing. Cloud, ch. XLVI, p. 209f. James Walsh speaks of the *ludus amoris* tradition in his introduction to the Cloud, pp. 77, 86, 209 n.306.

4. Hugo Rahner argues that the playfulness of God is the only way we also understand what it means to be human. "Plato refers to man as a *paignion theou*—a plaything of God, and sees in this the highest perfection a creature can attain.... It is only after we have spoken in all reverence of *Deus ludens* [a God who plays] that *Homo ludens* [the playful human being] can be understood." *Man at Play* (New York: Herder & Herder, 1972), pp. 11–12.

5. Alan Watts, *The Book: On the Taboo Against Knowing Who You Are* (New York: Collier, 1966), p. 12.

6. See Jerome R. Mintz, *Legends of the Hasidim* (Chicago: University of Chicago Press, 1968), p. 344.

7. Francis Thompson, *The Hound of Heaven,* ed. Michael A. Kelly (Philadelphia: Peter Reilly, 1916), p. 31.

8. In his commentary on Genesis 22, Martin Luther spoke of this hidden God as "playing" with Abraham and his son on Mount Moriah, inviting them to regard death itself as a sport and jest. *Luther's Works,* ed. Jaroslav Pelikan (Saint Louis: Concordia Publishing House, 1964), vol. 4: Lectures on Genesis, chaps. 21–25, pp. 115–22.

9. T. H. White, *The Book of Merlyn* (Austin: University of Texas Press, 1977), p. ix.

10. *Luther's Works,* vol. 54: Table Talk, pp. 19–20.

11. "O Jesus," she prayed in her *Story of a Soul,* "how happy your little bird is to be feeble and little. What would become of it if it were big? It would never have the audacity to come into your presence and then go to sleep." See Simon Tugwell, *Ways of Imperfection* (Springfield, Ill.: Templegate Publishers, 1985), pp. 223–25.

12. See Belden C. Lane, "*Chutzpa K'lapei Shamaya:* A Christian Response to the Jewish Tradition of Arguing with God," *Journal of Ecumenical Studies* 23:4 (Fall 1986), pp. 567–86.

13. Anne Sexton, "The Rowing Endeth," *The Awful Rowing toward God* (New York: Houghton Mifflin Co., 1975), pp. 85–86.

CHAPTER 7 · Attentiveness, Indifference, and Love
The Countercultural Spirituality of the Desert Christians

1. Edward Abbey, *Desert Solitaire: A Season in the Wilderness* (New York: McGraw-Hill Book Co., 1968), p. 267.

2. Evagrius, *Praktikos,* introductory letter to Anatolius, in Evagrius Ponticus, *The Praktikos; Chapters on Prayer,* ed. John Eudes Bamberger (Spencer, Mass.: Cistercian Publications, 1970), p. 14.

3. Antoine de Saint-Exupéry, *Wind, Sand and Stars* (New York: Reynal & Hitchcock, 1940), pp. 173–236. Saint-Exupéry was finally found by a bedouin caravan crossing the desert, twelve miles from the ancient monastic settlement at Wadi Natroun. Stacy Schiff, *Saint-Exupéry: A Biography* (New York: A. A. Knopf, 1994), p. 262.

4. Bruce Berger, *The Telling Distance: Conversations with the American Desert* (Portland, Ore.: Breitenbush Books, 1990), p. 1.

5. Peter Reyner Banham, *Scenes in America Deserta* (Salt Lake City, Utah: Gibbs M. Smith, Inc., 1982), p. 44.

6. John Crowe Ransom, *God Without Thunder: An Unorthodox Defense of Orthodoxy* (Hamden, Conn.: Archon Books, 1965).

7. Richard Cartwright Austin, *Baptized into Wilderness: A Christian Perspective on John Muir* (Atlanta, Ga.: John Knox Press, 1989), p. 90.

8. *Agrupnia,* meaning "wakefulness" (literally, "not asleep") is contrasted here with *apatheia* or "detachment" (literally, "without passion"). These two terms are chosen for contrast

because of the preference of the alpha privative or negative form in the history of the apophatic tradition. Two other words in Greek are used to describe *agrupnia* or attentiveness. *Prosochi* refers to "vigilance" or "attention"; *nipsis* carries a sense of "watchfulness" or "sobriety." See Philok, vol. I, p. 366.

9. *Apatheia* is defined here as "indifference," not after the ancient Stoic pattern of impassiveness but after the early Christian use of the word as referring to one's struggle with temptation in the spiritual life. Active indifference became a way of focusing one's attention on that which was most worthy of love. See G. Bardy, "Apatheia," in DictSp, I, p. 744.

10. In the "Principle and Foundation" to the *Spiritual Excercises,* Ignatius said that "we ought to keep ourselves indifferent [*indiferencia*] to all created things." See *Ignatius Loyola: Spiritual Exercises,* ed. Joseph Tetlow (New York: Crossroad, 1992), pp. 54–55; Karl Rahner's *Spiritual Exercises* (New York: Herder & Herder, 1965), pp. 23–27; and Harvey Egan's article "Indifference" in *The Westminster Dictionary of Christian Spirituality,* ed. Gordon S. Wakefield (Philadelphia: Westminster Press, 1983), pp. 211–13. Note that in his twentieth annotation Ignatius also suggested the separation and isolation of the desert as a valuable setting for experiencing the exercises.

11. Quoted by Daniel O'Hanlon, S.J., in Jacob Needleman, *Lost Christianity* (Garden City, N.J.: Doubleday, 1980), p. 150. Cf. Daniel O'Hanlon, "Zen and the *Spiritual Exercises,*" *Theological Studies* 39:4 (December 1978), p. 744.

12. T. S. Eliot, *Complete Poems and Plays* (New York: Harcourt, Brace & World, 1971), p. 61.

13. Ladder, Steps 20, 29, pp. 196–98, 282–85.

14. Baba Bathra 73b, quoted in Joshua Schwartz, "Sinai in Jewish Thought and Tradition," *Immanuel: A Bulletin of Religious Thought and Research in Israel* 13 (Fall 1981), p. 8.

15. Evagrius, *Chapters on Prayer,* 149, in Bamberger, *Evagrius Ponticus,* p. 79. Saint Hesychios, abbot of the monastery at Sinai, also emphasized attentiveness in his eighth-century work "On Watchfulness and Holiness," in Philok, I, pp. 162–65, 177–79.

16. John Cassian, *Conferences,* I, 1–2, in *John Cassian: Conferences,* trans. Colm Luibheid (New York: Paulist Press, 1985), pp. 37–38.

17. Tom Brown, Jr., *The Tracker* (Englewood Cliffs, N.J.: Prentice-Hall, 1978), p. 16.

18. Saint-Exupéry, *Wind, Sand and Stars,* p. 138.

19. Joseph Wood Krutch, *The Desert Year* (New York: William Sloane Associates, 1952), p. 4.

20. Jones, *Soul Making: The Desert Way of Spirituality* (San Francisco: Harper & Row, 1985), p. 89.

21. *New York Times,* 14 February 1960, sec. 1, p. 6.

22. W. L. Rusho, *Everett Ruess: A Vagabond for Beauty* (Layton, Utah: Peregrine Smith Books, 1983).

23. Stanley Hauerwas and William Willimon, *Resident Aliens* (Nashville, Tenn.: Abingdon, 1992), p. 93.

24. The sayings of the fathers are filled with stories of older monks who readily sacrificed their notoriety in the spiritual life for the sake of younger brothers. In one case, a revered master even went with a younger monk to a brothel, pretending to be tempted to sin along with him in order to talk the prostitute into dissuading him from breaking his vows. AP-anon, quoted in Columba Stewart, ed., *The World of the Desert Fathers* (Oxford: SLG Press, 1986), pp. 3–4.

25. AP-anon, in F. Nau, *Revue de L'Orient Chrétien* 7 (1912), p. 206. See Benedicta Ward, *Wisdom of the Desert Fathers* (Oxford: SLG Press, 1975), p. 50.

26. It was in this vein that Thomas Merton spoke of the contemplative as "anarchist" or outlaw, cutting against the grain of a dominant culture. *Wisdom of the Desert* (New York: New Directions, 1970), pp. 4–5.

27. William Golding, *The Paper Men* (New York: Farrar, Straus, & Giroux, 1984), p. 155.

28. Wallace Stegner, *The Sound of Mountain Water* (New York: E. P. Dutton, 1980), p. 153.

29. A similar theme is found in the mystical tradition of Islam, in Farid Ud-Din Attar's "The Conference of the Birds. " See Belden C. Lane, "In Quest of the King: Image, Narrative, and Unitive Spirituality in a Twelfth-Century Sufi Classic," *Horizons* 14:1 (Spring 1987), pp. 39–48.

30. Samuel Clemens, *Roughing It* (Hartford, Conn.: American Publishing Co., 1872), p. 388.

31. D. H. Lawrence, *Phoenix: The Posthumous Papers,* ed. Edward MacDonald (London: Heinemann, 1966), pp. 141–47.

32. Abbey, *Desert Solitaire,* p. 192. The phrase is taken from the last line of Spinoza's *Ethics.* See Edwin Curley, ed., *The Collected Works of Spinoza* (Princeton, N.J.: Princeton University Press, 1985), p. 617.

33. "Attention and Fascination: The Search for Cognitive Clarity," in *Humanscape: Environments for People,* ed. Stephen Kaplan (North Scituate, Mass.: Duxbury Press, 1978), pp. 86–87.

34. Lawrence Durrell, *The Alexandria Quartet* (London: Faber & Faber, 1969), p. 18. The description is taken from his "notes for landscape-tones" found at the beginning of the novel *Justine.*

35. Saint Anthony spoke of temptations coming to him in the form of terrifying beasts, enchanting women, and gold scattered on the desert floor. See Athanasius' *Life of Antony,* 5–7, 12, in *Athanasius: The Life of Antony and the Letter to Marcellinus,* trans. Robert C. Gregg (New York: Paulist Press, 1980), pp. 33–37, 40.

36. The destructive power of the suppressed *anima* is brilliantly described in chapter eight of Charles Williams's novel *Descent into Hell* (Grand Rapids, Mich.: William B. Eerdmans, 1980). Lawrence Wentworth, fascinated by a younger woman named Adela Hunt, makes his descent into the hell of his own imagination through an endlessly self-absorbed pursuit of his craving. He comes to prefer his manufactured image of Adela, an idolized reflection of himself, far more than he ever did the actual woman.

37. Donald Nicholl, *Holiness* (New York: Paulist Press, 1987), p. 91.

38. John Cassian, *Institutes,* XI, 4, in Philok, I, p. 91.

39. Philok, I, p. 92.

40. Eros was the word used by the Greek writers to refer to "that intense aspiration and longing which impel man towards union with God"; *epithymitikon* referred to the appetitive aspect of the soul (its desiring power) as originally identified by Plato. Some of the Greek fathers even affirmed *pathos* ("passion") as an impulse placed in humans by God at their creation. See Philok, vol. I, pp. 357–63.

41. Athanasius' *Life of Anthony,* 35, in Robert C. Gregg, Athanasius, pp. 58. The word he uses for "desire" here is *pathos,* or "passion." Jean Leclercq develops this theme of desire in the history of the monastic life in *The Love of Learning and the Desire for God: A Study of Monastic Culture* (New York: New American Library, 1961).

42. *Vita Sanctae Pelagiae, Meretricis,* in PL:73.663–672. The fourth-century story of Nonnus and Pelagia is retold in Helen Waddell's *The Desert Fathers* (Ann Arbor, Mich.: University of Michigan Press, 1966), pp. 177–88. Cf. Benedicta Ward, *Harlots of the Desert: A Study of Repentance in Early Monastic Sources* (Kalamazoo, Mich.: Cistercian Publications, Inc., 1987), pp. 57–75.

43. Ladder, Step 30, p. 287.

44. Ibid., pp. 286–87.

45. Francis de Sales, *Treatise on the Love of God,* trans. Henry B. Mackey (Westminster, Md.: Newman Book Shop, 1942), Book 6, ch. 3, pp. 239–41.

46. Hesychios, *On Watchfulness and Holiness,* 5, in Philok, vol. I, p. 163. Simone Weil stresses

this same desert pattern in her "Reflections on the Right Use of School Studies with a View to the Love of God," *Waiting for God* (New York: Harper & Row, 1973), p. 105–16. There she defined prayer as "the orientation of all the attention of which the soul is capable toward God."

47. Bernard McGinn, John Meyendorff, and Jean Leclercq, eds., *Christian Spirituality* (New York: Crossroad, 1989), vol. I, p. 404. Abba Macarius simply prayed over and over the words, "Lord, help."

48. John Cassian, *Conferences*, X, 10, in Luibheid, *John Cassian*, pp. 132, 238.

49. Ladder, Step 28, pp. 275–76.

50. After its compilation in the eighteenth century by Saint Nikodimos of the Holy Mountain of Athos and Saint Makarios of Corinth, *The Philokalia* was subsequently translated into Slavonic and was influential in reviving Russian spirituality in the nineteenth century, as seen in the popular *Way of a Pilgrim* and the writings of Fyodor Dostoyevsky. See Philok, vol. I, pp. 11–18.

51. Saint-Exupéry, *Wind, Sand and Stars*, p. 58.

52. "It is not a perfect prayer," said John Cassian, "in which the monk is conscious of himself or understands his prayer." *Conferences*, IX, 31, in Luibheid, *John Cassian*, p. 120.

53. Father Sylvan, a contemporary desert monk, quoted in Needleman, *Lost Christianity*, p. 207.

54. Carretto, *Letters from the Desert* (Maryknoll, N.Y.: Orbis Books, 1972), p. 61. This image is drawn from the Cloud, ch. VI, p. 131, where the author says, "You are to smite upon that thick cloud of unknowing with a sharp dart of longing love."

55. Saint-Exupéry, *Wind, Sand and Stars*, p. 130–31.

56. Weil, *Waiting for God*, p.111–12

57. Jones, *Soul Making: The Desert Way of Spirituality*, p. 29.

58. Weil, *Waiting for God*, p. 114.

59. Ibid., p. 115.

60. AP-anon, in F. Nau, *Revue de L'Orient Chrétien* 8 (1913), p. 143. See Ward, *Wisdom of the Desert Fathers*, p. 61.

61. Adapted from AP:anon, translated in Columba Stewart, ed. *World of the Desert Fathers* (Oxford: SLG Press, 1986), pp. 12–13.

62. Ward, *Wisdom of the Desert Fathers*, p. xii.

63. Cloud, ch. LX, p. 238.

64. Saint-Exupéry, *Wind, Sand and Stars*, pp. 138–44.

65. Ibid., p. 143.

MYTHIC LANDSCAPE · Scratchings on the Wall of a Desert Cell

1. Blaise Pascal, *Pensées*, trans. John Warrington (London: J. M. Dent & Sons, 1973), no. 136, p. 42.

2. Rowan Williams, *Christian Spirituality* (Atlanta, Ga.: John Knox Press, 1980), p. 94. The quotes from the desert fathers are from AP-anon, in F. Nau, *Revue de L'Orient Chrétien* 3 (1908), p. 279. See Benedicta Ward, *Wisdom of the Desert Fathers* (Oxford: SLG Press, 1986), p. 24.

3. Michael Ventura, "The Talent of the Room," *The Sun: A Magazine of Ideas* 217 (January 1994), pp 21–23.

4. Some interpreters of the desert monastic experience suggest that the relentless "demons" enountered by the desert fathers in their stillness actually served a therapeutic function in helping to focus their attention on that which demanded change and growth. See Richard Valantasis, "Daemons and the Perfecting of the Monk's Body: Monastic Anthropology, Daemonology, and Asceticism," *Semeia* 58 (1992), pp. 47–79.

5. AP-alph, Macarius the Great, 16, in PG:65.269B. Evagrius echoed the same theme, saying, "For fear that you may go wrong, stay rooted in your cell. . . . If a jar of wine is left in the same place for a long time, the wine in it becomes clear, settled and fragrant." *On Asceticism and Stillness in the Solitary Life,* in Philok, vol. I, pp. 34–35.

Conclusion
Rediscovering Christ in the Desert

1. C. S. Lewis, *The Lion, the Witch and the Wardrobe* (Harmondsworth, Eng.: Penguin Books, 1966), pp. 117, and *The Magician's Nephew* (Harmondsworth, Eng.: Penguin Books, 1966), pp. 99–100.

2. W. D. Davies affirms this as a natural consequence of the incarnation: "The Doctrine that the Word became flesh, although it resulted in a critique of distinct, traditional, holy places, demanded the recognition that where the Glory had appeared among men all physical forms became suffused with it." *The Gospel and the Land: Early Christianity and Jewish Territorial Doctrine* (Berkeley: University of California Press, 1974) p. 366. See also Geoffrey R. Lilburne's discussion of "the Christification of Holy Space" in his book *A Sense of Place: A Christian Theology of the Land* (Nashville, Tenn.: Abingdon Press, 1989), pp. 89–110.

3. Teilhard de Chardin emphasized God's work in "luring" the whole of creation toward an Omega point of increasing consciousness and love. See *The Phenomenon of Man* (New York: Harper & Row, 1961), pp. 264–72. Poet and physicist Bryan Swimme argues that "this alluring activity permeates the cosmos on all levels of being." *The Universe is a Green Dragon* (Santa Fe, N.M.: Bear & Co., 1984), p. 46.

4. Denys Turner, *The Darkness of God: Negativity in Christian Mysticism* (Cambridge: Cambridge University Press, 1995), p. 209. Jean-Pierre de Caussade criticized many "devotional practices" for this very reason. "We must be detached from everything," he said, "even from detachment; we must abandon into God's hands even our self-abandonment. The last thing we should do is try to *feel* our own submission to God." *Lettres Spirituelles,* ed. Michel Olphe-Galliard (Paris: Desclee, 1962–1964), vol. I, pp. 195, 197; vol. II, p. 19, 49 See Simon Tugwell, *Ways of Imperfection* (Springfield, Ill.: Templegate Publishers, 1985), p. 213.

5. There are two doors in the next life, someone once suggested—one is labeled "heaven" and the other "lecture on heaven." Everyone from the West is lined up outside the second door.

6. "Lift up your heart to God," writes the *Cloud* author, "with a humble impulse of love; and have *himself* as your aim, not any of his goods." Cloud, ch. III, pp. 119–21.

7. John of the Cross, DkNight, I.12.6, p. 323.

8. Evagrius, *On Discrimination in Respect to Passions and Thoughts,* 9, in Philok, vol. I, p. 44.

9. Richard Rohr and Andreas Ebert, *Discovering the Enneagram* (New York: Crossroad, 1990), pp. 146–61.

10. AP-alph, Syncletica, 21, in Jean Claude Guy, *Recherches sur la Tradition Grecque des Apophthegmata Patrum, Subsidia Hagiographica* (Brussels, 1962), vol. 36, pp. 34–35. Cf. Ward, The *Desert Christian: Sayings of the Desert Fathers* (New York: Macmillan, 1980), p. 234.

11. Terry Tempest Williams, *Refuge: An Unnatural History of Family and Place* (New York: Pantheon Books, 1991), pp. 148, 202.

12. Annie Dillard, *Teaching a Stone to Talk* (New York: Harper & Row, 1982), p. 15. In a similar way, Sue Hubbell speaks of the importance of "becoming feral," writing in *A Country Year: Living the Questions* (New York: Random House, 1986) that "Wild things and wild places pull me more strongly than they did a few years ago, and domesticity, dusting and cookery interest

me not at all." See Lorraine Anderson, ed., *Sisters of the Earth: Women's Prose and Poetry about Nature* (New York: Vintage Books, 1991), p. 134.

13. Quoted in Diana Eck, *Encountering God: A Spiritual Journey from Bozeman to Banaras* (Boston: Beacon Press, 1993), p. 142.

14. Harold Bloom, *The American Religion: The Emergence of the Post-Christian Nation* (New York: Simon & Schuster, 1992), pp. 25–33, 46–55.

15. Walter Brueggemann, *Israel's Praise: Doxology Against Idolatry and Ideology* (Philadelphia: Fortress Press, 1988), p. 40.

16. In her reconstruction of a ecological theology, Sallie McFague radically questions traditionally monarchical, triumphalistic, and patriarchal imagery for God, yet recognizes (especially in the liturgy) the continuing value of personal language in speaking of God's deeply embodied relationship to the earth. See *The Body of God: An Ecological Theology* (Minneapolis: Fortress Press, 1993), p. 142.

Epilogue

1. Ruth Kirk, *Exploring Death Valley* (Stanford, Calif.: Stanford University Press, 1977), p. 5. Cf. Edwin Corle, *Death Valley and the Creek Called Furnace* (Los Angeles: Ward Ritchie Press, 1941), pp. 3ff.

Index